RATIONAL ANALYSIS
PROBLEMATIC
WORLD

OWL

RATIONAL ANALYSIS FOR A PROBLEMATIC WORLD

Problem Structuring Methods for Complexity, Uncertainty and Conflict

Edited by

Jonathan Rosenhead

JOHN WILEY & SONS
Chichester · New York · Brisbane · Toronto · Singapore

Copyright © 1989 by   John Wiley & Sons Ltd
Baffins Lane, Chichester,
West Sussex PO19 1UD, England,
Telephone (+44) 1234 779777

Reprinted July 1990, February 1992, December 1993,
September 1994, December 1995, October 1996
July 1997, September 1998

Other Wiley Editorial Offices:

John Wiley & Sons, Inc., 605 Third Avenue,
New York, NY 10158-0012, USA

Jacaranda Wiley Ltd, 33 Park Road, Milton,
Queensland 4064, Australia

John Wiley & Sons (Cananda) Ltd, 22 Worcester Road,
Rexdale, Ontario M9W 1L1, Canada

John Wiley & Sons (SEA) Pte Ltd, 37 Jalan Pemimpin 05-04,
Block B, Union Industrial Building, Singapore 129809

Library of Congress Cataloging-in-Publication Data:

Rational analysis for a problematic world : problem structuring
  methods for complexity, uncertainty, and conflict / edited by
  Jonathan Rosenhead.
       p. cm.
    Bibliography. p.
    Includes index.
    ISBN 0 471 92285 4. — ISBN 0 471 92286 2 (pbk.)
    1. Decision-making. 2. Decision-making—Case studies. 3. Problem
  solving. 4. Problem solving—Case studies. I. Rosenhead,
  Jonathan.
  HD30.23R38 1989   10014714o4
  658.4'03—dc20   89-14719
                                                            CIP

British Library Cataloguing in Publication Data

Rational analysis for a problematic world : problem
  structuring methods for complexity, uncertainty and
  conflict.
  1. Organisation and methods
  I. Title
  658.4'034

  ISBN 0 471 92285 4
  ISBN 0 471 92286 2 (pbk.)

Typeset by Acorn Bookwork, Salisbury, Wiltshire
Printed in Great Britain by Redwood Books, Trowbridge, Wiltshire

Contents

Contents

Contributors

Peter Bennett

University of Strathclyde, Department of Management Science, Livingstone Tower, 26 Richmond Street, Glasgow G1 1XH

Peter Bennett studied physics at Southampton University and Philosophy of Science at Sussex, before moving into operational research. He has researched and published widely on decision-making in conflicts, and on helping with complex, 'messy' decisions in general. He has been involved in applied research and consultancy work in a variety of public and private sector organizations. He is currently senior lecturer (and postgraduate course director) in the Management Science Department, Strathclyde University.

Peter Checkland

Department of Systems and Information Management, University of Lancaster, Bailrigg, Lancaster LA1 4YX

Peter Checkland worked for 15 years in ICI, where he became manager of a Divisional Research Group of 100 people working on new products and processes in fibre-making technology. He joined the University of Lancaster in 1969 as Professor in the Department of Systems. He led research into the application of systems engineering in real-world management problem situations, resulting in the development of Soft Systems Methodology (SSM). He is the author of the classic account of SSM: *Systems Thinking, Systems Practice*. His research continues with recent major involvements in both industry and the public sector.

Steve Cropper

University of Strathclyde, Department of Management Science, Livingstone Tower, 26 Richmond Street, Glasgow G1 1XH

Steve Cropper holds degrees in town planning, and spent four years with Sussex University Operational Research Group exploring the relationships between various problem structuring methodologies in practice. He has undertaken applied work in various settings, including local government, the probation service, and with community groups. Having moved to Strathclyde in 1987, he is currently engaged in research with Government and the NHS into the impact of decision support on planning strategic guidance and appraisal systems.

Colin Eden

University of Strathclyde, Department of Management Science, Livingstone Tower, 26 Richmond Street, Glasgow G1 1XH

Colin Eden is Professor of Management Science at the Strathclyde Business School in Scotland. He started his career as an operational researcher and subsequently worked as a management consultant before joining the University of Bath. He has been director of the Strategic Decision Support Research Unit at Bath and at Strathclyde University. He has acted as a consultant to a wide variety of public and private organizations, both small and very large in size. Professor Eden has published several books and numerous papers in operational research and management journals.

Contributors

John Friend
IOP Consulting, Barleyland, Thornhill Lane, Thornhill, Bamford, Nr Sheffield S30 2BR

John Friend graduated from Cambridge University with a degree in mathematics and worked for ten years as a statistician and operational research scientist in the steel, civil aviation and chemical industries, before joining the Tavistock Institute's new Institute for Operational Research (IOR) in 1964. Working with social scientists, he discovered the complexities of public planning through the pioneering study of city government in Coventry which resulted in his first book, written with the late Neil Jessop, *Local Government and Strategic Choice* (Tavistock, 1969; second edition, Pergamon Press, 1977). He then developed a programme of applied work in which interorganizational issues became increasingly significant. Since leaving the Tavistock Institute in 1986, he has been extending these interests further in association with various academic and consulting groups. His recent book with Allen Hickling—*Planning under Pressure*, Pergamon Press, 1987—is recognized as the authoritative text on the strategic choice approach.

Allen Hickling
Allen Hickling and Associates, No. 2 The Bakery, Long Itchington, Rugby CV23 8PW

Allen Hickling qualified as an architect in Bristol after an early career which involved experience as a sailor, railway porter and semi-professional magician. Moving to North America, he worked as a planner, design consultant and racing driver before taking his Master's Degrees in Architecture and City Planning at the University of Pennsylvania. After joining the IOR Coventry office in 1971, he took responsibility for a wide range of action research projects, producing a handbook on the strategic choice approach which was translated into French, Dutch and Portuguese. Since starting his own consultancy in 1980, he has become deeply involved in applying strategic choice principles and methods to policy-making, in collaboration with civil servants, industrialists and others, especially in The Netherlands.

Nigel Howard
Nigel Howard Systems, 10 Bloomfield Road, Moseley, Birmingham B13 9BY

Nigel Howard describes himself as 'the world's only freelance game theorist'. He developed the theory of metagames in the late sixties at the Wharton School, under a contract with the US Arms Control Agency, and applied it to nuclear proliferation, planning the first SALT agreement, and preparing for the Vietnam peace talks. The publication of *Paradoxes of Rationality* (MIT Press, 1971) was followed by business applications of metagame analysis. He now runs a private consultancy to develop and market the CONAN program. This is used by large companies for policy planning, by managers in the British NHS and to coordinate marketing strategy among teams of salesmen. His most recent theoretical work is on 'soft' games, defined as games which change while being played under the stress of emotions, deceit, disbelief and mutual persuasion.

Chris Huxham
University of Strathclyde, Department of Management Science, Livingstone Tower, 26 Richmond Street, Glasgow G1 1XH

Chris Huxham studied operational research at the University of Sussex, and then held a lectureship at Aston University before moving to Strathclyde. She is Assistant Director of the MBA programmes at Strathclyde Business School, and manager of the IBM Business Education Project. She is also director of an action-research project concerned with linking Glasgow's year as European City of Culture with longer-term strategies for the city.

Jonathan Rosenhead
Operational Research, London School of Economics, Houghton Street, London WC2A 2AE

Jonathan Rosenhead is Professor of Operational Research at the London School of Economics. He has degrees in mathematics and statistics, and work experience in the steel industry and in management consultancy. His long-standing concern with methods for flexible planning has broadened into an involvement with approaches to structuring decision situations which are sufficiently transparent to facilitate participation. He is an advocate of the extension of the methods of operational research to community groups and other non-conventional clients, and was President of the Operational Research Society in 1986 and 1987.

Peter Simpson
Bristol Business School, Bristol Polytechnic, Coldharbour Lane, Frenchay, Bristol BS16 1QY

Pete Simpson is on the staff of the Bristol Business School of Bristol Polytechnic. He has been a researcher and consultant with a particular interest in working with community groups. He gained his first degree and doctorate from the University of Bath, and his research interests are in better understanding the role of faith in decision making.

Preface

Why this book has been written

The purpose of this book is to provide an introduction to a range of methods for structuring decisions and problems, rather than 'solving' them. Accounts of some of these methods have been available previously in scattered articles in technical journals. Others have been expounded in books, each offering a substantial presentation of one particular methodology (Checkland, 1981; Eden, Jones, and Sims, 1983; Friend and Hickling, 1987). However, even such lengthy accounts can present an obstacle as well as an opportunity to the potential user of 'soft' methods, as they are sometimes called. It is a considerable commitment to embark on reading a 300-page book. How can I know that *this* is the particular approach which has something to offer in my particular circumstances? How can I know that *any* of these methods could help me sort out my predicaments?.

The present volume has been designed to make access to these problem structuring methods less of a problem. Each of six methodologies is presented in a linked pair of chapters. For each approach, the first chapter lays out the justification for the method (what sorts of situation it addresses, and why these are significant), develops the conceptual apparatus which is employed, and describes the sequence of activities by which the method is applied. The second chapter of each pair illustrates the application of the method by means of a practical case study.

This format should make it possible for the reader to establish an informed view of what each methodology claims to be able to do. It will not, of course, convert the reader into a skilled exponent of the method. However, it should enable her or him to decide which of the approaches merits follow-up, whether through further reading, attendance at training sessions, or consultation with an experienced practitioner.

The book has another purpose. There has been a gradually growing recognition that the methods described here, and others like them, constitute a significant new direction for operational research and the systems movement. Do these methods have, despite their diversity, an underlying unity? Here they can be seen, not just as separate developments, but in conjunction with each other. Reading the assembled accounts, with their conceptual borrowings, cross-references and parallel formulations, re-inforces, I believe, the view that they constitute a distinct and radically different paradigm of decision-aiding. This book, hopefully, can assist in the establishment of a coherent identity for the new field.

Scope

The six methodologies which make up the core content of this book are:

Strategic Options Development and Analysis (SODA), with its technical component of cognitive mapping.

Soft Systems Methodology (SSM).

Strategic Choice, including the Analysis of Interconnected Decision Areas (AIDA).

Robustness Analysis.

Metagame Analysis.

Hypergame Analysis.

In each case the authors include the principal architect of the method.

It is in the above sequence that the topics feature in the book. The sequence does *not* correspond to any sequence of stages in problem solving or decision making; none of the approaches can easily be corralled within (say) 'appreciating the problem', or 'making choices'. The sequence is, in fact, to an extent arbitrary, though it does preserve certain connections. Thus both SODA and SSM offer perhaps the most articulated approaches to problem structuring—the identification of those factors and issues which should constitute the agenda for further discussion and analysis. Strategic Choice is also a general purpose approach to the structuring of complex situations, but places less emphasis on the psychological constructions of those involved. Strategic Choice and Robustness Analysis share a focus on uncertainty and ways of managing it, while both Metagame and Hypergame Analysis analyse in particular the conflictual aspects of decision situations.

There are, of course, useful contrasts and comparisons which can be made between these approaches, and some will be drawn out in the concluding chapter of the book. One characteristic which they do have in common is that they all address the provision of appropriate elements of structure for strategic problem situations. They are not, however, the only methods which make a contribution in this area. The approaches which have *not* been included in the book, but which might be thought to have a claim, include the Analytic Hierarchy Process (Saaty, 1980), Decision Analysis (Watson and Buede, 1988), Decision Conferencing (Phillips, 1989), Dialectical Inquiring Systems (Churchman, 1971), Idealized Planning (Ackoff, 1974, 1979), the LAMSADE School (Moscarola, 1984), and Strategic Assumption Surfacing and Testing (Mason and Mitroff, 1981). A case could also be made for such burgeoning areas as expert systems, or the use of spreadsheet packages.

Evidently it would not be possible to do justice in one book to such a gallery of approaches, even if all were true siblings of the methods which have been selected for inclusion in this volume. It is not necessary to argue here the reasons for particular exclusions. Instead of an exclusion rule, I have preferred the more positive, though equivalent, concept of an inclusion rule. Those approaches which are included here not only score individually on grounds of transparency, incorporation of conflict, activation of judgement, and intrinsic interest and applicability. Collectively they also constitute a new and distinctive British contribution to the art and craft of structuring problems. This focus is not the result of a misplaced nationalism: the methods described here need no special justifications, and can stand without crutches on a world stage. However, there is a great advantage in grouping together a set of approaches which have sprung from the same (or very similar) cultural matrix. A disjointed eclecticism can be avoided, enabling the coherence of the subject matter to emerge more sharply.

There are a number of audiences for this book. For graduate and even undergraduate students in a range of disciplines, this book can serve as a text for the courses which are now beginning to be taught. For the practitioner whose student days pre-dated the emergence of such courses, it offers at least the first stage of updating in a significant new area. And for the manager with a sophisticated interest in the potential of analysis, it offers an accessible state-of-the-art summary. All the contributors have enthusiastically cooperated in avoiding the need for any particular level of mathematical preparation. This is not to say that the material in the book is easy—but just that the difficulties are not mathematical.

Readers of this book will also find Bryant (1989) of direct relevance.

References

Ackoff, R. L. (1974). *Redesigning the Future*, Wiley, New York.
Ackoff, R. L. (1979). 'Resurrecting the future of operational research', *J. Opl Res. Soc.*, **30**, 189–99.

Bryant, J. (1989). *Problem Management: a guide for producers and players*, Wiley, Chichester.

Checkland, P. B. (1981). *Systems Thinking, Systems Practice*, Wiley, Chichester.

Churchman, C. W. (1971). *Design of Inquiring Systems*, Basic Books, New York.

Eden, C., Jones, S., and Sims, D. (1983). *Messing About in Problems*, Pergamon, Oxford.

Friend, J. K., and Hickling, A. (1987). *Planning Under Pressure*, Pergamon, Oxford.

Mason, R. O., and Mitroff, I. I. (1981). *Challenging Strategic Planning Assumptions*, Wiley, New York.

Moscarola, J. (1984). 'Organizational decision process and ORASA intervention', in *Rethinking the Process of Operational Research and Systems Analysis* (Eds. R. Tomlinson and I. Kiss), pp. 169–86, Pergamon, Oxford.

Phillips, L. D. (1989). 'People-centred group decision support', in *Knowledge-based Management Support Systems* (Eds. G. Doukidis, F. Land, and G. Miller), Ellis Horwood, Chichester.

Saaty, T. L. (1980). *The Analytic Hierarchy Process*, McGraw-Hill, New York.

Watson, S. R., and Buede, D. M. (1988). *Decision Synthesis: the principles and practice of decision analysis*, Cambridge University Press, Cambridge.

Acknowledgements

The emergence of this book owes much to the constructive suggestions of the contributing authors on chapters other than their own. To a significant extent, this is a collective enterprise.

Diane Taylor of John Wiley has judiciously combined forebearance with firmness in overcoming any temporary decline in motivation or momentum. My thanks are also due to Taz Johnson, who has performed secretarial exertions beyond the call of duty—having had to process not only the book in your hands, but also its polymorphic precursors.

1
Introduction: old and new paradigms of analysis

Jonathan Rosenhead

There is, today, a new generation of methods to assist in the analysis of decision problems. These methods are, as yet, less widely known, practised, and understood than their predecessors—the algorithmic and optimizing tools of operational research. Distinctive features of these novel approaches include an aim of partial structuring of previously unstructured situations (rather than the solution of well-structured problems), and a process involving participation as a key component.

The crisis

The function of this introductory chapter is to set the scene for the particular methods described in Chapters 2–13. I shall not offer précis or descriptions of these methods—since these are provided later in the book by those best qualified to do so.

In this chapter I shall try to establish the nature of the crisis which has afflicted more conventional methods of rational analysis. The chapter will give evidence for the existence of such a crisis, review the criticisms which have been advanced against the traditional approach, and indicate the general nature of the alternative approach which these criticisms imply. The six methods described in this volume constitute attempts, mostly

Rational Analysis for a Problematic World
Edited by J. Rosenhead. © 1989 John Wiley & Sons Ltd

deliberate, to demonstrate that there is, indeed, another way. I will leave to the concluding chapter (Chapter 14) an assessment of the extent to which this alternative is adequate to the tasks which it has set itself.

Foremost amongst the formal decision-aiding practices which have sprung up over the past half-century is operational research (OR). Most of the methods featured in this volume have emerged out of operational research, and are considered by their practitioners to be a part of OR. Indeed for a period during the 1988 Operational Research Society Annual Conference, every contributor to the book, bar one, was realized to be fleetingly present; so was our editor, and a brief review of progress proved possible. It is, then, in the context of OR that the crisis will be discussed here, though very similar issues and arguments have also arisen in the systems movement—with systems analysis and systems engineering subjected to severe criticism (Checkland, 1983).

The concept of scientific 'paradigms' which at times compete, stems from Kuhn (1970). Broadly, a paradigm consists of a set of implicit rules for identifying a valid scientific problem, and for recognizing what would constitute a solution to it. Suggestions of a paradigm crisis in operational research were advanced as early as 1973 (Thunhurst, 1973). In 1977 the leading British operational researcher K. D. Tocher criticized the dominant tendency in the subject in similar terms (Tocher, 1977). By 1981, the concept formed the organizing principle of Dando and Bennett's paper 'A Kuhnian crisis in management science?' (Dando and Bennett, 1981). The authors identified three conflicting paradigms ('official', 'reformist', and 'revolutionary') contending for ascendancy.

Indeed, the signs of paradigm crisis accumulated rapidly over this period. Major turmoil erupted in the world's two largest OR societies over plans to 'professionalize' the British operational research community (1972–73), and over the Operational Research Society of America's attempts to establish a code of conduct and discipline offenders (1971–72). Disputes of a non-technical nature flared in the normally sedate columns of respected journals. The ORSA code unleashed a torrent of critical comment (ORSA, 1971; Botts et al., 1972; Churchman et al., 1972). Ackoff engaged in an extended exchange with radical critics (Ackoff, 1974, 1975; Chesterton et al., 1975; Rosenhead, 1976); he himself launched a scathing attack on mainstream OR practice (Ackoff, 1979a,b) which evoked support for his diagnosis but not for his proposed remedy. The work of Ackoff, Churchman, and Checkland came under renewed critical scrutiny from Jackson (1982), once more provoking a substantial debate (Jackson, 1983; Rosenhead, 1984). Tinker and Lowe (1984) penned an assault on the one-dimensionality of management science which the journal *Interfaces* published with great reluctance—and a derisive commentary. And so on.

2

Within these, mostly ill-tempered, exchanges Dando and Bennett's three paradigms can be clearly discerned. Reformists, notably Ackoff and Checkland, criticize the official paradigm for its limiting, technical emphasis; in this they are joined by 'revolutionaries'. However, the latter seek a change in the clientele and establishment stance of the subject, rather than just a change in its methods—and are therefore sceptical about the claims of the reformists for the significance of their methodological innovations.

There is no need here to explore these positions in detail. What is relevant is that these multiple disputes led to a pervasive malaise in at least the English language OR communities—reinforced by the consequences for OR employment of the downturn in the world economy. By the mid-1980s the critics were clearly in the ascendant. Recognition of the crisis, and of something like the reformist route out of it, gained semi-official international authority from an IIASA volume of conference proceedings published in 1984 (Tomlinson and Kiss, 1984).

The critique

A crisis in the methods and practice of mainstream operational research has been widely acknowledged. We need to understand the criticisms which have been made—the 'where', 'why', and 'how' of OR's shortcomings —if we are to see the relevance of the alternative methods introduced in this book.

There are now a substantial number of critical dissections of the subject, in addition to those already referred to—see, for example Ackoff (1976, 1987), Eden (1982), Jackson (1987), Jackson and Keys (1984), Keys (1984), Rittel and Webber (1973), Rosenhead (1981, 1986), Rosenhead and Thunhurst (1982). Each offers a rather different emphasis or framework— though there is agreement on the serious, even dire nature of OR's predicament. The account which follows draws on all of these, though selectively, to produce a particular shaping of the material.

We may take as a starting point that operational research is an example, perhaps the exemplar, of 'rational comprehensive planning' (Rosenhead, 1980). This is a prescription for planning, policy formation or decision making consisting of five stages:

1. Identify objectives, with weights.
2. Identify alternative courses of action.
3. Predict consequence of actions in terms of objectives.
4. Evaluate the consequences on a common scale of value.
5. Select the alternative whose net benefit is highest.

In the specific case of operational research, stage 1 is the identification of the objective function, stage 3 is the modelling of cause–effect relationships, and stage 5 is the (normally computer-based) technique for identifying an optimal solution.

In its heyday of the 1960s and early 1970s this approach was widely seen as the rational way to take decisions. However, it came under attack from a variety of different perspectives (see Faludi, 1973). Critics, notably Lindblom, held it to be both socially undesirable and practically infeasible. Undesirable, because of the implicit assumption that a single agency could and should deploy a unitary set of agreed objectives—a recipe, it was claimed, for a holistic planning which would override more pluralistic arrangements. Infeasible, because of the lack of data, and of theory linking action and consequence, and because of the excessive intellectual demands on policy makers.

Some of these counter-arguments have a clear political motivation: rational comprehensive planning is portrayed not just as a tool of centralization, but as a step on the slippery slope to Soviet-style state planning. Resistance to rational comprehensive planning is here coupled with an ideological commitment to the market as the ideal mechanism for the allocation of resources. However, the attack on the *infeasibility* of rational comprehensive planning relies not on dogma but on evidence. The methods which had seemed to work well on more limited problems fell apart when given a chance to show their paces on more ambitious projects (Lee, 1973). The 'moon-ghetto metaphor', that methods capable of getting a person on to the moon could with advantage be employed on such lesser matters as solving the problems of inner city ghettos, proved to be a delusion (Nelson, 1974).

Much of this debate, though it applies more widely, has sprung from US experience. Particularly relevant to operational research is an analysis of the RAND Corporation's work in New York City (Greenberger, Crenson and Crissey, 1976). There RAND attempted to apply its cause–effect modelling and optimizing approach, honed on aerospace and defence problems, to the dilemmas of big city local government, with very mixed results. Success and implementation were obtained where the city agency was structured as a quasi-military hierarchy, and few if any of its members were analytically sophisticated; where the agency performed a well-defined task whose repetition generated reliable data suitable for quantitative manipulation; and where priorities between alternative objectives commanded almost universal consensus. The prime example of this congenial environment was encountered in the fire service; its diametrical opposite, and comprehensive failure, was found when RAND tackled the city's public health administration.

We can extend from the particular New York City–RAND experience to the more general criticism of operational research's dominant practice. Evidently the conditions for success are to be found principally, perhaps exclusively, at the tactical level. This corresponds to Ackoff's (1979a) observation that in US business enterprises, OR has been largely demoted from the corporate level, and is seen as appropriate only for secondary problems.

Certainly, improving the efficiency of operations is a thoroughly worthwhile task. However, the tactical is necessarily subordinate to the strategic. It is decisions at the higher level which set the context, determining the nature of those operations which, perhaps, OR may get a chance to optimize. And determining much else besides—management style, personnel policy, research and development strategy. ... From areas like these, operational research has been largely excluded. To a considerable extent it has excluded itself.

What have operational researchers been willing to recognize as falling within their remit? According to Checkland (1981), it has been that class of problems for which 'there is a desired state, S_1, and a present state, S_0, and alternative ways of getting from S_0 to S_1. "Problem solving", according to this view, consists of defining S_1 and S_0 and selecting the best means of reducing the difference between them.' Another way of putting this is that 'hard systems thinking', of which OR is an example, consists of 'systematically-ordered thinking concerned with means-definition in well-structured problems in which desirable ends can be stated'. There is seen to be only one problem 'out there'. The task of the analyst is to recognize it, and then turn the handle on the analytic sausage-machine. The method is, in principle, practitioner-free (Checkland, 1983).

How can so much be taken as 'given' in the traditional OR study? It is precisely because superordinate commitments are assumed to have been made at the level of policy formation, of design, of strategy. A focus limited to means–end linkages can be adequate if objectives have already been set (provided, of course, that consideration of—perhaps even the existence of—alternative objectives is rigorously excluded). The *context* of the technical task of OR is treated as frozen—held steady by dictat of legitimated decision makers, or by supposedly unproblematic assumptions of the analysts themselves. That task may nevertheless be of daunting complexity, calling forth dazzling feats of technical virtuosity—leading to Ackoff's (1979a) characterization of OR as 'mathematically sophisticated but contextually naive'.

A 'well-structured problem' will not just have unambiguous objectives, firm constraints, and establishable relationships between causes and effects. It will also, as a result of this specificity, have one clear solution.

There will be 'one best way'; and since it exists out there with the problem, the operational research technique's task, like that of a well-trained gun dog, is to go out and retrieve it.

Academic operational research has become dominated by the search for computable methods which can solve (in this sense) bigger problems, or solve problems of any given size more quickly; or for novel formulations which can trap recalcitrant problems within the algorithmic-optimizing net. The dominance is less strong in Britain than in the United States or continental Europe, but still clearly in evidence.

Practitioner groups have necessarily been more pragmatic. Some consultants have carved out a niche as purveyors of particular techniques. For external consultants this offers a marketable commodity to be exploited by repeat sales. For internal consultants it offers a reliable downhill path to a role of minor technical auxiliary. In either case the original OR orientation has been stood on its head. Whereas formerly the nature of OR was dictated by the nature of the problematic situations it faced, now increasingly the situations it faces are dictated by the techniques at its command (Ackoff, 1979a, 1987).

Of course, not all OR practitioner groups function like this, and few can do so exclusively and survive. What has been described here is an ideal type rather than a template. Those OR groups which flourish and continue to operate at strategic levels have found ways of avoiding the conceptual straitjacket. They do so through a network of organizational contacts, and through the maintenance of an internal culture which recognizes that problems are broader than the technical-fix orientation of traditional OR methods. But the general OR culture, and its proven techniques, offer them precious little help.

While OR remains shackled to its tool-box of models/techniques/solutions, it has little chance of a breakthrough on a broad front from resource allocation into system design, from the tactical into the strategic domain. When the commitments are made which set the context for lower level tasks, constraints are commonly ill-defined, or are themselves matters for policy clarification. Each decision situation is unique, because any commitment changes the configuration of resources, and so takes the organization into uncharted territory. Possible alternative ways forward need to be judged in relation to the threats and opportunities of the day after tomorrow, as much as to any present objectives. The dilemma, as experienced by those who have the responsibility for action, is commonly incompletely structured, or structured only in segments which fail to mesh. The clarity of the well-structured problem is simply unavailable, and an OR approach which asserts otherwise does violence to the nature of the situation.

The conditions under which one-of-a-kind strategic problems are confronted are the antithesis of those which permit algorithmic OR some scope for success. Consider the availability of data. There will be gaps because data collection on routine operations will not have covered aspects of the system which now prove to be of interest. There will be gaps because elements of the system under consideration, and the data relevant to it, will be under the control of others. There will be gaps because there are intangible dimensions of the possible outcomes which though crucial are resistant to quantification. And so on.

One key distinction between tactical and strategic situations is the uncertainty so characteristic of the latter. Not undemanding, domesticated uncertainty which will be satisfied with a diet of probabilities. For clarity, this can be better labelled as 'risk'. Non-risk uncertainty concerns unknown and sometimes unknowable dimensions of the present and the future. How will a relevant system respond to an unprecedented intervention? What actions will another actor in the drama take because of, or even in ignorance of, our decisions? What outcomes will be preferred in the future, or now, for that matter? These uncertainties present intractable difficulties in many problematic situations. Putting numbers on them does not reduce them to docility (Friend and Hickling, 1987).

According to Hopwood (1980), uncertainties have a direct effect on the manner in which organizational decision making is carried out. When uncertainties over the consequences of action, and over the objectives of action, are both low, the appropriate mode is 'computation'. If the former uncertainty (only) is high, the appropriate mode is 'judgement'; if only the latter uncertainty is relatively high, it is 'bargaining'; and if both are high, it switches to 'inspiration'. The typology was developed in the context of budgetary processes, but seems to apply more widely. Operational research has largely produced 'computational' tools. It has, therefore, been largely confined to problem situations where uncertainties (and hence the stakes) are low.

Where mainstream operational research has made an attempt to broaden its range, it has done so by treating the pulsating uncertainties of the strategic as if they can, indeed must, be fossilized as certainties, or at least tranquillized into probabilities. For what can an algorithm, untouched by human judgement, do with an unquantified uncertainty? With certainty, however, OR can optimize outcome. With probabilistic risk, OR can at least optimize 'expected' outcome.

Sandberg (1976) has called this approach 'colonizing the future'. Existing relationships in the decision environment, which generated the historical data, are projected out into the future, and these projections form the basis for the decisions which are taken. The resulting tendency is to congeal existing relationships, including power relationships, and so make the future, in its essence, the same as today. To Ackoff (1979a) this is the 'predict-and-prepare' paradigm. The future, with all its disparate behaviour, is assumed to unwind mechanistically and predictably under known causal laws. The OR task is simply to prepare (optimally) for the supposedly known future. But that future will be the product of many decisions made by many individuals and groups like our own. They too will, like us, be attempting to exercise deliberate choice despite a welter of uncertainties. If our decision is not pre-programmed and predictable, why should theirs be?

Evidently one of the significant sources of uncertainty is conflict. In conflict situations, parties will adjust their behaviour to take account in advance of possible opposing manoeuvres, and then in response to the ripostes which actually materialize. Thus interaction between different interests can occur both prospectively, as one or more parties tries to understand how far the threats block the opportunities, and as the play unfolds.

The only recognized orthodox OR approach which in any way incorporates the conflict dimension is the theory of games. However, the classical theory can handle only a thin caricature of the richness of real situations. Practitioners have made virtually no explicit use of game theory, leaving it as the preserve of academics of an unusually abstract disposition. Perhaps they are right—for these refined formulations are quite unsuitable as tools to facilitate the process of interaction.

This is not, of course, to say that the tools which OR *has* deployed have been any more appropriate. The classic OR formulation of the objective function to be maximized, whether under certainty or risk, amounts to an assumption that there is only one decision maker, with corresponding objectives, to be considered. In other words, any problem situation is treated as if it were a one-player game. The objective function is precisely a representation of what any one (who matters) most wants to achieve most fully. Because the formulation is based on an assumption that goals are agreed, or authoritatively laid down, conflict cannot be accommodated.

Furthermore, the one player whose game is recognized by OR is always on the same side. OR has worked almost exclusively for the managements of large organizations disposing of substantial resources, and controlling the labour of most of their members through the employment relationship (Rosenhead, 1986; Tinker and Lowe, 1984). Other types of organizations, especially those formed to promote or defend shared interests, exist, and have problems of decision making under complexity, uncertainty, and conflict. (These organizations differ from country to country. In Britain, examples include housing cooperatives, unemployed workers' groups, community health councils, environmental pressure groups, tenants' associations, trade union branches, community centres, etc.) Concerted moves to develop a practice of 'community operational research' have emerged only in the late 1980s. OR's neglect of these potential clients has contributed to its perception as an approach of only limited application.

What can be expected to happen when a methodology of this sort is all that those who profess to be expert in the analysis of systems have to offer? The answer is exclusion, but it comes in many varieties. Those who must take responsibility for decisions may simply exclude the analysts and analysis from involvement in the problem—because the formulation doesn't fit, or because of the opacity of the mathematical manipulations. Or the decision maker may decide to employ the method precisely *because* of its opacity. Other parties with less analytic capacity may be persuaded to accept the outcome as being an optimum scientifically determined by an incomprehensible technique. Their exclusion from understanding may be experienced as disabling, and potentially turbulent negotiations could then perhaps be bypassed—a less than honourable role for analysis. Or, most likely of all, the analysts will exclude themselves, finding that the unpacified nature of the problem situation leaves them nothing relevant to contribute.

Conflict also operates, in a way which undermines the classical OR approach, at a quite different level. For disagreement does not only occur between independent parties with irreconcilable interests. Analysis is used most often not for individuals but for organizations, which are aggregates of individuals. An organization is not an individual. It does not breathe, eat, or in any comparable sense have objectives. Decisions and actions emerge out of interactions between a variety of actors *internal* to the organization. Each may, indeed will, have an individual perspective or world-view (*Weltanschauung*) through which the actions and statements of others are interpreted. What the constraints are, what the priorities should be, what the problem actually is, may be perceived quite differently (Checkland, 1981; Eden, 1982, 1987).

A process of accommodation between participants is necessary before a problem focus can emerge which will carry assent and commitment to consequential actions. Yet the classical analytic approach asserts that an agreed organizational objective is required before analysis can start. Only in those relatively simple problems confined within the jurisdiction and competence of a unitary decision maker is this plausible. By denying or ignoring the need for mutual shaping of the problem definition, analysis renders itself largely irrelevant or even destructive to internal decision processes.

Classical operational research fails to see the world in which decisions get taken or problems get resolved as being peopled by purposeful human beings, and by groups of such individuals aggregated by imperfectly shared interests. This is a crippling limitation on its breadth of application. It is restricted to those cases (if any—views might differ here) in which it is legitimate or feasible to treat people as if they were machines. Operational researchers have tended to identify not only as scientists, but as natural scientists. Though their subject matter consists of purposeful systems of human and social activity, it has been approached just as if it were inert matter. Elements and relationships are treated as if they were unproblematical as to interpretation, and as predictable and stable as behaviour under natural laws. Social science perspectives have entered only rarely, and then most commonly in the form of behavioural science. Here the purposes of those who make up the system under study are indeed recognized, but only so that they may be manipulated (Rosenhead, 1989). The notion that these disparate and conflicting purposes might form active principles for, rather than passive objects of, analysis has been strikingly absent.

We have now completed a cursory tour of some of the major dimensions of criticism which have been directed at the conventional 'hard systems thinking' of which OR is a prominent part. The picture which has emerged, I believe, is of a dichotomy of problem situations, for which operational research has deployed a unitary paradigm appropriate to only one of the two classes. This dichotomy has been presented here as that between tactical and strategic problems. Others have coined more vivid terminology to dramatize the difference. Ackoff (1979a, 1981) distinguishes 'problems' from 'messes', and Rittel and Webber (1973) characterize 'tame' versus 'wicked' problems.

According to Ackoff (1979a) 'Managers are not confronted with problems that are independent of each other, but with dynamic situations that consist of complex systems of changing problems that interact with each other. I call such situations messes. Problems are abstractions extracted from messes by analysis; they are to messes as atoms are to tables and chairs.' It follows that optimal solutions to individual problems cannot be added to find an optimal solution to the whole mess: the behaviour of the mess will depend on how the solutions to its various parts interact. (Design processes are quintessentially of this character.) Instead of attempting to solve problems, we should be attempting to manage messes—which involves not solution but planning. If we insist on the 'solution' mode, we will be relegated to problems which are nearly independent, while messes go inadequately managed.

For Rittel, a 'tame' problem is one which can be specified, in a form agreed by any relevant parties, ahead of the analysis, and which does not change during the analysis. A 'wicked' problem, by contrast, is ill-defined. There are many alternative types and levels of explanation for the phenomena of concern, and any selected type of explanation determines the nature of the solution. Any wicked problem can indeed be seen as only a symptom of another wicked problem. Alternative solutions are, in any case, not true or false, but good or bad—and there are interested parties with conflicting perspectives who are better qualified to make such judgements than the analysts. The formulation of the problem, therefore, is only finally arrived at when a solution or resolution has been evolved. According to Rittel 'the methods of Operations Research ... become operational ... only *after* the most important decisions have already been made, i.e. after the [wicked] problem has already been tamed' (Rittel and Webber, 1973).

In less picturesque language, Ravetz (1971) offers constructive insights about the distinction between the two types of problem, which he calls 'technical' and 'practical', and the analytic methods appropriate to them. Technical problems are those for which at the inception of the study there exists a clearly specified function to be performed, for which a best means can be sought by experts. For a practical problem, by contrast, there will exist (at most) some general statement of a purpose to be achieved. The output of any study, to be useful, does not consist, essentially, of a specification of optimal means. It must propose, rather, an argument in favour of accepting some particular definition of the problem which leads to a corresponding means of solution.

For technical problems, expertise and technical authority are at a premium. For practical problems, the realm of expertise is confined to the technical derivation of means from ends. The larger questions, of the appropriateness of ends, are not addressable by techniques in any way comparable. These questions demand, rather, an argumentation based on an interaction of judgement and analysis—and experts in analysis have no monopoly of judgement.

The dilemma for those who perceive the two types of problem, and see no alternative to the technical methods of traditional operational research, has been well captured by Donald Schon (1987):

> In the swampy lowland, messy, confusing problems defy technical solution. The irony of this situation is that the problems of the high ground tend to be relatively unimportant to individuals or society at large, however great their technical interest may be, while in the swamp lie the problems of greatest human concern. The practitioner must choose. Shall he remain on the high ground where he can solve relatively unimportant problems according to prevailing standards of rigor, or shall he descend to the swamp of important problems and non-rigorous inquiry?

The next section will explore the desirable attributes of formal methods, rigorous or not, which can help to make sense of the otherwise trackless swamp.

The way forward

The present author has suggested elsewhere (Rosenhead, 1981) that the dominant paradigm of operational research has the six characteristics shown in Table 1.

Evidently many of these features have been highlighted in the preceding survey of criticisms of operational research and the 'hard systems' approach of which it is a part.

The purpose of the present section is to move on from critique or diagnosis towards prescription. How could a formal, systematic approach avoid these pitfalls, and so be capable of illuminating decision making, design choice, and problem resolution in situations which cannot be fully structured in advance?

One simple, even simplistic, way of envisioning what such an approach might look like is to turn the dominant paradigm on its head. For, if the orthodox approach is so inappropriate, surely its dialectical opposite must have much to offer. So we might consider an approach with the characteristics listed in Table 2.

Table 1
Characteristics of the dominant paradigm of operational research

1. Problem formulation in terms of a single objective and optimization. Multiple objectives, if recognized, are subjected to trade-off on to a common scale.
2. Overwhelming data demands, with consequent problems of distortion, data availability, and data credibility.
3. Scientization and depoliticization, assumed consensus.
4. People are treated as passive objects.
5. Assumption of a single decision maker with abstract objectives from which concrete actions can be deduced for implementation through a hierarchical chain of command.
6. Attempts to abolish future uncertainty, and pre-take future decisions.

Table 2
Characteristics for an alternative paradigm

1. Non-optimizing; seeks alternative solutions which are acceptable on separate dimensions, without trade-offs.
2. Reduced data demands, achieved by greater integration of hard and soft data with social judgements.
3. Simplicity and transparency, aimed at clarifying the terms of conflict.
4. Conceptualizes people as active subjects.
5. Facilitates planning from the bottom-up.
6. Accepts uncertainty, and aims to keep options open for later resolution.

When these characteristics of an alternative paradigm were first proposed in the late 1970s they seemed quite theoretical—at best, a blue print for a form of analytic assistance which might perhaps one day come into being. It was encouraging, though, that this sketch for a paradigm, like the orthodox version which it challenged, was internally consistent. The orthodox version, aiming in effect to provide methods for resource allocation within a bureaucratic organization, is characterized by deskilling, centralization, and control (Rosenhead, 1986). The alternative paradigm is similarly coherent, but with its bases in reskilling, decentralization, and liberation.

In fact it has become increasingly evident that methods with this orientation are not just theoretical possibilities. They exist; and some of them are described in this volume. Indeed most of these existed, though in a relatively underdeveloped form, before the existence of such a paradigm was postulated. Robustness Analysis, Strategic Choice, and Metagame Analysis were all conceived in the late 1960s. Soft Systems Methodology can be traced to the early 1970s, and Hypergame Analysis and Cognitive Mapping emerged in the later part of that decade. However, their relative prominence is quite new. The methods themselves have grown in sophistication; and analysts and decision makers have become more aware of the deficiencies of the orthodox inheritance. Only recently has it seemed not overly ambitious to identify them as a distinctive, coherent, and significant new paradigm in being.

This is not meant to imply that each of the methodologies described in this book exhibits all of the six characteristics of Table 2. Certainly some of the methodologies concentrate more on particular aspects (conflict, for example, or uncertainty) than others. And some of the characteristics, bottom-up planning in particular, require more than a cultural, conceptual or methodological shift to bring to full life. But it is also probably true that few if any particular techniques developed within the orthodox paradigm show all the hallmarks of *that* approach, either. The paradigms represent, as it were, ideal types, from which any practical example will deviate to some extent.

There is no call, here, to run the methodologies described in this volume past this, or any other, checklist of attributes. They are able, as it were, to speak for themselves at length in the following chapters. (How well the methodologies fit the alternative paradigm will be given some consideration in the final chapter.) It will be more useful, instead, to conclude this introduction with some general observations arising out of the contrast between the two paradigms. These will focus, in particular, on their assumptions about the nature of the decision process which the analysis is intended to aid, and about the role for technique.

Practitioners of the hard systems approach have failed to concern themselves over much with how the decisions they analyse actually get taken. There has even been rejection on principle, along the lines that 'the function of operational research is simply to provide decision makers with *information* on which to base decisions—it should not concern itself with the decision process itself' (Adelson and Norman, 1969). As early as 1969, this quotation was part of an attack on the rejectionist position it described. More recently, especially as awareness of an 'implementation problem' grew, so too did an acknowledgement that simply finding the 'right answer' for decision makers was not enough. Some advice about the craft of staying in touch with, improving communication with, your manager became commonplace in methodological articles. However, this was scarcely seen as affecting the methods to be used—only how you could get the analysis accepted and the recommendation implemented. Anyone who evinced a deeper concern about how the managerial decision process might affect OR's methods tended to get written off as unhealthily introverted.

This tunnel vision can be understood at a number of levels. One is that the natural science bias of OR and related approaches appeals particularly to those who prefer to exclude ambiguity and subjectivity in favour of a world of clean certainties. However, there is a less psychological level of explanation. An approach which attempts to substitute theory and analysis for judgement sets itself a stiff challenge. The resulting techniques are complex and opaque, and consequently exclude lay participation. Judgement is thereby largely sealed off, and the need for comprehensive complexity of technique is reinforced. The process of mutual exclusion of analysis and judgement is self-reinforcing. Such techniques guarantee a denuded social process of decision making.

But the converse is also true. If simpler, more transparent, less ambitious analytic tools are deployed, lay participation can be a reality. Precisely because of this activation of social interaction and judgement, methods do not need to be so complex. This process also is self-reinforcing. One can have a complex technology and a minimal social process; or one can have a rich social process of decision making and a correspondingly modest technology.

The alternative methodology attempts to exploit the potential of the second of these two possibilities. Though the importance of process does not figure as an explicit category in Table 2, it is implicit in several of those which are listed, and made possible by others.

A vestigial social process of decision making may be tolerated under particular circumstances—either those of authoritarian rule, or those of tactical autonomy. The scope which these circumstances offer to operational research and its siblings is, however, limited. As de Neufville and Keeney (1972) have stated 'Typically large decisions are not made by a single group of like minded people ... they are, rather, the result of extended negotiations, either implicit or explicit, between representatives of different points of view'.

Near the shop-floor, the command relationship may predominate. But at higher levels, where more strategic questions must be decided, the neat bureaucratic lines break down. It is necessary to assess information from both quantitative and non-quantitative sources, provided out of a range of expertises (engineering, legal, industrial relations, marketing, accounting) resistant to hierarchical ordering. The issues which are thrown up will be debated and reshaped from a variety of different perspectives. The threats and opportunities posed by uncontrollable elements must receive close attention, in order to assess the scope for collaborative or conflictual activity.

These aspects of strategic decision making have been expressed in terms of the decision processes of a conventionally structured organization. But they apply still more forcefully when the decision making is inter-organizational, or when (as in community operational research) the organization is democratically rather than hierarchically controlled. In all these types of situation, commitment to decision cannot be expected to follow a linear sequence of formulation–analysis–solution–implementation. Commitment will result, rather, from mechanisms such as coalition formation, consensus building, debate, negotiation.

For formal analysis to be helpful in these circumstances it has to be tailored to the requirements of a highly interactive process. If it cannot achieve fit with the time-scale, the dynamic, the language of these processes, it will impede and be excluded. If the decision under consideration has a high content of complexity, uncertainty and conflict, the absence of appropriate analytic assistance will be a handicap for the participants. The process of resolving the issue will be lengthier, more abrasive, less educational and, quite possibly, less effective than it should be.

Those who develop and practise the more interactive problem structuring methods described in this book are, and need to be, more acutely aware of this organizational environment. Checkland (1981), for example, distinguishes between customers, actors, and problem owners, in what has also been called the 'client system' (Tomlinson, 1984). Eden (1982, 1987) addresses the different social processes by which problems are constructed, and by which work is terminated as participants disengage. And so on. Clarity on such issues is seen not as an academic or intellectual bonus, but as the key to effective analytic participation in the management debate.

Effective participation in the process of formulation, debate, and refocusing can take many forms. There can be both visible and invisible products (Friend and Hickling, 1987)—plans, designs, and recommendations, but also changes in understanding and in relationships. Authors in this book differ in the significance which they attribute to these two types of analytic products. The tension between helping to provide answers to problems, and helping to improve decision making (Howard, 1986), is a healthy one. It is largely absent from the dominant OR paradigm.

It remains only to consider briefly what sort of tools, techniques or methodologies can contribute helpfully to such social processes of decision making—briefly, because the following chapters provide extensive accounts of such methodologies, and of how they work in practice.

One evident restriction on any formal methods is that overt (or even covert) mathematics of any complexity is likely to render the analysis inaccessible to most of its potential clientele. How then can complexity be represented, grasped and manipulated? Common sense and experience both suggest that graphical methods have much to offer. Diagrams can display in spatial terms quite intricate networks of influence, causality, similarity or compatibility. Representations of considerable complexity, capturing perhaps provisional understandings of a situation, can be apprehended visually with surprising ease. Even those without previous experience in the particular graphical notation are often able to adopt the language readily, and use it to suggest modifications to the 'model'. Such models (and there are several employed later in this volume) are necessarily non-quantitative. However, if the purpose is to survey possibilities rather than identify solutions, the loss is slight.

This perception leads on to a further positive property for alternative analytic methods. If the purpose is not to find a single solution, this implies that the 'solution space' as a whole is of interest. The set of all feasible future systems, designs, eventualities or whatever may be unmanageably large. Methods which can screen out the infeasible, scan the solution space, explore the effect of alternative constraints, and throw up contrasting possibilities are what are required—and also in short supply.

To render this option scanning both manageable in scale and also comprehensible to those who must take and live with any decisions, another act of analytic self-denial is called for. Continuous variables, with all the seductive appeal (to mathematicians) of calculus, may have to be sacrificed. Instead, a small number of representative discrete options will need to stand in for the theoretically infinite spectrum of alternatives. The relative advantages of these options can then be displayed in ways which focus the act or process of choice.

Complexity is not the sole indicator that appropriate analysis could have a job to do. Uncertainty is another prime confuser of the intuition. Techniques generated out of the orthodox paradigm have sought to order this chaos through the use of probabilities. Where data are available from previous experience in comparable circumstances, this mathematization is legitimate. However, these conditions are only met in tactical decision making. For unrepeatable situations, previous experience offers no reliable anticipation of uncontrollable or unforeseen events, or of outcome.

Decision theorists have attempted to escape from this impasse through the use of subjective probabilities—a quantification of how likely certain events are *felt* to be. (There are, in fact, 'harder' and 'softer' varieties of decision theory. What follows applies less strongly to the latter.) The resulting clarity is achieved, however, at unreasonable cost. The problem is removed whole from the swamp to the high ground, where mathematicians and economists can play with it and determine a best answer. But this 'best' is based on weighting the various possible outcomes by their probabilities, and averaging out. Such statistical 'expectations' can be highly appropriate for repetitive situations, where one can 'play the averages'. But a strategic commitment does not determine only what some pay-off will be. It can also influence a whole train of future events, many under the control of others, which will determine the next problematic situation to be faced. As a general guide, one could say that probabilities are likely to be a useful aid to choice only when what is at issue is of less than compelling importance.

This understanding has implications for any alternative methodology suitable for assisting with less tame problems. They cannot employ probabilities (and none of the methods in this book does so). Instead of the calculus of probabilities, we need a calculus of *possibilities*. Methods should structure and manipulate the events or outcomes which participants see as relevant to the issues which confront them. Which of these are perceived as relevant may depend on likelihood of occurrence, or gravity of consequence, or both.

What is important is that methods do not force the problem into a particular quantitative straitjacket. It must be possible for participants to identify events or outcomes which need to be taken into account, without being obliged to place (quite possibly meaningless) numbers on their significance. One example of this more appropriate approach is the use of scenarios. Placing pressing decisions in the context of alternative future environments is a way of opening up discussion about threats and opportunities. Forecasting just one future, or attempting to put probabilities on the unknowable so that it can be averaged over, is a way of closing discussion down.

Methods with the characteristics which I have been discussing are quite underdeveloped. The intellectual investment so far made in them is only a fraction of that which has been poured into optimizing algorithms. What is available is limited in scope and variety. In particular situations there may be no alternative method which fits the bill. Those providing analytic assistance may not have the luxury, or luck, of being able to invent the wheel while the vehicle is in motion. Often then, the most constructive option will be the radical re-use of existing technology. For example, techniques designed as optimizing routines can be used to explore the pattern of alternative optima under different assumptions. (This goes beyond orthodox sensitivity analysis, which investigates by how much assumptions would need to change before the identified optimum would be dethroned.) In this and others ways, it may be possible to ride pick-a-back on the investment of the optimizers, while subverting their implicit message.

Recognition of the likely need for improvisation is, of course, no reason for remaining inadequately informed about the alternative methods which do exist. The following chapters provide introductions to a range of such problem structuring methodologies. We will return to more general questions at the end of the book.

References

Ackoff, R. L. (1974). 'The social responsibility of operational research', *Opl Res. Q.*, **25**, 361–71.

Ackoff, R. L. (1975). 'A reply to the comments of Keith Chesterton, Robert Goodsman, Jonathan Rosenhead, and Colin Thunhurst', *Opl Res. Q.*, **26**, 96–9.

Ackoff, R. L. (1976). 'Does quality of life have to be quantified?', *Opl Res. Q.*, 27, 289–303.

Ackoff, R. L. (1979a). 'The future of operational research is past', *J. Opl Res. Soc.*, **30**, 93–104.

Ackoff, R. L. (1979b). 'Resurrecting the future of operational research', *J. Opl Res. Soc.*, **30**, 189–99.

Ackoff, R. L. (1981). 'The art and science of mess management', *Interfaces*, **11**, 20–6.

Ackoff, R. L. (1987). 'OR, a post mortem', *Opns Res.*, **35**, 471–4.

Adelson, R. M., and Norman, J. M. (1969). 'Operational research and decision-making', *Opl Res. Q.*, **20**, 399–413.

Botts, T. *et al.* (1972). Letters to the Editor, *Opns Res.*, **20**, 205–46.

Checkland, P. B. (1981). *Systems Thinking, Systems Practice*, Wiley, Chichester.

Checkland, P. B. (1983). 'O.R. and the Systems Movement: mappings and conflicts', *J. Opl Res. Soc.*, **34**, 661–75.

Chesterton, K., Goodsman, R., Rosenhead, J., and Thunhurst, C. (1975). 'A comment on Ackoff's "The Social Responsibility for Operational Research",' *Opl Res. Q.*, **26**, 91–5.

Churchman, C. W. *et al.* (1972). 'Discussion of the ORSA Guidelines', *Mgmt Sci.*, **18**, 608–29.

Dando, M. R., and Bennett, P. G. (1981). 'A Kuhnian crisis in management science?', *J. Opl Res. Soc.*, **32**, 91–103.

Eden, C. (1982). 'Problem construction and the influence of OR', *Interfaces*, *12*, 50–60.

Eden, C. (1987). 'Problem-solving or problem-finishing', in *New Directions in Management Science* (Eds. M. C. Jackson and P. Keys), pp. 97–107, Gower, Aldershot.

Faludi, A. (Ed.) (1973). *Planning Theory*, Pergamon, Oxford.

Friend, J. K., and Hickling, A. (1987). *Planning Under Pressure*, Pergamon, Oxford.

Greenberger, M., Crenson, M. A., and Crissey, B. L. (1976). *Models in the Policy Process*, Russell Sage, New York.

Hopwood, A. G. (1980). 'The organisational and behavioural aspects of budgetting and control', in *Topics in Management Accounting* (Eds. J. Arnold, B. Carsberg, and R. Scapens), pp. 221–40, Philip Allen, Deddington.

Howard, N. (1986). 'Usefulness of Metagame Analysis', *J. Opl Res. Soc.*, **37**, 430–2.

Jackson, M. C. (1982). 'The nature of "soft" systems thinking: the work of Churchman, Ackoff and Checkland', *J. Appl. Sys. Anal.*, **9**, 17–29. See also replies in the same issue.

Jackson, M. C. (1983). 'The nature of "soft" systems thinking: comment on the three replies', *J. Appl. Sys. Anal.*, **10**, 109–13.

Jackson, M. C. (1987). 'Present positions and future prospects in management science', *Omega*, **15**, 455–66.

Jackson, M. C., and Keys, P. (1984). 'Towards a system of systems methodologies', *J. Opl Res. Soc.*, **35**, 473–86.

Keys, P. (1987). 'Traditional management science and the emerging critique', in *New Directions in Management Science* (Eds. M. C. Jackson and P. Keys), pp. 1–25, Gower, Aldershot.

Kuhn, T. (1970). *The Structure of Scientific Revolutions*, University of Chicago Press, Chicago.

Lee, D. B. (1973). 'Requiem for large-scale models', *J. Am. Inst. Planners*, **39**, 163–78.

Nelson, R. R. (1974). 'Intellectualizing about the moon-ghetto metaphor: a study of the current malaise of rational analysis of social problems', *Policy Sci.*, **5**, 375–414.

de Neufville, R., and Keeney, R. L. (1972). 'Systems evaluation through decision analysis: Mexico City Airport', *J. Sys. Eng.*, **3**, 34–50.

ORSA *Ad Hoc* Committee on Professional Standards (1971). 'Guidelines for the practice of operations research', *Opns Res.*, **19**, 1123–258.

Ravetz, J. R. (1971). *Scientific Knowledge and its Social Problems*, Oxford University Press, Oxford.

Rittel, H. W. J., and Webber, M. M. (1973). 'Dilemmas in a general theory of planning', *Policy Sci.*, **4**, 155–69.

Rosenhead, J. (1976). 'Some further comments on the social responsibility of operational research', *Opl Res. Q.*, **27**, 266–72.

Rosenhead, J. (1980). 'Planning under uncertainty I: the inflexibility of methodologies', *J. Opl Res. Soc.*, **31**, 209–16.

Rosenhead, J. (1981). 'Operational research in urban planning', *Omega*, **9**, 345–64.

Rosenhead, J. (1984). 'Debating systems methodology: conflicting ideas about conflict and ideas', *J. Appl. Sys. Anal.*, **11**, 79–84.

Rosenhead, J. (1986). 'Custom and practice', *J. Opl Res. Soc.*, **37**, 335–43.

Rosenhead, J. (1989). 'Operational research—social science or barbarism?', in *Operational Research and the Social Sciences* (Eds. M. C. Jackson, P. Keys, and S. Cropper), Plenum, New York.

Rosenhead, J., and Thunhurst, C. (1982). 'A materialist analysis of operational research', *J. Opl Res. Soc.*, **33**, 111–22.

Sandberg, A. (1976). *The Limits to Democratic Planning*, LiberForlag, Stockholm.

Schon, D. A. (1987). *Educating the Reflective Practitioner: toward a new design for teaching and learning in the professions*, Jossey-Bass, San Francisco.

Thunhurst, C. (1973). 'Who does operational research operate for?' Paper presented at Operational Research Society Annual Conference, Torquay (mimeo).

Tinker, T., and Lowe, T. (1984). 'One-dimensional management science: the making of a technocratic consciousness', *Interfaces*, **14**, 40–56.

Tocher, K. D. (1977). 'Planning systems', *Phil. Trans. R. Soc. Lond. A*, **287**, 425–41.

Tomlinson, R. (1984). 'Rethinking the process of Systems Analysis and Operational Research: from practice to precept—and back again', in *Rethinking the Process of Operational Research and Systems Analysis* (Eds. R. Tomlinson and I. Kiss), pp. 205–21, Pergamon, Oxford.

Tomlinson, R., and Kiss, I. (Eds.) (1984). *Rethinking the Process of Operational Research and Systems Analysis,* Pergamon, Oxford.

2

Using cognitive mapping for strategic options development and analysis (SODA)

Colin Eden

Introduction

Strategic Options Development and Analysis (SODA) is a method for working on complex problems. It is an *approach* which is designed to help OR consultants help their clients work with messy problems. These are generally problems which demand an ability to use model building to help with both quantitative *and* qualitative aspects of the problem. It is an approach which aims to encourage the consultant to bring together two sets of skills. Firstly, the skills of a facilitator of the *processes* involved in getting a team to work together efficiently and effectively. Secondly, the skills to construct a model of, and appropriately analyse, the *content* which each member of the team wishes to address. The process management issues are not taken as independent of the content management issues. Rather, each aspect informs the way in which the other skill is best utilized. (Eden, 1986).

Thus with SODA the traditional model building and analysis skills of the operational researcher are used to handle the complexity which faces a team working on a messy issue. However, the nature of both the model and its analysis are powerful *facilitative devices*. They facilitate the better

Rational Analysis for a Problematic World
Edited by J. Rosenhead. © 1989 John Wiley & Sons Ltd

management of the process by which the team will arrive at something approaching *consensus* and *commitment* to action. Indeed the aim of seeking consensus rather than compromise, and commitment rather than agreement produces a distinctive and multifaceted measure of success for the use of the SODA approach.

Underlying this notion of success is a view of problem solving that focuses on the point at which people feel confident to take action. This is in contrast to the idea of striving for the 'right answer'. (One way of conceptualizing this difference is as an orientation to 'problem finishing/alleviation' rather than 'problem solving'—see Eden, 1987.) Thus SODA's success cannot be measured by the rationality or optimality of the action portfolio in terms of content alone.

For SODA, one can only evaluate success through a consideration of the personalities, roles, politics, and power dimensions of the *specific* group of individuals that make up the decision-making team. (The same may be said of Soft Systems Methodology and Strategic Choice.) Some practitioners (for example Machol, 1980) have alleged that the recourse to social considerations is an attempt to shelter behind the obfuscation provided by 'sociological jargon' and so excuse improper OR practice. One could argue the contrary, that the exclusion of such considerations has often been a factor limiting OR's acceptability.

An OR consultant will be interested in employing a SODA approach to problems *only* when some or all of the following conditions prevail. Firstly, the consultant is personally interested in the practical aspects of social psychology and cognitive psychology, that is in being explicit and reflective about managing a social process. The consultant will often be more happy operating 'on the hoof' than 'in the backroom'. The consultant will tend to *seek out* theories and methods which help analyse the potential tensions between members of the problem solving team.

Secondly, the consultant tends to relate personally to a small number (three to ten persons) of 'significant' people as client. This is in contrast to some consultants who see themselves acting with respect to 'the organization' as client.

Thirdly, the consultant will tend towards a contingent and cyclic approach to working on problems. The approach will be 'to proceed flexibly and experimentally from broad concepts to specific commitments, making the latter concrete as late as possible' (Quinn, 1980). This tendency is to be distinguished from that of working steadily through a linear and deterministic process towards a clear goal. The consultant will be as pleased to work in a 'quick and dirty' manner as in a 'thorough and complete' manner.

Finally, the consultant will be more interested in designing and managing problem solving workshops rather than in research and analysis of the problem characteristics. The personality of the consultant will be such that action satisfies more than discovery.

These characteristics are not better than other laudable profiles for the 'good' consultant. They are intended to help the reader gain a rough impression of the sort of person most likely to enjoy working with SODA. Similarly, they importantly encapsulate the sort of client who will feel comfortable working with SODA. The client will need to be sympathetic to the above characteristics. In particular, the client group will be looking for *help* in thinking through the issue they face, without expecting the consultant to act as an expert with respect to content. The expectation (Eden and Sims, 1979) to be established by both parties is that the consultant will contribute professional expertise in bringing together different perspectives, analysing the implication of those perspectives, and formulating a process for agreeing action.

A framework and context for 'SODA'

The framework of concepts shown in Figure 1 shows the four important and interacting theoretical perspectives that imply the need for an approach such as SODA. The figure shows four perspectives about the *individual*, about the *nature of organizations*, about *consulting practice*, and about the role of *technology and technique*. Each of these perspectives leads to the core notion that drives SODA: the application of a *facilitative device*. The following narrative discusses each of these perspectives in more detail.

The SODA approach has its foundation in 'subjectivism'. Each member of a client group is held to have his or her own personal subjective view of the 'real' problem. The wisdom and experience of members of the team is a key element in developing decisions with which participants feel confident. It is because of the complexity and richness that arises from attention to subjectivity, that a focus for SODA work is on the managing of *process* as well as content. This view of behaviour, judgement, and decision making in organizations sees experience-gathering as an act of scientific endeavour. This endeavour is more valid to the decision maker than the formal experimentation which we normally designate science.

The manager is taken to be involved in the psychological *construction* of the world rather than the *perception* of an objective world—'if men define situations as real, they are real in their consequences' (Thomas and Thomas, 1928). So it is the interpretation of an event that is reality, rather than the perception of it. Action arises out of the meaning of situations, and the meaning will vary from one individual to another even if the character-

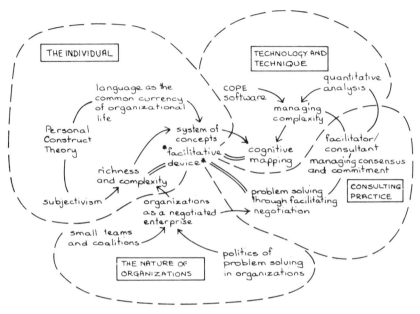

Figure 1
Theory and concepts guiding SODA

istics of the event are agreed by both individuals to be similar. Thus individuality is legitimate and allowed to blossom within a SODA project. Protecting individuality is designed to ensure that the outcome of the project is both creative and also consensual.

This orientation is different from that which drives the 'Systems Movement'. It is most easily differentiated through the distinction Silverman (1970) makes between the Systems Framework and the Action Framework (this distinction is explored more fully in Eden and Graham, 1983). Thus

> while behaviour may be viewed as a reflection of the organisational structure and its problems, . . . it is equally as valid to suggest that an organisation itself is the outcome of the interaction of motivated people attempting to resolve their own problems. . . . The environment in which an organisation is located might usefully be regarded as a source of meanings through which members defined their actions and made sense of the actions of others. (Silverman, 1970)

In organizations, teams are deliberately created in order that each member of the team may bring a different perspective to an issue. A different construction of problems comes from having a different role and from a different set of experiences and wisdom. In the SODA approach we simply aim to exploit this fully as a benefit. However, exploiting individuality implies deliberately encouraging more richness in problem construction by accentuating complexity within problems.

This focus on the individual, or on the *psychology* of problem solving, is guided by the 'Theory of Personal Constructs' (Kelly, 1955). This particular body of psychological theory is a *cognitive* theory. It argues that human beings are continually striving to 'make sense' of their world in order to 'manage and control' that world. In this way it implicitly sees the individual as a problem finder/problem solver, using concepts rather than emotion to guide action. Therefore, it suits the particular purpose of working with individuals who are constrained by a need to *explain* their actions within their organizational world. (Other psychological theories are appropriate for other purposes.) Within SODA, construct theory has practical significance because cognitive mapping, the technology and technique (in Figure 1), works with 'language as the common currency of organizational life'. A 'cognitive map' is a model of the 'system of concepts' used by the client to communicate the nature of a problem. The model represents the *meaning* of a concept by its relationship to other concepts.

The individual, within an organizational setting, will use all methods of communication in order to negotiate with and persuade others. However, SODA focuses on that form of communication which is most legitimate in organizations, i.e. language. This means ignoring, to a very considerable extent, the role of non-verbal communication in its own right. It assumes that the consultant will use language as an adequate (to the client) modelling medium to capture the meaning that derives from emotion expressed through intonation, body movement, and personality.

The above has discussed the segment labelled 'the individual' in Figure 1. Following the figure in an anticlockwise direction leads to a consideration of 'the nature of organizations'.

A facilitator considering the use of the SODA approach needs to be clear about, and in sympathy with, a particular view of decision making in organizations. This is one which emphasizes the role of the individual, in contrast to an inclination to 'reify' the organization or parts of it as if it were an individual. Many practitioners prefer to work with 'the organization' or 'the department' as the focus of attention. I do not wish to argue here that this is wrong, but rather to be clear that it does not inform the SODA approach.

A view of organizations which focuses on the individual will inevitably also focus on the organization as a changing set of coalitions in which politics and power are significant explanations of decision making. This view relates to March and Olsen's (1976) notion that an organization has a 'garbage can' of problems passing it by, out of which individual managers will arbitrarily select those that most fulfil their personal ambitions. That is to say, 'organizations are a negotiated enterprise' (Strauss *et al.*, 1963), whose participants are continuously negotiating and renegotiating their roles within it.

These two perspectives, on organizations and individuals, come together to form a 'consulting practice' (the third segment of Figure 1) which centres on the role of negotiation in effective problem solving. The consultant is the instrument for facilitating this negotiation, and for managing consensus and commitment. The consultant is taken to have a central professional role in both *designing and managing* this negotiation.

These three perspectives on the individual, the nature of organizations, and the characteristics of consulting practice each derive from seeing an organization as a negotiated enterprise. Through appropriate 'technology and technique' (the final segment of Figure 1) these building blocks come together through the concept at the core of Figure 1 — 'a facilitative device'. Our approach is aimed at providing a device which can be used to facilitate managing the messiness of deciding on action. In this way we are attempting to create an analytically sound method of dealing with both content *and* process.

In the case of SODA the technique is 'cognitive mapping', and the technology to help manage complexity is computer software called COPE.

Cognitive mapping as an OR modelling technique

The technique or methodology of 'cognitive mapping' does not exist independently of the framework described above. It exists, rather, as one of the key techniques which are employed in the prosecution of SODA. SODA is the *approach* to working with clients, out of which has grown the particular *technique* of cognitive mapping.

'Cognitive mapping' is the label for the general task of mapping a person's cognitions within the field of psychological research on perception. The term cognitive map was first used by Tolman in 1948, and has been used widely since then by researchers in a wide variety of disciplines. In this chapter we are introducing a version of cognitive mapping which has been specifically developed to help internal and external consultants/ facilitators deal with some important aspects of their job. It is also distinctive because it is a modelling approach which is directly derived from a substantive theory within cognitive psychology (Kelly, 1955).

The SODA-based version of 'cognitive mapping', as a modelling system, is founded on the belief expressed in Figure 1 that language is the basic currency of organizational problem solving. Whorf (1956) has vividly expressed the underlying view—that 'the world is presented in a kaleidoscope flux of impressions which has to be organized by our minds—and this means largely by the linguistic systems in our minds ... we cut nature up, organize it into concepts, and ascribe significances as weights largely because we are parties to an agreement to organize it in this way'.

A cognitive map is a *model*—a model amenable to formal analysis. It is a model designed to represent the way in which a person defines an issue. It is not a general model of someone's thinking, neither is it intended to be a simulation model of decision making. It is a network of ideas linked by arrows; the network is coded from what a person says. The arrows indicate the way in which one idea may lead to, or have implications for, another. Thus a map is a network of nodes and links (a 'directed graph'). Some years ago it seemed helpful to devise computer software that would help with storing the maps and with their analysis. In consequence, software called 'COPE' (Eden, Smithin, and Wiltshire, 1980, 1985) was developed to act as an aid in developing the methodology for working with teams. It became an integral, but not essential, part of the process of working on problems. I shall comment later upon the increasing role that the software COPE and associated computer technology is now playing both in the management of process, and in the management of content complexity.

When managers talk about an issue, and what should be done, they use language which is designed to argue why the world is 'like it is and how it might be changed'. Take a simple example of one person expressing a view about profit sharing.

> The latter-day Labour party, aiming to appeal upmarket, is in a more ambivalent position. At a time when they are looking for a concordat with the unions, union opposition to profit sharing—because of the fear of weakening the role of collective bargaining—is hard to avoid. American experience with Employee Share Ownership Plans since the early 1980s has led to a drop in union membership in firms with these profit sharing schemes.
> [Extract from the *Guardian* newspaper 'Who gains from profit sharing?' by Jane McLoughlin, 14 May 1986 (slightly modified).]

Figure 2 shows how this piece of written, rather than spoken, argument may be converted into a cognitive map. Important phrases are selected to capture the essential aspects of the arguments. An attempt to capture the meaning of each phrase is made by trying to identify the contrasting idea. Thus 'Labour support for profit sharing' is contrasted with 'ambivalence towards profit sharing', and 'upmarket appeal' is contrasted with 'working class appeal'. This latter contrast is a possibly incorrect attempt by the

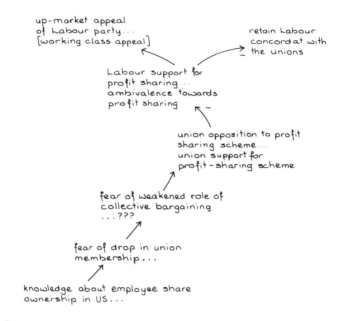

up-market appeal
of Labour party...
[working class appeal]

retain Labour
concordat with
the unions

Labour support for
profit sharing...
ambivalence towards
profit sharing

union opposition to profit
sharing scheme...
union support for
profit-sharing scheme

fear of weakened role of
collective bargaining
...???

fear of drop in union
membership...

knowledge about employee share
ownership in US...

Figure 2
An example of a small cognitive map ('...' is read as 'rather than' and separates the first pole of the concept from the contrasting pole)

coder to understand the meaning of 'upmarket' by making a guess. The *meaning* of a phrase together with its contrast (a 'concept') is further elaborated by considering the argumentation that links the concept with others. In a cognitive map this is shown by linking arrows.

Thus 'concept A leading to B and explained by C and D' has a different meaning from 'concept A leading to E and explained by C and F'. The meaning of a concept is given by the contrasting pole plus the explanatory and consequential concepts, not by any dictionary definition.

The phrases and linking arrows are not precisely a replication of the language used by the person speaking: they have been modified to reflect the need for an *action orientation*. Each of the concepts in Figure 2 is written as a 'call to action' and is intended to suggest an option for changing the nature of the situation in a positive way. Similarly, the argumentation (direction of the arrows) is such that an option always leads to a desired outcome, with the most important outcome hierarchically superior to others. The means to an end is always the subordinate concept, and placed at the tail of the arrow linking two concepts. In Figure 2 the highest order goal is taken to be the 'Labour party seeking an upmarket appeal', alongside the other presumed goal of 'retaining Labour's concordat with the unions'. All the options are taken to have implications for these goals.

In addition, the map indicates the nature of the argumentation by adding a negative sign to the end of an arrow if the first phrase of one concept relates to the second phrase of the other concept. Thus 'union opposition' leads to 'ambivalence *rather than* support'. The reasons for coding so that a negative sign is needed are several, it is not designed deliberately to complicate the map! The most obvious reason is that chains of argument often join together, so that one or other chain will need a negative sign in order for them to come together. An example of a more subtle reason is that it is sometimes helpful for the map to be constructed so that the first poles of concepts are those at the forefront of the client's thinking. In this way a map depicts the overall definition of the situation. Sometimes a glance at all the first poles (the definition of the situation which is predominant for that person) reveals that a situation is problematic because, in effect, the 'world is tumbling around about me, and I don't like it'. In other cases it will reveal that the client sees the situation as problematic because 'my world could be a better place, and I'm not there'. In the first case the client sees disaster and wants to remove himself or herself from it, in the second the client sees a better future and is striving to get there. This difference in construing the situation will have some bearing on how the consultant sets about managing the problem solving process. Early in a project it is important to build a map that reflects the client's orientation to the problem.

Changing the language used by the client, so that it becomes orientated to action rather than problem description, without the client losing 'ownership' of the model, is not a trivial exercise. Equally, deciding which concept is the goal/outcome/end and which is the action/option/means of a linked pair of concepts is a crucial step in the model building. For example, 'looking for a concordat with the unions' sounds like a goal, and so has been coded as a goal in Figure 2. However, if I were able to converse with Jane McLoughlin (as would be the case if she were a client), then I would be keen to establish whether 'a concordat' is regarded as a goal, or as an option which contributes to 'ambivalence towards profit sharing'. The overall sense of the text on its own makes me feel uncertain about my coding. Nevertheless, in some circumstances the hierarchical order of concepts can be decided more easily. When a concept is a generic label for a variety of possible options, then it will be hierarchical to each of the possible options that are encompassed by the generic label. Thus if I say 'helping the reader understand the point I am making leads me to include a diagram' then it would not be coded as spoken (arrow from 'helping' to 'diagram'). Instead, 'helping' would be the generic concept of which 'diagram' would be one option leading to the outcome of 'help'.

Working with cognitive maps

The map in Figure 2 is exceedingly small. Typically, a map created when working with one member of a problem solving team might contain 40 to 100 concepts; that for the issue as represented by the aggregation of maps for several team members could consist of several hundred. 'Strategic management' maps, which are to be used over long periods of time as a part of a managerial decision support system, can contain several thousand concepts. Nevertheless, the above example will demonstrate the principles of analysing the structure of maps.

There are two principal ways of working on a map with the client. The first is to explore the goal system further, and then gradually work down the map towards increasingly detailed options to achieve goals. Alternatively, one can start from the detailed options and gradually work up the map towards goals by exploring each concept in turn as a potential option. Which of these two approaches is chosen depends upon the professional judgement of the consultant about process issues concerning client attitudes. Some clients will become more excited by expending energy on elaborating and questioning the goals implied by their view of the problem. Others, in contrast, may regard the goals as self-evident and be more motivated by working on possibilities for action. This issue is discussed in more detail in the case study presented in the next chapter.

Each of these ways of working with a single client presumes that the consultant is satisfied that the model is a fair representation of the situation as it is seen by the client, and so is likely to be 'owned' by the client. The model above was constructed from written text; this origin apparently simplifies but actually complicates the process of understanding a client.

Working from text denudes the meaning that derives from intonation, from body movement, and more significantly from the results of consultant –client *interaction*. One of the powerful attributes of mapping as a model building method comes from the ability to create the model as the client is talking. This makes it possible to explore the implications of the model, with the client, during the interview. Therefore, it is more likely that ownership will be assured, because the consultant can check possible misunderstandings as the interview unfolds. This way of working also ensures that the consultant develops the questions asked during the interview from the interview data itself, rather than from an agenda of prepared questions. This allows for a warmer, more trusting consultant–client relationship to grow. This style of operating allows the consultant to move in a gentle fashion from an 'empathetic' to a 'negotiative' paradigm of consultant–client relationship (Eden and Sims, 1979). The process of working with the client for checking and further elaboration slides into working on options which are defined in enough detail that they can be acted upon.

As checking for an adequate model becomes less important, the consultant will move to one of the two more proactive, or negotiative, modes of working mentioned above—working with the client on an analysis of the goal system and then down the model towards options, or working from options towards goals.

Working in the first mode, with the goal system, implies concentrating on the concepts at the 'top', or hierarchically superordinate, part of the map. Consultant and client together will consider the overall network of goals, and their relationship one to another. In our example this means concentrating on questions such as 'why is upmarket appeal important to the Labour Party?' The client is invited to expand the chain of goals by moving to successively higher levels in the hierarchy. In this case we may suppose that something like 'wider electoral appeal . . . appeal to electorate in the North' might be a further elaboration. Both client and consultant may find it illuminating to go on extending such questions until it becomes 'obvious' to both that the concept at the top of the model, with no further consequences, is 'self-evidently' a 'good thing'. Once this stage has been reached the client may be invited to work back gradually down the hierarchy by answering the question 'what options come to mind for changing this situation, other than those already mentioned?' For example, 'what other ways come to mind for shifting "ambivalence towards profit sharing" to "support", other than "reducing the fear of a weakened role in collective bargaining"?'

The second mode of working with the client focuses on action by identifying each 'tail' (the concept at the bottom of a chain of argumentation, that is with no further explanations) and testing it as a possible intervention point. Therefore, 'knowledge about share ownership in the United States' is tested as a possible option—is there any way in which this 'first pole' of the concept creatively suggests a 'contrasting pole'? It may seem more natural to regard this particular concept in the example as simply a part of the context within the original statement, rather than as a means to the end of 'reducing fear of a drop in union membership'. However, consideration of such concepts as potential options often leads to creative suggestions for action—in this case 'rubbishing the knowledge from the United States' might be such an option. The next part of the problem solving process is to consider other means by which it might be possible to reduce the 'fear of a drop in union membership'. So, we proceed to elaborate the map by inserting new options/tails as subordinate concepts to that being considered.

Further exploration of options moves up the concept hierarchy, by considering ways of making 'weakened role' an option. This is done in the same way as in the above example: in this case I had supposed that there was an action which might be taken to 'reduce the fear of a weakened role for collective bargaining', and had inserted '???' in Figure 2. This was to serve as a prompt for guiding the client to consider possible contrasting poles. In addition I would invite the client to consider other ways of 'reducing fear', by asking 'are there any other reasons why unions have a fear of weakened role of collective bargaining?' For example, the client might respond by suggesting that the contrasting pole is 'weakened role seen as strength', not 'reduced role' as I had thought. If the client suggested this contrasting pole, I would seek to discover from the client how such a view might come about. For example 'delegating negotiating power down to local shop stewards' may be proferred as a possible explanation. This additional concept now becomes a new 'tail', as an explanation for 'weakened role seen as strength' (an arrow into the 'role' concept from 'delegating', with a –ve sign on it). After working with the client on other ways of countering 'weakened role' by developing other new 'tails' I would then move to the next concept up the hierarchy and consider other ways of countering 'union opposition'. And so on, elaborating the map by seeking to discover further explanations for why the situation is as it is.

Looking for options in this way reveals the importance of trying to identify contrasting poles of concepts—for the contrast is the essence of action. For example, in considering how to counter 'weakened role' it is important to identify the nature of the contrast. This might have been 'strengthened role' or 'less weakened role', or the contrast suggested above of 'weakened role seen as strength'. Each contrast has significantly different implications for identifying possible interventions and further explanations ('tails'). Each explanation, in its own way, becomes a new option to be considered in the same way as the 'tail' 'knowledge about employee share ownership in the United States' on the original map.

A 'SODA' project

Figure 2 is a 'cognitive' map because it is a model of the *thinking* of one person. In a SODA project the cognitive map of each member of the client team will be merged to form an aggregated map called a 'strategic map'. This process of merging maps is a crucial aspect of how the consultant takes account of process as well as content issues. The aim is to produce a 'facilitative device' to promote psychological negotiation amongst team members so that, in the first instance, a definition of the problem can be established. During the initial model building with individual clients, the aim was to help them 'change their minds' about the nature of the problem through a combination of self-reflection with respect to the map, and gentle negotiation with the consultant. The map is used as the device to facilitate the negotiation.

Similarly, the initial purpose of the merged map is to change the minds of each member of the client group, without their feeling compromised. The aim is to secure *enough* agreement about the nature of the problem that each team member is committed to expending energy on finding a *portfolio* of actions, where that portfolio *is* the strategy for dealing with the issue.

Because the aim is to facilitate negotiation, the individual maps are merged with a significant regard for the anticipated dynamics of negotiation. This means that when a concept on one map is overlaid on a similar concept on another map, it is a matter of concern as to which person's wording is retained on the strategic map. Similarly, as the strategic map is analysed prior to creating an agenda for a SODA workshop, attended by all or most team members, then the extracts from the strategic map that are to be used in the workshop are carefully monitored to ensure balanced representation from key team members.

Consider the (unlikely) possibility that Jane McLoughlin is a member of a problem solving team and that one of her colleagues had said:

> It is possible that the Labour Party might support profit sharing schemes if opinion polls demonstrated support from Union members ... however the tabloid newspapers would need to give some education on profit sharing instead of continuing to ignore the idea ... with support from these newspapers it is likely that some popular support might result—at the moment there is support only from the middle classes ... it is also important that the 'man-in-the-street' is made aware of the benefits US workers have seen from profit sharing schemes in the US ... the trouble for the Labour Party is that if there were popular support then other opposition parties might also support profit sharing ... nevertheless I believe the crucial question for the Labour Party is whether their support could decrease antagonism from key members of the CBI ... I suspect that if there were mechanisms for applying profit sharing to public sector workers then this would be a powerful argument for the party supporting something which at present only seems to apply to the private sector.

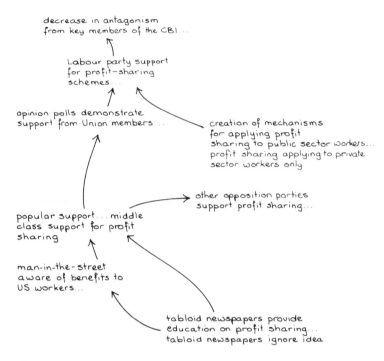

Figure 3
Possible cognitive map for a second team member

These views might have resulted in the map shown in Figure 3, which would need to be merged with that of Figure 2.

The cognitive maps built with each team member might be merged along the lines shown in Figure 4. I might overlay the two concepts that relate to profit sharing (concepts 1 and 5 in Figure 4), and then link concepts elsewhere within the two maps (4 leads to 2, 6 leads to 9, and 14 leads to 12 and 13). Unless there is a process reason for doing otherwise (for example, if the concept that is to be overlaid belongs to the boss then it *might* be worth considering deliberately retaining regardless of other consider-ations), then the concept that is lost is that which is less rich. Thus in this example concept 5 will be lost in favour of concept 1 which has a contrasting pole. As other concepts are linked, the consultant uses judge-ment to maintain the hierarchical relationships within the final merged map. This judgement is not to be treated lightly, for the consultant will be beginning a process of negotiating his own view of the problem on to the model by inserting new links between 'owned' maps. For example, in the

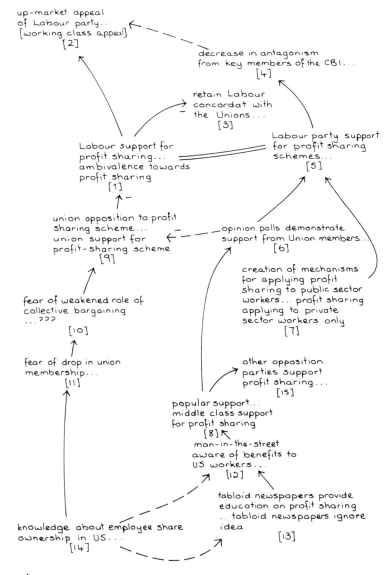

Figure 4
Merging two cognitive maps

merged model, I have decided to *suggest* that a 'decrease in antagonism from key members of the CBI' will have the likely consequence of creating 'upmarket appeal'. By so doing I am implicitly (and later during a workshop explicitly) inviting consideration of options for 'decreasing antagonism' other than that of providing support for profit sharing.

Figure 4 shows instances of two paths of argumentation from one concept to another. For example, in the merged map concept 1 leads directly to concept 2, and indirectly through concept 4. In these circumstances it is helpful to ask whether there are genuinely two paths—it is often possible that the direct route is the same as the indirect route, the indirect route being a useful elaboration of the direct route. If both paths indicate different argumentation—as appears to be the case in the above map—then it will be useful to add in at least one further concept to explain the different means to the same end. In the example we might ask the clients to elaborate, and this might result in a further concept such as 'Labour seen to be supporting trendy new ideas'. We may also note that there are now ten(!) paths of argumentation from concept 14 to concept 2 (a path is any unique sequence of concepts, for example the path 14,13,12, 8,6,1,2 is different from 14,12,8,6,1,2). The option represented by concept 14 of 'rubbishing knowledge' is a *dilemma* in that it leads to a desirable outcome following some paths and an undesirable outcome following others. It is also tempting for the consultant to insert a tentative negative link from the current undesirable goal of 'other opposition parties support profit sharing' to 'upmarket appeal'.

The SODA process is built around working with a team, on their aggregated data, having paid the fullest possible attention to the individuality of problem construction. The process is designed to facilitate negotiation and the broadening of problem definition, that is, a deliberate attempt to increase complexity rather than reduce it. And it must be noted that increasing complexity can be disabling (Eden *et al.*, 1981) to a client, unless the consultant has a method for managing this complexity *without* losing richness and subtlety. The process is also structured to decrease the possibility of 'group think', and increase the possibility of identifying creatively pleasing strategies. The most important element of the methodology is a SODA *workshop*. The workshop is carefully designed to address the aggregated data in a manner which does not lose any of the richness and detail of the owned cognitive maps.

After maps have been merged, the consultant must analyse the content and structure of the model in order to generate an agenda for the workshop—an agenda which has sensibly managed complexity without losing richness. While this can be done manually, it is obviously easier using a computer and associated software—the strategic map is likely to be of several hundred concepts. The overall richness of the structure of the data will be difficult to appreciate fully without the help of sophisticated clustering and mapping algorithms. The initial task is to analyse the data to identify 'emerging themes', and 'core concepts' (Eden, 1988).

The computer software (COPE) which performs these tasks has been designed at the Universities of Bath and Strathclyde with support from British Telecom and ICL. It is passive software which is non-prescriptive in use or outcome. It is deliberately designed to help the skilled professional consultant manage the complexity and richness that arises when working large amounts of interrelated qualitative data. It contains several algorithms for automatically drawing maps, for identifying clusters, for comparing subsets of data, for 'collapsing' maps, for creating expert system specifications, and for allowing clients to interact directly with a large strategic database. It provides the user with the opportunity to custom design analysis routines through the use of its own high level language. The software is most often used in real time in conjunction with VDU projector facilities as the core technology in a SODA workshop (Eden and Ackermann, 1987). However, the use of COPE is *not* essential to the approach, and in many projects is deliberately excluded because it would not fit with the style and culture of the client group, or alternatively because time constraints do not make it efficient.

The design of the SODA workshop is initially influenced by an identification of the *system of interacting problems that make up the issue* being addressed. A variety of methods for analysis of the data is available to the user of the software. These help the consultant to use professional judgement to identify clusters within the map. In this way clusters of about 15–30 concepts are identified. Each represents a problem arena within which there will be problem-related goals at the 'head' of the cluster, strategic options within the cluster, and options at the 'tail' of the cluster. Each cluster will probably be linked to other clusters. The goals of one problem lead to the options of another, and the options within one problem are consequences of the goals of a subordinate problem.

Figure 5 shows the principle of clustering maps. In this example complexity has been managed by visually (rather than mathematically) breaking the map into three clusters which are relatively independent of one another. (Deleting the relationships from concept 4 to concepts 2 and 10 would make each cluster completely independent.) The clustering in this example has been undertaken with no regard for the content and complete regard for structure; this is always a good starting point but rarely a good finishing point for the analysis of maps. A structural analysis must then be followed by attention to content and process, and the clusters modified accordingly. Similarly, each cluster is tested by making a judgement about

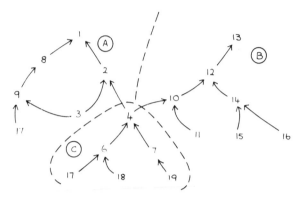

Figure 5
An example of clustering

the validity of the analysis in suggesting a sensible problem with goals and options.

It is only by using judgement that the essentially reductionist cluster analysis guides the consultant towards capturing the holistic properties of the aggregated data. Each cluster may be given a label to describe the 'nub of the problem' it represents. An overview map may then be constructed which identifies the problems/clusters and their hierarchical relationship one to another.

The 'SODA' workshop

Armed with these clusters, each produced either by hand or by the computer as large (newsprint size) maps, and taking full account of the process issues, the consultant must establish a rough agenda for the workshop. Typically, a workshop will be arranged to take anything from 2 hours to 2 days, depending on the availability of team members and the perceived importance of the issue. The scheme for the workshop is, in principle, similar to that for the interaction between consultant and single client. The consultant may choose to start from a goal orientation or an action orientation. An important consideration is to design an agenda which will allow a *cyclic process* to unfold. (See Friend and Hickling, 1987 for further discussion of the nature of cyclic processes in problem solving workshops.) The objective of working with a cyclic process is to ensure that participants in a workshop are helped with the process of gradually absorbing the overall emerging issues, yet get to grips with the detail, and move to action.

This can be achieved most effectively by taking participants quickly through an overview of the *system of key goals*, the *interrelated problems*, key *options*, and *assumptions*. This first pass through the data is undertaken by the consultant without extensive discussion—it is 'billed' as an introductory pass. The aim of the first pass is to begin the process of participants 'taking on board' alternative views—the gradual psychological negotiation to a new construction of the problem. In addition, the first pass is aimed at gaining ownership by a controlled 'walk' through the model to demonstrate that concepts belonging to each participant have been included in the model. The potential for each of the participants 'changing his or her mind' is largely dependent upon the help the model provides in extending ownership beyond those concepts which belong to a single participant. Extending ownership occurs by a participant seeing his or her own concepts now set within the context of concepts that are known to belong to other participants. Cycling through the data on several occasions gives the time for each participant to absorb the change in *meaning* implied by a new context for concepts. This is the model acting as *facilitative device*, whereby a person can concentrate on the concepts themselves rather than who is presenting them, or on the social needs of debate.

The first pass creates a 'backdrop' against which the second pass, focusing on individual issues/clusters, can unfold. The preparatory work on the agenda for the workshop will have located the key issues, their interdependence, and the order in which they will be addressed. The consultant must decide whether to work on a cluster top-down (goal system mode) or bottom-up (option mode). In this second pass the 'rules' change and discussion is encouraged. As discussion continues the consultant will be publicly elaborating and extending the maps. (See Eden and Ackermann, 1987 for discussion of this process as a computer assisted group decision support system.)

For the operational researcher, the clusters within the strategic map will have alerted him or her to opportunities for more extensive project work. It is usual for a SODA workshop to identify opportunities for further analysis, such as financial model building, simulation modelling, market research, and statistical analysis. The software has provision for 'collapsing' an ideas oriented map down to a smaller map focusing on those concepts that may form the basis of an 'influence diagram' for use in system dynamics model building. Alternatively, the same sort of collapsed model can provide a direct input to 'spreadsheet' software. However, the attraction of undertaking this further work, for both consultant and client, lies in the clear understanding that it will be carried out within the context of broader qualitative issues. This means that work within one problem/cluster will have known ramifications for work on other interacting problems. For example, it is not unusual to discover key relationships (arrows), within a cluster/problem, about which there is a high level of uncertainty. Often these relationships express a crucial belief about how the market place works. When such circumstances occur the client may call for market research to validate particular concepts and their links.

Review and summary

The aim of this chapter has been: (i) to set out the key assumptions which underlie the SODA approach to working with teams; and (ii) to exemplify this approach through the use of 'cognitive mapping' as the core technique within SODA. Others choose to use the technique of cognitive mapping as either a content analysis tool, for example within the field of political science (Axelrod, 1976), or as an 'influence diagram' for disciples of system dynamics simulation modelling (Forrester, 1961; Coyle, 1977; and more recently Richmond, 1987). As I hope I have shown in this chapter and in the following case study, the SODA approach and cognitive mapping as a *consultancy* tool has been developed independently of other work, because it has a different purpose and a different body of theory and concepts underlying it.

As readers evaluate its appropriateness or otherwise for their own practice, I would suggest that the following questions be considered. Firstly, does the body of theory and the concepts that have been outlined here make sense to you? If you draw upon your own experience of organizations and consulting, does the view of organizational life and the nature of problems presented here fit with that experience? Does the emphasis on the design and analysis of process fit your own personal style and capabilities? Secondly, do you believe that the SODA approach, and cognitive mapping, adequately relate to the theory, concepts, and declared aims? And thirdly, does the application of the analytical techniques designed into the software seem to be a useful and powerful addition to the package of tools available to you? These questions are intended to be hierarchical—it is possible to answer 'yes' to the first questions and 'no' to the others, 'yes' to the first two sets of questions and 'no' to the last, or 'yes' to all three—in any of these events the reader might expect some part of this chapter to inform professional practice. However, the reader should not adopt the method without being in sympathy with the underlying theory and aims.

Finally, as with all of the methods reported in this book, using the SODA approach with cognitive mapping can look deceptively easy. The experience of a wide range of practising consultants is that it is not easy. Its power derives from the ability of the consultant to employ contingently a coherent body of theory and concepts within the practical world of small group problem solving. Nevertheless, as with any other powerful approach of substance, some training and practice coupled with commitment is a basis for many consultants becoming skilled and valued facilitators of this approach.

Our experiences of training practitioners and other consultants suggests that it is an approach which others can learn. Nevertheless, a difficulty with SODA, Soft Systems Methodology, Strategic Choice, and Metagame Analysis is that there is likely to be disappointment with first use. This is particularly likely if the user believed that a cursory absorption of the principles would suffice.

References

Axelrod, R. (1976). *The Structure of Decision*, Princeton Univ. Press, New Jersey.

Coyle, R. G. (1977). *Management System Dynamics*, Wiley, London.

Eden, C. (1985). 'Perish the thought!', *J. Opl Res. Soc.*, **36**, 809–19.

Eden, C. (1986). 'The future consultant—finding the multiplier', University of Bath, School of Management.

Eden, C. (1987). 'Problem solving or problem finishing?', in *New Directions in Management Science* (Eds. M. Jackson and P. Keys), Gower, Aldershot.

Eden, C. (1988). 'Strategic decision support through computer based analysis and presentation of cognitive maps'. Presented to Alfred-Howle Seminar, University of Laval, April.

Eden, C., and Ackermann, F. (1987). *SODA—using a computer to help with the management of strategic vision*, IBSCUG/ISA conference paper, London Business School.

Eden, C., and Graham, R. (1983). 'Halfway to infinity', *J. Opl Res. Soc.*, **34**, 723–8.

Eden, C., Jones, S., and Sims, D. (1979). *Thinking in Organizations*, Macmillan, London.

Eden, C., and Sims, D. (1979). 'On the nature of problems in consulting practice', *Omega*, **7**, 119–27.

Eden, C., Smithin, T., and Wiltshire, J. (1980). 'Cognition, simulation and learning', *J. Experiential Learn. Sim.*, **2**, 131–43.

Eden, C., Smithin, T., and Wiltshire, J. (1985). *Cope Users Guide and Reference Manual*, Bath Software Research, Bristol.

Eden, C., Jones, S., Sims, D., and Smithin, T. (1981). 'Intersubjective issues and issues of intersubjectivity', *J. Mgmt Studies*, **18**, 37–47.

Forrester, J. W. (1961). *Industrial Dynamics*, MIT Press, Massachusetts and Wiley, New York.

Friend, J., and Hickling, A. (1987). *Planning Under Pressure—the Strategic Choice Approach*. Pergamon, Oxford.

Kelly, G. A. (1955). *The Psychology of Personal Constructs: a theory of personality*, Norton, New York.

Machol, R. E. (1980). 'Comment on "Publish or Perish"', *J. Opl Res. Soc.*, **31**, 1109–13.

March, J. G., and Olsen, J. P. (1976). *Ambiguity and Choice in Organizations*, Universitetsforlaget, Bergen.

Quinn, J. B. (1980). *Strategies for Change: local incrementalism*, Irwin, Homewood, Illinois.

Richmond, B. (1987). *The Strategic Management Forum: from vision to strategy to operating policies and back again*, High Performance Systems.

Silverman, D. (1970). *The Theory of Organizations*, Heinemann.

Strauss, A., Schatzman, L., Ehrlich, D., Bucher, R., and Sabshin, M. (1963). 'The hospital and its negotiated order', in *The Hospital in Modern Society* (Ed. E. Friedson), 147–69, Macmillan.

Thomas, W. I., and Thomas, D. S. (1928). *The Child in America: Behaviour problems and progress*, Knopf, New York.

Tolman, E. C. (1948). 'Cognitive maps in rats and men', *Psychological Review*, **55**, 189–208.

Whorf, B. (1956). *Language, Thought and Reality*, MIT Press, Cambridge, Mass.

3
SODA and cognitive mapping in practice

Colin Eden and Peter Simpson

A developing consultant–client relationship

This chapter is about a recent project which will illustrate how the 'precepts' of SODA and cognitive mapping are used in practice. The *general* structure employed in this project is one that has been found to be effective on a number of occasions, but this is nevertheless a unique project. All projects are unique, and professional judgement in designing the programme of the consultancy is always necessary. To attempt to apply the contents of this chapter as a 'precise formula' in other circumstances would be to court disaster. In order to appreciate this point more fully, contrast this case study with another previously published case study 'Perish the thought' (Eden, 1985).

The project which forms the centre of the story was taken on for two reasons. Firstly, we are keen to undertake projects with a community orientation—and the project fell into this category. Secondly, the potential of the project for reporting in case-study format was recognized. This is difficult with the majority of our consultancy/action-research based projects, which are for large international companies, involving highly confidential work on product development and strategy formulation.

Our involvement in this project began when one of the authors was talking to the 'budding client' about business in general. During the conversation the client began to discuss his own business. He felt a sense of unease about the way in which it was developing, and that he was having problems deciding how to improve the situation. The client was aware that

Rational Analysis for a Problematic World
Edited by J. Rosenhead. © 1989 John Wiley & Sons Ltd

we act as consultants to small teams and management groups, but was unclear about what we did with them. He tentatively enquired about the possibility of our helping him with his problems. As a result of this initial chance discussion, a more formal meeting was set up on the client's premises. The nature of this early episode in establishing a consultant–client contract has characteristics which are similar to those reported by many OR managers, and is certainly typical of most of the projects with which we have found ourselves involved, some on a long-term basis. The experience that we have had in a wide range of situations with a variety of potential clients has highlighted the importance of personal relationships in establishing the nature of the consultancy contract. Particularly as a consultant group without a hard (solution) package to sell, we have found that there is a need for a high level of trust if the client is to invest time in the whole process.

The company involved is a relatively new organization. It is a small recruitment and employment agency established about a year before this account starts. Set up in association with a national pressure group, it specializes in providing employment opportunities for individuals, in the fields of computing and electronics, who wish to find non-defence-related work. Without being anti-defence, the emphasis of the agency is the promotion of the peaceful use of the country's skills in computing and electronics. The directors of the agency intend to operate the business as a commercially viable operation, but not as profit-takers: they will be using the profits to further the ideological aims of the organization.

This detail has been given because the nature of the client-organization is a significant factor in designing and prosecuting a project. In this case we were inevitably to discover the complex and, characteristically, often conflicting goals which influence the problems members of the organization felt they must address.

The initial contact was with one of the Directors, John,* who was largely responsible for the formation of the agency. Previously a successful reliability engineer, John had given up his work in that field to dedicate himself full time to the work of the agency. John impressed us as an individual with considerable vision and commitment, combining an entrepreneurial spirit with a strong sense of social responsibility. Alongside John were two other Directors, Will and Brian, who worked one day per week in the early stages of the company.

The client was not in a position to pay for the consultancy. Nevertheless, the notion of striking a bargain was helpful in establishing a relationship

---

*The names have been deliberately changed, but the characters are real.

that would not be too one-sided. This bargain entailed an agreement in principle (though subject to a residual client veto) for the initial interview to be recorded on videotape for teaching purposes.

The contract that is established significantly influences the nature of the consultant–client relationship, and consequently affects the outcomes. In this case as the project developed there was a need to continually re-establish the nature of the contract. For example, in a meeting with the other Directors, Brian suggested a possible course of action to which John commented 'Well, that does depend on whether Colin and Peter want to take this any further'. To have this expressed so explicitly was helpful: it gave an easy opportunity to make a clear declaration of our commitment to the project for a significant time into the future and our reasons for such a commitment. Without this knowledge of whether the work is going to continue, let alone where it is going to lead, the clients will be unable to engage fully in the process. They themselves will then, quite reasonably, fail to give the commitment necessary for a successful involvement. This is true for the consultant as well! Attention to establishing realistic and explicitly stated consultant–client expectations throughout the project is always important. Even though each party may have hidden agendas, it is still important that expectations are stated in a richer format than traditional 'terms of reference'.

We have found that the practice of 'setting expectations' provides direction and clarity for both the client and consultant alike. Before our first formal involvement with the company, we discussed what we, as consultants and members of an academic research unit, wished to achieve from the involvement. Did we want to develop the project? To what end? To what extent? The answers to such questions can only ever be in terms of general intention rather than specific goals. We carefully determined that this was indeed a potentially attractive project for us. We were able to declare that it would contribute to developing research, provide suitable case-study material, and satisfy our personal interest in non-profit-making work. In line with this intent, some 'milestones' were discussed which we, and they, wished to achieve along the way. At this early stage these did not project too far into the future. We limited ourselves to seeking to gain a commitment from John to engage in a project with us, and to establishing a rough agenda for that project with him.

Taking pains to *manage* the client's expectations is equally important. For example, at the end of the first interview with John we took the opportunity to explore our mutual future expectations. We were careful to take a 'laid-back' approach to the significance of what we might be able to do to help. This is typical of our approach early in a project, when we seek to establish reasonable expectations about the nature of our involvement.

It is important that the client recognizes the importance of *his* contribution to what we do, that we are not able to offer a general panacea. We carefully attempted to lay out a couple of 'milestones' which would not involve too much commitment on either side. In this case we suggested that 'there may not be any further work but it might be useful to fix a second meeting to have a look at the outcome of further analysis—if nothing comes of it we can call it a day'. We went on to explain a little of what we would do between now and then—'use some computer software [an allusion to a little "magic"], see what themes emerge and what they suggest in terms of further work, if any'.

We continue this process of managing expectations throughout the period of any consultancy project, setting milestones and evaluating progress at every stage. However, we always seek to establish that we do not expect to put in writing detailed 'terms of reference' or to write a final report (Eden, 1982).

Problem construction

Our first act of involvement in the problem was to interview John. This interview with John was carried out by one interviewer: both he and John sitting comfortably in easy chairs rather than at a desk or table. The intention was to put John as much at ease as possible. The fact that the session was being filmed did not assist in this, forcing the chairs to be located in one particular part of the room for best lighting, and slightly closer together than would normally have been arranged. The camera was large and obtrusive, making it very plain that 'every word and action was being recorded'. This was not a satisfactory situation, but holding a second interview later served to alleviate many of the difficulties caused. In other projects it has been possible to omit second interviews, but in this case a second session was essential.

We used 'cognitive mapping' to record the interview as John was talking. This allowed the interview to be run in a non-directive manner, the map providing 'prompts' once the interview was underway. Being 'non-directive' can encourage 'rambling' (Eden, Jones, and Sims 1983). Rambling 'throws into the air' a large number of ideas that can be lost easily by the interviewer. Mapping is a particularly effective means of capturing these ideas. The technique is fairly simple but like most skills will improve with practice. It is probably worth outlining a few simple guidelines to the practicalities of mapping during an interview.

We use a sharp pencil (preferably of the 'propelling pencil' variety which does not need resharpening and is available in a variety of lead sizes) and underlined 11×8 inch pads of paper, resting on a clip-board. This allows the interviewer to write on their knee while sitting in easy chairs. This often contributes to a more relaxed atmosphere. The sharp pencil and unlined paper allows one to write small and all over the page. Typically a 30–40 concept map will fit on to one page.

Starting about one-third of the way down the page, in the middle, the first few concepts should be recorded without any attempt at linking them together. This allows time to gain more of an appreciation of the wider context and meaning of the non-verbal, as well as verbal, information being gathered. Following that, make linkages as appropriate. Position concepts in the vicinity of related concepts, or place them in uncluttered parts of the paper if the idea is not related to others already recorded. As the interview progresses the sheet will become messy and cluttered, but will provide sufficient structure and order to provide prompts. Missing lines of argumentation at this stage is not too important; it is more important to capture concepts.

The significance of the interview as both a cathartic experience and a chance for the client to reflect on the problem should not be underestimated. For example, in the first interview which we had with Will he commented that 'It's very flattering the way that you are writing so much down'. This sort of thing is of benefit in itself, enhancing the relationship and developing levels of trust and commitment. The interviewer in this case chose to take the opportunity to share the map with the interviewee: a further step towards countering the alienation that is often felt in interview situations. Using the map, the interviewer was able to ask 'I don't fully understand what these ideas were about, as you can see they have finished up as a cluster of thoughts that are independent of all the others. . .'. This prompted the response 'Oh yes, I should have said some more about that. It's very important and has something to do with this bit up here.'

Even where it is not appropriate to show the interviewee the map, the interviewer can use isolated concepts as prompts for more discussion: 'You mentioned [XYZ]. Can you tell me some more about why that is important?' In the way which was outlined in the previous chapter, 'heads' and 'tails' of chains may be used as prompts for questioning: 'Earlier you were talking about [head] which is influenced by [explanation]. Is [head] important in influencing anything else, or is it important in its own right?' Similarly, 'You mentioned that [tail] will lead to [consequence]. How might you bring about [tail]?' Or 'Are there any other ramifications of doing [tail]?'

One of the major difficulties in the first interview is getting beyond what may be called 'prepared scripts'. First interviews can often be threatening for the interviewees, no matter how senior or experienced. As a consequence there is a tendency to switch into a set of well-worn statements about the world which do not get to the root of what is important to them. Even so, prepared scripts do have their advantages. These are evident in the very different context of social events, where such 'safe ground' allows people to interact at a level which facilitates the development of trust and openness. It is only with time that a person will divulge things of importance. One of the ways in which we seek to minimize this problem is to pay attention to opportunities presented by informal social occasions.

'And later, in the bar . . .' In our first interview with John the video equipment served to exacerbate the difficulty of generating an atmosphere in which he felt free to talk about the things that were important to him. 'Nuts and bolts' issues do not generally sound as impressive as 'motherhood and apple pie', but we were to discover that it was in the day-to-day work of the company that John was truly most interested. Once the video equipment was turned off and the interview had 'ended', the discussion went on to a consideration of a variety of more 'mundane' problems. For example, the conversation progressed to the issue of the importance of the agency's image with potential clientele, and a decision was made to improve the quality of the signs at the doorway. Deliberately allowing 'wind-down' time at the end of an interview will often enable the client to comment on the 'real concerns'.

Informal data collection can most easily occur at the end of a formal session, perhaps while packing away, or walking down the corridor together before parting, or better still over a drink in the bar unwinding at the end of the day. Without the cloak of formality, conversation becomes more relaxed and trusting. Without being deceitful, remaining aware of the importance of your client's conversation can prove very fruitful in developing an understanding of the situation.

Information gathered informally may rightly be incorporated in the model which was developed in the formal part of the interview. However, perhaps with these data more than any other, discretion needs to be shown in omitting comments that are obviously intended to be 'off the record'. This is an integral part of establishing a trusting collaborative relationship with the client. (Issues relating to listening and interviewing skills in OR consultancy are discussed in more detail in Eden, Jones, and Sims, 1983 and Charles, Fleetwood-Walker, and Luck, 1985.)

The importance of 'informal times' can be a significant influence on the consultant's involvement in the work. We have found that approaching the informal times with a sense of purpose can serve to generate a strength of relationship with the client which might otherwise not arise. A contribution to building the consultant–client relationship is a significant outcome in itself, but we have found that it also serves to develop a sense of 'belonging' to the client group on the part of the consultant. Early on in the project reported here we were invited to join the staff and Directors at the 'Christmas Dinner'. This accelerated our involvement and sense of belonging in the group.

The difficulty of entering a perhaps very cohesive group and expecting to have an impact should not be underestimated, and is a social skill that few of us possess naturally. Developing this sense of belonging will help to generate a greater commitment to the work rather than 'going through the same old routine'.

The map that was constructed during the first interview with John is shown in Figure 1. This is a photocopy of the state of the notes immediately after the interview. It is clear from this photograph that we do not expect the map of an interview to be: (i) tidy; (ii) easily readable by anyone other than the note-taker; (iii) complete; or (iv) a map with many contrasting poles. Within a short time after the interview the interviewer must use these initial notes to prompt his memory as a basis for completing the map. This completion of the map starts by exploring each 'head' and asking 'so what?' Did the client say anything that gives further clues as to why the outcome, suggested by the head, is regarded as desirable? Similarly with each 'tail', and also across 'clusters' of concepts: 'Should these concepts be linked in any way to this group of concepts?'

Each concept is inspected to establish whether the client gave any clues as to the nature of the contrasting pole. These are often discovered by simply asking 'what did the client mean by this concept?' By persisting with this process the map will gradually become a fuller record, representing more of the interviewee's ideas and understanding of the situation.

The process of extending and rebuilding the interview map can be aided by the use of COPE—software designed to allow the user to store and work on cognitive maps. The cognitive map is recorded as a 'model' within COPE. It is then possible to analyse the model and generate output in a variety of forms: lists of all the concepts, just the heads, just the tails, those concepts with most links, those with no links, and so on. Figure 2 shows some examples of listings.

One particularly important feature at this stage is the facility to 'group' concepts into 'clusters'. Each group will tend to focus on a particular theme, although there will be links 'across clusters'. This process has been described in the previous chapter and elsewhere (Eden, 1989). It is then possible to obtain printed maps of these different parts of the model. The notes shown in Figure 1 resulted in a final model of 65 concepts and 80 relationships, which 'clustered' into six groups. Figure 3 shows pictures of some of the six maps.

At this stage of the project the interview and formal mapping meant

Figure 1
The two pages of notes (in cognitive map form) from interview 1

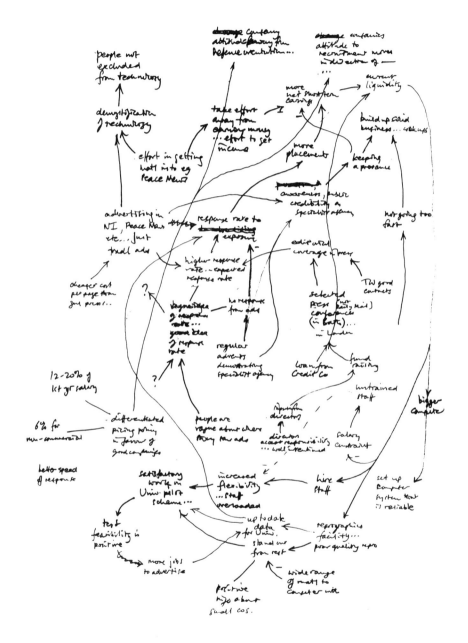

Figure 1 (cont.)

```
model:ERDEMO               C O P E                    clip:
   1    People not excluded from technology . . . [not]People not excluded from t
  12    vague idea of response rate . . . good idea of response rate
  18    building up solid business . . . making great mess-ups
  28    set up computer system that is reliable . . . [not]set up computer system
  48    ER has cooperative perspective . . . ER a 'true' cooperative
  66    industry attitude away from defence orientation . . . [not]industry attit


COPE>              LIST OF HEADS
[ lh              ]                                    Ready
```

```
model:ERDEMO               C O P E                    clip:
   3    effort in getting material into eg Peace News . . . [not]effort in gett
   5    cheaper costs per page than glossies . . . [not]cheaper costs per page
  14    regular adverts demonstrating specialist agency . . . [not]regular adve
  15    people are vague about where they saw ads . . . [not]people are vague a
  16    loan from credit Co/Mercury Trust . . . [not]loan from credit Co/Mercur
  22    TW has good contacts . . . [not]TW has good contacts
  23    selected press (not Daily Mail) conferences (in Bath) . . . (in London)
  26    directors accept responsibility . . . directors well intentioned
  35    more jobs to advertise . . . [not]more jobs to advertise
  38    wide range of material to compete with . . . [not]wide range of materia
  44    6% for non-commercial . . . [not]6% for non-commercial
  49    no-one has experience of co-ops . . . [not]no-one has experience of co-
  50    TW has experience of running a business . . . [not]TW has experience of
  51    ER obtain funds of 10-20K . . . [not]ER obtain funds of 10-20K
  54    TW set up a system that will run itself . . . [not]TW set up a system t
  61    directors all committed to ER ideals . . . [not]directors all committe
  63    staff selection influenced by their desire for social change . . . [no
  68    tell candidates about company attitudes . . . [not]tell candidates abo
  70    Co show positive effort to change . . . [not]Co show positive effort t
  72    charge nothing to some . . . [not]charge nothing to some
COPE>              LIST OF TAILS .
[ lt              ]                                    Ready
```

Figure 2
Some examples of listings from COPE

we were becoming familiar with the various facets of the situation: organizational type, number and character of individuals involved, and the sorts of issue which were of importance. Although this understanding was not yet detailed, we were in a position to 'get a feel' for whether our form of consultancy would be appropriate, and what form that involvement might take.

One of the major aims that we had for the second interview, a follow-up interview with John, was to begin to define our involvement with the agency. There is little point in wasting time doing something that one or both parties will find neither rewarding nor effective. This applies as much to the consultant as to the client. The consultant needs to work on a problem or set of problems which are personally engaging and challenging. Building the project must involve a process of negotiating a problem that both are interested in. The problem which is focused on can never be solely defined by the client's interests (Eden and Sims, 1979).

In this case we had a reasonably good idea of a useful way to proceed which would satisfy a number of our aims, while also fruitfully addressing the difficulties our client was facing. The idea was to seek the involvement of the other Directors. A rough short-term plan was to meet with both Will and Brian, with the intention of interviewing each of them twice. One major objective from these interviews would be the generation of their personal cognitive maps. The final part of our short-term plan was to run a

```
model:ERDEMO                    C O P E                      clip:
  7     ER financially sound in long term . . . ER not generat      10.0
 42     differentiated pricing policy                                8.0
 33     satisfactory work on Univ pilot scheme                       6.0
 39     reprographics facility . . . poor quality repro              5.0
  4     advertising in NI, Peace News etc . . . just tradition       4.0
  8     current liquidity                                            4.0
 18     building up solid business . . . making great mess-ups       4.0
 19     ER generate public credibility as specialist agency          4.0
 21     ER maximise regular editorial coverage in the press          4.0
 36     up to date data for Univ                                     4.0
 46     stand out from the rest                                      4.0
 71     fees/income obtained                                         4.0
  2     Demystification of technology                                3.0
  9     more placements                                              3.0
 10     ER get good response rate to exposure                        3.0
 11     ER get higher response rate . . . expected response ra       3.0
 17     keeping a presence                                           3.0
 20     deliberately not going too fast                              3.0
 30     taking account of untrained staff                            3.0
 40     company attitude away from defence orientation               3.0
COPE>                  MOST LINKED CONCEPTS .
 [                        ]                                        Ready
```

Figure 2 (cont.)

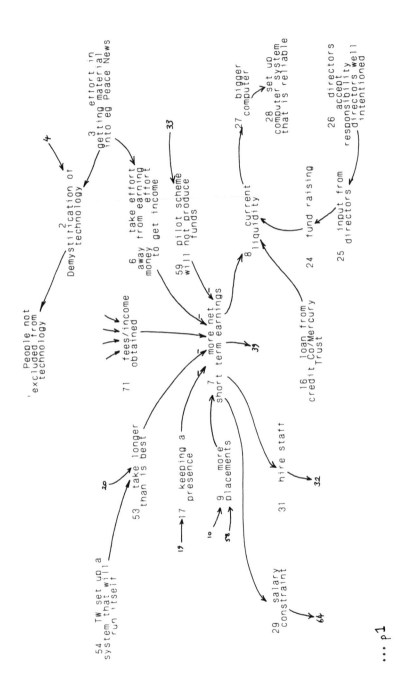

Figure 3
Four of the six maps that were generated after the first interview with John

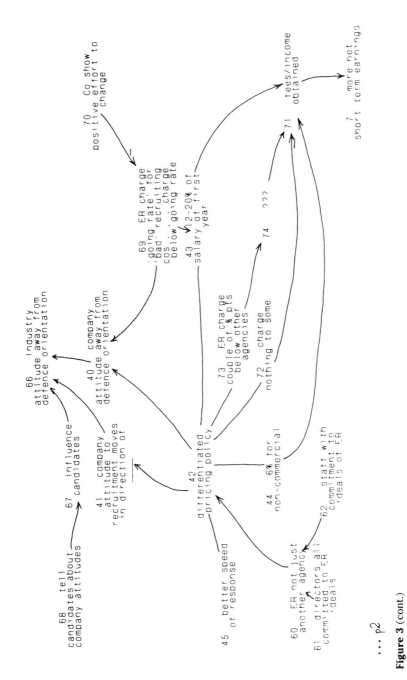

Figure 3 (cont.)

... p2

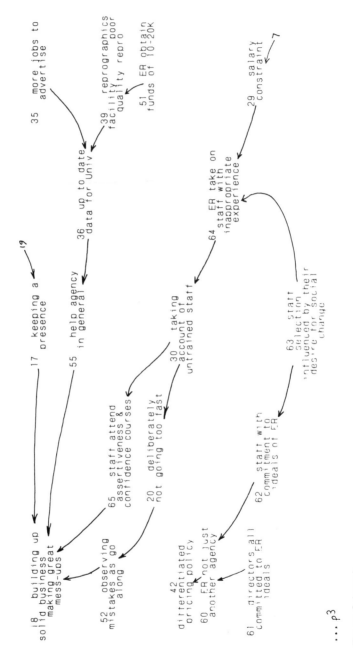

35 more jobs to advertise

39 reprographics facility poor quality repro

51 ER obtain funds of 10-20K

29 salary constraint

36 up to date data for Univ

64 ER take on staff with inappropriate experience

17 keeping a presence

55 help agency in general

30 taking account of untrained staff

63 staff selection influenced by their desire for social change

65 staff attend assertiveness & confidence courses

20 deliberately not going too fast

62 staff with commitment to ideals of ER

18 building up solid business making great mess-ups

52 observing mistakes as go along

42 differentiated pricing policy

60 ER not just another agency

61 directors all committed to ER ideals

... p3

Figure 3 (cont.)

56

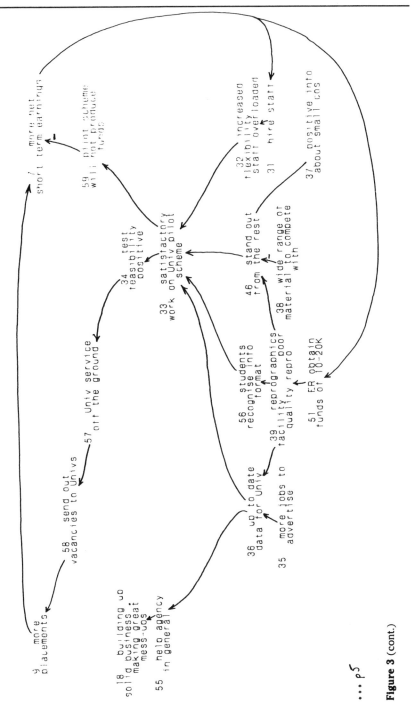

Figure 3 (cont.)

... p5

workshop with all three of them, which we would facilitate using the merged maps from all previous interviews.

The second interview

Six maps, some of which are shown in Figure 3, were prepared for use in the second interview with John. We had ample time to prepare these maps. However, if you are working to a very tight schedule and there is insufficient time, limited tidying up must suffice to prepare the interviewer for the second interview. Judgement must be exercised in deciding whether any of the material generated by the first interview should be presented back to the client. The result of not doing so will be that the second interviews will be very similar to the first interviews, though providing clarification and the opportunity for some fresh thinking.

In this case the six maps were to be used as the focus of attention. Since the previous session with John, we had tidied up the initial map that we had made (Figure 1), organizing it into half a dozen maps which seemed to focus on particular themes. This work had been carried out using the COPE software.

The maps themselves had also been produced using the software, and were printed out on a plotter and photocopied. The result was a booklet containing a model of John's ideas as we thought they had been expressed in the first interview.

The preparation process is time consuming because the volume of data can be considerable (anywhere between 30 and 120 concepts from a one-hour interview). It is not a trivial task to tidy up the rough map which forms the output from the interview, to review the linkages between concepts, and finally to structure all of the data in way that will be effective. However, the result is a model which will be used throughout the consultancy. The effort is a good long-term investment of time: once done, elements of this basic model will be used again and again in a variety of ways.

The intention of cognitive mapping as a modelling technique is that it forces the consultant to be clear about his or her understanding of the client's problem. The time spent getting a map 'right' is designed to meet this end and not the end of technical precision. The technique must not get in the way of its purpose.

The time required for the computer to produce the printed maps is less than a minute for each mapped group of between 10 and 30 concepts. To take advantage of this facility, however, requires appropriate hardware (at least a 640K IBM AT compatible PC, and flexible printer), and of course the software. These restrictions need not be crucial. Operating entirely without computer support is perfectly feasible, drawing maps by hand. However, this is considerably more laborious, and lacks much of the power and flexibility of working with the computer.

We approached John's second interview with a clear framework for developing the work at the back of our minds. However, uppermost in our minds was the need to run the interview in a way which was going to be engaging and useful for John. The chance of introducing our ideas for developing the work further would depend on a successful session with John. Consequently we adopted a fairly contingent attitude towards the interview.

In common with most of our clients, John was unfamiliar with cognitive maps. We had already given some consideration to the best way of introducing them to him. It is sometimes possible that a client ignores the maps after politely acknowledging their 'correctness'. If the map is to be used as an *interactive model* then the client must not be put off by excessive complexity of too much information on a single map. We 'hold the hand' of the client by taking a few simple foci of attention that are highlighted (using coloured highlighting pens), and 'walking around' the map from the start point.

The approach which we judged most likely to be effective in this instance was to highlight what seemed to be the key goals expressed in each of the maps. As the person heading up the organization, his maps encompassed a variety of strong visionary thrusts knitted in to the fabric of an operational definition of how the agency was functioning at the time. Thus, although John was engaged in the day-to-day work of the agency, his interest was in managing the tension set up between current reality and organizational aims. Consequently, focusing on the push and pull of these goals seemed likely to be a meaningful entry point into John's maps.

In contrast, the second interview which we later carried out with Brian was to require a very different emphasis because of his different character and personality. As with John, we had carried out a first interview, and from that session had prepared a booklet of about half a dozen maps. However, on the basis of our understanding of Brian from that first interview, and from an analysis of the maps, it was evident that Brian was not excited by exploring the goals of the organization. Brian seemed to be more interested in action. Indeed, one of the explanations which he gave for his involvement in the work of the agency was that he was interested in '*doing* things', such as 'running projects for the development of socially useful products'.

Thus, in talking about the agency and what was important to the organization, Brian might begin with the higher order aims, similar to those expressed in John's maps, but swiftly be drawn into an elaborate discussion of aspects of the work which were contributing to those goals. In contrast to John's map, in which highlighted concepts were at the heads of chains of concepts, many of the concepts we chose to highlight were in the middle of chains, or at their tails, being actions.

Let us return to the second interview with John. This was deliberately conducted in a relaxed setting, sitting side by side in easy chairs with a small coffee table on which to spread out the maps. With John talking about the individual concepts picked out with a highlighter pen, the maps were gradually used to explain how we understood what he had said at the previous meeting. We regularly checked that his meaning had been understood correctly. As John was encouraged to qualify and elaborate aspects of the maps, his comments were written on to the maps in pencil, and linked in to the concepts which were already there. This was all going on in front of John, and during the interview he focused his attention more and more on the maps, until he was talking about concepts on the map without any prompting.

John was invited to comment on what most interested him, rather than to feel that he must address all of the maps equally in order to please the interviewer. In the event we spent a large part of the interview concentrating on the topic of 'advertising'. 'Becoming known in the market place' was a particular aim at the time. All other goals, although needing to be taken into account, and therefore usefully held in the background by their presence in the model, were not 'key' to John *at that time* (Eden, 1987).

We discussed this theme, making a number of revisions to the maps. As we investigated potential courses of action these large maps came into their own. We were able to make a considerable number of additions to the 'Advertising' map without spreading on to another sheet of paper. We were able to make additions and then reflect upon them throughout the session.

The 'Advertising' map which stimulated this discussion is shown in Figure 4. A photocopy of the map together with the amendments made throughout the session is shown in Figure 5. The messiness of the developed map is not as much of a problem to the client as it is likely to be to you, the reader. This is because the map is developed with the participation of the client, who directs elaboration and corrections. There is a clarity that comes with familiarity, and with ownership of the material.

There are many benefits of working on the existing map rather than on a clean sheet of paper, not least the facility to link across to other areas of the map. This can be seen in Figure 5, where arrows are drawn across the map from one sub-cluster to another. In order to be thorough, and not to miss out important sections of the map unintentionally, a 'tick' was placed against concepts as they were covered in discussion. The map was thus acting as our agenda, providing a structure to the session.

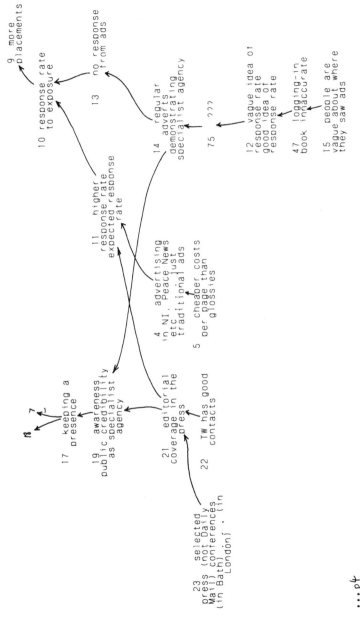

Figure 4
The map that was worked on to produce Figure 5

61

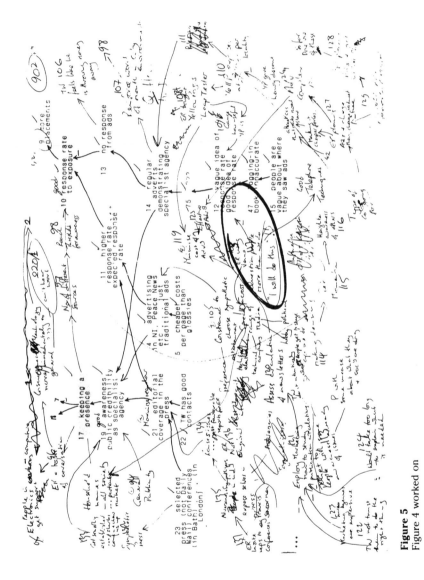

Figure 5
Figure 4 worked on

The interest with which John received the maps was demonstrated by his request to take a copy to use at a forthcoming planning meeting.

The agency had very limited resources to play with, but needed to invest in relatively expensive advertising campaigns if it was to promote market awareness. John was concerned that he did not really know how and why the agency was getting approaches from candidates for employment, or from prospective employers. Were such enquiries a response to advertisements? Or to editorials and word of mouth? What return was the agency getting on its advertising investment? We routinely asked John what explanations might lead to their having a 'good idea of response rate' (one of the concepts in Figure 4). His reply to this was that 'we might question people on the telephone more than we do ... instead of just attending to the call itself'. Figure 6 demonstrates how this was recorded on the map.

When John was routinely asked 'So why don't you do that?', he replied 'Well, I'd never thought of it before'. 'So ... what's stopping you from doing it?' 'Nothing,' he said, 'We'll do it!'

Although not the most world-stopping decision ever made, the sense of achievement was notable. The process was enhanced by such a 'simple' and yet powerful milestone. Reflecting on the content of the maps is in itself generally very rewarding for clients. It helps to settle things in their minds, and to provide structure for previously mysterious or unfathomable complexity of floating and darting ideas. However, the process usually moves beyond reflection towards decision making and a commitment to action. When a client makes this commitment to prospective action, the consultant will often feel a sense of the decision being 'obvious'. Yet for the client it was not obvious, and only became possible through a change in his understanding of his problem.

The next stage of the project was to interview Will and Brian individually. These first interviews were also conducted in an 'open' style with minimal direction, encouraging the interviewees to talk about whatever seemed of importance to them. Our intention was to capture as much of

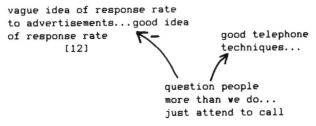

Figure 6
Further elaboration

their intelligent ramblings as possible. These first interviews provided a vital foundation, modelling a kernel of personal wisdom from which all else started to grow. At this stage the quest on the part of the interviewer was to gain an empathetic understanding of how the interviewees saw their world.

Some of the content of these first interviews was material designed to impress the consultant (as the consultant also attempted to impress the client with understanding and professionalism). This is quite normal, but the consultant should be aware of this and use professional judgement to weigh particular statements accordingly.

Because of the way this and many projects unfold it is often important to distinguish between 'first interview' and 'first interviews'. The very first interview can be different in that it forms an entrance to the group or organization. A one-hour interview with John was our first systematic introduction to the operations of the organization. Although the approach is not entirely different in succeeding interviews, this interview was unique in the sense that it very strongly 'set the scene' and so guided our direction afterwards. It is worth deliberately approaching it in such a way. Beyond this, the general points that we have to make about all first interviews apply also to this first interview.

We had already carried out the second interview with John by this stage in the project. Normally we would carry out first and second interviews with each of the principal participants if time allowed, followed by a 'workshop' involving everyone. In this case, we carried out first and second interviews with John and Brian, who both lived and worked locally. Will, who was based in London, proved more difficult to contact. After two failed attempts to interview him, time was moving on. The possibility of losing continuity with John and Brian forced a revision of the schedule. In the end there was time to carry out only one interview with Will. There was consequently no opportunity to allow him to see the results of that session. This was unfortunate both in terms of the effectiveness of our interaction with Will, and of the development of his model.

Who is the client?

A general issue which it is appropriate to cover at this stage in our story is that of thinking about 'who is the client?' The initial contact was with John, a senior member of the organization, so one might reasonably assume that he was the client. However, let us consider the situation further. Although John identified with many of the problems of the agency so strongly that they were his own, if John were to leave would we be able to, or indeed be interested in, carrying on the involvement? If so, is there someone other than John, or some coalition, who can better serve as our client? Having built relationships with the other Directors this question attains greater importance: if we then retained the view that John was our client, would this produce an imbalance in our interactions with the others? Would this give too much power to John in a situation where this was not desirable or desired? And desirable to whom?

This last question had particular significance, in the light of John's expressed desire that the other Directors be given more of a voice and greater opportunity to influence the running of the agency than had previously been the case. John's predominant influence arose from his position as the only Director employed full time by the company. Although one might consider this to be an advantageous situation for John, the need for some others to share the problems and responsibilities was high on John's list of priorities. Had we adopted John as our client without giving careful thought to the implications of doing so, this delicate situation could have been exacerbated.

Determining who the client is to be is important in the early stages of any involvement. This will often prove to be a key to managing the politics of the project. Deciding upon your client means deciding upon the party you will seek to support, and whose aims you will seek to attain.

It has been our experience that it is of considerable value to identify a particular person, or a very small group of persons, as the client. The alternative may appear to be more 'objective', more in keeping with a 'professional' approach without bias. But the outcome is almost sure to be a less effective project in which a lower level of commitment is attained.

Identifying a client is not a trivial matter. The following questions highlight some of the areas of consideration. Does the person identified as your client have the power to act on the issues that form the nub of the project? If not, does your client 'have the ear' of someone who does? It is of little purpose determining a course of action if it can never be implemented. This argument extends to seemingly more mundane issues. For example, when communicating with your client-organization, is your chosen client in a suitable position to act as your 'go-between' with other members of the client group? Will others take sufficient notice of messages that come from your client? Is your client reliable in the role? Does your client understand, at least to an extent, why you wish to do things in certain ways? If not, does your client trust you sufficiently to go ahead on your say-so?

There is yet another factor to consider. We have not taken into account our own wishes in the matter: who do *we* wish to work for? How will *our* aims be best fulfilled? In general our aims are that participants and ourselves are happy to describe the project as 'successful'. Consequently, we would be looking for a client with sufficient power to develop a project that will have impact within the organization, and who has an aptitude for the way in which we work. Over and above this, social factors will influence our choice of client. For example, if there is a choice between a person who sails and a land-lubber, Colin will choose the former every time! This is not merely a pleasantry, for it has practical ramifications in terms of the quality and (sea)worthiness of the consultant–client relationship.

As has already been suggested, the 'client' is not necessarily an individual, but could be a small team. The 'client' might also change, depending upon the particular stage of the project. However, it is worth taking care over determining the client. If the consultant–client relationship is left too loose, none of the relevant individuals or groups may be sure whether they are the client or not. This may result in a crucial shortfall in the commitment that is needed to drive the process onwards. For example, if neither John, Will nor Brian perceives himself to be a client, as part of the client–consultant relationship, then there is a great danger that we could be left 'high and dry'—not because of a lack of interest on their part, but because of a lack of sufficient understanding of what role they should be playing. The *role of client* brings with it a set of role expectations which are powerful in guiding effort and providing legitimacy for action. Without sufficient definition in the minds of those concerned, these necessary adjuncts to successful social action are lost.

In this project John was selected as our 'client', and has remained so throughout the period of our involvement. He was interested in the project and sympathetic to our style of work. He would frequently call us just for a chat about how things were going in the comapny. As the Managing Director he had a powerful position within the company. Working with a coalition of the three Directors, including Will and Brian, would probably have been more in keeping with the organizational culture; however, the fact that they were not involved in the day-to-day operations of the company made this impracticable.

Developing the project

The record of the interviews presented several possible routes in which we might encourage the project to move. For example, there was a need to articulate more fully the goal system for the agency, in order to highlight what appeared to be strongly conflicting goals. This tension was particularly evident between the agency's strong ideological aims, and the more usual business aims of a commercially viable employment agency. There was a problem/cluster which related specifically to the involvement of other Directors. There was a problem/cluster which related to financial planning and forecasting, and a cluster related to anticipating the relationship between demand, advertising, and staffing. And there were several other interrelated problems of a subordinate nature.

Analysis of the models suggested a number of ways of developing the project. There was the possibility of proposing a number of interlinked traditional OR projects: a simple financial planning model (such as a spreadsheet analysis), a forecasting/simulation model of demand which might be linked to the spreadsheet, and a carefully designed programme of workshops to explore a coherent goal system for the agency. We chose to bring the participants together in a workshop situation as the most appropriate next stage, without ignoring the other opportunities as future stages. We felt that the group would respond to an opportunity to share their vision of the organization and its problems, and that any other projects should 'fall out' of the workshop.

The SODA workshop

Our preferred method of running group sessions like this workshop is to use a merged model of the participants' personal models, as outlined in the previous chapter. The wealth of insight which is contained within a merged model is useful and effective in engaging the interest of the participants, and serves as an opportunity to develop the ideas and proposals already contained in the model.

That Will had not been seen for a second time caused some difficulty. Was it valid to include his interview data in the merged model to be presented to the other Directors? Will had had no opportunity to correct aspects of the model which might have been misinterpreted from what he had said at the interview. At best this was unsatisfactory, at worst it could seriously damage consultant–client relations. Further, without having seen his thoughts and comments recorded in 'map form' in a model of his own, there was a possibility that Will would lose ownership of the data incorporated in a joint model, partly because of a lack of familiarity with the method of representation.

Despite our reservations we decided to proceed with a model which included Will's ideas. In our judgement, the degree of trust between the Directors made such a course of action unlikely to cause Will discomfort. We also judged that our relationship with our client was sufficiently robust to allow us to take such a risk.

We contacted John a few days before the workshop to ask him what he hoped to achieve from the afternoon. Like most clients, he was a little perplexed by the question. Clients have, by this stage of the project, developed confidence in the consultant. The 'cathartic' experience of the interviews and the personal orientation of the initial work seems to leave many clients believing the workshop will be successfully managed. Nevertheless, we always spend some time in advance with the most senior and/ or powerful members of the client team, discussing the aims of such a workshop. The purpose is to establish some realistic expectations about the likely outcome.

In this case we particularly wanted John to realize that some of the aspects of the agency and its goals which were clear to him were not self-evident to the other two members of the team. Indeed, he should be prepared for time to be spent comparing and contrasting different views of the agency and its future. We emphasized that this would have positive value; there was the potential for a great deal of synergy from bringing together the different perspectives.

John expressed the desire that the other Directors should have the opportunity to discuss these issues, particularly as he felt that they might then become more involved in addressing them. In line with this, we suggested that an important agenda item might be 'The Role of Directors', which had fallen out of the COPE analysis as an important cluster of concepts. He agreed that this would be useful.

The workshop was organized round an agenda of 'key concepts' with which we led the Directors through the model, allowing them freedom, even encouraging them, to discuss topics or issues as they wished. Using this process to introduce them to one another's ideas, the afternoon developed smoothly and successfully.

The use of colour is particularly effective when working on a large model of this type. While preparing the model for the session, concepts of three different 'types' were identified: goals, strategic options, and options. These were differently coloured to make them readily identifiable to the participants and so help reduce complexity. (The definition of these terms, and their conceptualization within the context of the use of COPE is discussed elsewhere: see Eden, 1989.) An example of a strategic issue is that of 'Developing the Role of Directors'. A number of options always lead into a strategic option.

The agenda was generated by examining strategic options which were judged to be of particular importance. Each of these was explored, taking a look at the goals which would be affected and at the options which could be implemented to achieve the strategic thrust implied by the strategic option. Thus the possible strategic thrust in this case might be 'to prosecute an effective role in the organization'.

The process of working on the combined model served to generate discussion naturally on the strategic option 'Developing the Role of Directors'. Each Director became more informed of the breadth and complexity of the issue by considering the merged ideas and perspectives of the others. In particular, Brian and Will, each with a part-time involvement, gained insight into aspects of the work, and possible roles for each of them, which they had not previously considered. Being presented with an overview of the whole model, Brian commented that he had 'not consciously realized quite how much there was to be done and considered'. In the event the topic proved to be an exceedingly appropriate strategic option to explore: the evidence of John arriving at the meeting obviously exhausted from overwork was symbolic of the significance of the issue. The timing of the meeting was not ideal, on a Friday afternoon, but John was noticeably more tired than the others. As the discussion progressed Will and Brian began to agree that they ought to be sharing more of the burden and identify how they might effectively do this.

The effectiveness of the afternoon in giving Will and Brian 'more of a voice' is difficult to assess: John was too tired and overworked to pick up immediately on any new contributions that they might make. However, this came to assume a secondary importance to the need, as perceived by Will and Brian, to fulfil their roles as Directors more effectively in supporting John. At one point in the discussion, Will apologized to John for not supporting him as he should have. Subsequently the discussion around many of the identified options focused on relieving John of some of the responsibility for action. The discussion focused on those ideas which could lead Brian and Will, in their part-time capacities, to take on some of the burden. During this discussion John found a new lease of energy and became very engaged with the model and with adapting it to encompass the ideas and views that Will and Brian were now elaborating. The model was beginning to act truly as a 'negotiative device'. The model itself began to take on the role of 'problem solver', with the consultant able to devote more energy to the management of the process.

After three hours Will had to leave to catch his train back to London and so the decision was made to finish. The workshop had gone well, serving to generate better relations and understanding between the Directors, and to stimulate enthusiasm to proceed further. The three Directors had committed themselves to several courses of action which were expected to 'Develop the Role of Directors', and they had also agreed to the importance of other key strategic options that would require further research, analysis, and a similar workshop.

This workshop had not specifically addressed the financial state of the company either now or in the future, nor did it attempt to forecast future business, nor indeed any other issues that an outsider might have regarded as the most concrete. This focus on more intangible strategic issues is typical of the *early* stages of a SODA project. It is our belief, and it seems to be the belief of our clients, that it is a focus on these 'softer' issues at the beginning of a project which later enables the participants to use more traditional analysis in an effective manner. In this project subsequent workshops explored a selection of the other issue clusters; in so doing a number of specific analyses were undertaken to enable options to be selected in a more informed manner.

In this sense the project was unfolding in a fairly typical manner. The problem construction aspects that dominate the beginning of a project generally continue to re-emerge, as a group cycles through more traditional analysis. After each analysis the insights gained would be set back within the qualitative aspects of the COPE model in order that the final decision would fully reflect both qualitative and quantitative considerations. The intention of a SODA method of working is not that it should replace traditional OR analysis, but rather that it should act in a complementary manner.

References

Charles, D., Fleetwood-Walker, P., and Luck, M. (1985). 'Communication skills: Information-seeking interviews', *J. Opl Res. Soc.*, *36*, 883–90.

Eden, C. (1982). 'Problem construction and the influence of OR', *Interfaces*, **12**, 50–60.

Eden, C. (1985). 'Perish the thought', *J. Opl Res. Soc.*, *36*, 809–19.

Eden, C. (1987). 'Problem solving or problem finishing?', in *New Directions in Management Science* (Eds M. Jackson and P. Keys), Gower, Aldershot.

Eden, C. (1989). 'Cognitive maps as a visionary tool: Strategy embedded in issue management', *Long Range Planning*, in press.

Eden, C., and Sims, D. (1979). 'On the nature of problems in consulting practice', *Omega*, **7**(2), 119–27.

Eden, C., Jones, S., and Sims, D. (1983). *Messing About In Problems*, Pergamon.

4
Soft systems methodology

Peter Checkland

The only man-made object on our planet which is visible to astronauts in space is the Great Wall of China. Its creators over several thousand years, or, to take a more recent and less awe-inspiring example, the creators of the American telephone network in the early years of this century, must have been engineers and managers of considerable skill. In both cases they successfully accomplished what in today's language would be called major 'projects', though that word has become popular only in recent times. The notion of a project implies bringing together the materials and skills necessary to create both some complex object and the way it will be used. A project implies the exercise of a combination of engineering and management skills. In the case of the latter, not only does the project itself have to be managed, but also the project content must include creating a way of using (managing) the physical object or objects. In the case of the Anglo-French Concorde project, for example, the overall task was to create both the world's first supersonic passenger aircraft and ways in which it could be manned, flown, serviced, and fitted into airline operations.

Given the number of impressive projects throughout human history, it is perhaps surprising that it is as recently as the 1950s and 1960s that ways of defining and carrying out projects were set down formally in a methodology to be followed by aspiring project managers. What is less surprising is that engineers played a big part in that development. The thinking of engineers extended from designing and making single objects to creating *systems*, the latter thought of as both a connected set of objects and the way of using them. In the 1950s, phrases such as 'the systems engineer' and 'systems engineering' became current, and methodological accounts of how to do systems engineering—something intuitively grasped by the builders of the Great Wall and the engineers of the American telephone

Rational Analysis for a Problematic World
Edited by J. Rosenhead. © 1989 John Wiley & Sons Ltd

network—began to appear. Hall's classic account of 1962, *A Methodology for Systems Engineering*, was generalized from the experiences of Bell Telephone Laboratories in carrying out research and development projects, and the approach is now well established.

This kind of systems engineering is both the intellectual and the practical parent of the Soft Systems Methodology (SSM) to be described in this chapter. SSM is best understood in relation to its origins. It is the problem solving approach developed from systems engineering when that approach failed. And systems engineering—impressive enough as a way of carrying out technological projects—failed when attempts were made to apply it, not to projects in the sense described above, but to the messy, changing, ill-defined problem situations with which managers have to cope in their day-to-day professional lives.

In this chapter the nature of systems engineering will be described briefly, in order to explain the conditions under which it will inevitably break down. An account will then be given of the emergence of SSM as a response to that breakdown, and an account of it as a problem solving methodology suitable for messy problem situations will be given. Finally, it will be useful to reflect on just how far the systems thinking in SSM has moved beyond that in systems engineering.

In the following chapter a detailed account of SSM in action will be given.

Systems engineering

Professional engineers make sense of their world by thinking about it in the following way. A specification is produced which gives a careful description of something which is required, whether a physical object (for example, a particular kind of valve for an oil rig) or a complete system (for example, a petrochemical complex). The professional skill of the engineer is then used to meet the specification in the most efficient, economic, and elegant way. Finally, the finished object or system has to be described— often in 'manuals'—in ways which enable others to use it. The acclaimed engineer is the person who invents new ways of meeting a specification (for example, a jet engine instead of a piston engine) or who finds solutions which use less materials, perform better or are more elegant (for example, basing a bridge on the idea of the keystone).

How, then, does the engineer go about his or her task of *meeting the specification?* Engineering thinking is teleological; it asks: what is the *purpose served* by the object or system? The engineer works back from the purpose, or objective, and creates an object or system which will achieve that objective. The whole design realization process is driven by the discipline of having to meet a declared objective (Machol, 1965; Chestnut, 1967; Wymore, 1976).

Out of this kind of thinking, which, in the case of Bell Telephone Laboratories, was 'generalized from case histories' (Hall, 1962), comes a methodology for systems engineering as a series of steps in a process. These steps start by defining the need to be met and the objectives of the system which will meet them. Alternative systems are appraised in the light of the objectives, and the most promising alternative is selected for development. The criteria for 'promising' include such considerations as fitness for purpose, and economic aspects. Finally, the selected system is realized, operated, and maintained. Many techniques exist to help with each stage of this process.

In a sentence, the essence of the approach is *the selection of an appropriate means to achieve an end which is defined at the start and thereafter taken as given.* The American moon landing provides a sharp example of this. The President himself defined the objective as 'before this decade is out ... landing a man on the Moon and returning him safely to Earth' and declared an open-ended commitment to providing whatever resources were required (Kennedy, 1961). Once the NASA project was underway, questioning the objective was inconceivable.

This is the core of the systems engineering approach whose failures in normal management situations led to the emergence of SSM. In fact the thinking which has been described here as characteristic of the engineering tradition parallels in time, and matches in content, the thinking underlying the establishment in the 1950s and 1960s of the whole group of methodologies for rationally intervening in real situations in order to bring about improvements. These go under different names and were developed in somewhat different contexts.

'Systems analysis', for example, as originated by RAND Corporation and subsequently developed by many different groups (Smith, 1966; Optner, 1965; Quade, 1975; Miser and Quade, 1985, 1988) brings together ideas from engineering and ideas from economics and seeks to help a real-world decision maker faced with carrying out a major project. As described by one of its pioneers, the systems analysis approach assumes an objective we desire to achieve; alternative systems for achieving it; costs or resources required by each system; models showing the interdependences of objectives, systems, resources, and environment; and a criterion for choosing the preferred alternative (Hitch, 1955).

'Operational research', as we now know it, grew out of the application of the scientific method not to unchanging Nature but to wartime military operations. OR discovered that the scientific method could be used to understand, if not the unique idiosyncrasies which characterize human situations, at least *the logic of situations* (Blackett, 1962; Waddington, 1973). Operational researchers went on to work out the applied mathematics of the logic of some common situations which recur, such as managing queues, locating depots, deciding when to replace capital equipment, or assembling an investment portfolio (see any university textbook on classical OR, such as Wagner, 1975). Traditionally, the approach seeks to apply the empirical method of natural science to real-world operations. It does this by defining the objective to be achieved in a real-world activity, and then exploring how that objective might be achieved by manipulating a model. The well-known algorithms of OR are simply ready-made manipulations for some well-structured problems which recur.

It is obvious that the fundamental thinking underlying systems engineering, systems analysis, and operational research is very similar. Though they have different names as a result of their different histories, these three approaches to rational intervention in human affairs can readily be shown to represent *one* approach (Checkland, 1981, 1983). They all assume that an important class of real-world problems can be formulated as a search for an efficient means of achieving objectives known to be desirable. The search can be conducted systematically by defining the objective to be achieved and manipulating models of the situation or of alternative forms it might take. This approach has been named as 'hard' systems thinking, to distinguish it from the 'soft' systems thinking which grew out of it (Checkland, 1985).

The emergence of SSM

With hindsight the emergence of SSM from failed attempts to use the methodology of systems engineering seems inevitable. At the time, of course, the usual confusion which characterizes any research programme in a changing subject, seemed to reign supreme! The research intention, in a university postgraduate Department of Systems, was to find out what happened to systems engineering methodology when the word 'engineering' was read in its broad sense (you can 'engineer' an agreement, as well as a nitric acid plant) with the approach applied to typical managerial problems in organizations, rather than to the better-structured projects of systems engineering embodying 'hard' systems thinking.

'Hard' systems thinking entails starting from a carefully defined objective which is taken as given. This is the starting point in systems engineering, systems analysis, and classical (textbook) OR. But in many, perhaps most, managerial problems at any level the questions—What are the objectives? What are we trying to achieve?—are themselves part of the problem. In our research we found ourselves seeking an approach to problem solving which would cope with messy situations in which objectives were themselves problematical.

In one formative experience the work was being carried out in a textile company with 1000 employees which was in grave difficulties. The company had spent its spare cash on a new technology (extrusion of polypropylene tape) which it had failed to master. And it had failed to pay a dividend for the first time in its history. It had recruited from outside (also for the first time in its history) two senior managers, a Marketing Director and a Finance Director, who felt very uncomfortable in the parochial culture of the firm. Every aspect of the company activity—production planning, controlling quality, distribution, etc.—exhibited many obvious deficiencies.

We were asked to do whatever seemed helpful to ensure company survival. The Managing Director declared that the objective was 'to survive', but this was hardly an *operational* definition. What exactly should survive: the traditional business, a rationalized version of it, or one based on the new polypropylene technology? Senior managers had very different ideas on what should be done. The Production Director, for example, attributed the company's problems to the Marketing Department's failure to lay down achievable technical standards for each of the company products. More important, the managers lacked any mechanisms for exploring different views and achieving agreement on action.

The methodological model provided by systems engineering seemed quite irrelevant to this mess. What was 'the need'? What 'system' would meet that need? What were 'the objectives' of that system? These seemed very naive and simplistic questions in the face of the failings, fears and farce of the actual situation. Systems engineering—like the other 'hard' approaches—assumes a relatively well-structured problem situation in which there is virtual agreement on *what* constitutes the problem: it remains to organize *how* to deal with it. However, for most managers most of the time both what to do and how to do it are problematical, and questions such as: What is the system? What are its objectives? ignore the fact that there will be a multiplicity of views on both, with alternative interpretations fighting it out on the basis not only of logic but also of power, politics, and personality. An approach which assumes these questions have been settled, and concentrates only on getting together a response, will pass by the problems of real life, applicable though it may be once a particular project has been decided upon.

Another formative experience was a study of the Anglo-French Concorde project, based in the British Aircraft Corporation. Again we had the situation, welcome for research purposes, that 'the problem' was not tightly defined. We were to make a study and see where systems thinking could contribute to the success of the project. This was a very much more sophisticated environment than that in the textile firm which could not cope with polypropylene extrusion! But this perhaps made it more difficult for us to see how our methodology was failing us. The context of the work was that serious consideration was being given at that time as to how computerized information systems could and should be introduced into BAC, and our study could be seen as part of that effort. We had recently, in a quite different study, developed a way of modelling information flows by deriving them from models of operational decisions which recur, these being forerunners of the activity models which are now a central feature of SSM (Checkland and Griffin, 1970).

With some vague idea of using this method to define the basic information flows necessary in the Concorde project, and examining existing flows, we did not pause over questions of objectives at the start of the systems engineering methodology. We took it without question that the need was *obviously* to develop the innovative aircraft and get it into service. 'The system' was the Concorde project; and 'the objectives of the system' were to develop, jointly with the French, an aircraft to meet a particular specification within a certain time at a minimal cost. All this was taken to be completely obvious, and it was anticipated that work would eventually concentrate on alternative ways of meeting the information-flow requirements of such models.

It was subsequently extremely difficult for us to appreciate that the models we produced, which represented projects to develop Concorde, were simply *not meaningful* to the managers with whom we tried to discuss them and their implications! Since 'the Concorde project' was the phrase everyone used, it was not easy for us to step back and perceive that project thinking was not in fact the way BAC managers made sense of their world, even though the need for a supersonic passenger aircraft was taken as given. BAC was not then managed, as are many aircraft manufacturers, on the basis of project management. BAC was organized at that time in functional groups, with *ad hoc* task forces formed to tackle particular crises, and what was referred to as 'the project' at BAC at Filton had only a reporting, not a managing, role, the reporting being to the government in Whitehall.

Here again, our systems-engineering-based methodology was not capturing the richness of the situation. We did not stop to consider whether to take the Concorde project to be essentially political (collaborating with the French; beating the Americans to at least one advanced technology), economic (providing much employment in the British engineering industry), legal (the question of possible cancellation as costs soared) or technological. The most obvious technological objective was taken as given. And we failed to perceive that the project-management language of our models did not get heard in the particular culture we were in. Here was a case in which, even though what was called 'the Concorde project' had been established, the methodological concepts of systems engineering, with their focus on the logic of achieving an objective, missed much of the human richness of the specific problem situation in BAC. And there are few human situations in which getting the logic right is enough to bring about action.

These experiences in management situations in the textile and aircraft industries, like many similar experiences in the early years of the research programme, emphasized that the use of systems engineering methodology in 'soft' (multi-perspective) problem situations had severe limitations. Any situation in which human beings try to act together will be complex simply because individuals are autonomous. Shared perceptions—essential for corporate action—will have to be established, negotiated, argued, tested, in a complex social process. Any human situation, in fact, will be characterized by more than facts and logic. It is true that a distribution means will *have* to be appropriate to the product distributed, that continuity of product supply will be contingent upon a continuity in supply of raw materials, etc. But the facts and logic will never supply a complete description of a human situation. Equally important will be the myths and meanings by means of which human beings make sense of their worlds. Systems engineering, by taking objectives as given, assumes that the myths and meanings are in place, and static, and that effort can focus on the facts and logic. This is explicitly recognized. In a significant passage near the end of their book on *Systems Analysis for Engineers and Managers* de Neufville and Stafford (1971, p. 251) remind analysts of their limited role:

> It is important that engineers, planners, and economists recognize not only their incapacity to determine a social welfare function, but also the legitimacy of the political process to decide social priorities.

This is clear advice to engineers, planners, and economists to stick to their fields of facts and logic, leaving aside broader social issues.

In many public projects, for example in health care or public water systems, the political process will be embodied in *representative* institutions which will generate the objective to be taken as given. In a company or other organization there is unlikely to be a political system based on representation, but politics in whatever form will still have an important bearing on the priorities which determine whether a project goes forward or not. De Neufville and Stafford, in the quotation above, are reminding users of the 'hard' approach they describe that politics, much concerned with myths and meanings, is *outside its scope*, that their approach assumes 'whats' have been decided and gets down to providing an efficient 'how'.

A systems-based methodology for general management problem solving would evidently have to change significantly the process of systems engineering. That is what happened. A rudimentary form of SSM as an alternative emerged in a dozen projects of the kind discussed briefly above (Checkland, 1972). What is now to be described is a mature version of SSM several hundred projects later, to which very many users in industry, the public sector, and universities have contributed.

Soft systems methodology

A full account of the emergence of SSM and some rethinking of systems ideas which that entailed has been given elsewhere (Checkland, 1981, 1984, 1988; Wilson, 1984). Here will be summarized the main features of the approach as they appear to be in the late 1980s after much experience in organizations large and small, public and private, together with some experience in studies not based within organizations, an area which needs to be further extended.

Whereas systems engineering methodology is a system concerned with achieving objectives, SSM is a learning system. The learning is about a complex problematical human situation, and leads to taking purposeful action in the situation aimed at improvement, action which seems sensible to those concerned. SSM articulates a process of enquiry which leads to the action, but that is not an end point unless you choose to make it one. Taking that action changes the problem situation. Hence enquiry can continue; there are new things to find out, and the learning is in principle never ending. This learning process or cycle can be thought of as a sequence of stages, and will be described later in this chapter in this way, even though the user does not necessarily have to plod through from Stage 1 to Stage 7. But first it is useful to describe some general features of this approach, some assumptions which it takes as given, which make it the process it is.

Firstly, SSM is a process for managing, and must therefore take a particular view of what 'managing' is and what a manager does. Managing is interpreted very broadly as a process of achieving organized action; it is not restricted to the activities of the particular professional class which emerged as a result of the Industrial Revolution. In the broad sense relevant to SSM, the activities of a peasant craftsman, of an industrial company, of a cooperative, of a trade union, of the NHS, of a terrorist cell or

The lifeworld : a flux of interacting events and ideas

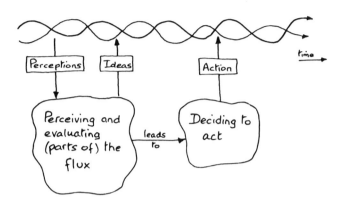

Figure 1
A broad concept of 'managing' (after Checkland and Casar, 1986)

an anarchist political group all have to be *managed*, in that they all entail deliberate, thought-out action, not simply random thrashing about. And the view of this deliberating which SSM takes, is that anyone who is a manager in any field of activity is reacting and trying to cope with an ever-changing flux of interacting events and ideas. The world immerses all of us in such a flux. 'Managing' means reacting to that flux: perceiving and evaluating (parts of) it, deciding upon action, and taking action which itself becomes part of the on-going events/ideas flux, leading to new perceptions and evaluations and further actions. Although management 'problems' may occasionally be temporarily 'solved' out of existence, this is only a special case of the continuing process. Choose the right time frame and all is seen to be flux. The process is shown in Figure 1 (based on Checkland and Casar, 1986).

Given this broad view of managing, SSM then assumes that different individuals and groups, being ultimately autonomous, will make different evaluations leading to different actions. This creates 'issues' with which the manager must cope. Gregarious life would not be possible if perceptions and evaluations did not to some extent overlap. Such an overlap is virtually a condition for the existence of what we call 'an organization'. But the overlap will never be complete, and the issues which arise from the mismatch provide much of the substance of managerial work. The issues themselves will derive both from interpreting the facts and logic of a situation and from engaging with the myths and meanings through which other managers and participants make sense of it.

The third major assumption of SSM is that in consciously articulating the process of Figure 1, systems ideas will be helpful. 'System' is a concept of a whole which has properties as a single entity, so-called 'emergent properties' (Checkland, 1981, Ch. 3). (For example, the ability to confer degrees is an emergent property of a university as an entity: the property has meaning only in relation to the institution as a single whole.) Since the world outside ourselves appears to be densely interconnected—more like a hedge than a handful of marbles—it seems worth exploring the extent to which systems ideas can be mobilized to help explain the tangled reality we perceive.

The fourth general assumption behind SSM stems from the experience of developing it. When this was done in the 1970s, systems thinkers had already developed the concepts of 'natural systems' (a possible name for wholes created by Nature) and 'designed systems' (a name for wholes created by Man). Such ideas had been helpful in understanding such things as frogs and foxgloves, tramcars and telescopes. They did not, however, seem rich enough concepts to cope with the complexity of human situations. These, in every study we undertook, wherever situated, involved human beings trying to take purposeful action. The idea was, therefore, developed that a set of activities linked together in a logical structure to constitute a purposeful whole (the ability to pursue the purpose being an emergent property of that whole) could be taken to be a new concept of system to set alongside 'natural sytem' and 'designed system'. The name adopted for the new concept was 'human activity system' (the phrase being borrowed from Blair and Whitston's book on industrial engineering, 1971).

In order to make use of this idea, however, by forming concepts of human activity systems and trying to map them on to real-world action, it was necessary to achieve some important learning about the way in which people talk and think about purposeful activity.

Where it will be possible fairly easily to get an agreed and testable account of a frog regarded as a natural system, or a bicycle treated as a designed system, accounts of purposeful activity are usually given in terms of an *interpretation* applied by the speaker. Ask someone how he or she would regard a prison as a purposeful human activity system and he or she will usually describe it as 'a rehabilitation system' or 'a punishment system' or 'a system to protect society' or, more cynically, 'a system to train criminals'. These answers, all *relevant* to debating, or understanding, the notion of 'a prison', are all heavy with interpretation. It is rare to get an answer as relatively neutral as 'a system to accept and store labelled people for a defined length of time'.

This readiness to talk of purposeful activity only in terms of a particular interpretation, bias, prejudice or value system means that we have to accept (a) that there will be multiple possible descriptions of any named real-world purposeful action, and (b) that any description of purposeful activity which is to be used analytically will have to be explicit concerning assumptions about the world which that description takes as given. German has the strongest word for this. We need in naming a system of purposeful activity to declare the *Weltanschauung* which makes that description meaningful. The usual translation is 'worldview', but that has a rather bland air, as does 'point of view'. Our *Weltanschauungen* are the stocks of images in our heads, put there by our origins, upbringing and experience of the world, which we use to make sense of the world and which *normally go unquestioned.* It is a difference of *Weltanschauung* which causes the Government of Nicaragua in the 1980s to describe the guerillas known as the Contras as 'terrorists' while the President of the United States refers to them as 'freedom fighters'. Systems engineering ignores *Weltanschauungen.* SSM cannot afford to.

In order to engage with the concept of using systems language to give accounts of purposeful activity, SSM was *forced* to take account of the need to describe any human activity system in relation to a particular image of the world. And similarly it had to accept that any real-world purposeful action could be mapped by several human-activity-system descriptions, based on different assumptions about the world.

These considerations lead to the fifth basic characteristic of SSM as an enquiring process. SSM learns by *comparing* pure models of purposeful activity (in the form of models of human activity systems) with perceptions of what is going on in a real-world problem situation. Thus we could learn about real prisons by comparing what goes on in them with the activities in a set of models which might include, among other possibilities, a rehabilitation system, a punishment system, a system to protect society, a system to train criminals and a storage system. Intuitively this seems to be what we do anyway in the process of consciously thinking about something. We try out various mental constructions; indeed, our ability to do this consciously seems to be one of the significant things which distinguishes us from cats, crabs, and cuckoos. SSM simply provides a highly explicit kind of comparison based on system models used in an organized process which is itself a learning system.

The purpose of this comparison, carried out in the later stages of the SSM approach, is to achieve a readiness to take action purposefully in the problem situation in question, action which is defined in the debate initiated by the comparison stage (model versus perceptions of the real world).

Thus, finally, SSM is an articulation of a complex social process in which assumptions about the world—the relevant myths and meanings as well as the logics for achieving purposes which are expressed in the systems models—are teased out, challenged, tested. It is thus intrinsically a *participative* process because it can only proceed via debate. SSM does not in principle call for a professional expert who makes a study and draws conclusions, although the legacy of attitudes in the management science world in which it was developed means that it has on many occasions been used in that mode. Of course, someone familiar with the approach, who is skilled at naming human activity systems and building models of them, can greatly facilitate a study. But the most important aim of such a person is to give away the approach, to hand it over to people in the problem situation, to leave behind not only some specific action taken but also the process by which the decision on that action was reached.

The stages of soft systems methodology

Having described five important general features of SSM, we are now in a position to give an account of it as a sequence of well-defined stages. This will be done for the sake of clarity in description, but it will be pointed out that in an actual application it is not essential slavishly to follow the sequence from Stage 1 to Stage 7. SSM articulates the process of Figure 1 by means of organized finding out about a problem situation, the finding out then leading to taking deliberate action to bring about improvement in the situation. In the everyday world a common route from finding out to taking action is to rely upon experience. Experience is certainly not to be despised, but SSM supplements it by an explicit use of systems thinking, in the process shown in Figure 2. The systems thinking starts by naming (in so-called 'root definitions') some systems of purposeful activity (human activity systems) which are hopefully *relevant* to exploration of the problem situation. This oblique approach is necessary because, as has been argued above, it is never possible simply to describe real-world purposeful activity once and for all. We can only describe a range of interpretations which are relevant to *debating* the real-world processes and structures. There will always be many possible, more or less plausible, accounts of a prison, a production process, a distribution function or a health care system. We have to learn our way collaboratively to the most relevant perceptions in a particular situation in order to take action to improve the situation.

Activity models are built of a number of named relevant systems. These models are brought into the everyday world of the problem situation, and compared with real-world action going on there. The models, being only logical machines for pursuing a purpose, built on the basis of declared pure

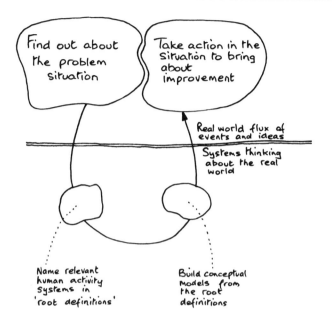

Figure 2
The basic structure of soft systems methodology

Weltanschauungen, will not in general precisely map the observed real-world action. If they do, then more radical root definitions are needed!

The purpose of the comparison is to provide the structure of a debate about possible changes, that debate focusing on differences between models and real-world action. The object of setting up the debate is to *learn your way to possible implementable changes*, changes which are expected to constitute improvements in the problem situation. In general, the implementable changes will represent an *accommodation* between the different conflicting views developed and presented in the debate. An accommodation does not eliminate conflict—which is endemic in human situations—but may make corporate purposeful action possible. The purpose of the debate is to find the way to that action.

Since human situations embody myths and meanings as well as facts and logic, the search is for changes which meet two criteria simultaneously. The changes must be both *systemically* desirable (on the basis of the logic of the models), and *culturally* feasible for the people in the problem situation, given the unique history of the specific situation in a particular culture. The debate both defines changes which would bring about improvement, and seeks to motivate people to take action to implement the defined changes.

83

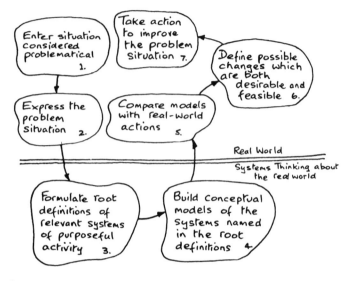

Figure 3
The learning cycle of soft systems methodology

The problem situation—a portion of the flux of events and ideas in Figure 1—may well have been changed by the systems thinking about it; it certainly will be changed by the action taken to improve it. A cycle of learning and action is thus complete, the flux moves on, the cycle of learning and action can begin again ....

Figure 3 shows the whole cycle of SSM in more detail. Its separate stages will now be further described, although it should be emphasized that straightforward linear progress from Stage 1 to Stage 7 is not necessarily the way in which users of SSM operate its cycle. As long as the logical connections between the stages are kept in mind, the actual problem solving activity can move flexibly amongst them.

Stages 1 and 2: Finding out

It will not be possible for any would-be problem solver, whether an outsider or part of the problem situation, to simply 'find out' about the situation in a neutral manner. The personality traits, experience, knowledge, and interests of our investigator will all affect what is noticed and what is taken to be significant. The finding out has to be done, seriously but lightly, with this in mind.

Three phases in developing ways of finding out, and expressing, the problem situation can be discerned in the evolution of SSM. Initially, pictures of the situation in question were assembled by recording elements of slow-to-change *structure*, recording the dynamic elements of continuously changing *process*, and forming a view of how the two relate to each other in creating the *climate* of the situation. Examples of this are described in Checkland (1981). The approach was found to be helpful, especially the representation of important relationships in the situation literally in 'rich pictures', but many people found these guidelines too abstract when faced with the specific, often alarming, energy and emotion in a human situation regarded as problematical.

An alternative approach was developed of using the cycle of SSM itself to do the initial finding out. This was done by quickly moving to Stages 3 and 4, building models of systems to carry out some declared, official, primary task relevant to the situation (e.g. the storage and loan of a body of written and recorded material, in the case of a library) and using the comparison between these models and real-world action to direct and constitute the finding out. This approach has been successful in many cases but suffers from the disadvantage that it can tend to channel subsequent thinking in only one (somewhat boring) direction, namely improving the efficiency of existing operations.

Recently, experiments with a third approach have proved promising. This can be seen as a return to the initial approach but using more elaborate guidelines. 'Finding out' is now carried out through three related analyses. Analysis One takes the intervention in the situation as its subject matter and identifies the occupiers of the roles 'client(s)' [who cause(s) the intervention to take place] and 'would-be problem solver(s)' [who conduct(s) the study] (see Checkland, 1981, pp. 237–40). Then, whoever is in the latter role names a list of possible people who could be taken to be 'problem owners'. This list will normally include whoever is 'client', but also many different people with an interest in the situation or likely to be affected by changes in it. This list is a good source of potentially relevant systems for Stage 3 of SSM as a whole.

Analysis Two looks at the problem situation as a 'social system'—using that phrase in its everyday-language sense. Analysis Two establishes what social roles are significant in the situation, what norms of behaviour are expected from role holders, and by what values performance in role is deemed to be good or bad. This analysis ensures that basic attention is paid to the problem situation as a *culture*.

Finally, Analysis Three examines the situation *politically* by asking questions about the disposition of power. This is done by asking through what commodities power is manifest in the situation, and finding out how these commodities are obtained, used, preserved, passed on. (Typical commodities included role-based, sapiential or charismatic authority;

85

privileged access to certain people or information; command of resources, etc.) The three analyses are described more fully in Checkland (1986). They yield a rich picture from which some systems of purposeful activity relevant to exploration of the problem situation can now be selected.

Stage 3: Formulating root definitions

The formal expression of systems thinking in SSM begins by writing down the names of some systems for carrying out purposeful activity, systems thought to be *relevant* to that deeper exploration of the problem situation which will lead to action to improve it. In the early years of SSM much effort was spent in trying to select the most relevant of all possible relevant systems. This is now seen as wasted effort. As the user becomes familiar with the approach, he or she finds that insight is most effectively generated by entertaining many possibilities. Thus we *learn* our way to those which turn out to be most relevant by passing quickly round Stages 1–5 a number of times.

Early in the research 'root definitions' (RDs), as the names of relevant systems are called, were written rather casually, covering essentially only the purpose which the system in question pursued. Later, when RDs from many studies were examined against a completely general model covering any purposeful activity (Smyth and Checkland, 1976) a rule was derived for ensuring that RDs are well formulated. RDs should be constructed by consciously considering the elements of the mnemonic CATWOE, which is explained and illustrated in Figure 4.

The core of an RD is T, the transformation process which changes some defined input into some defined output. This simple concept is frequently misunderstood, and the systems literature is full of inadequate representations of system inputs and outputs. Figure 5 illustrates the idea and some pitfalls. The usual error is to confuse the system input (that entity which gets changed into the output) with the resources needed to bring about the transformation, quite a different concept. Everyone who has ever used systems thinking will have made the mistake more than once! However, it is very important to get a correct representation of T, since once that exists, model building in Stage 4 is straightforward. What is looked for in Stage 3 is the coherent formulation of some RDs which can be related to the CATWOE questions and from which models can be built.

When the work which yielded the CATWOE mnemonic was carried out, it was noticed that historically we had been very prone to write RDs which excluded both A (the actors who would do the activities of the system) and O (the system owner who could demolish it). The reason for this, it was eventually realized, lay in the legacy of systems engineering ideas which

Formulation of Root Definitions

Consider the following elements : CATWOE

C customer   Who would be victims/beneficiaries
               of the purposeful activity ?

A actors   Who would do the activities ?

T transformation   What is the purposeful activity
  process   expressed as

               input $\longrightarrow$ $\boxed{T}$ $\xrightarrow{\text{output}}$?

W Weltanschauung   What view of the world makes
                   this definition meaningful ?

O owner   Who could stop this activity ?

E environmental   What constraints in its environment
  constraints   does this system take as given ?

Example :

A professionally-manned system in a manufacturing company
which, in the light of market forecasts and raw material
availability, makes detailed production plans for a defined period

CATWOE analysis —

C people in the production function

A professional planners

T need for production plan $\longrightarrow$ need met ; or :
  information $\longrightarrow$ plan

W rational planning of production is desirable and is a
  possibility ; there is the degree of stability needed
  to make rational planning feasible

O the company

E staff and line roles ; information availability

Figure 4
Formulation of root definitions

87

Purposeful systems as transformation processes

Input → T → Output
I → O

T changes, transforms I into O. I must be present in O but in a changed state.
An abstract I must yield an abstract O.
A concrete I must yield a concrete O.

Example: Possible T's relevant to a football match:

Players ⟶ Tired players
Pitch ⟶ Churned-up pitch
Rules ⟶ Rules having been applied
Football skills ⟶ Football skills developed
Team spirit ⟶ Team spirit increased/diminished
Need for entertainment ⟶ Need met by mounting a football match

Two wrong answers:

Players ⟶ Football skills displayed

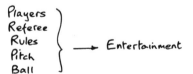

Players
Referee
Rules ⟶ Entertainment
Pitch
Ball

Figure 5
The concept 'transformation process'

were only gradually being stripped off as SSM evolved. We had tended to miss A and O in CATWOE because we had been far too ready to think only of notional systems whose boundaries corresponded with real-world organization groupings such as sections, departments, divisions—in which case A and O were too obvious to be noticed. This readiness to think of real-world departments, etc., as *being* systems, a common thought in hard systems thinking, gave far too much importance to organization boundaries, which are in the end arbitrary, created by human beings, hence changeable.

Nowadays we would always try to include amongst the relevant systems not only some 'primary task' definitions expressing official, declared, tasks but also 'issue-based' definitions which lead to systems not likely to be institutionalized in the real world (Checkland and Wilson, 1980). For example, in an organization which carries out a number of disparate tasks, a useful issue-based RD might express the idea of 'a system to resolve conflicts on resource use'. You would not expect to find a department of conflict resolution in the organization: nevertheless such systems, which cut across organizational boundaries, are very useful in freeing up thinking, and in generating new ideas at the comparison stage. Selected relevant systems should always include some with issue-based root definitions.

In summary, a well-ordered Stage 3 yields a handful of well-formulated RDs, both 'primary task' and 'issue-based', which can then be modelled in Stage 4.

Stage 4: Building conceptual models

In SSM the core of the language for modelling activity systems is very simple and very sophisticated: simple because the user knows it already—it is 'all the verbs in English'; and sophisticated because there are a great many verbs in English, allowing fine nuances of meaning to be expressed!

The model-building process consists of assembling the verbs describing the activities which would have to be there in the system named in the RD and structuring them according to logical dependencies. An arrow from activity x (say, 'obtain raw material') to activity y ('convert raw material to product') shows that y is *contingent upon* x. These considerations govern the assembly of the operational part of the system which would achieve the transformation process(es) named in the RD. It is a useful aim, for most models, to describe the operational activities in 'the magical number 7 ± 2' activities. The quoted phrase is from Miller's famous paper in cognitive psychology (Miller, 1956) in which he suggests that the human brain may have limited channel capacity for processing information: 7 ± 2 concepts we can perhaps cope with simultaneously.

The final model is that of *a system*, that is to say a notional entity which could adapt and survive, via processes of communication and control, in a changing environment. Because of this it is necessary to add to the operational sub-system a monitoring and control sub-system, which examines the operations and takes control action to change and/or improve them. Any system model is thus a combination of an operational system and a monitoring and control system.

We may unpack the concept 'monitoring and control' by asking: how could the system fail? In general there are three kinds of answers to that (Forbes and Checkland, 1987). Firstly, failure could stem from doing the wrong thing. For a purposeful 'system to do x', the question as to whether x is the right thing to do tests the *effectiveness* of the system in its wider context. Secondly, the system must show a means of pursuing the purpose expressed in the RD which in principle could actually work. Asking whether the selected means does work tests the *efficacy* of the system. Finally, an effective system with an efficacious means could still 'fail' because the operations of the system do not achieve the desired end with economy of resource use. The degree to which achieving the transformation uses up resources measures the *efficiency* of the system. Any monitoring and control system must pay attention to all three of these 'Es'. For example, consider setting up a notional system to wash cars in which a small boy works with a bucket of water and a cloth. Monitoring effectiveness means asking the question: do we, in this situation, want to devote our time and effort to providing a car washing facility rather than doing something else? Monitoring efficacy asks whether or not the small boy with his limited resources could in fact do the job. Finally, we need to ask if the small boy is making a minimum use of resources (here, time and materials) while producing cleaned cars: we need to measure the system's efficiency in that sense.

These considerations show that having expressed the purposeful activity as an input–output transformation, we need to ask what would serve as measures of effectiveness, efficacy, and efficiency. Having defined these, we can in principle observe the system at work and take control action if it is not performing well according to these measures. This leads to the general structure for any model of the kind discussed here shown in Figure 6: when building such models it is always wise to think about what the measures of performance could or would be.

More detailed consideration of the concept of monitoring and control shows that in circumstances in which questions of effectiveness are paramount, it may be useful to express the structure of the systems modelled in the form shown in Figure 7. This is a more sophisticated version of Figure 6, and draws attention to the fact that questions con-

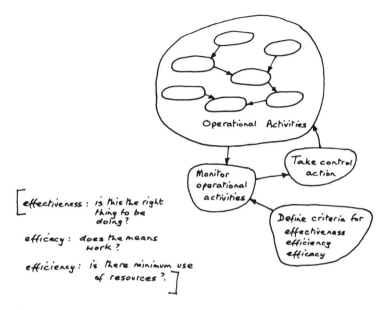

Figure 6
The general structure of a model of a purposeful activity system

cerning the effectiveness of a system can be answered only by taking account of the wider system(s) of which the system in question will be a part. The owner of a system described in an RD (CATWOE's 'O') will reside in a wider system and could in principle decide to demolish the operations of the system and do something else instead. One of the reasons for including 'system owner' in CATWOE, in fact, is to ensure that thinking is not restricted to one level (that of the system as a logical machine pursuing its purpose). Thinking about 'O' forces us to take into account the meta-level which can discourse *about* the system in question.

This last consideration is an example of the importance of the system concept of 'hierarchy'—or, if you want to avoid the unhelpful coercive connotations of that word, 'stratified order'. According to this idea, no system can ever be conceptualized in isolation, only as existing at one level in a stratified order of sub-systems, system and wider systems, etc.

A second way in which the concept is important in model building is that it allows detailed models of notional systems to be built without breaking the useful rule of '7±2 activities'. Having built a complete model with a handful of activities in the operational sub-system, we may now make any or all of those activities sources of root definitions which can themselves be modelled in more detail: 'obtain raw material' can be expanded into the

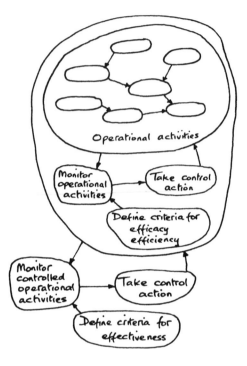

Figure 7
The structure of a model of a purposeful activity system indicating that effectiveness is decided in the wider system which owns this system

structured set of activities which make up 'the system to obtain raw materials'. Similarly, the system originally modelled may itself be regarded as *one* purposeful activity in a wider system, one whose root definition will be suggested by examining the effectiveness criteria. For example, conceptualizing a system to provide health care for the elderly might lead to modelling the wider system which provides all health care services, and has to weigh the priority given to each.

We have worked in some studies with detailed models containing more than 200 activities, but we would not have known how to build them except in a stratified order of wider systems, systems, sub-systems and sub-subsystems!

Perhaps the greatest difficulty in conceptual model building lies in disciplining oneself to work only from the words in the root definition. Since RDs are relevant to real-world activity, it is easy to slip into feeding into the model elements from real-world versions of the purposeful activity being treated as a system, elements not justified by the words of the RD.

Model Building :

A defensible logical structure for a model may
be derived from a root definition even though
knowledge of any real-world version of the
purposeful activity is lacking!

Root Definition

> A dag-owned gor tonking system which,
> within legal constraints, tonks those gors
> which meet criteria gog.

C   gors
A   not stated (skilled tonkers implied)
T   gors ⟶ tonked gors
W   gor tonking is a good thing to do
O   dag
E   legal constraints

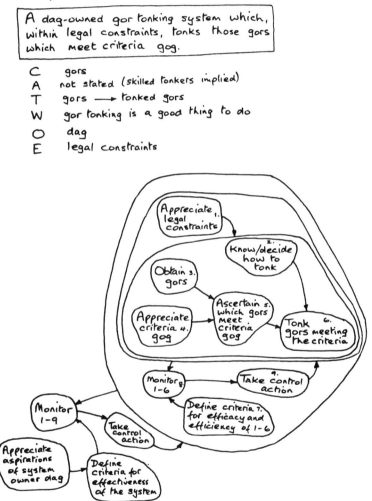

Figure 8
Model building from a root definition and CATWOE

Root Definition

> A hospital-owned system which provides records of spending on drugs so that control action by administrators and doctors to meet defined budgets can be taken jointly.

C   Administrators, doctors

A   Not stated

T   Need to know → Need met by
    Spending on drugs   recording information

W   Monitoring spending on drugs is possible and is an adequate basis for joint control action

O   Hospital

E   Hospital mechanisms; roles administrators and doctors; defined budgets

Figure 9
Another example of model building

Model building should focus only on the RD; every phrase in it will lead to particular activities in the model; every element in the model should relate to a particular part of the RD. The aim is a *justifiable* combination of RD and conceptual model. It is not expected that different modellers will derive *exactly* the same model from an RD, simply because words carry different connotations for different people. What is sought is a model which is coherent and defensible rather than 'correct'.

Figures 8 and 9 give examples of RDs and the models which derive from them. The model in Figure 8 cannot possibly include unjustified real-world knowledge since it is, deliberately, an RD without meaning. It is included to show how a defensible logical structure for a model can be created from an RD, even though the RD does not refer to the everyday world.

In summary, this stage yields a number of models of activity systems, some of them probably related hierarchically, each built according to a particular pure view of the world which is declared in the W of CATWOE.

Stage 5: Comparing models and 'reality'

The models from Stage 4 provide a means for perceiving reality afresh and initiating a discussion from which changes to improve the problem situation can be sought. This is achieved by focusing upon differences between the models and perceived reality. Since the models are all based upon pure, carefully expressed worldviews, the discussion directs attention to taken-as-given assumptions about the world, highlights alternatives and, in general, provides an opportunity for rethinking many aspects of real-world activity. Stage 5 is always an exciting, sometimes a painful experience! And it is very often the point from which one recycles to earlier stages in the methodology, as learning is achieved through the comparisons between models and real world.

Four ways of conducting the model/real-world comparison have emerged. Whichever approach is adopted, the initial comparison is usefully done at the level of the RD itself. How does it reflect current perceptions? Could it? Should it? For example, in a study aimed at improving the operations of a local public library, an RD might be based on viewing the library, not as a well-understood mechanism for book and record loan, but as a part of the local education system. It would be useful, even before considering the model, to compare and contrast this concept with those of the professional librarians, potential actual users of the library and local educationists.

When it comes to comparing activity models with what is currently going on in the situation, we are at the point at which the often unquestioned, informal and intuitive perceptions of reality are brought up against the systems constructs. The constructs (both issue-based and primary task) are those considered *relevant* to reconsidering present perceptions and activities, with a view to improving them. Since human situations are diverse, it is not surprising that different ways of carrying out the comparison stage have seemed sensible in different studies.

The first of four ways of conducting this stage is the least formal: simply record differences which stand out between the handful of models and current perceptions and happenings. List the differences and discuss whether or not they matter. This approach is often relevant where roles and/or strategies are an issue. If the concern is more detailed—improving operations and necessary information flows, for example—then a more formal listing of differences yields the second approach. Here, each model is used to define a series of specific questions concerning activities, and links between activities, for which answers are then sought in the situation itself; this often involving further finding out beyond that carried out initially in Stages 1 and 2. Thus we can ask of every activity and every link in the model: Does this happen in the real situation? How? By what criteria is it judged? Is it a subject of concern in the situation? Tables of answers to such questions are assembled. This ordered questioning is the most common way of carrying out this stage (Checkland, 1981).

A third approach is to 'operate' the activity system, on paper, and so write a scenario describing how things might happen given the RD in question. Such scenarios can often be compared with historical happenings known to people in the problem situation.

The fourth method of comparison consists of trying to build a model *of* a part of reality similar to a model thought to be *relevant* to it, following as closely as possible the structure of the latter model itself. If this can be done then overlay of the two models reveals the differences starkly. (In the unlikely event that the two models were identical—unlikely because reality is more rich and complex than logical models—this would mean that more radical RDs were needed.) This is the most formal method of doing the comparison, and naturally it can only be used if there is in the real world some fairly direct manifestation of the purposeful activity of the model. This is not as common an occurrence as might be thought, given that the models are intellectual constructions intended to structure debate, not would-be descriptions of reality. So this fourth method of doing the comparison often cannot be used.

In summary, this stage provides the structure and substance of an organized debate about improving a situation thought of as problematical.

In practice it merges into the next stage in which changes to be implemented are defined.

Stage 6: Defining changes

The purpose of the comparison stage is to use the differences between models and reality to discuss possible changes which could bring about improvement in the problem situation. The models are not necessarily thought of as designs, as happens in 'hard' systems engineering. Here the thought may be to make reality either more *or less* like the models: the purpose is to make the debate a coherent one.

What is looked for in the debate is possible changes which appear to those taking part to constitute potential improvements worth trying. Such changes have to meet two rather different criteria simultaneously. Firstly, the comparison of a fecund reality with a number of models (which are simply logical machines) will generate ideas for changes which are *systemically desirable*, such as instituting mechanisms for assessing effectiveness, making sure resources are appropriate, ensuring that logical dependencies are reflected in real-world sequential actions, etc. But this logic is not enough. People will not always be motivated to implement change which is justified merely by logic! The debate must find its way to changes which are also *culturally feasible* in the particular human situation in question. (The history of the situation, its myths and meanings, for instance, will always affect this issue.) This is one reason why it is so important to think carefully about the *Weltanschauung* of each RD and model: CATWOE's W is a way of ensuring the cultural aspects cannot be completely ignored.

This need for cultural feasibility as well as systemic desirability is something which scientists and engineers sometimes find difficult; they tend to overemphasize the importance of logic, and fail to notice cultural aspects which in fact determine whether or not change will occur. In one study the logic of information flows required by an activity model to monitor expenditure on drugs in a large general hospital had little impact in the face of the heavily defended clinical autonomy of the hospital consultants. And the example has already been given of the project models which were simply not meaningful within the engineering culture of the British Aircraft Corporation at the time of our study.

If both logical and cultural criteria are not kept in mind, then the chance of achieving change will be much reduced; though equally it must be said that what is culturally feasible in a given situation will itself be changed in and by the debate of Stages 5 and 6. Cultures are never completely static, and SSM can be seen as a way of exploring them and enabling them to change.

97

Stage 7: Taking action

When some changes accepted as 'desirable and feasible' have been identified, then the cycle of SSM is completed by implementing these changes. The readiness to make the changes, of course, changes perceptions of the initial problematical situation—which in any case will have been moved on by the very processes of SSM. There is now a somewhat more structured problem situation, and addressing it (that is, implementing the changes) can itself be tackled by using SSM in further cycles. 'Relevant systems' will now include 'a system to implement the defined changes', and modelling it via RDs and CATWOE can help make implementation a coherent process.

The cycle of SSM, and the recycles which normally occur within any application of it, thus provides a way of articulating the cycle of Figure 1, an approach to 'managing' in a broad sense of the word. It is an approach, 'validated' by having been found useful in several hundred studies as well as transferable to users other than those who developed it. It makes use of systems ideas together with a concept of purposeful activity, in a combination which tries to address not only the facts and logic of a problem situation, but also the myths and meanings through which the people in the situation perceive it and relate to it.

Conclusion

How different is SSM from the systems engineering (SE) which spawned it? In particular, how different is the systems thinking in 'soft' systems methodology from that in 'hard' systems engineering?

SE works with a defined need or objective, and systematically finds its way to a system to meet the need, achieve the objective. In the experiences which produced SSM, it was found necessary to regard as problematical precisely what is taken as given in SE, namely the need or objective. SSM treats *what to do* as well as *how to do it* as part of the problem. It does so via the device of modelling systems which pursue a pure purpose from a declared point of view. It accepts that real-world action will be much messier than these pure models, and uses the models to structure a debate in which different conflicting objectives, needs, purposes, interests, values can be teased out and discussed. In this way it tries to encompass cultural myths and meanings as well as publicly testable facts and logic. It thus seeks to articulate a process in which an accommodation between conflicting interests and views can be sought, an accommodation which will enable action aimed at feasible improvement to be undertaken. This means that SSM is a learning, not an optimizing system; learning has to be participative, so that SSM is not—or should not be—the skill of an external expert.

Finally, it will be clear that ending a systems study which uses SSM is an arbitrary act: the flux of events and ideas moves on, there are no permanent solutions, and systems thinking has to be envisaged as a process which is in principle never ending.

All these differences between SSM and SE make SSM the general case of which SE is a special case. The special case becomes relevant when ends are agreed (or can be imposed), and the question is not what to do but only how to do it.

SE takes 'system' to be the name of something in the world which could be 'engineered'. SSM takes 'system' to be the name of an epistemological device which can be used to investigate some of the problems in the world. Thus the crucial distinction between the hard and soft systems approaches is that the former takes the world to consist of systems, whereas the latter shifts systemicity from the world to the process of enquiry into the world: in SSM 'the system' is not something out there in the situation but is the process of enquiry, a process which happens to make use of pure systems models (Checkland, 1983; 1985).

In the next chapter an application of SSM as a process of enquiry leading to real-world action will be described.

References

Blackett, P. M. S. (1962). *Studies of War*, Oliver and Boyd, Edinburgh.

Blair, R. N., and Whitston, C. W. (1971). *Elements of Industrial Systems Engineering*, Prentice Hall, Englewood Cliffs, NJ.

Checkland, P. B. (1972). 'Towards a systems-based methodology for real-world problem solving', *J. Sys. Eng.* **3**, 87–116.

Checkland, P. B. (1981). *Systems Thinking, Systems Practice*, Wiley, Chichester.

Checkland, P. B. (1983). 'OR and the systems movement: mappings and conflicts', *J. Opl. Res. Soc.*, **34**(8), 661–75.

Checkland, P. B. (1984). 'Systems thinking in management: the development of soft systems methodology and its implications for social science', in *Self-organisation and Management of Social Systems* (Eds. H. Ulrich and G. J. B. Probst), pp. 94–104, Springer-Verlag, Berlin.

Checkland, P. B. (1985). 'From optimizing to learning: a development of systems thinking for the 1990's', *J. Opl Res. Soc.*, **36**, 757–67.

Checkland, P. B. (1986). 'The Politics of Practice', IIASA Roundtable, 'The Art and Science of Systems Practice', Laxenburg, Austria, November 1986.

Checkland, P. B. (1988). 'Soft systems methodology: overview', *J. Appl. Sys. Anal.*, **15**, 27–30.

Checkland, P. B., and Casar, A. (1986). 'Vickers' concept of an appreciative system: a systemic account', *J. Appl. Sys. Anal.*, **13**, 3–17.

Checkland, P. B., and Griffin, R. (1970). 'Management information systems: a systems view', *J. Sys. Eng.*, **1**, 29–42.

Checkland, P. B., and Wilson, B. (1980). 'Primary task and issue-based root definitions in systems studies', *J. Appl. Sys. Anal.*, **7**, 51–4.

Chestnut, H. (1967). *Systems Engineering Methods*, Wiley, New York.

de Neufville, R., and Stafford, J. H. (1971). *Systems Analysis for Engineers and Managers*, McGraw-Hill, New York.

Forbes, P., and Checkland, P. B. (1987). 'Monitoring and control in systems models', Internal Discussion Paper 3/87, Department of Systems, University of Lancaster.

Hall, A. D. (1962). *A Methodology for Systems Engineering*, Van Nostrand, Princeton, NJ.

Hitch, C. J. (1955). 'An appreciation of systems analysis', in *Systems Analysis* (Ed. S. L. Optner, 1965), pp. 19–36, Penguin, Harmondsworth.

Kennedy, J. F. (1961). Message to Congress on urgent national needs.

Machol, R. E. (1965). *Systems Engineering Handbook*, McGraw-Hill, New York.

Miller, G. (1956). 'The magical number 7 ± 2', *Psych. Rev.*, **63**, 81–96.

Miser, H. J., and Quade, E. S. (Eds.) (1985). *Handbook of Systems Analysis: overview of uses, procedures, applications, and practice*, North-Holland, New York.

Miser, H. J., and Quade, E. S. (Eds.) (1988). *Handbook of Systems Analysis: craft issues and procedural choices*, North-Holland, New York.

Optner, S. L. (Ed.) (1965). *Systems Analysis*, Penguin, Harmondsworth.

Quade, E. S. (1975). *Analysis for Public Decision*, Elsevier, New York.

Smith, B. L. R. (1966). *The Rand Corporation*, Harvard University Press, Cambridge, Mass.

Smyth, D. S., and Checkland, P. B. (1976). 'Using a systems approach: the structure of root definitions', *J. Appl. Sys. Anal.*, **5**, 75–83.

Waddington, C. H. (1973). *OR in World War 2*, Elek Science, London.

Wagner, H. M. (1975). *Principles of Operations Research*, Prentice-Hall, London.

Wilson, B. (1984). *Systems: Concepts, Methodologies and Applications*, Wiley, Chichester.

Wymore, A. W. (1976). *Systems Engineering Methodology for Interdisciplinary Teams*, Wiley, New York.

5

An application of soft systems methodology

Peter Checkland

The previous chapter described the approach now known as soft systems methodology (SSM), and did so by relating it to the history of its development. As has been described, this arose out of failed attempts to use the methodology of systems engineering in the kind of messy ill-structured situation which faces anyone who tries to bring a little order into human affairs. The outcome was a methodology for coping with the complexity of human affairs which is in the form of an enquiring or learning system, one making use of systems ideas.

It is the essence of a *methodology*—as opposed to a method, or technique—that it offers a set of guidelines or principles which in any specific instance can be tailored both to the characteristics of the situation in which it is to be applied and to the people using the approach: users of SSM have to discover for themselves ways of using it which they personally find both comfortable and stimulating. Chapter 4 has described the version of SSM which has been generalized from a large number of studies. In any specific application its guidelines are there to help, but should not be used in cookbook fashion. Such is the variety of human problem situations that no would-be problem solving approach could be reduced to a standard formula and still manage to engage with the richness of particular situations. Flexibility in use is characteristic of competent applications of SSM, and the reader should not look for a handbook formula to be followed every time.

What follows is an account of a use of SSM by a problem solving team in a manufacturing company (Checkland, 1985). It is intended to amplify and

Rational Analysis for a Problematic World
Edited by J. Rosenhead. © 1989 John Wiley & Sons Ltd

extend the general account of SSM in the previous chapter. This story is a mainstream application of the approach, neither as plodding as early studies in which the methodology was being established, nor as *avant garde* as recent examples in which the stages of SSM are used out of sequence with extreme flexibility.

It is obvious that a number of problems face anyone trying to describe a real experience. For one thing, it will be impossible for any written account to approach the rich complexity of lived experience. This would be true even if we were to abandon the would-be scientific approach and write a novel out of the experience. For the novel would be from the author's point of view: is that the 'true' account? Is there in fact any 'true' account of the study, given that the happenings were experienced by a group of people each having his or her own (changing) *Weltanschauung*. And even if all participants agreed an account of the study, and agreed on the study's value—an unlikely event in itself—then that account, if regarded as advocating the approach adopted, would be defenceless against a number of criticisms. There is no answer to anyone who asserts that the study should have been done more quickly or more competently, or that some other approach would have been more effective. Since the same human problem situation cannot be tackled twice, such criticisms are not ultimately very interesting, being incapable of refutation; but they do indicate that case histories are tender flowers, easily trampled under the boots of unreason.

Given these problems, the author can only declare the stance from which the study is described, and hope that he gets readers ready to see if the story provides some learning for them! What is described here, then, is an account from the author's point of view of a systems study using SSM in which he participated. In the true spirit of SSM, the study was carried out by three people in the problem situation in question, three people who were managers rather than professional SSM practitioners. My role, and that of my colleague Iain Perring, was to help the study along. We provided occasional *enabling* help.

In order to make the account of the study as useful as possible to the reader, communication of two kinds is needed. Not only will an account of the study be given, but also an occasional commentary on it, focusing upon the methodological issues. The commentary is carried by the passages indented on the pages that follow.

The study context

The study was carried out in the information and library function of a successful well-managed UK company in a science-based industry. The company attached great importance both to research and, more generally, to information provision, and the latter function was organized as a department: the Information and Library Services Department (ILSD). Its head at the time of the study was an experienced manager near the end of his career. He saw his final task with the company as improving the performance and credibility of ILSD. This he was trying to do at a time when the company as a whole, here called 'Regal Chemicals', was striving for greater effectiveness and efficiency. Following a study of its performance in comparison with that of its international competitors, Regal had become convinced that survival in international markets depended upon improving performance significantly. The Board had expressed this dramatically by saying that survival required productivity improvements which were the equivalent of running the business with 30 per cent fewer people. Such conclusions were not uncommon amongst well-run companies in the United Kingdom at the time. Early retirements were encouraged, and each department had been set target numbers to be reached over a year or two: in the case of ILSD a reduction from 32 to 25 people. The head of ILSD said that he sought 'an improvement in the level of thinking in the department, in its problem solving capability', as well as the reduction in numbers. He decided on a systems study, describing its theme as 'the role of information, and ILSD, in the slimmed-down business'. Having attended a one-week course on SSM he knew that although studies can be done by practitioners brought in as external experts, it is in the true spirit of SSM that studies are best done by people in the problem situation itself—with help if necessary. Help *was* necessary here, in that the three senior members of ILSD who were asked to carry out a systems study using SSM knew nothing of that approach! The three managers were to work on the study one day a week, and my colleague and I were to work with them on occasional days. The head of ILSD did not include himself in the team because he was shortly to retire, and in any case wanted the team to generate and 'own' the outcome of the study.

Although the three managers were somewhat daunted at being asked not only to do the study, but to do it following a particular methodology of which they had never heard, the general morale was not low. The head of ILSD had convinced his people that the difficult situation faced by the Department—and by Regal as a whole—was an opportunity as well as a threat. Here was a chance to rethink their role and make their operation more effective and efficient.

Methodologically the starting point was thus an ill-structured problem situation which the head of ILSD, understanding SSM, did not try sharply to define as 'a problem'. Although the reduction of numbers from 32 to 25 was clearly on the agenda, he discouraged the team from starting with a detailed look at

103

posts and roles in the Department with a view to eliminating some of them, which would have been the traditional approach. He encouraged an examination of the whole problem situation, confident that the question of numbers would emerge in context in the course of the study, as indeed it did. In real-world problem situations sharp definitions of 'the problem' are always misleading, and much effort can be wasted in trying to achieve such definitions.

Finding out: stages 1 and 2

Involvement with the team began with a two-day meeting, during which I outlined some basic systems thinking and we together made sense of those ideas by beginning work on the study. Expression of the problem situation was achieved using the structure/process/climate guidelines and Analysis One, as described in the previous chapter, together with some informal use of the ideas which were later formulated as Analyses Two and Three.

In Regal Chemicals this exploration recorded the several structures of ILSD: the library; computerized information systems enabling Regal scientists to consult databases in California; a collection of specimens of every compound the laboratories had ever synthesized; a secure collection of company reports with their defined security classifications, etc. Processes were those associated with providing a professional information service to the company as a whole, but mainly, it emerged, to the Research Department. The climate of the situation (the relation between structure and process), as I perceived it from this initial exploration, was essentially reactive. There was professional pride in being able to respond quickly and efficiently—with technical competence—to requests for information related to Regal's business, and especially its science base. This early analysis revealed an important source of informal power for ILSD, namely its relations with certain key users of its services. These were individuals with whom ILSD had a productive relationship, and who, either as a result of their formal roles or knowledge, or because of their personality traits, were 'intellectual gatekeepers' in different parts of the company. ('If you want to influence the market researchers, make sure Tom Smith is on your side first, even though he's not Section Head.')

Moving to a more formal 'Analysis One' (as described in the previous chapter), possible occupants of the role 'problem owner' included potential and actual users of ILSD's services, the ILSD professionals, the Company itself, the study team and the Head of Department. The rich picture assembled suggested many possible relevant systems; the problem was to select an initially manageable number which was highly relevant.

Initially there was some understandable reluctance on the part of the team to pause on the expression of the problem situation. After all, they knew ILSD and its environment intimately from their day-to-day professional involvement: why bother to express it on paper? In the end they justified this activity to themselves because of the need to make sure that I and my colleague had a reasonably full appreciation of ILSD's situation. In fact, the general finding in the research on SSM is that a formal expression of the situation addressed, using—I would now say—Analyses One, Two, and Three, is a very useful way of beginning to see a problem situation with fresh eyes. Day-to-day familiarity, although it *feels* rich, includes much unexamined acceptance of activities, structures, and attitudes. These unarticulated assumptions benefit from being questioned through the use of a semi-formal framework.

The first methodological cycle: stages 3, 4, and 5

The expression of the problem situation led to ample discussion of problem themes, and very quickly we had a daunting list of 26 ideas from which choices of relevant systems could be made. Not wishing to formulate 26 root definitions and build 26 conceptual models, we *used the methodology itself* to reduce the plethora of ideas to a handful.

The original 26-strong list contained such ideas as:

– respond to manpower constraints;
– improve liaison with, and feedback from, users;
– cope with escalating cost of materials;
– appreciate, absorb, and exploit technological development;
– decide how to define acquisition, retention, discard policy;
– define the evaluative aspects of information provision;
– improve/integrate procedural systems.

Each of these could be made the source of a relevant system, or, indeed several! All entries in the list were regarded as important: the problem was to assign priorities and so select a handful of relevant systems. The only way to do this seemed to be to look at the 26 items from a higher level, so that they could be compared and ranked in importance. The higher level concept was provided by a rudimentary model of wealth-generating operations which, in order to function, need the enabling activity of support units. The concept is shown in Figure 1. The wealth-generating operations O, existing in an environment E, need the help they get from enabling support functions such as S. R is the relation between S and O.

At a high level of abstraction the EROS model of Figure 1, is a conceptual model of an activity system which can be mapped on to Regal Chemical's structure of wealth-generating operations, the manufacture and sale of

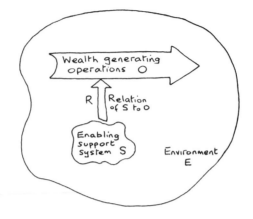

Figure 1
The rudimentary EROS model of operations and enabling support

chemicals, supported by various enabling functions which include ILSD. It is in fact a basis for a rudimentary 'primary task' root definition and model, and it was generated in order to enable the 26 ideas for relevant systems to be appraised.

Setting this model against each of the 26 ideas for relevant systems enabled each of them to be labelled according to whether it focused most sharply on E, R, O or S. The groups of ideas which this produced were then examined and subjectively ranked in importance. The process was less simple than this account of it, but using the EROS model in this way did enable the team gradually to form views on the priority of ideas in the list. Out of the debate structured by this initial 'comparison stage' came a reasonably confident selection of ideas for a handful of relevant systems:

1. An environment-appreciating system.
2. A relationship (O–S) establishing and maintaining system.
3. An 'information as a resource' managing system.
4. An 'aiding the business' system.

> Methodologically, this activity produced a carefully formulated outcome from Stage 2, namely a list of relevant systems which could be turned into root definitions and then modelled in detail. This point had been reached by passing quickly round the cycle of SSM from Stage 1 to Stage 5 in a first pass. Stages 1 and 2 produced the 26 ideas for relevant systems. The EROS model was generated in Stages 3 and 4 as a first relevant system, relevant that is to making judgements about the 26 ideas. Stage 5 then consisted of setting each of the ideas for relevant systems against the EROS model, in order to discuss the nature and potential importance of the 26 ideas. This discussion yielded

the four systems thought by the team to be most relevant. We could now move to Stage 3 of a second cycle of SSM. The first methodological cycle occupied the team for an hour or two.

The second methodological cycle: stages 3, 4, and 5

Of the four relevant systems listed above, No. 3 is the most central, in the sense that the other three would be linked to it in different ways. In order to manage information as a resource, it would be necessary both to appreciate the environment (the first relevant system) and to establish and maintain a relationship with those making use of the information resource (the second). 'Aiding the business' (the fourth relevant system) is what managing information as a resource is supposed to do. Thus, Nos. 1, 2, and 4 are ancillary to No. 3, which therefore would be worth modelling first.

Two root definitions were based upon relevant system No. 3, these being definitions of systems to manage information as a resource from the points of view of the Regal Board and of users respectively:

Root Definition 3a
A system to manage for the Regal Board an information resource, involving the creation and manipulation of a database from locally generated and bought-in material, covering the Company's present and possible future research and business activities as an aid to decision making, within manpower and financial constraints.

CATWOE analysis
C Regal Board and the Company
A information professionals (implied)
T need for a managed information resource $--\blacktriangleright$ that need met
W this kind of staff support function is needed and is feasible
O Regal Board
E structure of staff and line functions; manpower and financial constraints.

Root Definition 3b
A Regal-owned system for satisfying the potential and stated information needs of the user by the timely provision of a comprehensive, readily accessible collection of information, together with a facility/service to meet information needs.

CATWOE analysis
C the user
A information professionals (implied)

T   user with information needs $--\blacktriangleright$ user with those needs met
W   it is possible to define and provide for users' information needs in Regal
O   the Company
E   staff and line functions; various conditions: timely, comprehensive, etc.

A model of root definition 3a is shown in Figure 2. Now followed a period, spread over several months, of one-day-a-week working, in which root definitions were formulated and modelled and compared with the real world of ILSD activity. Such comparisons are often initially carried out informally. Sophisticated users of SSM, for example, will never write a root definition without mentally carrying out some Stage 5 comparison, since the ultimate aim is some models which are *neither* descriptions of the world as it is, *nor* descriptions so far from present 'reality' that they have no meaning for the people in the problem situation. Of course, what does have meaning will evolve during the course of the study and be affected by it, possibly profoundly.

In the Regal study, what happened during this period was that the building of the models (with which we initially provided some help to the team), and the carrying out of comparisons, enriched and modified the way the team had habitually thought about their world. Gradually attention focused on particular models and particular comparisons. The changing thinking seemed to me, as an outsider, to represent a shift in the concept of ILSD with which the ILSD professionals were comfortable. They moved from thinking of ILSD as a reactive function, responding quickly and competently to user requests and having the expertise to do it, to ILSD as a proactive function, one which could on occasion tell actual or potential users what they *ought* to know.

Figures 3 and 4 illustrate two of the models used during this phase. The model of Figure 3 is another model of a service system from a user's point of view. That of Figure 4 is from the point of view of the professional providers of an information service.

The team spent several days making detailed comparisons between models and real world. They adopted the much-used tabular method. A left-hand column lists the activities and relationships in the model; a middle column records the real-world manifestation, if any; a third column adds value judgements about the real-world manifestation and how it is currently rated. If it is missing in the real world, is that a good thing? Does that matter? What are the implications of filling a gap? How might it be filled?, etc. This third column is a source of new root definitions, new perceptions of the real-world activities and, gradually, ideas about desirable and feasible change.

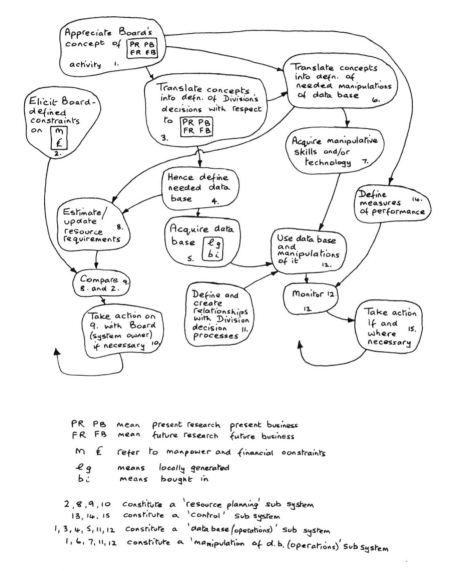

PR PB mean   present research   present business
FR FB mean   future research   future business

m £   refer to manpower and financial constraints

ℓg   means   locally generated
bi   means   bought in

2, 8, 9, 10   constitute a 'resource planning' sub system
13, 14, 15   constitute a 'control' sub system
1, 3, 4, 5, 11, 12   constitute a 'data base (operations)' sub system
1, 6, 7, 11, 12   constitute a 'manipulation of d.b. (operations)' sub system

Figure 2
A conceptual model from 'root definition 3a' (see text)

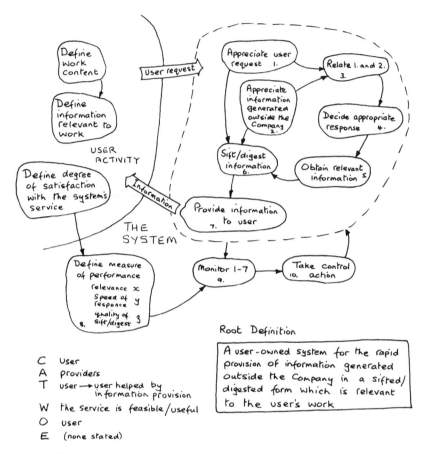

Figure 3
Root definition and model for a system which meets the user's information needs

Methodologically this was an orthodox cycling round SSM's Stages 2,3,4,5, with an eye to moving to a Stage 6 definition of desirable and feasible changes. It was a period in which the team acquired familiarity with the idea of models of purposeful activity systems used as a device for the cogent examination of familiar real-world activity. The strangeness of such models quickly diminished for the team, though users of SSM should never underestimate the degree of culture shock occasioned by presenting managers of any kind, at any level, with *completed* models: better to build the models cooperatively. Quickly, in this study, the methodology became transparent and the team could concentrate on substantive issues.

This second methodological cycle occupied about 20 days spread over several months.

Root Definition

A system, organized by ILSD, which provides comprehensive information to active or passive users employing technical and other skills, assisted by modern technology, so that the service is regarded as comprehensive.

C   User
A   ILSD, some users
T   user → user helped by information provision
W   modern technology and the local culture make this feasible, useful
O   (implied) The Company using ILSD as agent
E   existing structure, modern technology, company resources

Figure 4
Root definition and model for an information provision system from the providers' point of view

The third methodological cycle: expansion of some models

During all of this phase, the function of SSM seemed to me to be to provide a means through which the team could examine their familiar world of professional activity in a fresh and coherent way. As the study made its rather stately progress (due to the one-day-a-week arrangement), the team were gradually forming new concepts of feasible roles for ILSD and were examining their implications. They were changing their readiness to see the world in a particular way, changing their 'appreciative settings', in Vicker's language (Vickers, 1956; Checkland and Casar, 1986).

In the course of this work, the model of Figure 4 was found to be particularly useful as a source of rich debate, so much so that the need was felt to develop part of this model (and parts of some other models) in more detail. Several of the activities of the Figure 4 model were made the source of new root definitions, the models from which gave the desirable increased level of detail. For example, the team chose to expand activities 4 and 5 of the model in Figure 4 ('Identify users and potential users'; 'Identify users' requirements') in the way captured in the following root definition:

> A system owned by ILSD which, together with users, identifies those scientific, technical and commercial staff in research, technical service, development, production, and business functions who require professionally provided information to do their jobs effectively, and key users in particular; and which identifies the level and nature of those requirements, i.e. breadth and depth of subject matter, detail and precision of output.
>
> C ILSD and users
> A ILSD and users
> T identification of users and users' needs
> W this mutual working can be an effective and efficient basis for ILSD processes
> O ILSD
> E existing organizational structure

This root definition was modelled, its activities hierarchically expanding part of the model of Figure 4.

This and similar expansions of other models to more detailed levels shifted consideration from *what* ILSD might do to *how* it might do it. It was at this stage in the study that it became relevant to turn to the question of numbers. Activity models were found to be a good route to rational discussion of manpower planning questions: what roles do these models suggest would be sensible, and how many people would be needed to fill them?

Discussion in the team now centred on the desirability and feasibility of the potential changes which were defined by comparisons at a detailed level between models and real world. The outcome of these discussions gradually emerged as a concept of a realigned and reorganized ILSD with defined staff numbers and roles.

The expansions of the models which seemed most meaningful to the team took the study into its third cycle. The first had solved the problem of the 26 candidate relevant systems; the second led to detailed comparisons and the gradual formulation of a new role for ILSD; the third led to more detailed consideration of real-world 'hows'. This third cycle occupied a few weeks of work spread over several calender months. Methodologically, it illustrated the way in which hierarchical model building can lead to specific consideration of 'hows' and the changes they would entail. The shift from Stages 3 and 4 (modelling) to Stages 5 and 6 (comparison and definition of changes) did not take place once and for all, in sequence. There was much iteration. However, if asked, at any particular moment, what they were now doing, I do believe that the team could have given a coherent answer in the language of SSM: 'Now we're expanding activity 5 of this model'. 'Now we're discussing the differences between this model and current tasks in Reports Section', etc. It is the function of SSM to provide such a language, and so enable the problem-solving activity itself actually to become more coherent.

The fourth methodological cycle: widening the debate

So far, the study had been an internal ILSD activity, involving only the team, other members of the department, and my colleague and me from Lancaster on occasional days. Now that a new concept of ILSD and its role had emerged, and was being expressed in terms of staff numbers and possible job descriptions, it was necessary to involve a wider audience in Regal Chemicals in the debate arising from the study. (Technically, we were involving them in Stage 6 of SSM.) This involvement took a number of different forms. Firstly, the team discussed the study with all members of ILSD (and, since my colleague and I were not present, the obvious joke could be exploited: 'We're being Lancastrated'). Secondly, a presentation to senior Regal managers was arranged. Thirdly, before that presentation was made, an internal report on the study was published by the team.

The report centred on a statement of the main message of the study which was the result of a half-day discussion between ourselves and the team. That statement, which all the members of the team agreed, was as follows:

1. We have made a fundamental appraisal of the role of ILSD.
2. The method was to examine several 'systems' relevant to ILSD and examine the forms they might take, depending upon how the fundamental purpose of ILSD is defined. Possible purposes examined ranged from 'respond quickly to requests for information' to 'manage information as a major resource'.
3. A particularly fruitful definition of ILSD purpose has been found to be both not too far from reality and suggestive of useful changes. That definition is:

    A system organized by ILSD to provide a continuing comprehensive information service to users, employing technical and other skills available within the system, and employing modern technology so that the service is effective in furthering Regal's business interests.
4. A system which would meet this definition looks like this . . .
5. We have compared this (and other) models with present operations and structures in order that the identification of differences can stimulate discussion about desirable and feasible change.
6. The comparison leads to identification of four major differences with major implications:
    (a) the modelled ILSD plays a more central role in the company;
    (b) a relationship with users is implied which requires 'active' users (trained by ILSD perhaps, to help themselves) and a richer user–ILSD dialogue;
    (c) ILSD would have to develop its training function;
    (d) a more organized monitoring and control of ILSD activity is implied. (Organizational implications are still being worked out.)
7. These implications imply some changes which ILSD can make, but some which require the active collaboration of others.
8. Hence we require endorsement at this stage.

The team's report which conveyed this message gave an account of the study structured according to its methodology. The final expanded version of the model whose first version is in Figure 4, was included as an illustration, together with a detailed account of its comparison with present arrangements. The exposition here was carefully written to be in terms of issues and events in Regal well known to the potential readers of the report. For example, the comparison between the real world and the expanded version of activities 4 and 5 drew attention to the solution to the problem—familiar to people within the company—of designing the file/index of references to 50 000 chemicals made over the years in Regal's laboratories. This information needed to be retrievable by researchers in terms of molecular structure, and of physical and techno-logical properties. The parties concerned in that design had been the user who owned the problem, an information specialist from ILSD with encod-ing/retrieval expertise, and a computer system specialist. This was offered as a sample illustration of the kind of collaborative intervention by ILSD which would increase if the new concept of ILSD became a reality.

The report also included as an appendix the most radical considerations from the study, ones which went beyond the departmental boundaries of ILSD. The message here, aimed at Regal's Board, was that during the 1980s it would become essential to manage information as a major resource at company level: it would be necessary to treat information as a resource on a par with personnel and finance, and organizational arrangements for doing so would have to be found. This appendix was my only contribution to the report. I did not, in fact, see the report in draft form before it was published; I took this to be a good sign that the study was fully 'owned' by the team.

By the time the report was written and published, the work had pro-gressed beyond it to the stage at which the team had a prepared argument for a particular number of people in ILSD (21, in fact) and for a particular set of roles in the department.

After publication of the report, and the team's presentation of an account of the study to all members of ILSD, it was still necessary to widen the debate about the issues addressed, since the report argued for changes whose implementation was more than an internal matter for ILSD. In fact, through the head of ILSD, it had already been arranged that a presentation would be given to a selected group of senior managers of Regal.

On the day, the team gave the main presentation, based on the written report. I made a short contribution covering the broader message con-veyed in the report's appendix, namely that there was a strong argument for Regal's appointing a Director of Information at Board level.

The meeting as a whole went well. It was a good example of the changing perceptions and judgements which Vickers calls the working of an 'appreci-ative system'. During the discussion after the presentation, one of the senior managers from the Research Department said that he had had a big surprise at the meeting. 'I have known and worked with ILSD for 20 years,' he said, 'and I came along this morning out of a sense of duty. To my amazement, I find I now have a new perception of ILSD.' This evidence of a change of perception by one of their major users encouraged the team, and added to their confidence in their own new perception of ILSD—one which had developed gradually during the study and was very different from their view at the start. For their part, the managers attending the presentation seemed to accept that a significant and useful rethinking of ILSD's role had been carried out. They indicated their readiness to help and support the new procedures where the collaboration of their own departments and sections was called for. (Discussion of the message of the appendix was much more wary! The picture presented there was of Regal in the 1980s as a set of semi-autonomous work groups linked in an information network. This idea was a long way outside the conventional outlook of most of the senior managers at that time.)

As a whole, the study changed the way in which the ILSD professionals thought about their world and took action in it; and it changed Regal's perception of its Information and Library Services Department. Tangible outcomes followed the study, and there is no doubt that the study helped to bring them about. The study alerted Regal to its information function, and to the new ideas and energy within it. The company invested in ILSD, following the systems study, in two forms. There was capital investment in the kind of information technology needed to foster a more proactive ILSD; and there was human resource investment. The latter took the form of the appointment, on the retirement of the manager who had initiated the study, of a new Head of Department drawn from the cadre of young up-and-coming managers. In the culture of Regal this was a significant act, signalling a shift towards treating information provision as an important function in the company.

> The third cycle of the methodology led to the fourth which took it beyond the team and their department and ended this study. In this fourth (informal) cycle, senior managers were drawn into the discussion of changes. In the team's eyes these managers were taking part in Stage 6 of ILSD's use of SSM—though the language of SSM was not much used in the team's presentation to senior management. It was necessary to bring in more senior managers at this point because the changes generated within the study had implications at a company level and needed resources which only the company as a whole could provide. ILSD had reached the limit of its political power, and the wider issues needed a wider forum and wider political endorsement. Stage 7, therefore, consisted of ILSD's making some internal changes and seeking endorsement of the larger changes from the company as a whole. Figure 5 shows the methodological history of the study.
>
> The study put new items on the agenda of company debate; it made a contribution to the company's readiness to perceive and interpret the world in a particular way; and it was now, in the sense in which it was originally conceived, completed. The story does, however, illustrate the methodological point in SSM that to end a study is essentially an arbitrary act. The study had contributed to producing a new problem situation—that of installing the new concept of ILSD, with its new technology and new management. The appreciative process goes on, whether or not you choose to continue to improve its articulation by the use of SSM.

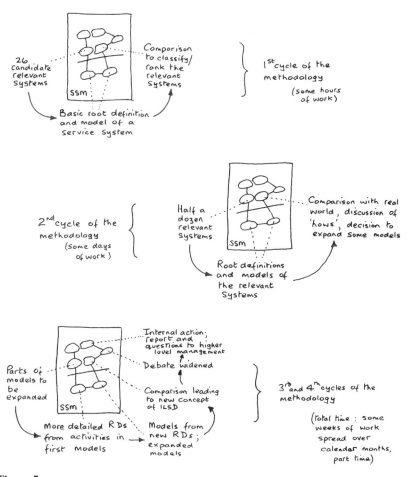

Figure 5
The methodological history of this study

Conclusion

The intention in this chapter has been to illustrate SSM by giving an account of its use. The account tries to describe the experience, but, of course, the experience itself was much richer than any account of it could be. This account has concentrated selectively on making the use of the methodology clear.

The study was 'successful' in that it made a significant contribution to bringing about change in a particular real situation. But the account of this

117

'successful' study is completely defenceless against assertions that it should have been done better, or quicker, or that some other approach would have been even more successful. Since the same human situation cannot be investigated twice, methodology is *undecidable*: 'successes' might have been greater with some other approach, and 'failures' might be due to incompetence in using the methodology rather than to the methodology itself (Checkland, 1972). An individual can only test a methodology by seeing if he or she finds it useful. Ultimately, the only powerful argument in favour of SSM is that it has been found to be transferable to people beyond those who developed it, has been used in several hundred studies and is still developing.

Finally, it is worth saying that the least perceptive criticism of the ILSD study (it is one which has been made!) is the assertion that it is 'obvious' that information provision functions in organizations should be proactive rather than simply reactive. Such a statement may, perhaps, in some circumstances, be a useful piece of rhetoric. But it is a blinkered remark on at least two counts. Firstly, it implies that change might be induced simply by making assertions, by rhetoric alone—by, for example, telling ILSD that it should be more proactive. Most people, however, do not initiate significant change as a result of being lectured to, but only as a result of experiencing something. SSM tries to provide an organized mental experience in which complexity can be comprehended and hence coped with, enabling confident new perceptions to emerge.

The second consideration which makes such criticism blinkered is that nothing is 'obvious' in an abstract general sense. Things are only 'obvious' in relation to a particular way of perceiving the world, to a particular culture. It is indeed important that the outcome of a systems study should, by the time it is reached, appear completely 'obvious' to the people who constitute the culture in which the study is taking place. What is interesting in organizations, regarded as cultures, is the process by which ideas of what is 'obvious' are formed, clash, and change. Soft systems methodology uses systems models in an organized learning system to improve and make more apparent the process by which 'what obviously ought to be done' emerges for particular people at a particular moment in time in a particular situation with its own unique history. SSM encompasses but also transcends the logic of situations; its focus is the cultural processes which lead to purposeful action.

References

Checkland, P. B. (1972). 'Towards a systems-based methodology for real-world problem solving', *J. Sys. Eng.*, **3**, 87–116.

Checkland, P. B. (1985). 'Achieving desirable and feasible change: an application of soft systems methodology', *J. Opl Res. Soc.*, **36**, 821–31.

Checkland, P. B., and Casar, A. (1986). 'Vickers' concept of an appreciative system: a systemic account', *J. Appl. Sys. Anal.*, **13**, 3–17.

Vickers, G. (1956). *The Art of Judgement*, Chapman and Hall, London. (Republished 1983, Harper and Row, London.)

6
The strategic choice approach

John Friend

Introduction

This chapter and the next are about an approach to coping with complexity —the strategic choice approach—which deals with the interconnectedness of decision problems in an explicit yet selective way. The most distinctive feature of this approach is the way it helps users in making incremental progress towards decisions by focusing their attention on alternative ways of managing *uncertainty*. Because it combines a concern for complexity with an emphasis on real-time decision making, the strategic choice approach has been described as an approach to *planning under pressure* (Friend and Hickling, 1987).

Origins and applications

The origins of this approach are to be found in the experience of two pioneering research projects, in which operational researchers and social scientists worked together in observing strategic decision makers in action and talking with them about the day-to-day dilemmas that they faced. One of these projects was concerned with communications in the building industry (Crichton, 1966), and the other with policy making in city government (Friend and Jessop, 1977). Both were conducted by mixed teams of operational research workers and social scientists from the Tavistock

Rational Analysis for a Problematic World
Edited by J. Rosenhead. © 1989 John Wiley & Sons Ltd

Institute of Human Relations, with some overlap in the membership of the respective project teams.

The insights obtained in the course of these two seminal projects were to provide foundations for the development of a set of relatively open, participative methods for representing the structure of interrelated decision problems and the various sources of uncertainty—technical, political, structural—which made them difficult to resolve. Subsequently, these methods were put to the test in a programme of collaborative 'action research' projects, in which operational research scientists acted as advisers to teams of decision makers faced with particular planning tasks. Gradually, the use of these methods has spread, to the extent that they are now being used in addressing complex decision problems in several parts of the world, at a variety of scales and in a variety of organizational and inter-organizational settings.

The case study to be presented in Chapter 7 offers one example of a comparatively high-level application to national policy making in the Netherlands. However, the approach is a versatile one which can also be applied quickly and informally at more modest levels of decision making. For the term *strategic choice*—in the particular sense to be used in this chapter—is intended to signify not so much a high *level* of decision making within any particular organizational framework, as a willingness to address interconnected decision problems in a strategic *way*.

It may be no accident that the principles of the strategic choice approach first emerged from research experience in two realms of decision making—the construction industry and city government—in which powers of decision are widely diffused, and much depends on collective processes of negotiation and debate.

Of course, complexity in the relationships between decision makers is by no means absent within the more conventional hierarchical control structure of the classical commercial firm. Yet the prevailing assumption has long been that it is the firm that offers the model for the design of effective decision processes, whatever the management and planning context. One important point which is demonstrated by the history of the strategic choice approach is that there is substantial scope for the transfer of innovation from other more complex organizational settings into the world of the commercial corporation; a scope which has for too long been undervalued or ignored.

Philosophy: the management of uncertainty

So the origins of the approach to be presented in this chapter are empirical rather than intellectual. They reflect not so much any idealized principles of sound decision making, as a more explicit recognition of some of the ways in which people, faced with complex decision problems in practice, learn to cope with the dilemmas of their work, even if only at an intuitive level.

In such situations, decision makers must learn to make judgements as to how broadly or closely to focus their attention; how to strike a balance between current commitment and future flexibility; and who else should be brought into the decision process, and when and how. The way in which such dilemmas are handled, when working under real-time pressures, can have deep influences not only on the decisions reached, but also on the way the decision process itself is steered through a labyrinth of possible organizational channels.

The strategic choice approach views the routeing of any non-routine decision process as governed by perceptions of the relative importance to be attached to three broad types of *uncertainty*, each calling for a different type of response. These three categories of uncertainty are described as follows:

Uncertainties pertaining to the working Environment: UE for short

This is the kind of uncertainty that can be dealt with by responses of a relatively *technical* nature: by surveys, research investigations, forecasting exercises, costing estimations. The response can range from an informal telephone conversation with an expert at one extreme, to the initiation of an elaborate exercise in mathematical modelling at the other. The type of concern which this response reflects is generally of the form '*this decision is difficult because we don't know enough about its circumstances, because we can't readily predict what the consequences of different ways forward might be ...*'

Uncertainties pertaining to guiding Values: UV for short

This is the kind of uncertainty which calls for a more *political* response. This response might take various forms—a request for policy guidance from a higher authority, an exercise to clarify objectives, a programme of consultations among affected interests. Again, the level of response may vary from the most informal of soundings to the most elaborate exercise for involving interest groups in the evaluation of alternative proposals. Here, the concern on the part of the decision makers tends to take the form '*this decision is difficult for us because there are so many conflicting objectives, priorities, interests. .., because we don't have a clear enough view of where we should be going. ..*'

123

Uncertainties pertaining to Related decision fields: UR for short

This is the kind of uncertainty that calls for a response in the form of exploration of the *structural* relationships between the decision currently in view and others with which it appears to be interconnected. The call here may be to expand the agenda of decision, to negotiate or collaborate with other decision makers, to move to a broader planning perspective—for the more linked decisions are to be considered, the more likely it becomes that time horizons will lengthen, and that some at least of the decisions will be 'owned' by other people. Again, the level of response may vary from the most informal exploration across organizational boundaries to the most formal planning exercise. The concern on the part of decision makers here tends to take the form *'this decision is difficult because we have been viewing it in too restricted terms, because we can't treat it in isolation from. . .'*

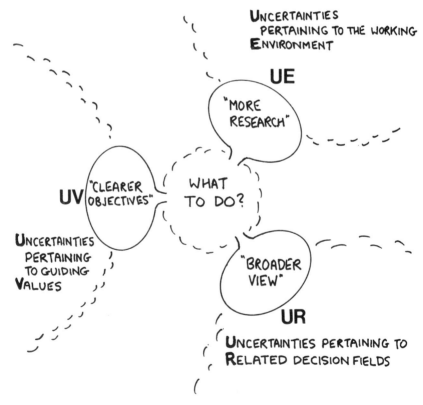

Figure 1
Three types of uncertainty

This view of three different categories of uncertainty, calling for different kinds of response, is summarized in Figure 1. The three types of uncertainty are here related to a 'snapshot' picture in which one or more decison makers are supposed to be experiencing some degree of difficulty in deciding what they should do. So the picture may appear to be a static one; but it is one which has profound implications for the wider *dynamics* of any complex decision process.

It is easy enough for any set of decision makers, faced with a complex and seemingly intractable decision problem, to agree that all three kinds of uncertainty are significant and should be vigorously addressed. However, this is in practice a counsel of perfection, ignoring both the *costs* of initiating different kinds of response, and also the likelihood that they yield different levels of *benefit* in terms of the confidence with which important decisions can be made. Research can be expensive and time consuming; so can consultation with affected interests; so too can large-scale planning exercises. And it is not hard to find examples of situations in which major investments of effort in any of these directions have yielded disappointingly meagre results.

So decision makers continually face important practical choices about how far to invest in different kinds of response to uncertainty. The return on investment can be conceived in terms of more confident decision making; while the outlay has to be seen not only in terms of scarce resources such as money and demands on the time of busy people, but also in terms of delays in the taking of decisions to which particular urgencies apply. The choice of how best to *manage uncertainty* at any moment is one which implicitly faces all decision makers trying to cope with complex problems—and it is this kind of choice in particular which the strategic choice approach aims to articulate in a more explicit way.

The dynamics of strategic choice

It is now time to move to a more dynamic view of a process of strategic choice, as a framework through which to introduce a set of simple yet appropriate concepts and techniques. This framework is one which distinguishes four complementary modes of decision making activity, defined as follows:

1. *The shaping mode* When functioning in this mode, decision makers are addressing concerns about the structure of the set of decision problems which they face. They may be debating in what ways problems should be formulated, and how far one decision should be seen as linked

to another. They may be considering whether their current focus should be enlarged or, conversely, whether a complex of related problems should be broken down into more manageable parts.

2. *The designing mode* When functioning in this mode, the decision makers are addressing concerns about what courses of action are possible in relation to their current view of problem shape. They may be debating whether they have enough options in view, or whether there are design constraints of either a technical or a policy nature which might restrict their ability to combine options for dealing with different parts of the problem in particular ways.

3. *The comparing mode* When functioning in this mode, the decision makers are addressing concerns about the ways in which the consequences or other implications of different courses of action should be compared. They may be considering all kinds of economic, social and other criteria, and debating in what ways assessments of consequences can be made. This is the mode in which uncertainties of the three types UE, UV, and UR tend to come most clearly to the surface—though they can arise when working in any of the other modes as well.

4. *The choosing mode* When functioning in this mode, the decision makers are addressing concerns to do with incremental commitment to actions over time. From a strategic choice perspective, this means not only considering whether there are particular commitments to substantive action that could be undertaken straight away, but also thinking about ways in which the future process might be managed. So it is in this mode that time becomes central, and alternative strategies for managing uncertainty through time must be reviewed.

Figure 2 presents a picture in which the opportunity exists to switch freely from work in any one of the four modes to work for a while in any of the others. It is not hard to see similarities between this model of a decision process, and other more familiar models in which a sequence of logical steps or stages is defined—often with feedback loops to allow for a deliberate return to earlier stages. Yet observations of decision making in groups suggest that, when faced by complex problems, people tend to switch their attention rapidly between one mode and another in the more fluid and adaptive way suggested in Figure 2.

Sometimes, this switching process may seem to be almost random, generating no more than a sense of going round in circles without any progress having been made. Yet at other times it may lead to a sharing of insights and perceptions which makes a valuable contribution in sustaining the sense of momentum in the decision process. For example, if one member of a group is arguing about the disadvantage of some proposed

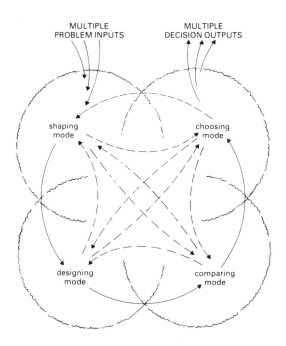

Figure 2
Four modes of decision making. (From J. Friend and A. Hickling (1987) *Planning under Pressure*, by permission of Pergamon Press)

course of action relative to others (comparing), this may prompt another to suggest some quite different course (designing). Other participants may then begin to argue that the whole problem should be restructured if it is to be realistically addressed (shaping); then others again, impatiently, may claim that the argument has gone on long enough and that it is now time to make progress towards decisions (choosing). But it may be that decisive action can only be agreed in relation to some parts of the problem—so there may be further shaping to be done in those other parts where commitment is to be deferred.

In terms of the framework of Figure 2, it can be seen that most of the more conventional management science techniques are addressed primarily to the activities of the designing and comparing modes. Some of them are concerned with a search for an optimum within a closely defined problem structure, and others with exploring the consequences of adopting alternative courses of action through the use of formal predictive models. In so far as uncertainties are explicitly considered, these are generally of the UE type.

However, it is now widely recognized that such techniques have severe limitations in coping with many forms of complexity encountered in practice—and it is these limitations that the strategic choice approach seeks to overcome. The next four sections will introduce a set of comparatively unsophisticated techniques designed to be used when working in each of the four modes in turn. Together, these form an appropriate—as opposed to an advanced—technology of strategic choice. But the strategic choice approach, as it has developed through practice, is more than just an alternative decision technology; it also embraces complementary dimensions of organization, process and product, and these other dimensions will be briefly reviewed in the closing section of this chapter.

Techniques for shaping

In the strategic choice technology, the starting point for the work of the shaping mode is the concept of the *decision area*. This is a very simple concept, of extremely wide application. For a decision area is no more than a description of any area of choice within which decision makers can conceive of alternative courses of action that might be adopted, now or at some future time. So there could be decision areas about *whether* to invest in a particular project; about *where* to locate some proposed new development; about *who* should be made responsible for some task; or about *when* some agreed action should be initiated. It is of the essence of the decision area concept that it can be used to describe decision problems of many different kinds, as a starting point from which to examine the structural relationships among the choices to be made.

Figure 3 presents an example of a set of nine decision areas which, it will be supposed, have been identified as facing decision makers in a well-established manufacturing company called Marintec Industries. This firm is in the business of making instruments for small boats; also, through a subsidiary on an adjacent site, it manufactures packaging materials both for its own use and for sale to other firms.* It will be noticed that the nine decision areas are of different types and levels; some of them relate to specific opportunities, while others relate to broader policy issues that may have been under discussion for some time, but may be highlighted anew by recent events.

Each of the nine decision areas is represented in Figure 3 by a labelled

---

*This is an adaptation of an exercise, based on a real company, which was first devised by Allen Hickling.

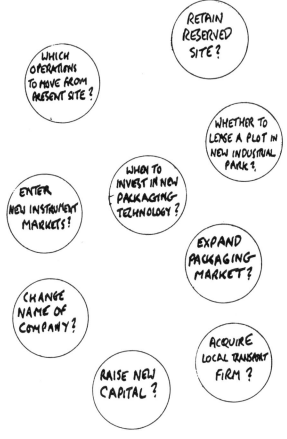

Figure 3
A set of decision areas

circle, describing a choice to be made—hence the question marks. A set of decision areas such as this provides a first basis for building a map of key decisions and the interrelationships between them. This is a process which is usually carried out not as a backroom exercise but through a discussion process, often involving a number of people who may have different perspectives and insights to contribute.

This process of mapping involves the construction of a *decision graph* in which connecting lines—known as *decision links*, or often simply as links—are drawn to connect some pairs of decision areas but not others. The inclusion of a decision link merely indicates a working assumption that those two decisions are directly interconnected, in the sense that

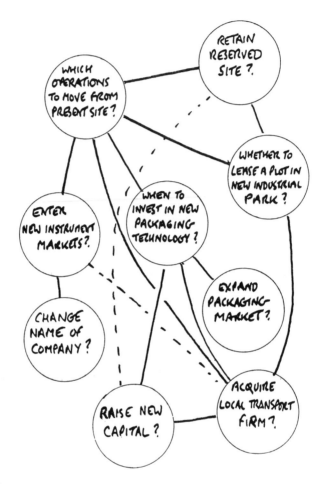

Figure 4
Introducing decision links

there is thought to be a significant possibility of a different outcome if the two choices were considered together rather than one at a time.

Figure 4 illustrates the idea of a decision link by introducing a set of links connecting some pairs of decision areas, but not others, amongst those that face Marintec Industries. Two of the links are thought by the decision makers to be more doubtful than the rest, and are represented by broken lines. For the judgement as to whether a particular decision link should be included can often be a highly subjective one, over which there may be disagreement between one decision maker and another.

There may be many different lines of reasoning behind the inclusion—or exclusion—of decision links. For example, the link between the retention of the reserved site, and the issue of which operation to move, might arise from an assumption that this particular site would be suitable for relocation of the packaging factory, but not the instrument side of the business. On the other hand, the link between the choice of which operation to move, and that of when to invest in new packaging technology, might reflect an assumption that it would be uneconomic to install this technology at this time if the packaging operation were later to be relocated.

The use of directed links is discouraged in the building of decision graphs. For decision links are not intended—as in some other methods of mapping relationships—to convey any implications of causality, or of the sequence in which decisions should be addressed. Nor does it matter, in terms of the logic of the graph, how the various decision areas are positioned in relation to each other. For the map is a topological one, in which the positioning of nodes can be altered without altering the structural information about relationships it contains.

It is, however, often worth spending some time rearranging the positions of decision areas on a graph, to bring out its structural relationships more clearly and minimize the kind of confusion that can arise from too many criss-crossing lines. In Figure 5, some of the decision areas in Figure 4 have been repositioned in a way that brings out more clearly the pivotal position of particular decision areas, such as that concerned with which of the two operations to move.

Some simple rules can help in identifying comparatively isolated decision areas and tightly interconnected clusters. Where the number of decision areas is larger than in this example—as is often the case in practice—then it can be useful to turn to a computer for help in this process. But the kinds of assumptions about linkage between decision areas which are introduced in this kind of preliminary problem structuring will often be too crude and tentative to justify much sophistication in analysis. And the more decision areas have been identified, the more this kind of caution will apply.

The greater the number of decision areas, the more important it is too to be sparing in the introduction of decision links. A graph in which practically every decision area seems to be connected to every other will not only be impenetrable to the eye; it will also contain much less structural information of a kind useful to decision making than one in which links have been inserted in a more selective way.

Wherever a decision graph contains more than three or four decision areas, it is rarely productive to switch into more detailed analysis of options and their implications without first attempting to restrict the focus

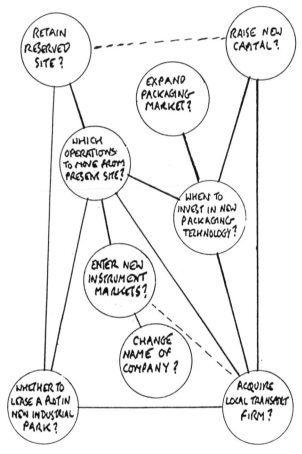

Figure 5
Rearranged decision graph

of attention within the decision graph. Indeed, for a problem of any complexity, the choice of an agreed *problem focus* for closer investigation can be seen as the main objective in the construction of a decision graph.

This point is illustrated in Figure 6, in which various additional types of information have been superimposed on the rearranged decision graph of Figure 5. Some decision areas have now been marked as more urgent than others, and some as more important. Although the structural information contained in the decision graph provides an important overall frame of reference in the choice of a preferred problem focus, it is important to recognize that other criteria of selection may also become significant at this stage.

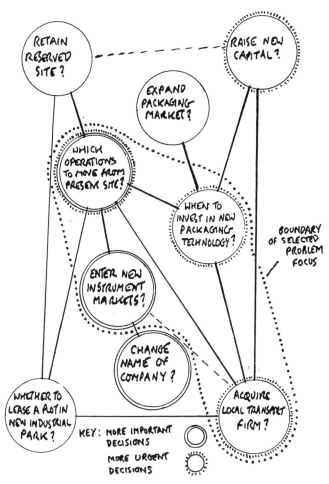

Figure 6
Choosing a problem focus

The dotted boundary line in Figure 6 encloses a set of four decision areas within the wider formulation of the Marintec problem, selected partly on grounds of importance, partly on grounds of urgency, and partly on grounds of connectedness within the overall graph. This focus could be replaced by any other—perhaps containing more decision areas, perhaps fewer—should the participants so agree. Or it could be altered at some later stage of the analysis, in keeping with the adaptive style of switching between modes suggested in Figure 2. Or, again, two or more different problem foci could be chosen simultaneously—with or without overlaps between them—and these might be assigned to different groups of people, for closer examination of alternatives and their implications.

Techniques for designing

One widely applicable method for exploring the specific courses of action available within a chosen problem focus is that of *Analysis of Interconnected Decision Areas*, usually referred to by the acronym *AIDA*. This is a simple enough method in its essence; it involves representing the range of alternatives available within any decision area in terms of a limited set of mutually exclusive *options*, and then introducing a set of tentative yes/no assumptions about whether options in different decision areas can be combined. This makes the generation of feasible combinations of options a straightforward logical process, in which computer methods can be used to save time if the number of decision areas is large. However, in practice it is usually preferable to restrict the problem focus to no more than three or four decision areas at a time, so as not to be working with more combinations of alternatives than people can easily comprehend.

Figure 7 lists a set of options representing the range of choice thought to be available within each of the four decision areas contained in the problem focus already selected for the Marintec problem. In each case, a set of at least two options is listed; it is rare in practice to work with more than four or five.

Sometimes, of course, the number of options within a decision area may seem to be more open-ended—for example, where it concerns the choice of some point along a continuous scale. In that case, the AIDA method requires a simplified representation of the range of choice, in terms of a few judiciously spaced points within what is thought to be the feasible range. Such a simplified representation may be unacceptable when applying more sophisticated techniques to a more highly structured management control problem; but it can be quite adequate for the purpose of an exploratory analysis of the type of non-recurrent problem situation to which the strategic choice approach is normally applied.

The important point is that the set of options within a decision area should be not so much exhaustive as broadly representative of the range of choice believed to be available; so far as possible, they should be mutually exclusive as well. Sometimes, a set of options on closer inspection may not appear to meet this latter condition, in which case additional composite options can be added; or—preferably in many cases—the decision area itself can be reformulated so that the mutual exclusiveness condition applies. For example, it might be asked why the instrument market might

DECISION AREA   OPTIONS

WHICH OPERATIONS TO
MOVE FROM PRESENT SITE?

- INSTRUMENTS
- PACKAGING
- BOTH

ENTER NEW
INSTRUMENT MARKETS?

- AGRICULTURAL
- LIGHT AIRCRAFT
- NONE

ACQUIRE LOCAL
TRANSPORT FIRM?

- YES
- NO

WHEN TO INVEST IN
NEW PACKAGING
TECHNOLOGY?

- NOW
- LATER

Figure 7
Options within decision areas

not be extended to cover *both* agricultural vehicles and light aircraft. Perhaps such a step could be ruled out on grounds of too much risk. If not, however, the decision area about new instrument markets could be split into two—one to do with whether or not to move into the agricultural market and the other to do with whether or not to move into the light aviation field. This illustrates the important point that there will often in practice be various equally valid ways in which the same problem can be formulated in AIDA terms.

The task of designing feasible alternatives within an AIDA formulation of a problem is essentially a combinatorial one. For it involves identifying the full set of combinations of options, one drawn from each decision area, which do not violate any assumed feasibility constraints. The most usual form of constraint introduced into an AIDA problem formulation is an assumption that a particular option in one decision area should be treated as *incompatible* with a particular option within another decision area.

In AIDA language, a judgement that two options from different decision areas are to be treated as incompatible is termed an *option bar*. In Figure 8, a matrix arrangement is used to show the pattern of option bars judged to apply between options in the first two of the decision areas in Figure 7. The names of the decision areas and options are here abbreviated, and crosses are used to indicate incompatibilities—with question marks to indicate cases where doubt or disagreement exists. The second matrix presents similar information for the first decision area in conjunction with the third; and in this way a larger array of small matrices can be built up covering other pairs of decision areas as well.

Some option bars may derive from the inherent logical structure of a problem. Others, however, may represent working assumptions as to what combinations of options are to be considered acceptable, reflecting a range

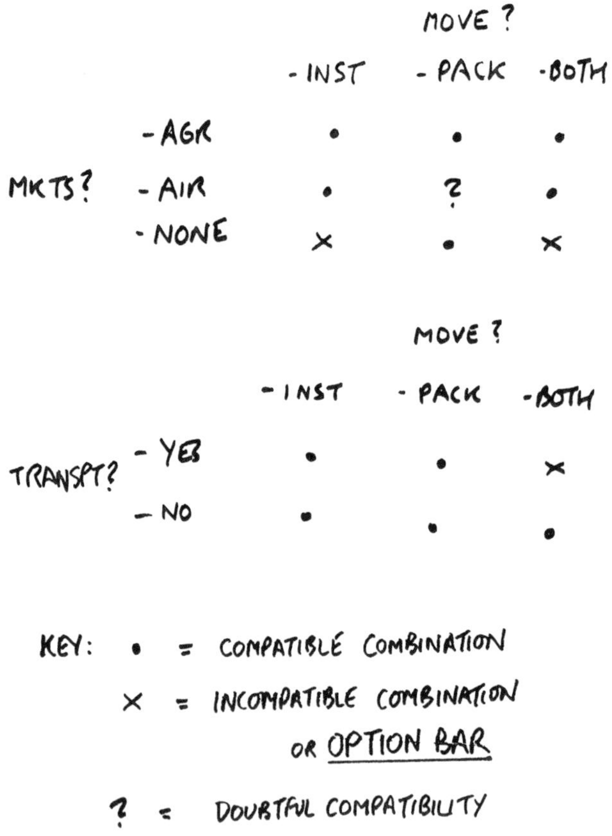

Figure 8
Introducing option bars

of different kinds of judgements—technical, economic or political. It is always useful to debate any such assumptions in a critical spirit—and to make a record of them so that they can be altered at a later stage of analysis should it be agreed.

The overall pattern of option bars within a problem focus can be represented either as a set of small matrices such as that in Figure 8 or, alternatively, in a graphical format known as the *option graph*. Figure 9 shows an option graph which includes a full set of option bars for the four decision areas in the Marintec problem focus. The option graph representation builds on the basic conventions of the decision graph. One difference is that the options within each decision area within the problem focus are now identified. Also, the decision links connecting particular pairs of decision areas are now replaced by a more detailed pattern of links between specific options—each of them representing the assumption of an option bar, with broken lines again used to indicate any doubtful cases.

It might seem strange at first that the connecting lines on the option graph are used to indicate incompatible rather than compatible pairs of options. However, experience soon confirms that it is in most cases only a

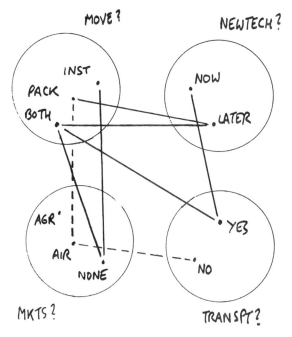

Figure 9
An option graph

minority of option combinations that are ruled out by option bars—so a graph which shows incompatible rather than compatible combinations is almost always simpler to drawn and to interpret in practice.

Unless the option graph is small, with only two or three decision areas and only a few option bars, it is usually far from easy to identify all the feasible combinations merely by inspection. Instead, it is necessary to go through a logical process of elimination, taking the decision areas in a chosen order and exploring all possible paths through the problem, eliminating a path whenever an option bar is found.

The result of this process can be presented in the form either of a conventional list or of a logical 'option tree' as shown in Figure 10. This format is rather similar to that of a decision tree in classical decision analysis; but the tree is here used merely to display the range of choice available within a given pattern of logical constraints as represented by option bars. In the example of Figure 10, it can be seen that there are eleven feasible combinations of options across all four decision areas within the Marintec problem focus—of which those combinations with question marks at the end are only feasible if the doubtful option bars are removed. Each of these feasible combinations of options is known as a feasible *decision scheme*.

To illustrate the logic involved in checking paths for feasibility, each path through the tree in Figure 10 which encounters a firm option bar is marked with a cross, and thereafter closed. In some cases, an option is incompatible with the option immediately before it in the sequence, as can be seen by referring back to the option graph in Figure 9; in other cases, a path is closed because of an option bar relating to an option in a decision area further back down the line. One way of reducing the size of the tree is to omit each of the 'dead branches' ending in a cross; the value of including the closed branches in this example is merely to allow the logic of the process of elimination to be followed more clearly.

Each feasible decision scheme can be given a code for later reference; and in Figure 10 an alphabetic code has been used. It is always possible to rearrange such a tree in a different order, for example to bring the most important or urgent decision areas to the front; and such changes of sequence can often help when it comes to the work of the choosing mode, concerned with making incremental progress through time.

The process of logical elimination of those paths which are ruled out by option bars is one that can be carried out quite quickly for a small problem focus, without any computational aids—but if need be it can be carried out by computer, as the logic is straightforward enough. This can be useful where there are five or more decision areas within the problem focus, or

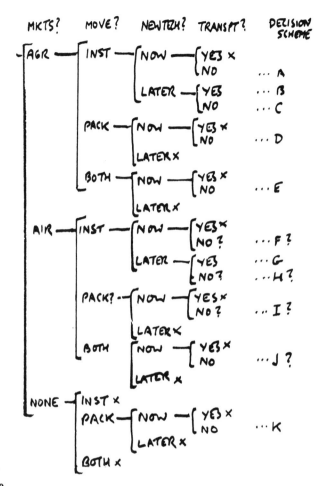

Figure 10
Identifying feasible decision schemes

where it is desired to test quickly what the effect would be if particular options or option bars were added or removed.

If the number of decision schemes appears too large to handle, then the assumptions as to what combinations are admissible can be tightened up, or more doubtful options can be removed. But this process of cutting down the range of choice by introducing new constraints is one that it can be unwise to pursue too far. For the purpose of work in the designing mode is not to come up with a single 'optimum' answer, but rather to generate a rich yet manageable set of alternatives amongst which explicit com-

139

parisons can be made, taking a range of considerations—and of uncertainties—into account.

Techniques for comparing

In principle at least, almost any method for predicting the effects of proposed courses of action, or evaluating one against another, is compatible with the strategic choice philosophy. However, what is important is that the chosen method should allow uncertainties of all kinds to be brought to the surface, so that they can be consciously managed. In dealing with complex issues affecting many interests, it is especially important not to suppress uncertainties about appropriate value judgements—in strategic choice terms, uncertainties of type UV. This requirement points towards the desirability of a multi-criteria approach to evaluation, as opposed to the more supposedly objective type of approach which seeks to reduce as many types of consequence as possible to a single—usually monetary—scale.

The term *comparison area* will be introduced as an alternative to the more usual term 'criterion' at this stage. Like the concept of a decision area, the concept of a comparison area may be defined at any level, broad or narrow. Its usage is not confined to areas in which effects can be quantified; rather, a comparison area is simply an area of concern to those involved in the decision process, within which it is desired to compare alternative courses in some way.

Figure 11 illustrates the general concept by listing a set of comparison areas for the Marintec problem—only one of them in this case with a clear scale of measurement in which to work. If desired, an initial set of comparison areas such as this can be expanded, condensed, amended or completely restructured as the analysis proceeds.

Where the shape of the problem may evolve through time, the activity of comparing different ways forward also has to be conceived in dynamic terms. Where a problem focus includes several linked decision areas, and there are many schemes among which to make comparisons, it is unrealistic to compare them simultaneously at a level which allows all effects to be considered and all areas of uncertainty to be critically exposed. So it is usual, in the spirit of dynamic comparison which characterizes the strategic choice approach, to alternate between crude comparisons of many decision schemes and closer comparisons of a selected few, using each perspective to generate insights of value to the wider process.

So, faced with a set of many possible combinations of options, a practical first step is to develop a *working shortlist* by filtering out the majority of

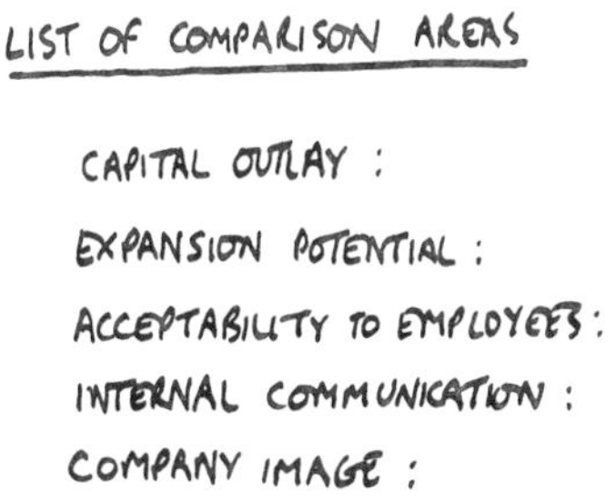

LIST OF COMPARISON AREAS

CAPITAL OUTLAY :

EXPANSION POTENTIAL :

ACCEPTABILITY TO EMPLOYEES :

INTERNAL COMMUNICATION :

COMPANY IMAGE :

Figure 11
A set of comparison areas

them by means of relatively crude constraints within a few of the more important comparison areas. Then the schemes that remain can be compared more closely in terms of a wider set of comparison areas, leading to fuller consideration of relevant areas of uncertainty and ways in which they might be managed. This does not mean that those schemes omitted from the working shortlist are discarded for all time—for they may re-enter the analysis later, in the light of insights gained through comparisons at the more closely focused level.

Figure 12 illustrates this principle by showing one way in which a working shortlist can be formed for the Marintec decision problem as formulated earlier in Figure 10. Crude comparisons are made on three of the five comparison areas, by using various simplified scales. In the case of the *capital* assessment, estimates are given in money values (thousands of pounds, dollars or whatever). Depending on the situation, the estimate for each scheme can either be arrived at by viewing it as an entity, or by summing separate estimates for its constituent options. The other two assessments are here presented in terms of purely judgemental scales, defined in relation to extreme points. For example, scheme K is judged to have the least expansion potential (1) and scheme J the most (9), with other schemes located at intermediate points within this range.

Using value judgements on what is thought likely to be acceptable, constraints on some or all of these assessments—no more than this amount of capital expenditure, at least this level of expansion potential, at least this level of acceptability to employees—are then introduced to reduce the length of the list of schemes. The level of any of these constraints can of course be modified to produce whatever length of working shortlist is desired.

Within a shortlist of three or four schemes, it becomes possible to compare selected pairs of alternatives in more depth, introducing additional comparison areas. It also becomes possible to introduce assess-

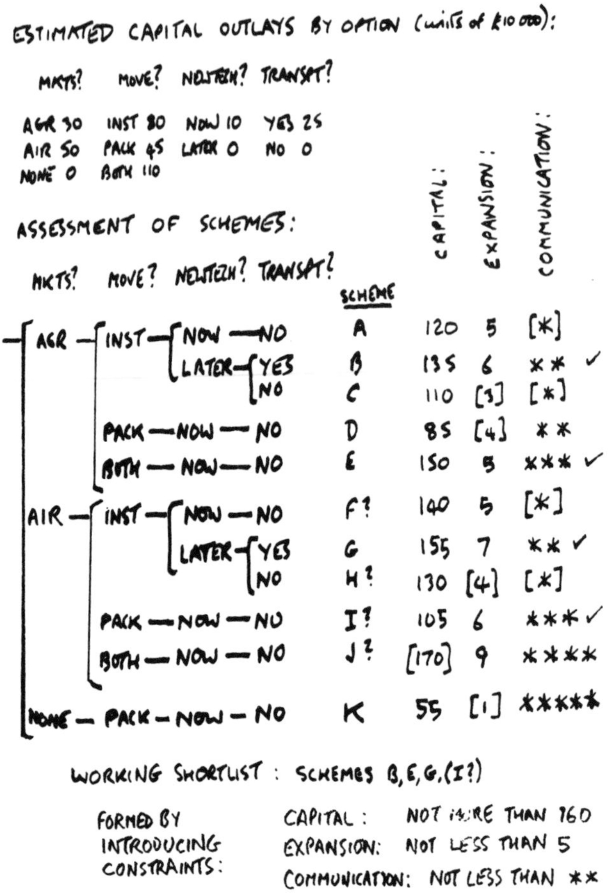

ESTIMATED CAPITAL OUTLAYS BY OPTION (units of £10 000):

MKTS?   MOVE?   NEWTECH?   TRANSPT?

AGR 30   INST 80   NOW 10   YES 25
AIR 50   PACK 45   LATER 0   NO 0
NONE 0   BOTH 110

ASSESSMENT OF SCHEMES:

MKTS?   MOVE?   NEWTECH?   TRANSPT?

SCHEME	CAPITAL	EXPANSION	COMMUNICATION	
A	120	5	[*]	
B	135	6	**	✓
C	110	[3]	[*]	
D	85	[4]	**	
E	150	5	***	✓
F?	140	5	[*]	
G	155	7	**	✓
H?	130	[4]	[*]	
I?	105	6	***	✓
J?	[170]	9	****	
K	55	[1]	*****	

WORKING SHORTLIST : SCHEMES B, E, G, (I?)

FORMED BY
INTRODUCING
CONSTRAINTS:

CAPITAL : NOT MORE THAN 160
EXPANSION: NOT LESS THAN 5
COMMUNICATION: NOT LESS THAN **

Figure 12
Forming a working shortlist

ments expressed not just in terms of point estimates on simplified scales, but in more subtle ways which can begin to bring indications of uncertainty more clearly into view.

In Figure 13, two of the four short-listed Marintec schemes—those labelled B and I—are compared with each other in terms of all five comparison areas that were listed in Figure 11. It now becomes possible to add various further forms of comparative information to the crude assessments that were used as a basis for short-listing in Figure 12. Much of this new information is expressed in the form of words—words which reveal something about the levels and sources of uncertainty as perceived by

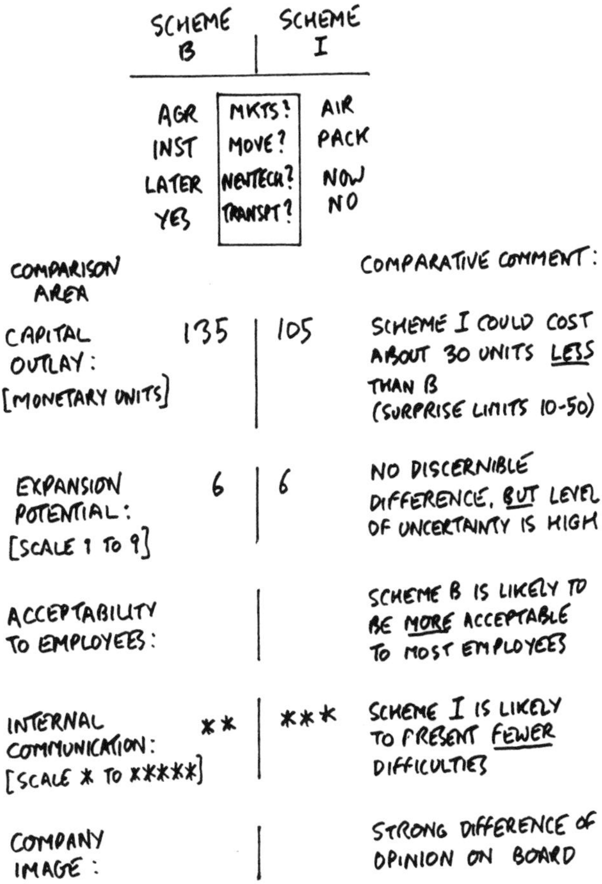

Figure 13
Comparison under uncertainty

those involved in the assessment process. Even the use of seemingly evasive words such as 'about' or 'likely' begins to convey at least some information about perceived uncertainties; while a term such as 'strong difference of opinion' suggests a conflict between decision makers, pointing to uncertainties to be managed within the category UV.

In one of the comparison areas of Figure 13—capital outlay—information about uncertainty is expressed not only in words, but also in terms of a range of possible figures within which the difference between the two schemes is thought likely to lie. The limits of the range are known as 'surprise limits' in strategic choice terminology. The concept is akin to the

143

statistical concept of confidence limits; however, in practice, surprise limits may be the outcome not of rigorous statistical analysis, but of personal judgement based on experience, or cross-questioning of one or more experts in the field.

Issues of judgement arise at many levels in making assessments within comparison areas. However, some of the most difficult and value-laden judgements rise when assessments within different comparison areas come to be weighed against one another in the attempt to form an overall preference judgement. In practice, such judgements often become highly political, with uncertainties of type UV very much to the fore.

Rather than search for some apparently value-free 'objective function' based on a monetary or other numerical scale, it is more in keeping with the strategic choice philosophy to turn to a means of balancing differences across comparison areas which can be more directly shaped to the political context in which decisions are being addressed. This can be done by introducing an overall judgemental scale of *comparative advantage* between two alternatives, as illustrated in Figure 14.

The pair of alternatives being compared in this way may be either two options from a single decision area, or two schemes representing feasible combinations of options across decision areas. The purpose of the 'balance sheet' format is to help people not merely to form a view of where the overall balance of advantage between alternatives lies, but also to explore the various forms of uncertainty that may combine to make this a difficult task. For serious uncertainties are always likely to arise, not only in assessing differences within comparison areas, but also in relating each comparison area to a common advantage scale—which itself can scarcely be calibrated in any objective way.

The convention used in Figure 14 is to calibrate the common scale with reference to successive levels of perceived advantage to either alternative, expressed in terms not of numbers but of words. The words used—negligible, marginal, significant, considerable, and extreme—are themselves such that they have to be given meaning in relation to the specific context within which decisions are to be made. This can be no simple task; indeed, the same precise level of difference in capital expenditure—say 50 000 pounds, dollars or whatever—might be regarded as extreme in one organizational context yet negligible in another.

However, the *attempt* to relate all assessments to such a politically based scale is itself an important element in the comparison process. For the value judgements it demands can serve to bring uncertainties of type UV directly to the surface, allowing them to be viewed in perspective alongside other uncertainties that may have arisen in trying to make assessments within the chosen comparison areas taken individually. In Figure 14, a view

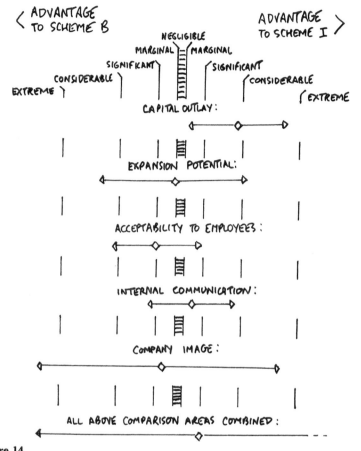

Figure 14
Analysis of comparative advantage

of the overall influence of uncertainty on the comparison of the two alternatives is built up by the use of ranges to indicate the limits within which it is thought conceivable that the balance of advantage will lie. This is done for each comparison area taken on its own, and then for the set of all the comparison areas, using the 'surprise limits' approach already described.

The process of amalgamating the ranges across comparison areas can be handled either through a statistical sum-of-squares approach or, with a little practice, in a more informal way. It is important that the calibration of the comparative advantage should be allowed to evolve gradually all the time—preferably as part of an interactive process in which a range of relevant value perspectives can be brought to bear.

145

Sometimes, the end result of this process will be a clear conclusion that the overall balance of advantage lies to one alternative or the other. Very often in practice, however, a substantial level of uncertainty will remain: and the choice then arises of whether to carry out further pair comparisons; whether to switch to further shaping or designing activities; or whether to proceed to the choosing mode, to consider in what ways the key uncertainties might be managed in making progress towards decisions.

Techniques for choosing

In order to make progress in handling complex problems, decision makers must find ways of managing uncertainty through time. It is usually when working in the comparing mode that users of strategic choice methods become most conscious of particular areas of uncertainty that get in the way of clear decisions. Yet uncertainty can surface, too, during work in the shaping and designing modes; indeed, the story of the Marintec problem so far illustrates how doubts can arise in agreeing whether or not to include particular decision links, options or option bars.

It is a useful discipline to record all potentially significant areas of uncertainty on a list as soon as they are recognized. This list will then gradually lengthen as work proceeds from one mode to another, and may require rearrangement and consolidation from time to time. The eventual purpose of this listing is to develop a set of *uncertainty areas* to which to refer when working in the choosing mode—just as decision areas formed the main reference point for the work of the shaping mode, and comparison areas for the work of the comparison mode. Indeed, it is quite usual for some areas of concern which were initially formulated as decision areas to be reformulated later as either comparison areas or uncertainty areas, or vice versa.

It is at moments when alternative courses of action are being weighed against each other across several comparison areas—as in the comparative advantage chart of Figure 14—that different areas of uncertainty fall most clearly into perspective in terms of their significance for the decision process. This point is illustrated in Figure 15.

Figure 15 lists a set of uncertainty areas, of various kinds, which might be thought to have a significant bearing on the comparison of schemes B and I within the Marintec problem focus. Each is described in words, and some of them, like decision areas, are also given briefer labels. The convention is introduced of placing a question mark in front of the label, to distinguish an uncertainty area from a decision area, where the convention is to place the question mark at the end.

UNCERTAINTY AREA: LABEL: TYPE: SALIENCE:

? POSSIBLE INFEASIBILITY OF MOVING
INSTRUMENT MANUFACTURE IF
ENTERING AIRCRAFT MARKET UE •

FROM CAPITAL OUTLAY COMPARISON:
? EXTRA COST OF MOVING
INSTRUMENT MANUFACTURE UE •

FROM EXPANSION POTENTIAL COMPARISON:
? GROWTH POTENTIAL OF AIRCRAFT ?AIRPOTL UE (UR?) ••
MARKET
? POLICY VALUE OF EXPANSION TO UV •
COMPANY

FROM ACCEPTABILITY TO EMPLOYEES COMPARISON:
? CHOICE OF NEARBY OR REMOTE ?FARSITE UR ••
RELOCATION SITE

FROM INTERNAL COMMUNICATION COMPARISON:
? CHOICE OF NEARBY OR REMOTE ?FARSITE UR ••
RELOCATION SITE (SEE ABOVE)
? INVESTMENT IN TELECOMMUNIC'NS UR •

FROM COMPANY IMAGE COMPARISON:
? VALUE TO THIS COMPANY OF ?VALIMAG UV •••
ESTABLISHED MARITIME IMAGE
? DECISION ON CHANGE OF NAME ?NEWNAME UR ••

Figure 15
Identifying and comparing uncertainty areas

The first uncertainty area in the list is one which was originally identified when working in the designing mode; this concerns whether or not scheme I is to be considered feasible, because of a doubtful option bar. The others reflect sources of doubt encountered either in comparing B and I within particular comparison areas, or in judging how assessments in different comparison areas are to be translated to the common comparative advantage scale.

Having identified and labelled a working list of uncertainty areas, a next step is to try classifying them according to the UE/UV/UR categories. This can be done by asking whether each is of a kind which could be tackled by more technical forms of investigation; or by explorations of a more political nature; or by extending the problem focus to cover other related decision areas—which may in turn mean considering how to relate to other decision makers. Sometimes, the classification of an uncertainty area may be far from clear. This may be because it embraces elements of more than one category; in that case, the principles of sensitivity analysis can be used, whether formally or informally, to disentangle the elements and arrive at judgements over which of them are more important.

In Figure 15, a rough-and-ready scoring system has been used to grade the uncertainty areas for their relative importance, or *salience*, in relation to the current focus of comparison. This is essentially a matter of personal or collective judgement, but it can help in making such judgements to refer back to information built up in the course of earlier work. For example, the comparative width of the ranges in Figure 14 indicates that the level of uncertainty in judging the balance of advantage between schemes B and I is greater in some comparison areas than in others.

When considering how uncertainty might be managed at any point in the process, it is usual to start by looking at those uncertainty areas which have been given a higher salience grading; for it is unlikely to be worth investing serious effort in actions to deal with uncertainties of lower salience so long as more salient ones remain. For each of the more salient uncertainty areas, the next step is to ask whether it is possible to conceive of any possible *exploratory options* through which the current level of salience might be reduced. Depending on the UE/UV/UR classification of each uncertainty area, such options could take the form of proposals for research or other investigation; for policy soundings; or for liaison or negotiation with other parties.

Figure 16 uses the device of an *uncertainty graph* to illustrate how a set of different kinds of exploratory option might be identified for four of the most salient uncertainty areas that were listed in Figure 15. It is not essential to move to such a graphical form of representation at this stage; but to do so helps to illustrate the principles being used. In Figure 16, the more salient of the uncertainty areas are located in labelled circles closer to the centre of the graph. In each case, one possible form of exploratory option has been identified—technical, political or collaborative—and an arrow is used to indicate what effect this action is thought likely to have on the salience level of the uncertainty area concerned. In effect, the arrow shows how far the pursuit of that exploratory option—as opposed to the 'null option' of accepting the current level of uncertainty—is expected to push that uncertainty area outwards towards the periphery of the graph.

This kind of analysis helps in forming a view of the relative effectiveness of different exploratory actions in improving the level of confidence with which decisions can be made. For example, from Figure 16 it appears that informal soundings with key company stakeholders could lead to the most

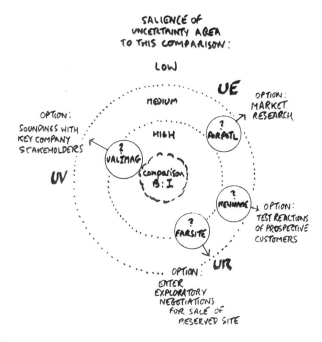

SALIENCE of
UNCERTAINTY AREA
TO THIS COMPARISON:

LOW

MEDIUM

UE
OPTION:
MARKET
RESEARCH

OPTION:
SOUNDINGS WITH
KEY COMPANY
STAKEHOLDERS

HIGH

? ARATL

? VALIMAG

UV

comparison
B:I

? NEVIMAGE
OPTION:
TEST REACTIONS
OF PROSPECTIVE
CUSTOMERS

? FARSITE

OPTION:
ENTER
EXPLORATORY
NEGOTIATIONS
FOR SALE OF
RESERVED SITE

UR

Figure 16
Identifying exploratory options

salient of the uncertainty areas becoming much more marginal. Market research would have a much more limited impact on an area of uncertainty which is already less salient in relation to the comparison of alternatives that is currently in view.

Exploratory options can differ not only in their effectiveness judged in terms of confidence in decision making, but also in terms of their costs. There are two main forms which these costs can take in practice. One is the cost in terms of claims on scarce *resources* such as money, professional skills or the time of busy decision makers; the other is the cost in terms of *delay* to the decision process while the exploratory action proposed is being followed through.

In theory at least, it is possible to compare different exploratory options in the same analytical way as more substantive alternatives—starting in this context with the three basic comparison areas of confidence; claims on scarce resources; and decision delay. Such a comparison will of course be likely to expose new areas of uncertainty, not least of the UV type. How much, for example, would those responsible for budgets be willing to pay for some specified increase in the confidence with which decisions can be taken; and how long will others deeply affected by the decision be prepared to see it delayed?

To pursue such questions in any depth will mean taking the whole process of strategic choice to another level. For the issue now is one of how to manage uncertainty in deciding how uncertainty itself should be managed; and such questions could, given time, be pursued in infinite regress. However, it will be only rarely in practical decision processes that it is worth pausing to explore these higher order subtleties. It is the *principle* rather than the formal method of analysis that is important; and, when working in the choosing mode, people are always more likely to be concerned with moving towards action than with refinements of analytical method.

The question of how far to defer decisions while pursuing exploratory actions is one that becomes more subtle when there are several interconnected decision areas within the problem focus. For some decisions will usually be more urgent than others; so in practice there will often be an opportunity to adopt a 'mixed strategy' in which decisions are made now in some at least of the more pressing decision areas, while options are kept open in others. This is where the principle of *robustness* enters into a process of strategic choice—a principle which is discussed more fully in Chapters 8 and 9.

One way of bringing out these differences in the urgency of decisions is to rearrange the presentation of a set of feasible decision schemes so as to bring the more urgent decision areas to the earlier branches of the tree. In the Marintec problem, for example, it may be considered especially urgent to make a decision on whether to buy up the local transport firm; and also on whether to include the investment in new packaging technology in this year's capital programme or to defer it till a later year. In Figure 17, these urgencies are reflected by rearranging the tree of Figure 10 to bring these two decision areas to the left. By an extension of the strategic choice terminology introduced so far, each of these combinations of options in the more urgent decision areas can be termed an *action scheme*.

It can be seen from Figure 17 that one of the three possible action schemes appears more attractive than the others in terms of the flexibility of future choice that it retains. This is the action scheme consisting of not buying up the transport firm, yet going ahead now with the new packaging technology. For this combination allows options to be kept open as to which operations to move, and also (depending on whether a dubious option bar is allowed) what new markets, if any, to open up.

However, it still has to be judged to what extent this extra flexibility is beneficial. In this case, reference back to earlier steps in the analysis shows that the NO-NOW path leaves open no more of the four schemes short-

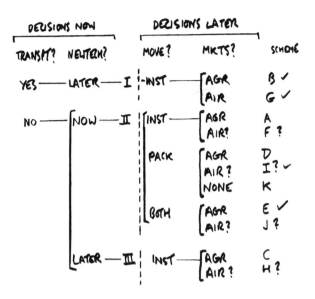

Figure 17
Comparing action schemes

listed in Figure 12 than the YES-LATER path: and one of these indeed is of doubtful feasibility. It is in making this kind of judgement that the idea of robustness becomes especially relevant, but at this point too it can become important to re-examine all the critical assumptions about the existence of options and option bars that were introduced when working in the designing mode.

When people are considering incremental steps forward at some moment in a decision process, it becomes important for them to begin drawing several aspects of the process together. For they have to consider the choice of immediate actions, if any; the choice of any exploratory actions to reduce the salience of any important areas of uncertainty; and the choice of any procedural or other arrangements for making decisions later in any areas where action is currently deferred. A broad framework for achieving this synthesis is provided by the strategic choice concept of the *commitment package*, which is illustrated in Figure 18.

DECISIONS NOW		FUTURE DECISION SPACE	
ACTIONS	EXPLORATIONS	DEFERRED CHOICES	CONTINGENCY PLANNING
TRANSPORT: WITHDRAW FROM NEGOTIATIONS TO BUY LOCAL TRANSPORT FIRM			RECONSIDER IF A MAJOR PRICE REDUCTION OFFERED SOON ✗
TECHNOLOGY: INCLUDE NEW PACKAGING TECHNOLOGY ORDER IN THIS YEAR'S PROGRAMME			
LOCATION/ MARKETS:	EXPLORE CONSEQUENCES OF ALTERNATIVE LOCATIONS — SOUND OUT EMPLOYEE ATTITUDES	DECIDE 12 MONTHS FROM NOW: • WHICH OPERATION(S) TO MOVE • WHETHER TO RETAIN RESERVED SITE • MARKET DIVERSIFICATION • WHETHER TO PROMOTE NEW IMAGE & NAME	

✗ THEN RECONSIDER ALTERNATIVE PACKAGE
 - BUYING UP LOCAL TRANSPORT FIRM
 - DEFERRING INVESTMENT IN NEW PACKAGING
                                                    TECHNOLOGY

Figure 18
A commitment package

There are many variations of the commitment package framework which have been adopted in practical applications of the strategic choice approach. Figure 18 shows a relatively simple variant in which the framework is divided vertically into two main parts: one relates to decisions that it is proposed should be made now; and the other to decisions to be deferred until some future time. The former category is subdivided into two columns: the first is concerned with actions to be taken in relation to substantive decision areas; and the second with actions to be taken in response to particular uncertainty areas affecting future decisions.

It is important here to remember that the identification of exploratory *options* does not necessarily imply that these explorations should be set in train: for first, their relative 'resource effectiveness' must be explored. In

Figure 18, indeed, it may be noticed that the two proposed explorations did not figure in the set of exploratory options earlier identified in Figure 16. For the focus has now shifted from the comparison of schemes B and I to the comparison of future choices left open by the choice of action scheme II in Figure 17—among them, E and I within the short-listed set. So the salience of the uncertainties listed in Figure 15 now has to be reviewed afresh.

There is a logical link between the second column of the commitment package and the third, concerned with arrangements for deferred choices. It is the purpose of the explorations to pave the way for some of these deferred decisions, so it will make sense to arrange for them to be considered again at some time after the outcomes of the explorations are expected to be known. In some situations, however, it will be seen as appropriate to relate the taking of future decisions, not to the outcomes of explorations, but to certain key contingencies. Both for this reason, and to allow for proposed sequels to current actions should particular contingencies occur, a fourth column headed 'contingency planning' is usually included in the commitment package format.

Sometimes, it may be easy to reach agreement on the content of a proposed commitment package. In some situations, however, it will pay to design and compare two or more packages, differing either at the margin or in a more radical way. For a commitment package is intended as an aid to *choosing*; and, if it is to be submitted as a recommendation for moving forward to some individual or group in which is vested the authority to decide, they may well wish to review alternative packages before any formal decisions are made.

So the construction of a commitment package does not always mark the end of the process of critical debate. And such debate, in whatever context, can lead to further rounds of work in the shaping, designing, and comparing modes. For, the more complex the issues, the less realistic it becomes to suppose that the process of strategic choice will ever fully run its course.

Strategic choice in practice: dimensions of the approach

In this chapter, it has been possible to make no more than a brief tour of the set of concepts and methods used to guide work in the four complementary modes of a process of strategic choice—shaping, designing, comparing, and choosing. As will already be apparent, to apply these concepts and methods to practical decision problems can require a great deal of judgement; judgement of a kind that is discussed more fully in the principal textbook on the approach (Friend and Hickling, 1987).

When the approach is being used as an aid to participative decision making, it has been found useful to refer to a set of operational guidelines which transcend the four basic modes, and which describe broad aspects of the overall approach. These guidelines too are discussed more fully in the work referred to above; it is possible here to do no more than introduce them briefly, under the four main headings of *technology, organization, process*, and *products*.

Technology

The *technology* which has evolved in connection with the strategic choice approach extends beyond the various basic concepts and methods that have been already described. For if such tools are to be used interactively as an aid to communication, it is essential that the *media* of communication should be such as to allow people to participate as fully as possible—recognizing that it is in a group setting that the richest opportunities for interactive working are to be found.

The style that has developed for group interaction in strategic choice is one in which people are encouraged to work together not in fixed positions around a table, but in a setting in which they can move about freely, using graphical representations of the kind already introduced in this chapter to build up shared representations of the problems they face. This means writing on large sheets of paper which all can see, and making more use of wall space than of tables; which in turn means meeting in a spacious enough room, adequately equipped, with as few obstructions as possible either in the way of unnecessary furniture or wall fittings. Amongst the materials to be provided are a liberal supply of sheets of plain paper, usually in the form of A1 flip charts; removable adhesive such as blu-tack; and a supply of marker pens in varied colours—for colour distinctions can be a valuable aid to communication when working in this way.

Despite the emphasis usually placed on interactive work in groups, the approach can also be used to good effect by individuals, whether in the intervals between group sessions or as an aid to personal strategic thinking. It is in this context that another technological aid—the microcomputer—begins to come into its own. Software for strategic choice is under continuous development. The latest experience has been that strategic choice software can provide a very effective means of helping to structure the debate about complex problems within a small group of three or four people, even though it can inhibit the all-important process of group interaction when larger numbers of people are involved.

Organization

A group of between six and eight people provides an ideal size for a strategic choice 'workshop', combining informality, diversity of contributions and opportunity for all to participate without a tendency for some people to split off or become marginalized. Sometimes, it may be difficult to keep numbers as small as this without excluding important professional, departmental or organizational interests; but experience has shown that there are a variety of other ways of involving people in the wider decision process than through intensive participation in 'workshop' type activity. Some people with a stake in the decisions to be made may have too wide a range of responsibilities, or be too busy to wish to be drawn deeply into a workshop-type activity; yet they may have important roles to play either in authorizing actions based on the group's work or in enlisting the support of others.

There are many possibilities for involving such people in the process in a more *reactive* rather than an interactive way. Nevertheless, opportunities can be designed for drawing them into the interactive work from time to time, for example in the shaping of agendas and the assembly of proposals for incremental action. The case study to be presented in Chapter 7 illustrates some of the ways in which this can be done.

Process

Under the heading of operational guidelines for the management of process, some important points arise relating to the management of *time*, both during and between intensive periods of group interaction. Within an interactive group session, one of the most important matters of judgement concerns the balancing of time between work in the four modes of shaping, designing, comparing, and choosing; for time spent working continuously in any one of these modes can soon begin to yield diminishing returns. If a strategic choice workshop is to be productive, it is important to have at least one member of the group who is prepared to play a facilitating or 'process management' role. Such a person has to be experienced in making judgements as to when the time has arrived to switch from one mode to another—and also as to which of the other modes is likely to produce the greatest benefits at that particular stage in the process.

The key criterion in making such judgements is the opportunity for interactive *learning* to be realized through a switch to another mode. Experience has confirmed that there is particular value in switching to any mode that has been comparatively neglected in the process so far. Indeed, there can be value in moving rapidly—even prematurely—ahead to experience the activity of the choosing mode even at an early stage, when the work of shaping seems scarcely to have begun; or in switching back to a spell of shaping activity even at a stage when the pressures for decision are intense. As a guide to these shaping judgements, it is helpful to keep a key 'map' of the four modes, as in Figure 2, somewhere on the wall for reference. This allows not only the facilitator but also other participants to refer to it whenever they feel a switch of mode should be discussed.

Products

Any process of strategic choice can be expected to yield not only *visible* products in the shape of recommended actions and policy changes, but also a range of more subtle *invisible products*—including, in particular, adaptations in the outlooks, perceptions, and appreciative judgements of the individuals taking part.

The overall effect of the methods introduced in this chapter is to make more visible to the participants some of the products which would normally remain invisible. For the set of pictures of concerns and relationships that gradually builds up on flip charts around the walls of the room will have the cumulative effect of creating a record of shared progress within the group. It is a record which captures elements of interactive learning as well as progress towards decisions, for it allows people to retrace the steps they went through—including any false trails, differences of view and revisions to past assumptions along the way. Because such exploratory aspects of the process are so important, it is usual for all but the most trivial of 'mistakes' to be treated as part of the record, rather than erased.

It is, however, dangerous for the participants in a group process to assume that what they have created on flip charts on the walls will immediately make sense to other people who were not directly involved. For this kind of record will be full of shorthand terms and graphical 'jargon' which will have acquired meaning only to those directly involved in the process. It is, therefore, essential to go through a careful process of further interpretation of the visible products of a working session before presenting these products to others, either as recommendations, or as interim views to which some kind of response is sought.

Informal strategic choice

The emphasis in this chapter has been on methods of working which may seem comparatively 'soft' in relation to the more classical methods of management science, yet can still be expressed in formal, logical terms.

This element of formality has been necessary in order to demonstrate the methods explicitly, and to indicate their value as a neutral form of language to aid communication in multidisciplinary groups.

However, in conclusion, it is important to make the point that strategic choice ideas can also be used in a more informal, low-key, and selective way. For the whole approach is based on an appreciation of the practical experience of decision makers—individually and in groups—in developing ways of responding to complex problems which are appropriate to the subtle challenges that they pose, even though they may not often be consciously recognized.

If some of the insights offered here can make even piecemeal, momentary contributions to people's more personal decision processes, then that too can be considered to reflect the general philosophy of the strategic choice approach. For the more the acquired wisdom of experienced decision makers can be made explicit, the richer become the opportunities for reflection as well as communication—and the more the essence of that wisdom can be passed on to their successors in positions of responsibility both within organizations and between, so that they can build further on the understanding their predecessors have gained.

References

Crichton, C. (Ed.) (1966). *Interdependence and Uncertainty: a Study of the Building Industry*, Tavistock, London.

Friend, J. K., and Hickling, A. (1987). *Planning under Pressure: the Strategic Choice Approach*, Pergamon, Oxford.

Friend, J. K., and Jessop, W. N. (1977). *Local Government and Strategic Choice* (second edition), Pergamon, Oxford.

7

Gambling with frozen fire?

Using the strategic choice approach in the formulation of national policy on the storage, handling, transport and use of LPG in The Netherlands

Allen Hickling

Disaster strikes

The 1978 disaster in the small Spanish town of San Carlos de la Rapita involved over 400 horrifying casualties. An LPG* lorry had crashed into the crowded Los Alfaques holiday campsite creating a ball of fire which consumed everything in its path. Nearly 200 died on the spot, and many of the injured were not to survive (*The Times*, 12 July 1978).

This was the first really serious accident with this highly dangerous, but otherwise very useful substance. It came at a time in The Netherlands when there was a trend towards increased use of LPG. The main causes were the rising price of naphtha (for which LPG is a substitute as a chemical feedstock), and expected surpluses of LPG on the world market.

Dramatic increases were expected in the use of LPG as a chemical feedstock. It was also expected to take a larger share of the traditional market, serving as a substitute for petrol as a motor fuel.

Plans had already been drawn up by private companies for the development of LPG terminals in several locations in The Netherlands. These were intended to receive shipments from the Middle East, which would then be

---

*LPG stands for Liquefied Petroleum Gas. It consists mostly of propane or butane, and it can be a mixture of both. At room temperature under atmospheric pressure the substance is gaseous. It is transported and stored either under pressure (17 atm) or frozen ($-50\,°C$).

Rational Analysis for a Problematic World
Edited by J. Rosenhead. © 1989 John Wiley & Sons Ltd

used at facilities close to the terminal, or be transported to other users, including export to Germany.

But now, clearly, it was also a recognized hazard. The question had to be faced: 'Were we gambling with frozen fire?' (van de Graaf, 1985).

About the presentation of this case study

This is a case study of the use of the strategic choice approach in practice. It is not an idealized fiction of what a project might have been like if the approach had been applied 'according to the book'. In this it is unlike the example used by John Friend in the previous chapter, which he cleaned up and adapted in order to present the strategic choice approach as clearly as possible.

The experience is that tackling really difficult problems is messy. However, to describe what really happened would be to condemn the reader to an almost impossible task akin to unravelling the proverbial Gordian knot. For, in working with the strategic choice approach in practice, the messiness is handled through its characteristic non-linear development of understanding, which takes various forms:

– the essential looping and switching between the modes of work;
– the incompleteness of analyses, which is an inevitable result of the fast learning process;
– the replication of effort caused by the need to work things through with different groups.

Actually, to talk about analysis at all may be misleading. The normal perception of analysis is that of working through a problem using predetermined methods, techniques, and procedures in a pre-established order, which produces the solution to that problem. But strategic choice is not like that—it is a dynamic learning process.

Also there was a lot of work to be done. If one considers only the four-month period during which the strategic choice consultants were involved, there were probably 350 man-days put in by the team of eight alone. Of course not all of this could properly be described as strategic choice work—at least in the technical sense—and the consultants were only contracted for 30 man-days.

Thus only about fifteen days were spent in the typical interactive workshop sessions of strategic choice, which played a key role in directing the work undertaken in the intervening periods. Much of the team's time went into preparing working papers, consulting with colleagues and so on.

And there was the preparatory networking and 'back room' work which they had to do as an essential prerequisite to effective interactive working.

In an attempt to portray the spirit of the strategic choice manner of working, photographs of the original documents have been used in conjunction with the translated figures. Two characteristics are noticeable:

- the hurried writing which is a direct result of trying to keep up with the interactive process (exacerbated for the reader of this case study by Dutch being the working language);
- the many erasures and the over-writing which came from the cyclic 'learning-by-doing' nature of the approach.

In this case, the difficulties of presenting a full story have been accommodated by excluding some of the cycles and describing separately parts which were actually overlapping in time. Those parts of the work selected for detailed description are followed through only as far as the evidence will allow. However, every attempt has been made to demonstrate the contribution each part made to the end result.

The process of updating the interim policy is blocked

Four days after the disaster in Spain, there was an article about LPG in the *Sunday Times*. After another horrifying account of the accident itself, the situation was summed up as follows:

> And the rest of the industrial world, reminded of the growing stream of corrosive, poisonous, explosive and inflammatory substances constantly on the move past its front doors, is joltingly forced to ask: 'Could it happen here?'
> (*Sunday Times*, 16 July 1978)

The answer in The Netherlands was immediately positive. Public perception of the risks rose alarmingly. It soon became a hot political issue, and the Government reacted by setting up the necessary organization, and providing the necessary resources, to produce an immediate policy.

In 1979 interim policy guidelines were laid down in a White Paper. This restricted further development by confining landing activities to the Rijnmond area, with distribution by pipeline. More importantly, in terms of this case study, the policy explicitly included time for further studies into the risks involved, and for further policy analysis to be carried out. The process was to be guided by an inter-ministerial Government Commission (RPC).

As early as the end of 1981 it was becoming clear that the interim policy would not stand up for long. Thus it was decided that the process of preparing a new policy should be started without delay. Consequently, a small project group was set up to service the Government Commission. This group was comprised of civil servants representing four very different sections of government. Each was a well-established centre of power representing interests which were difficult to satisfy in combination:

– the Ministry of Economic Affairs;
– the Ministry of Transport and Public Works;
– the Environmental Hygiene arm of the Ministry of Environmental Affairs;
– the Physical Planning arm of the Ministry of Environmental Affairs.

And work on the new policy began.

Extensive risk analyses had already been carried out for the Commission by recognized experts in the field, and towards the autumn of 1982 many of the results were already available. It had been expected that, at this point, the way forward would be reasonably clear-cut. In the event it was not. Although the results were not yet final, it was becoming clear that they would not be enough. In fact all three of the classic characteristics of a difficult decision problem were clearly evident—complexity, uncertainty, and conflict.

Thus, late in the autumn of 1982, the scene was set for a prime example of a blocked decision process—and further, one which had reached a state of urgency. Not only was there a lack of any real progress towards a proper policy, but the level of conflict in the project group was also causing no little concern. And time was running out. A situation which seems to be not uncommon in government policy making.

It was at this point that the Government Commission sought the advice of two decision process consultants—Arnold de Jong and Allen Hickling. These two, both experts in the use of the strategic choice approach, were consulted in the first instance about the management of uncertainty. However, other related difficulties, with respect to the complexity and conflict, soon became apparent.

A decision focus for the shaping mode

As might be expected after eighteen months of deliberation over a revised policy, much work had already been done. Amongst other things there was the on-going risk analysis. Although this was heavily focused on uncertainties about the environment (UE) as opposed to those about values (UV) or related areas of decision (UR), it was none the less identifying some of the more important uncertainties.

There was also the work of the project group itself. They had spent some considerable time defining the LPG 'system' in and through The Netherlands. In addition they had already submitted 96 alternative so-called scenarios (actually theoretically possible combinations of policies) to the Government Commission (RPC, 1982).

This work had produced a useful level of understanding on which to base the shaping of the problem. Thus the first cycle through the shaping process was accomplished relatively quickly.

However, much of the shaping work typical of strategic choice was never used in any formal way. In its place a sort of translation was carried out, from the hard systems-thinking framework, which had prevailed before, to one which was decision-centred. This is entirely consistent with the strategic choice philosophy—accepting that there are many sensible ways to approach a problem.

This background accounts for the way in which that earlier systems thinking is strongly reflected in the results at this stage (see the left-hand side of Figure 1), although in successive cycles this became less obvious (see the right-hand side of Figure 1). Had the starting point been different —as, more usually, when strategic choice is used from the beginning— then the decision graph would have been different also, probably with a wider variety of decision areas at various levels of concern.

Analysis of the decision graph was used to identify a problem focus for further work. The connectedness of the decision areas had already been used implicitly during the process of translation, and had produced five main possibilities. Urgency, importance, and controllability were used as criteria to provide the basis for further discrimination.

The possible focus which had to do with market demand was easily identified as being uncontrollable, in the sense that it depended to a great extent on the future choices of others. In this way it was really a major uncertainty rather than a problem focus. As such it was felt to be a safe one to leave aside for the time being. There was, in any case, already an assumption that demand was going to increase, even though it would not reach the high levels earlier predicted. Indeed this was the reason for the project in the first place.

The other four possibilities represented the four main concerns of the project—the landing, storage, transportation, and use of LPG. Thus all of them would have to be addressed sooner or later. However, on the basis of the group's current understanding of the issues, it was relatively easy to identify two as being more important than the others.

As it happened these two, the choice of location for landing areas and

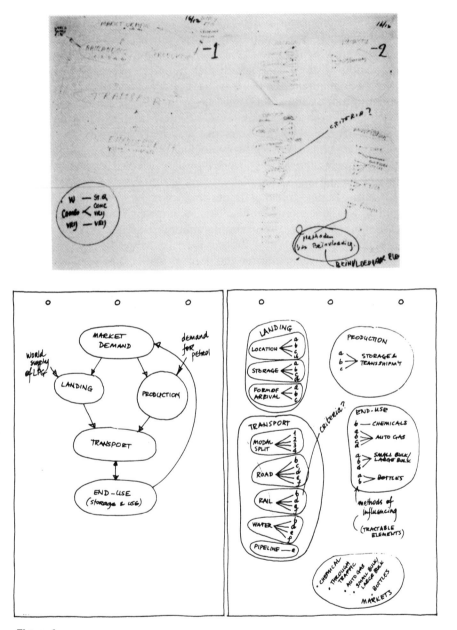

Figure 1
Shaping—the LPG system in decision graph form

the choice of which transportation system to favour, were also urgent in a political sense, the Government Commission having said that they wanted to look at them next. This being the case, the other two (together with the one about the market), could clearly be left aside for the time being.

During this process a record was also being kept of other decision areas of a more operational nature, which were going to be of concern later, in effect leaving them aside as well. For example:

- the choice of how to handle safety in trans-shipment;
- the choice of type(s) of technical improvement to be fitted to ships using inland waterways;
- the choice of alignment for the proposed pipeline (through Noord Brabant or through Belgium);
- and so on.

Actually any listing provides in itself a sort of implicit problem focus. But any shaping at the operational level tended to be carried out more informally. When the lower levels of concern came into consideration, decision areas such as these were just brought into the work as they became relevant.

As it happened, shaping at any level became the primary mode of work hardly at all in later cycles of the project. It was mostly carried out in the form of quick loops out of the other modes of the work, using the understanding achieved in earlier cycles as a basis for further development.

Each problem focus evolved over time, splitting and re-forming as the level of concern changed. For example, the transportation focus first evolved into one of 'modal split' (the balance between different forms of transport). Then in later cycles it split into two—one focused on 'mainstream' (bulk) transportation, and the other on 'diffused' (local) distribution. Soon after this, through traffic came back into consideration as a problem focus rather than an uncertainty, and was absorbed into the mainstream focus.

And there were, of course, other activities in other modes of work taking place concurrently. It is impossible to work exclusively in one mode at a time. Quick loops into other modes were taking place frequently and, while the results were not immediately used in the shaping mode, the understanding gained did enable the work to be better directed.

What is more, this work was not wasted. The results were recorded on the wall, along with the problem focus as it developed. In this way lists of aims, constraints, assumptions, and uncertainties were prepared for future use in other modes.

AIDA in the designing and comparing modes

Throughout the shaping work, asumptions were being made as part of the formulation process. Many of these were, in effect, the result of quick loops into the design mode of working made to clarify the definition of decision areas. Examples of such assumptions were:

- that the existing terminal and landing point in the Westerschelde could not be closed, while that at Rijnmond could not be increased in area;
- that the choice of any particular landing location(s) would not exclude the landing at others where the LPG was to be used directly;
- that no form of transportation could be altogether excluded, thus any choice would be about which form(s) to encourage and which to discourage;
- and so on.

These, plus the more operational concerns which had been listed at the same time, were the starting point for the use of the Analysis of Interconnected Decision Areas (AIDA). This required more detailed development of the decision areas, the options within them, and the option bars between them.

Unfortunately it is impossible here to follow progress through more than one problem focus. For this, the one about transportation has been chosen.

Taking the decision graph literally, it was thought that there would be five decision areas in the problem focus (see Figure 1): one each for choices about the pipeline; the railways; the waterways; and the road system—and one for the balance to be struck between them ('modal split'). In the event, each of these was quickly formulated as a cluster of four or five decision areas in its own right—a sort of lower level problem focus in fact.

The question of water transportation (canals) can be taken as an example. Early attempts to clarify the choices to be made led almost immediately to the identification of five separate decision areas (see Figure 2). In addition to the expected decision about the extent to which water transport should be used, there were choices to be faced about technical provisions on the vessels; physical improvements to the infrastructure; the introduction of selective routing; and the use of traffic control measures.

The group found it difficult to formulate the options within the decision areas at a consistently strategic level of abstraction. This is not uncommon. Options are not always discrete—nor mutually exclusive. However, it is necessary to start somewhere, even though it is inevitable that the results will have to be reworked almost immediately—and maybe several times.

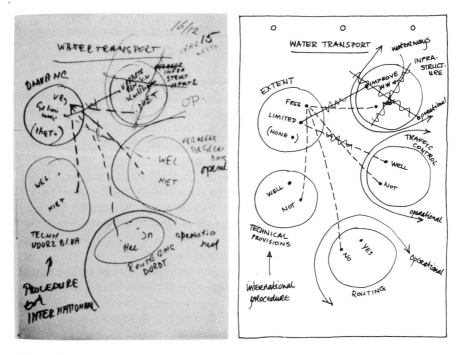

Figure 2
Designing—early option graph (water transport)

A form of representation was used here. For example, the two options 'free' and 'limited' were used to represent the extent of use of water transport. Although the former may indeed have meant totally unconstrained—thus providing a discrete option—this was certainly not so of the latter. The limited option actually represented a number of different levels of constraint. (One could imagine, in another case, options such as 'very limited'; 'somewhat limited'; and 'slightly limited'.)

In passing it should be mentioned that there was a third, discrete and mutually exclusive, option included in this decision area in the early stages. However, the extreme of prohibiting use of the canals for transportation of LPG ('none') was abandoned in the light of the assumption about impracticability which was listed earlier.

The choice about improvements to the infrastructure was the next decision area to be considered. At the outset the options were expected to be composed of different sorts of improvement and areas of application. Thus one option was identified as improvements to the canals themselves. However, further analysis showed that other improvements could be better

167

accommodated in the other decision areas, so that the only other option was to make no improvements ('none'). The structure of the options in the other three decision areas then followed this pattern, and they were all formulated in yes/no terms.

As is quite usual, the placing of option bars proved particularly difficult initially. Often at a strategic level of policy choice there are no logical option bars at all. This was not the case here, but there was reasonable certainty about only one—it was agreed that expenditure on improvements to the waterways was definitely incompatible with limiting the use of water transport.

There was a feeling of uncertainty about all of the other five option bars, which were therefore shown with broken lines. But it was difficult to relate this to specific external uncertainties. It was more to do with the formulation as a whole. For example, while a specifically formulated 'no' traffic control option might have been considered incompatible with a higher level one of 'limited' water transport in some cases, it could not be totally excluded. It depended to a great extent on how it was to be combined with the other operational choices—about improving the infrastructure and selective routeing.

It was concluded at this stage that two of the decision areas—those concerned with traffic control and routeing—should be put aside for reintroduction later at an operational level. A third—the one about improving the infrastructure—was at first eliminated, but later reinstated (notice the crossing out, and then the crossing out of the crossing out, in Figure 2) also for use at the operational level.

As time went on, this sort of analysis was carried out for all the clusters within the transportation problem focus. Some were more fully worked out than others—not always because they were inherently easier, but more due to the 'learning-by-doing' effect.

One of the more difficult ones was that about 'modal split'. This later turned out to be the only truly strategic level choice to do with transportation, and some of the difficulties of formulating options at this broad level began to emerge (see Figure 3).

One common way of handling this sort of difficulty is through use of representation. Thus the 'free' and 'limited' options, referring to the extent of use of water transport, were used again. However, another way of handling the difficulty is to concentrate on what one can actually do. The two options 'consciously controlled' and 'not consciously controlled' with respect to the railways, are of this type.

There is a danger that concentrating on what can be done can easily lead to formulation at too specific a level. For example, the options for the pipeline were formulated in terms of which of several alignments it could

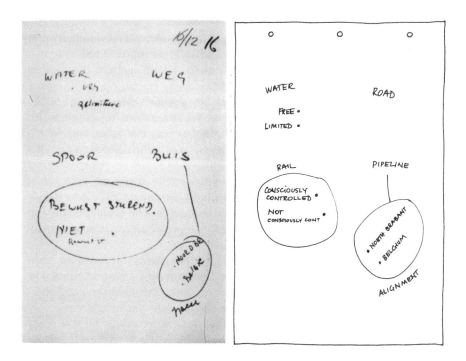

Figure 3
Designing—early option graph (modal split)

take, rather than the more strategic choice of whether to go ahead with one or not.

The purpose of showing this clearly incomplete part of the analysis is to demonstrate the value of 'learning by doing'. It is important to move ahead quickly simply because it speeds up the learning effect—especially in group situations. The work shown in Figure 3 also serves as a good example of how any analysis should be abandoned as soon as the learning effect drops off. No further work was necessary to draw two sorts of conclusion—one was visible and concerned with the content of the problem, and the other invisible and concerned with the process.

The former was simply that it is not sensible to adopt the promotion of a pipeline without limiting transportation by rail and water, and vice versa. The latter was that any formulation of the modal split choice would probably require four decision areas. And, although the options within them would have to be at a relatively high level of abstraction, they might need to be based on more detailed analysis in the first instance.

169

This learning was a signal for the start of a second cycle through the design mode. But at this point once again, in the interests of simplicity and given the space available, the full analysis has to be represented by only a part. For these purposes it has been chosen to pick up again on the choices surrounding the use of water transport.

In the following cycle, three decision areas were developed out of the original five (see Figure 4). The one about the extent to which water transport would be used came through unchanged. The other four, which had been posed at a more operational level, were reformulated as two at a broader level.

One decision area was designed to embrace technical improvements of all sorts, including physical improvements to the canals as well as engineering changes on the vessels and other apparatus. The second dealt with the selection of routes, which included the possibility of traffic control systems.

The options changed little, although the possibility of 'no water transport' at all was finally omitted from the decision area about extent of use. The other two retained their basic 'yes'/'no' form, but took on a considerably different meaning with the redefinition of their decision areas.

Two option bars were identified. What was not carried out was their annotation—keeping track of the logic on which they were based—probably in the interests of moving ahead fast at this stage. However, it is reasonably easy to reconstruct one argument: that the restriction of traffic to specified canals would hardly be consistent with free use of water transport. And the argument underlying the second option bar was similarly straightforward. The requirement of expensive technical up-grading of the vessels and other privately owned apparatus would be resisted strongly by their owners if, at the same time, their operations were to be limited.

The resulting decision schemes were listed on the same sheet of paper— and as it was such a simple option graph, this was done directly as an option table. More usually, if this is done at all, it is via an option tree which is easier to construct.

At this point the group chose to compare these decision schemes. Early work on comparison areas had taken the form of lists of national policies relevant to the project. Some were very broad and represented the basic rationale for the project as such. For example:

— energy saving and conservation;
— the limitation of air pollution;
— the promotion of economic development;
— and so on.

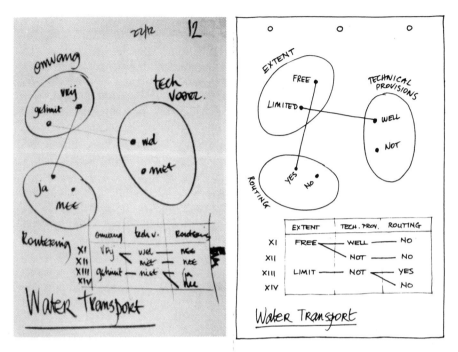

Figure 4
Designing—option graph and table (water transportation)

These were so fundamental that they were more in the nature of implicit constraints operating throughout the whole project—especially in the formulation of decision areas, options, and option bars. Others, which proved to be more applicable to the LPG problem, were more relevant to the work in the comparing mode. For example:

- the promotion of public safety;
- the promotion of diversification in sources of energy and raw materials;
- maintenance of the Dutch international position in the area of transportation;
- and so on.

This earlier work was taken up again at this point, and formed the basis for a set of comparison areas for the emerging decision schemes concerning transportation. These areas were the reduction of risk; flexibility in loading; transportation costs; effects on the Dutch economic position; and the demand on space—the last two being typical of criteria used throughout the Dutch National Government.

The comparison table formed by these comparison areas and the decision schemes (see Figure 5) was filled in as a group process. The source of knowledge used was the current level of understanding and common sense held by the participants, enhanced by the synergy created through the interactive work-style. This analysis took place in at least two cycles, one in which the main body of the table was completed, and another which can be seen in the workings on the extreme right. No numerical quantification was attempted—symbols representing relative effect were considered more appropriate to the rigour (or lack of it) of the exercise. The aim was not to select one best solution, but rather to find a number of good decision schemes for further analysis.

Looking now at only the transportation decision schemes, and taking the 'reduction of risk' comparison area as an example, the larger the black spot the greater was the estimated reduction in risk. Thus the decision scheme now identified as XII (see also Figure 4), allowing unlimited use of water transport with no special improvements of any sort, was given a very small spot indicating a very low rating with virtually no reduction whatsoever. On the other hand, the group rated the installation of technical improvements very highly, and decision scheme XI was given a correspondingly large spot.

A similar exercise was carried out for each comparison area in turn. Notice that the use of different symbols petered out after a while, and simple rankings took their place. These rankings, carried out for one comparison area at a time, are used extensively in strategic choice. The rank order is listed within the table—here numbered in reverse order simply because that is the way the group wanted to do it (the first is numbered '4', the second '3', and so on).

Understanding was recorded as it developed, even though it may not have been immediately relevant. Examples are the note attached to decision scheme XII, which was actually added later, and the question marks which can be seen in the comparison table. The latter indicated that the group were finding it very difficult to assess the transportation costs of decision schemes XI and XII, and attributed this to uncertainty. The exact nature of the uncertainty was not shown, because it was added separately to the growing list of those to be managed later.

There followed a simple evaluation to derive a working shortlist. Close inspection of these results enabled the group to identify decision scheme XII as being substantially inferior to decision scheme XI. Further, decision schemes XIII and XIV were seen to be dominated by decision scheme XI. This is not always a reliable criterion for reducing the number of alternatives under consideration, but it is a useful guide. In this case they were also thought to be so consistently low-scoring across all the comparison areas that they were crossed out.

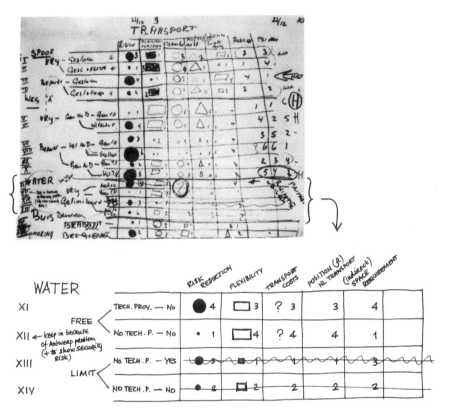

Figure 5
Comparing—preliminary work on decision schemes (with a focus on water transport)

On second thoughts, however, this meant that limitation of water transport was completely eliminated as an option, and the group were not ready for that yet. Consequently, alternative XIII, limitation of traffic by allowing the use of only selected routes, was brought back in again—hence the crossing out of the first crossing out. Thus decision schemes XI and XIII were carried forward for further analysis.

When this sort of analysis had been carried out for all four forms of transportation, the remaining decision schemes for each were used as options in a higher level option graph for the modal split question. In this way decision schemes XI and XIII were entered as options in the water transport decision area—with scheme XII being brought back in later (see Figure 6).

The work had now reached a stage where keeping track of the argumentation was beginning to be more important. The options were based on

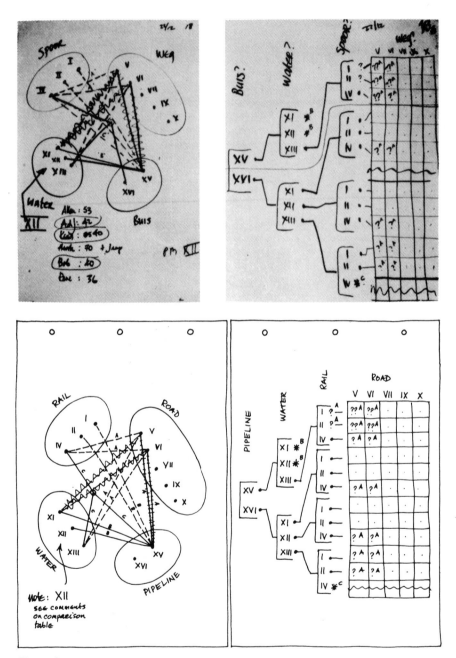

Figure 6
Designing—option graph, option tree and consistency table (modal split)

considerable analysis, and each simple roman numeral represented a quite detailed definition. (For example, 'XI' meant promoting free use of the waterways system, with the safety of vessels controlled only via regulations concerning technical provision.)

The option bars now also needed to be clearly defined. The underlying logic of each was recorded and linked to the relevant bar(s) by a code letter. This simplified the recording process where a number of bars were supported by the same argument. For example:

A   There was uncertainty about the viability of putting all transportation on to the road system.

B   Promotion of two forms of mainstream transportation at the same time would have been counter-productive (e.g.: pipeline versus water transport).

There was also a special form of option bar—a sort of three-way bar which connected options in three separate decision areas—meaning that all three used together would not work, although any one or two out of the three would be feasible. In this case the argument was as follows:

C   The limitation of all three forms of bulk transportation together would provide too low a level of service.

The decision schemes for the three 'heavy' transportation decision areas— pipeline, water, and rail—were listed in the form of an option tree. In this case, in order to save space, the fourth decision area to do with roads was added using a consistency matrix—a variation on the compatibility matrix described in the previous chapter.

While this use of the consistency matrix gave an indication of how many decision schemes to expect, and the pattern of compatibilities between the options, it did not make it easy to carry the analysis foward into comparison. But it did help in looping back into the shaping mode to reformulate the problem focus, so the chosen graphic structure served the team well.

They concluded from the analysis so far, and through discussion around it, that two main forms of distribution had to be provided for. One, described as 'mainstream', had to do with the major bulk transport flows to a few principal locations, while the other would serve a more diffuse network of destinations. Each of these now formed a separate problem focus. For common-sense reasons the pipeline was dropped from consideration for diffuse transportation, and to avoid traffic congestion road transport was dropped for mainstream transportation.

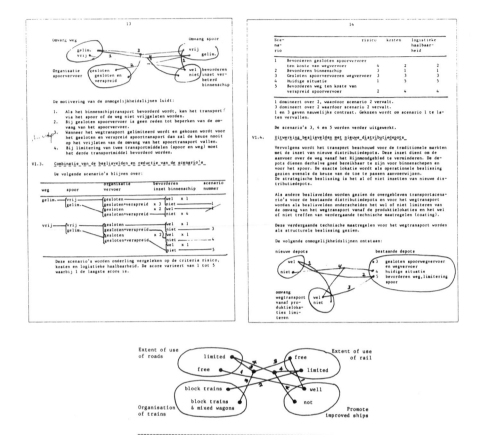

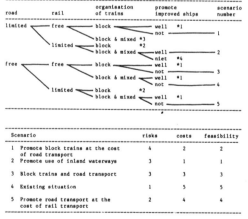

road	rail	organisation of trains	promote improved ships	scenario number
limited	free	block	well *1 / not	1
		block & mixed *3		
	limited	block *2		
		block & mixed	well / niet *4	2
free	free	block	well *1 / not	3
		block & mixed	well *1 / not	4
	limited	block *2		
		block & mixed	well *1 / not	5

Scenario	risks	costs	feasibility
1 Promote block trains at the cost of road transport	4	2	2
2 Promote use of inland waterways	3	1	1
3 Block trains and road transport	3	3	3
4 Existing situation	1	5	5
5 Promote road transport at the cost of rail transport	2	4	4

Figure 7
Interim presentation of local transport decision schemes (option graph, option tree and comparison table)

The next cycle of work using AIDA in the design and comparing modes was one of the last concerning policy about modal split, and the results were presented to the Government Commission in one of several working papers (RPC, 1983a). But, once again, it is impossible to follow the analysis completely through in all its aspects, and a part only must stand in as an example. For this purpose the analysis of the modal split for local transportation has been chosen.

Of the four decision areas in the analysis up to this point, two remained more-or-less unchanged—but now the group felt confident in going back to more broadly formulated (although paradoxically better defined) options. Thus the 'free' and 'limited' options reappear for the use of roads and rail (see Figure 7). The pipeline decision area had by this time fallen out of consideration. The fourth, about the inland waterways, was reformulated as a choice of whether to promote the technical improvements. An additional railway decision area concerning the organization of trains was introduced ('block trains' (all LPG) or 'block trains and mixed wagons').

The resulting decision schemes, of which there were five, were presented in an option tree and another cycle of comparison undertaken. For this the aims of the project, originally set up by the Government Commission and formulated while the shaping work was going on, were picked up again. Using these together with the experience gained in earlier comparisons, the group were able to identify three key comparison areas: risk, cost, and (logistical) feasibility.

In this cycle the five decision schemes were assessed only by rank order—within each comparison area separately. No weighting of the comparison areas, beyond that implied in their selection, was thought to be necessary at this stage. However, a simple dominance analysis revealed that alternative 2 was inherently inferior to alternatives 1 and 3.

Then further examination showed that alternatives 1 and 3 were so nearly the same that one could be selected to represent them both. Decision scheme 3 was so selected and the analysis continued with only three alternatives—numbers 3, 4, and 5.

At this point the use of a relative advantage analysis would have been very helpful. Unfortunately this technique was not so well developed at that time, and the project group chose another direction. Instead they started integrating the work which had been carried out on different foci. The three short-listed alternatives were brought together with the results of similar work on the location of depots and other local distribution centres.

This work was presented to the Government Commission, and decisions were taken leading on to the writing of policy statements—and the analysis switched more into the comparing and choosing modes.

Management of uncertainty in the comparing and choosing modes

The management of uncertainty played an important role throughout the project. At the outset this took the form of listing for future reference any areas of uncertainty as they were identified. For example:

- What were the intentions of Belgian Government with respect to regulation of inland shipping which had to pass through Dutch waters en route to Antwerp?
- How well developed was the new Walradar chain (an augmented shore radar system)? How far had it already been installed, and when could it be expected to be fully operational?
- How was the trade-off to be made between the costs of the various possibe measures and the level of risk?

Some of these could be reduced within the time-frame of the project through:

- seeking preliminary results from the on-going risk analysis (thus reducing uncertainty of type UE);
- use of the inter-organizational structure of the group (thus reducing uncertainty of type UR);
- interactive working which included consultation with others (thus reducing uncertainty of type UV).

Some areas of uncertainty emerged too late in the process, or were not amenable to quick reduction in this way. Thus, as time went on, it became more necessary to adopt working asumptions in order to make progress.

Choices were being made in all modes of work through repeated cycles of reformulation—some going deeper into more detail, others focusing more broadly and thus extending the scope of the analysis. In each case any significant assumptions were listed as they were made. From lists made in the shaping mode we have for example:

- the demand for LPG in The Netherlands would not grow as much or as fast as was predicted in 1979, but would be fairly substantial at least to the year 2000;
- in order for the pipeline to be feasible, all other forms of bulk transportation would have to be limited;
- and so on.

Constraints applied through the introduction of option bars, or in short-listing directly from the comparison table, were often based on assumptions about the availability of scarce resources, or about the behaviour of others. For example:

- the Government would continue to promote their policy on deregulation, with its concerted effort to reduce the exercise of control required of all levels of government;
- mutually satisfactory financing arrangements for the Walradar system could be negotiated with the Belgian Government;
- the spatial requirements for the safe shunting of mixed freight trains (including LPG wagons) would not be so great as to be impossible;
- and so on.

As the time for formal policy making approached, the explicit analysis of uncertainty became more pressing.

The lists of uncertainties—both those listed directly and those implied by the assumptions being made—had become quite considerable. And now they needed to be interpreted as uncertainty areas. Because it was not possible to analyse all of them, a selection had to be made.

Indeed a sort of selection process had been going on all the time—not all the uncertainties and assumptions were being recorded. Only those uncertainties which made the group feel less confident that they were doing the right thing, and those assumptions which threatened the validity of the results if they were proved incorrect, had made it into the lists.

One such cycle, in which a selected few of the outstanding uncertainty areas were analysed, is presented here as an example (Figure 8). The problem focus was the issue of 'mainstream' transportation which, at this stage, had been reduced to a combination of water and rail.

For the identification of such uncertainty areas, the synergy of the group process was used—in quick loops between the choosing and comparing modes. Judgements were based on the nature of the emerging decisions—whether they were to be full-blown long-term commitments, or of a more interim, delayed or contingent nature—in terms of the possibilities for accommodation to, and/or reduction of, the uncertainties. Seven uncertainty areas were identified in this way, although two of them were combined during the analysis (see the left-hand side of Figure 8).

At this point an uncertainty graph was introduced, and analysis of the uncertainty areas could begin. In this case the radial form was used (see right-hand side of Figure 8), with the uncertainties of types UV and UR on opposite sides to those normally used.

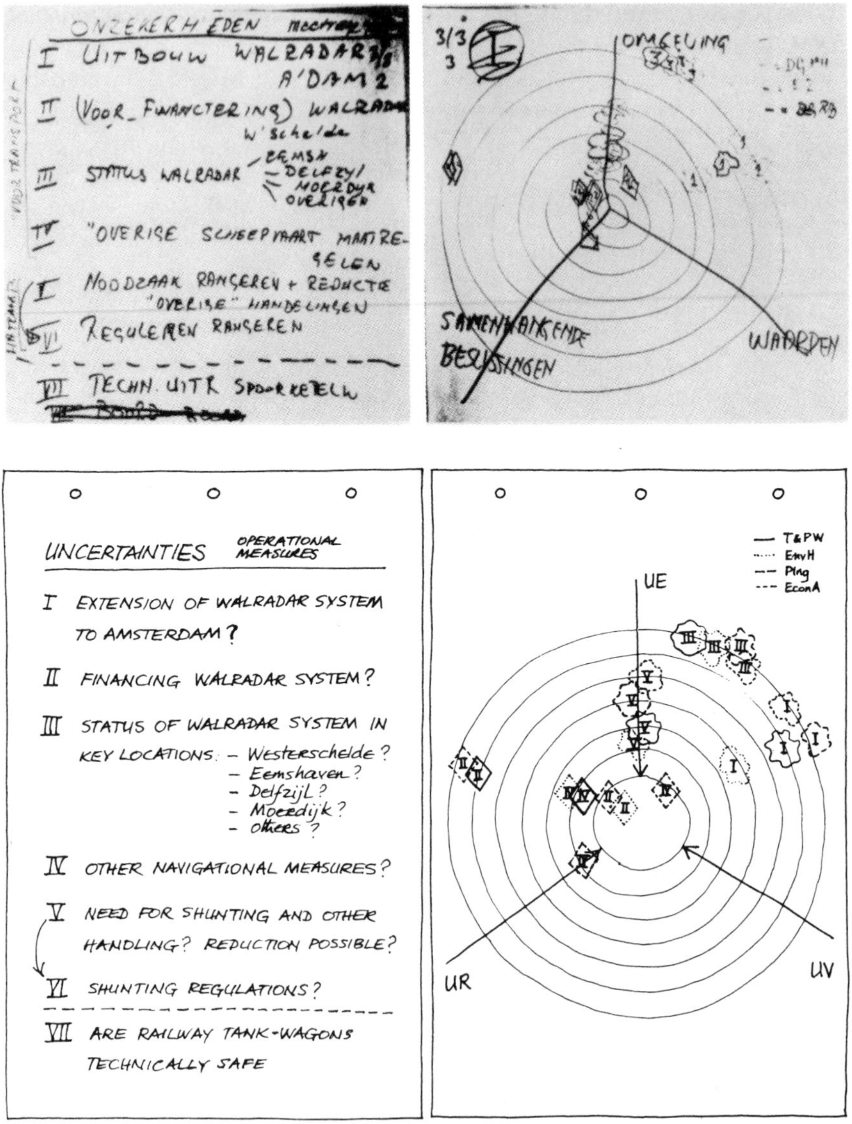

Figure 8
Analysis of uncertainty using an uncertainty graph

Uncertainties were plotted according to type by relating them to the three axes (UE, UV, and UR), with the more salient ones nearer the centre. What is more, in addition to the use of type and salience as characteristics by which to compare them, the group also used strength. Hard diamond shapes were used for those it was thought difficult to reduce, while soft jelly-like shapes were used for those more easily reduced.

One slight complication was that different opinions about the assessment of the uncertainty areas became apparent almost immediately. These differences were accommodated by allowing each of the four sectors of government represented in the group to plot the uncertainty areas separately, using a simple colour code to differentiate them.

As is commonly the case in using the strategic choice approach, the analysis was not carried out in full. Nevertheless, some useful conclusions could be drawn from it. There was, for example, strong consensus about uncertainty area III. And differences of opinion were only significant in the case of uncertainty area II—and then only in terms of its salience. That it was a mixture of uncertainties of type UR and UE, and that it was going to be very difficult to reduce, was agreed.

The identification of exploratory options was carried out quite informally in this case. These can be seen in the short-term work programme which was being compiled in parallel (see Figure 9). This interim product can be seen as a commitment package, though this framework was not used explicitly. However, the deadline was stated ('18 March'), and those responsible were noted ('T & PW', 'EnvH', and so on).

This programme was still quite tentative. Thus there was an emphasis on reducing uncertainty on all items. Nevertheless, preferred policy options could be implied from some of them. For example item 8 implied an already quite specific area for extension, and item 9 was taking the choice of pressure tanks in preference to refrigerated ones into its final stages (see right-hand side of Figure 9).

As it happened, the shift into more formal use of the commitment package framework occurred very shortly after this. The move took place quite quickly, and the work was completed in about half a day. The combination of being pressured to produce something and feeling ready to do so was enough to get the process going.

The group sat in the project room with the photo-reports of much earlier sessions and the more formal working papers on the table. On the wall was hung a selection of flip charts—mostly the more recent ones, but also key ones from earlier cycles of the process.

Also on the wall were a number of sheets with the empty commitment package already printed on them (see Figure 10 for the format). These provided the basic vertical structure of actions (*actie*), explorations

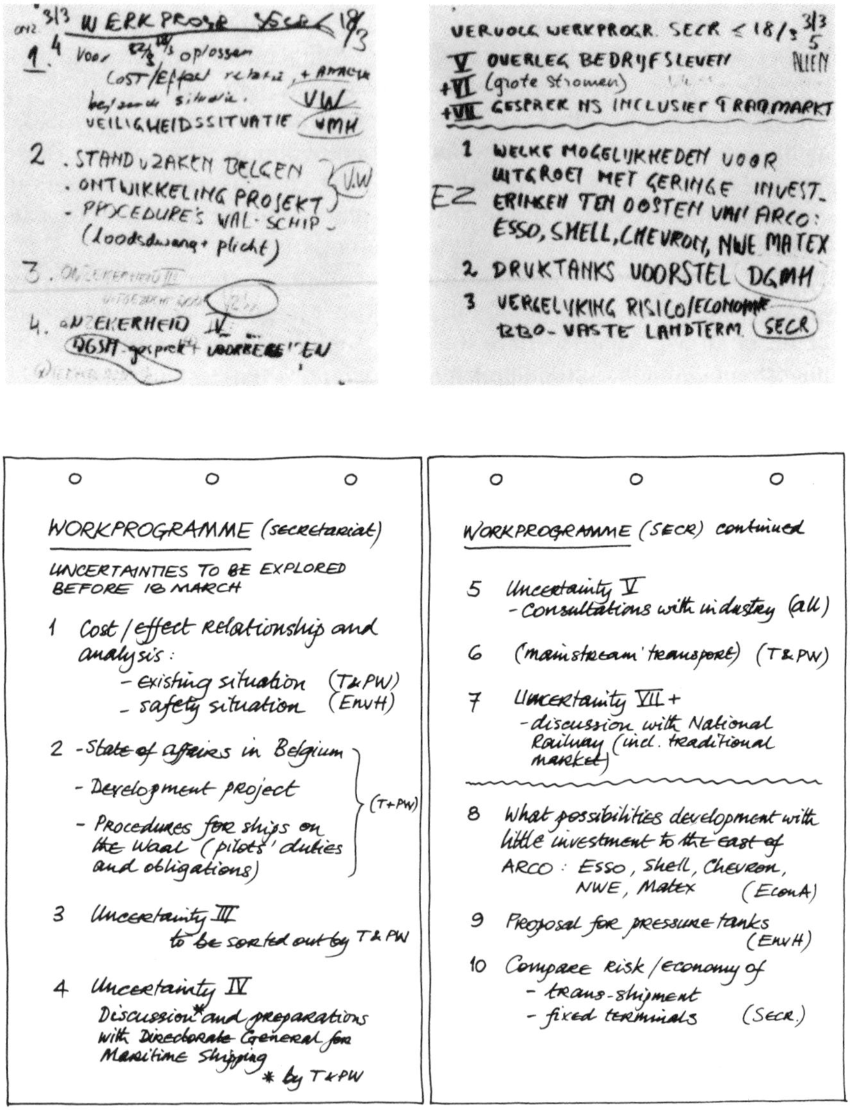

Figure 9
Choosing—an interim work programme

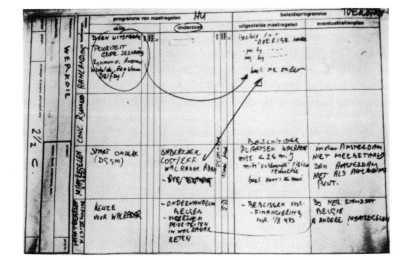

Figure 10
Choosing—use of a commitment package framework

(*onderzoek*), deferred choices (*uitgestelde maatregelen*) and contingency plans (*eventualiteitenplan*), and the horizontal structure of decision areas.

In addition, provision was made for the broader choices of who the commitment package was to be aimed at, in terms of who was the decision taker (*besluitnemer*); the primary orientation (*strategie, scenario, alternatief, enz*); and the time horizon (*tijdsperiode*). And the more operational issues of who was responsible for action (*wie*); the appropriate deadline (*wanneer*); and the available budget (*fl*).

These were filled in using the understanding gained through the learning process. Building on the working papers, recall was triggered where necessary by notes on the sheets and in the photo-reports. Unlike the practice in using more conventional methodologies, conclusions were not drawn out of the analysis, so much as they were out of the understanding which was obtained through the analysis.

The process of building up the policy began by identifying the decision taker which, on this occasion, was deemed to be the Government Commission. This was because such an identification would help in defining which decisions to focus upon, and in describing the choices made. What could be treated as a decision for one decision taker would, most usually, have to be treated as an uncertainty, or as the subject of an assumption, by another.

At the same time the orientation of the commitment package was identified which, in this example, was '2½C'. (This happened to be one of the variations on the scenario involving regional concentration of landing points with free use of the railways for mainline distribution.) The need for identification of the orientation was that it was still not clear which of the short-listed orientations was going to be chosen eventually. Therefore, work had to be done on both in order to understand the consequences of each in policy terms.

Each combination of decision taker and orientation was written up on several sheets of paper. Then decision areas were written in and the policy choices noted (see Figure 10). Each row accommodated the various types of choice concerning that decision area where applicable, with cells left blank otherwise. Particular relationships between choices were noted with the use of arrows.

For example, in the case of the *Westerschelde* (at the bottom of Figure 10), the choice was for the use of the Walradar system in any case. But there was also considerable uncertainty about:

– the possibilities of sharing its financing with Belgium (uncertainty of type UR);

– and the priorities that had been established in the Walradar chain up to that time (uncertainty of type UV).

These were to be the subject of explorations. The former was then made the subject of future decision (to be made before 1 August 1983). The arrow across the bottom indicated that the results of research into the latter were to be used as the basis for alternative measures in the event that negotiations with the Belgians went badly.

Of course, the White Paper was not written in the half-day it took to put together the first full set of policy choices. But, the main policies were certainly structured and agreed in outline at that time. The complete document was then drawn up during the following weeks.

The basic policy was to discontinue the licensing of one terminal in the Rijnmond area and its associated pipeline, which had been planned to serve as the main form of inland transport. Instead, the development of a limited number of terminals was to be allowed. The pipeline would not be built and in its place a combination of improved barges and trains (run as single-freight, closed transport) were to be the preferred mode of bulk transport. Road transport was to be used only for more diffuse local distribution.

The commitment package framework survived throughout the process of finalization and its headings were used explicitly in the final published version of the White Paper. A summary of the more operational policy measures was listed under these headings, filling seven typeset pages. As it is impossible to quote all of them, a few typical policy statements from each heading have been selected to serve as examples.

A typical action was related to the development of Amsterdam as a landing point:

> 1.4 For the seaway approaching Amsterdam, for a distance of 2.5 km to the west and 3.5 km to the east of the locks, but excepting the locks themselves, approaching or passing LPG freighters is prohibited. This ban also applies from a distance of 2.5 km to the west of the America Harbour to the harbour itself.
>
> *Integrale Nota LPG* (p. 109)

As is often the case, the choice of this action was made in the face of considerable uncertainty and involved the making of assumptions, which could have serious consequences if they were to be proved wrong. In this case they were about the expected amount of shipping. A reasonable increase in traffic could have raised the danger significantly, and a contingency plan had to be designed to accommodate such an eventuality:

> 4.2 If a terminal is to be built in Amsterdam, a suitable safety zone for LPG ships must be available. Should there be a substantial increase in imports, or in the number of shipping movements, then a refuge harbour should be built.
>
> *Integrale Nota LPG* (p. 115)

There were several actions concerning the handling of railway wagons in marshalling yards. For example:

> 1.10 In yards where LPG pressure-vessel wagons are marshalled, the points in use must be so secured that they cannot be switched when one or more wagons are near or on them.
>
> *Integrale Nota LPG* (p. 114)

As was revealed by the analysis of uncertainty (see Figure 8), there was some doubt about the issue of marshalling, and this was reflected in policy statements which, in strategic choice terms, were explorations:

> 2.4 Research will be made into the risks in marshalling yards. The strength of LPG pressure-vessel rail wagons, especially in connection with potential leakages, will be investigated. The special equipment on these wagons, required to prevent, or at least considerably delay a BLEVE,* will also be looked into.
>
> *Integrale Nota LPG* (p. 110)

Typically, this was then linked to deferred decisions on a stronger policy:

> 3.5 The results stemming from 2.4, concerned with the construction of pressure-vessel rail wagons, will be applied internationally (R.I.D.) with the intent of incorporating them in international regulatory directives.
>
> *Integrale Nota LPG* (p. 114)

The complete document, having been drawn up in draft form, then followed the more-or-less conventional six-month period of finalization. An extensive programme of consultation with other ministries and industry was undertaken. It was adapted and polished, and finally submitted to the Second Chamber of the Dutch Parliament.

---

*A 'BLEVE' is a Boiling Liquid Expanding Vapour Explosion.

Disaster strikes again

The LPG policy passed through its formal process of acceptance un-opposed on 20 November 1984.

That very night there was a massive explosion and fire on the outskirts of Mexico City. Flames 100 metres high engulfed the area. At the source was one of the city's main gas distribution centres—including 80 000 barrels of LPG. Hundreds of people died and thousands were injured. Witnesses said that birds were fried in the air. Over 4000 homes were destroyed, and the suburb of San Juanico was no more (*The Times*, 21 November 1984).

The news hit the newspapers in The Netherlands the next morning. If the LPG policy was going to be challenged, this would have been the time. But the reaction, unlike that after the accident in Spain six years earlier, was one of calm confidence. The policy, underpinned by the high level of consensus and commitment gained through the process, stood the test well.

Reflection, commentary, and conclusions

The story of the LPG policy in The Netherlands continues, even though there has been little of consequence to report in its first five years of operation. However, this case study, having been focused only on the use of strategic choice in that whole story, ends here. Thus it is at this point that it may be helpful to reflect on some of the lessons to be gained from the experience.

The approach-technology/organization/process/products framework, in-troduced in the preceding chapter, provides the structure for this review. Commentary is provided, on reflection five years after the event, by people who were centrally involved in the project.

The approach

The strategic choice approach was suggested at a point in the project when progress was almost at a standstill. Agreement was impossible even about which analytical techniques to use. Not only did those suggested have limited scope just as the risk analyses had—but each had the added disadvantage of being proposed by one of the participants, and thus tainted with their bias.

The strategic choice approach overcame these difficulties. The 'tool-box' idea provided a wide range of techniques, concepts, and frameworks suitable for various aspects of the problem. What is more, it was introduced by independent consultants. However, this by itself was not enough. Formal analytical techniques cannot help people come to grips with the social aspects of an impasse. Thus two other elements of strategic choice played an important role:

- the cyclic model of the process that provided the intial breakthrough;
- the interactive style of working that provided a favourable context within which it could be applied.

In addition the approach offered an essentially different way of thinking about uncertainty. It was no longer seen as something to be worked against—to be eliminated or controlled. Rather it was seen as something to be worked with and managed creatively ('. . . the system of management of uncertainties played an important role. . .'—Rene van Oosterwijk).

What is more, uncertainty is treated much more broadly within strategic choice. Up to that time the focus had been almost exclusively on uncertainties about the physical context—those of type UE. It was only when strategic choice was introduced into the project that uncertainties of types UV and UR were brought into consideration. ('Very interesting was the handling of the inevitable uncertainties in the decision making: defining the uncertainties at stake, giving them a role in the decision making and giving them their own place in the policy. . .'—Cees Moons.)

The technology

Strategic choice is decision focused, thus providing a technology which is easily accessible to all concerned. The participants changed from concentrating on their perceptions of the system they were trying to manage. Instead, they focused on the decisions they were facing. ('These tools are effective in stimulating a process in which the energy of the actors is focused on a solution-oriented framework'—Bob van de Graaf.)

The Analysis of Interconnected Decision Areas (AIDA) allowed a logical approach to the identification of a focus, in place of intuition based on naturally partisan views. ('Also the relationship between problems became clear, as well as the lack of relationship through which it was possible to see how part-problems could be isolated'—Henk Waardenaar.)

AIDA also provided the means of handling the complexity presented by the interrelatedness between decisions. The number of alternatives under consideration at any one time was limited to only those which were feasible. ('The way in which alternative solutions were listed and worked out was also found to be useful'—Cees Moons.)

At the time of the LPG project, strategic choice was less well developed to aid in the comparing mode of work than it is now. Some structure was used in the form of simple comparison tables. However, little else was provided other than the manner of writing everything on the wall to make the process more open. ('Strategic choice was less helpful in the "solution phase". Choosing is more of a creative process in which alternatives are combined to achieve an optimal result, rather than an analytical listing of possibilities'—Henk Waardenaar.)

Much of the early difficulty lay in the fact that an interdepartmental group, working on a policy problem, tends to work not as a team but as opponents in negotiation. While this cannot be totally changed, it was made much more manageable by the introduction of independent process consultants who operated in the role of facilitators. ('The success of the policy making in the LPG project, with its four competing government agencies, each with its own interests and views, owed much to the guidance of a more or less impartial "third party"'—Jan Jaap de Boer.)

But strategic choice also provided a set of concepts, based on the management of decisions, which together formed a common framework for communication. Thus it proved extremely valuable as an aid in the many interactive sessions, which involved working not around a table, but on large sheets of paper on the wall—in most cases aided by the facilitators. ('Through this method all those involved obtained a clear and shared picture of the LPG problem'—Cees Moons.)

The organization

At the time of the LPG project, many of the ideas about organization for strategic choice were in the early stages of development and were thus not applied as they would be now. However, they did provide a changed context which enabled partisan representatives to work jointly. ('Previously the discussion was usually influenced by misunderstandings, which caused feelings of fear in inter-ministerial discussions'—Cees Moons.)

In addition, the use of strategic choice promoted the development of more effective links with the 'home' organizations of the project group members. At the outset the primary interest of each lay in working with its constituency in its own field. Later their joint working became the primary interest. Consultations with their constituencies were selectively programmed, with strategic choice providing analysis and a common framework for communication. ('The team would generate solutions and would later present these to the various constituencies. Typically in this period there was a marked improvement in the social interaction among them'—Bob van de Graaf.)

The process

One of the main contributing factors to the blocked process, which gave rise to the invitation to try out strategic choice, was that the project group were adhering to a linear process. They were analysing one problem after the other, and trying to move from one decision to the next. ('The effect was like trying to get ahead by taking two steps back for every one taken forward'—Frans Evers.)

However, using strategic choice, explicit recognition was given to the cyclic nature of any creative learning process, allowing progress to be made with provision for adaptation in the light of experience. With this the need for a sequence of complete negotiated agreements to each step could be overcome. ('The breakthrough came with the concept of the cyclic process. Making decisions, running through the whole problem, and coming back again. Making and re-making decisions until a consistent set was found'—Bob van de Graaf.)

The products

The products of strategic choice are both visible and invisible, and based on the idea of incremental progress. For the visible ones, produced in the form of conventional documents, the commitment package provided a vital framework. It opened the way for decisions to be made with respect to time, under conditions of uncertainty and conflict. ('The most useful instrument in strategic choice, in my opinion, was the commitment package. In this way decisions were formulated so that the time element could be better taken into account. Commitments in the spirit of "we may agree that I am right now, but it may turn out later that you are right when certain occurrences become clear (e.g. through research and contingency plans)" could be clearly put into words'—Cees Moons.)

Joint commitment and mutual understanding were the principal invisible products. But they are, by their very nature, extremely difficult to demonstrate. In fact they were only experienced directly by those who were involved in the process, and even then they may only be recognized at some time in the future. ('The success of the policy-making in the LPG project with the competing government agencies, each with its own interests and views, ... depended in my view largely ... on the shared learning and use of the policy-making methods, on the shared information and mutual trust developed between all parties ...'—Jan Jaap de Boer.)

That the project was successful, at least in the eyes of the project group, can be seen from the commentary above. However, additional evidence can be found in the documents, especially in the White Paper itself—

Appendix 4 of which is a description of the methodology, presented as part of the justification of the policy proposed.

What is more, in 1986 a retrospective study of five different environmental policy-making projects in The Netherlands was undertaken by Professor Dr R. Hoppe of the University of Amsterdam. He conducted an opinion survey of people concerned with the five projects from both inside and outside the Ministry. Two principal measures of quality were used:

- the degree to which the project achieved its goals;
- the standard of the policy document itself.

In these terms the LPG project was rated the best, with scores of 100 per cent on both measures.

Further confirmation comes, if any is needed, from the fact that since 1983 the strategic choice approach has been chosen for use on many other policy-making projects in The Netherlands. The issues have ranged from the ageing of the population to the highly polluted silt dredged from the Rhine estuary. It is currently being used in, amongst other projects, the preparation of the National Environmental Policy Plan, which is to be put before the Second Chamber of the Dutch Parliament in 1989.

Acknowledgement

Photographs from the workshop on LPG policy are reproduced by courtesy of C. A. de Jong.

References and bibliography

Government Documents

Rijksplanologischecommissie (RPC) (1982). *Scenarios*, RPC-LPG nr 116, Vergadering 26 Mei 1982, Den Haag.
Rijksplanologischecommissie (RPC) (1983a). *Opbouw en Selectie van Scenarios*, RPC-LPG nr 159, Vergadering 20 januari 1983, Den Haag.
Rijksplanologischecommissie (RPC) (1983b). *Opbouw en Selectie van Scenarios*, RPC-LPG nr 165, Vergadering 24 februari 1983, Den Haag.
Tweede Kamer de Staten-Generaal (1984). *Integrale Nota LPG*, Vergaderjaar 1983–1984, 18 233, nrs. 1–2, Den Haag.

Case studies and reports

Environmental Resources Limited (1987). 'Case Study H: LPG Policy in The Netherlands', in *Risky Decisions: a Management Strategy*, ERL, London.

Gardenier, J. (1984). *New LPG Guidelines in The Netherlands*, Technical Report No. 23, ISSN 0111–2856, Town and Country Planning Directorate, Ministry of Work and Development, Wellington North, New Zealand.

van de Graaf, R. (1985). 'Strategic Choice in LPG Policy', in *Evaluation of Complex Policy Problems* (Eds. A. Faludi and H. Voogd), Delftsche Uitgevers, Delft.

Hoppe, R. (1987). *Naar Professioneel Management in VROM-Beleidsvorming: Resultaten Enquete*, University of Amsterdam, Amsterdam.

Personal communications

Many and various communications have taken place with members of the project team. Those quoted in the text are listed here in alphabetical order with their organizational affiliation at the time:

- Jan Jaap de Boer (Physical Planning arm of the Ministry of Environmental Affairs).
- Frans Evers (Environmental Hygiene arm of the Ministry of Environmental Affairs).
- Bob van de Graaf (Ministry of Economic Affairs).
- Cees Moons, (Environmental Hygiene arm of the Ministry of Environmental Affairs).
- Rene van Oosterwijk (Ministry of Transport and Public Works).
- Henk Waardenaar (Physical Planning arm of the Ministry of Environmental Affairs).

8
Robustness analysis: keeping your options open

Jonathan Rosenhead

If you and a group of friends were going out to dinner together tomorrow, how would you choose which restaurant to go to? One approach would be to collect menus from all the restaurants in the vicinity, get each of your intended companions to rate each of the main courses on a suitable scale of utility, and then combine these evaluations to identify the restaurant expected to achieve the highest aggregate satisfaction of desire. Alternatively, you could get a general sense from each of the participants of types of food they specially like or can't eat (fish? curry?) and then select a restaurant, either by menu or by general type, which provides a spread of options broad enough to encompass their tastes.

The fastidious among you will have noted that the first formulation is grotesquely oversimplified. What about starters? What about puddings? Don't we care about the wine list or the ambiance? If we are going to take seriously the task of maximizing expected satisfaction, then this sketched approach can only be the starting point for an elaborate and sophisticated exercise. In fact, I rather doubt it will be complete in time for tomorrow's dinner.

Evidently the second approach makes fewer demands on data, on the quantification of preferences, and on mathematical analysis. But the distinctive grounds for preferring it are to do with its handling of uncertainty. It does *not* require as a precondition for any analysis the identification

Rational Analysis for a Problematic World
Edited by J. Rosenhead. © 1989 John Wiley & Sons Ltd

today of what dish each diner will wish to eat tomorrow. It is reasonable not to do so, since that question cannot be answered today (tomorrow's taste buds will be conditioned by a complex of internal and external events which cannot be anticipated) and so it should not be asked. Answers, if given, will be speculative, and any apparent optimum will be spurious.

The 'eating out' example can serve as an appetizing introduction (*hors d'oeuvre?*) to the field of application of robustness analysis. Robustness provides an approach to the structuring of problem situations in which uncertainty is high, and where decisions can or must be staged sequentially. Its characteristic thrust is to identify decisions early in the sequence which will keep open a range of options for the future.

This chapter will outline the robustness approach, which is more a framework than a programmed sequence of operations. But first it will explore the reasons why planning under uncertainty is both important and difficult, and at the same time introduce the key elements which come together in robustness analysis.

Uncertainty

Uncertainty afflicts a wide range of problems a good deal more momentous than where tomorrow's dinner is coming from. The significance of uncertainty for a decision situation depends on the cost of reversing a commitment once made, the volatility of the environment, and the sensitivity of benefits to the occurrence of the unpredicted. It is when high uncertainty is coupled with (relative to the scale of the enterprise) high cost that uncertainty's invisible presence needs to be acknowledged and allowed for in any analysis. Such conditions are all too common. Town planners laying down infrastructure cannot predict whether future commercial development will justify it. Decisions on factory size will have different outcomes depending on the level of demand which materializes. Design of a product range may be vulnerable to changes in taste and in technology, and to competitive strategies. Acquisition of new weapons systems may be caught in a budgetary squeeze some years down the road. A child who doesn't know what she wants to do when she grows up must nevertheless select subjects to study at school. And so on.

The future, it has been suggested, is a combination of the known and the unknowable. The proportion of the latter tends to rise as the time-scale extends, graphically represented by the 'trumpet of uncertainty' opening out into a wide bell (Figure 1). There is another sense in which time is against us. Things certainly seem to have been getting worse lately. With the growth in scale and reach of dominant institutions, developed societies

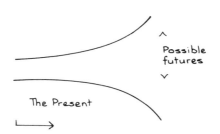

Figure 1
The trumpet of uncertainty

are evidently approaching Emery and Trist's (1965) 'turbulent environment'—not only the decisions of individual units, but also the interactions between them, produce endemic unpredictability. Less developed countries, through their relationships of dependency, experience the backwash of this turbulence without articulated internal structures which can soften its impact. Unforeseen change is no longer the exception—we live at best with 'punctuated equilibria' (Evans, 1987). It is only the nature of the surprises which will be a surprise.

Uncertainty and planning methods

This everyday, commonplace observation is routinely denied in practice by the planning methodologies still employed to guide society and its parts into the future. For example, the required planning method for British health authorities is to draw up a strategic plan of how their services will look a decade ahead, and then approach it operationally in yearly stages. Land-use planning in Britain has moved on from the rigid master plan only as far as the structure plan, in which a capacity to respond to changing circumstances is thought adequately preserved by the omission of too much specific detail. (Etzioni's (1968) 'mixed scanning' planning methodology incorporates this limited approach to flexibility.) Transport planning world-wide adopts an elaborate method balanced precariously on future forecasts. Business has perhaps been more realistic, but its realism has largely taken the form of a retreat from long-range planning into a search for shorter term entrepreneurial advantage.

The planning methods still in use were developed during the 1950s and 1960s for an expected era of smoothly continuing expansion. They are the technical manifestations of rational comprehensive planning, described in Chapter 1. The retreat into non-planning, by contrast, bears some of the hallmarks of its competitive philosophy, disjointed incrementalism. Superficially, incrementalism might appear to offer just that responsiveness to change which rational comprehensive planning lacks. Yet it is the responsiveness of drift, of flotsam on the ocean of circumstance. There is no place for purpose, beyond the purpose of staying afloat. The more demanding task of steering creatively through disturbed waters towards goals which are themselves impermanent is not even attempted (Rosenhead, 1980a).

The inadequacy of what is on offer can be brought home by analogy with a game of chess. Incrementalism proposes an opportunistic policy of short-term gains—take what pieces you can now. A sure recipe for disaster against an even moderately skilful player. Rational comprehensive planning will propose, after long and deep analysis, that we should focus all our efforts on achieving mate with a combination of queen, knight, and passed pawn on square KB6 at move 39. Such a strategy would be impossible to operationalize in the opening moves, and rapidly prove irrelevant as the middle game develops (as it will) unexpectedly.

The rational comprehensive approach has been described as 'moon-shot' planning. But in chess the target does not move in stately orbit—and life is far more complex than chess.

Forecasts and futures

The fundamental problem with moon-shot planning is that it requires knowledge of the middle- to long-term future which is, in principle, simply unobtainable. Sometimes this certain future is merely assumed, in which case the assumption is that tomorrow will be essentially the same as today (Lee, 1976). Occasionally the formalistic procedures of the DELPHI approach are used—for surely the experts could tell us what the future will be like, if only they would agree. Most often the future is captured by means of a forecast, the projection of current trends.

There is no need here to retell horror stories of forecasts their owners would rather forget. (In any case by the time this book is published there should be more.) By themselves failed forecasts prove nothing: indeed they can and are used by proponents of forecasting as evidence of the need for still more sophisticated forecasting. My argument is not that forecasts happen to be wrong, but that they are bound to be.

There are good reasons for believing that forecasts of any importance are inherently fallible. Our ignorance of what is happening *now* should not be underestimated. But this will be compounded by the succession of natural disasters, new discoveries, accidental conjunctures and conscious interventions which will lay their train across the future. Longer term or strategic planning cannot be firmly based on an attempt to predict what *will* happen, rendered infeasible as it is by the purposeful interactions of a host of human actors. A more limited task, of identifying a range of scenarios of what *might* happen, would be a modest and supportable basis for planning analysis.

There is no one form for such multi-future planning. Lee (1976) has advocated a mixed approach to forecasting in which regularities from the historical record are combined with various possible assumed structural changes. The value of this approach, he states, 'is less that it may yield forecasts which are proven accurate in the event than that it focuses attention on the specification of different sets of reasonable, or even unreasonable but not ignorable, assumptions. To put it another way, it promotes systematic speculation.' Royal Dutch Shell has developed an approach on very much these lines, producing on a regular basis a number of scenarios portraying alternative development paths for the world economy and the market in oil (Wack, 1985). These scenarios, however, do not serve as inputs to further specified stages of a planning process. They function, rather, as informative background material of which managers should be aware while taking their decisions.

A more positive multi-future approach, and one informed by a very different intent, has been formulated by Sandberg (1976). Instead of unconditional projections which colonize the future by assuming the continuation of existing relations, he proposes 'conditional projections', to act as a guide to more purposeful action. Conditional projections work out the consequences of 'what if ...' statements. *What if* this particular relationship, which seems to have operated in the past, were replaced by another? The purpose of the analysis, treating relationships as socially constructed rather than as natural laws, is to identify those whose rupture would open up more desirable vistas.

Multi-future forecasting is a clear advance on unconditional forecasting. It avoids the arrogance of misplaced certainty. However, unless we believe with Sandberg that we can struggle to some effect to bring about a future we prefer, then the multi-future perspective still leaves us with a problem. What do we actually *do*, now?

Sequential decisions

If one key to planning under uncertainty is the acknowledgement of multiple futures, the other is the recognition of a clear distinction between decisions and plans. I may *plan* in January to take a Mediterranean holiday in August, but my initial *decision* is to go to the local travel agent and collect brochures on a number of possible tourist centres. After further analysis I may from time to time take further decisions—to book a holiday, to pay for it, to insure my deposit, ... At each stage there remains an uncertainty whether the remaining stages of the plan will be implemented in the form originally envisaged, or at all. A letter from the bank manager, the illness of a close relative, growth of an insurrectionary movement— any of these and more could cause me to exercise my free will as a sequential decision maker.

The distinction can be put more formally. A decision is a commitment of resources which transforms some aspect of the decision maker's environment; the environment can be restored to its former condition, if at all, only by a further decision and at (at least) psychological cost). A plan consists of a foreshadowing of a set of decisions which it is currently anticipated will be taken at some time or times in the future, or an identification of an intended future state which necessarily implies such a set of future decisions. If a plan does not include within it decisions for implementation forthwith, then no commitment is made for the time being. The plan can in this case be revised or discarded without anything having been lost— except time. But, of course, nothing has been gained either.

The distinction between 'plan' and 'decision' has been laboured at some length as it is crucial to an understanding of how rational decisions can be taken under uncertainty. The frequent practice of eliding their meanings, so that a plan is viewed as a commitment rather than a working hypothesis about future actions, causes both confusion and rigidity. Further, it concentrates attention, counter-productively, on trying to get the right *plan*— a mis-direction of intellectual resources since it is highly implausible that the plan as specified will ever be enacted. (If it is, through bureaucratic momentum, so much the worse.) A clear appreciation of the plan/decision distinction focuses analytic effort on getting the *decision* right, with the plan as a framework to ensure that the longer term is not sacrificed to short-term advantage. The appropriate visual aid for the uncertain planner is a pair of bifocals, enabling her to focus alternately on the horizon and on the terrain at her feet.

The decision/plan distinction is embodied in the Strategic Choice approach's concept of the 'commitment package' (see Chapters 6 and 7). Strategic Choice and robustness analysis have a shared concern with the management of uncertainty—indeed the two approaches have been used in conjunction (Friend and Jessop, 1969; Centre for Environmental Studies, 1970). The specific focus of robustness analysis is on how the distinction between decisions and plans can be exploited to maintain *flexibility*.

Flexibility and robustness

There is more than one possible strategy when confronted by high levels of uncertainty. The very intensity of threat may elicit counter-productive reactions (such as those alleged of the ostrich). But there are alternative strategies even if we exclude the irrational. One might be to attempt to control the environment from which the uncertainty emanates. Another is to tighten up internal organization for quicker response when unpredicted change occurs. However, when none of these strategies is available, or in addition to them, flexibility may avoid untoward consequences. Indeed it may make it possible to take advantage of unexpected opportunities: the eventual manifestations of uncertainty are not always malign.

Once the unexpected has occurred it can be straightforward to see how policy or position should be modified. Such modification may, however, be impossible without damaging costs or sacrifice of other desiderata. How serious the consequences of change are will depend on how easily the previous posture can accommodate the necessary transformations.

Such flexibility may turn out to be available when demands on it are made. However, it is more prudent to attempt to *engineer* a high level of flexibility rather than rely on lucky accidents. Liquidity (in financial management), versatility (of military forces—Bonder, 1979), resilience (of ecological systems—Holling, 1973) and hedging (in the planning of investments) are all analytic tools developed in different planning environments to achieve this flexible capability.

'Robustness', and the analysis based on it, embodies a particular perspective on flexibility. It is concerned with situations where an individual, group or organization needs to make commitments now under conditions of uncertainty, and where these decisions will be followed at intervals by other commitments. With a robustness perspective the focus will be on the alternative immediate commitments which could be made, which will be compared in terms of the range of possible future commitments with which they appear to be compatible. Robustness analysis is a bifocal instrument.

Robustness analysis assesses the flexibility achieved or denied by particular acts of commitment. This decision focus arises naturally out of the operational research tradition. However, it does have pragmatic advantages. People and organizations become accustomed to living with uncertainty. Under normal circumstances there may be no opportunity to convene a forum in which strategies for coping with uncertainty can be proposed or reviewed. (If a threat of imminent dislocation is vividly perceived, it may be a little easier.) Proposing changes just because the environment is uncertain, just in order to generate flexibility, will appear

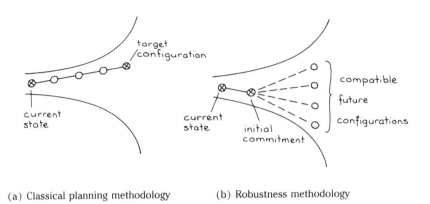

(a) Classical planning methodology   (b) Robustness methodology

Figure 2
Planning and the trumpet of uncertainty

gratuitous. But when resource commitments are in any case due to be made, in the normal course of business, an opportunity is provided to analyse them in terms of flexibility. Thinking on uncertainty and flexibility can thus, in principle, be integrated into the normal course of business, rather than appear as a disruption to it.

The contrast between this perspective and that of the classical 'planning-as-decision-making' methods of operational research is brought out in Figure 2. In Figure 2(a) an optimal system for an assumed future state of the environment is derived, and the plan consists of the necessary decisions required to transform the current system into that target configuration.

Figure 2(b) declines to identify a future decision path or target. The only firm commitments called for are those in the initial decision package—possible future commitments are of interest principally for the range of capability to respond to unexpected developments in the environment which they represent. (The term 'decision package' is used to indicate that initial commitments may come in integrated bundles.)

Graphical illustrations suggest but do not define a method. A more formal measure of the options left open is required, if initial commitments are to be compared. We define the *robustness* of any initial decision to be the number of acceptable options at the planning horizon with which it is compatible, expressed as a ratio of the total number of acceptable options at the planning horizon.

This definition can be expressed more formally through a minimal mathematical notation. Consider a planning situation in which we may denote the set of all options at the planning horizon by $\underset{\sim}{S}$, and the subset of

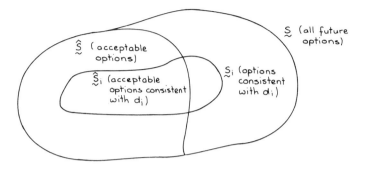

Figure 3
A categorization of future options

$\underset{\sim}{S}$ consisting of acceptable options by $\underset{\sim}{\hat{S}}$. Similarly the set of options attainable if a particular initial decision or decision package d_i is taken may be denoted by $\underset{\sim}{S}_i$, and the subset $\underset{\sim}{S}_i$ of these consisting of acceptable options by $\underset{\sim}{\hat{S}}_i$ (See Figure 3). We can then define the robustness of an initial decision d_i as

$$r(d_i) = n(\hat{\underset{\sim}{S}}_i)/n(\hat{\underset{\sim}{S}})$$

where n( ) is the number of elements in the relevant set.

Clearly the robustness of any initial decision must lie between 0 and 1, since $\underset{\sim}{S}_i$ can be no bigger than $\hat{\underset{\sim}{S}}$. The higher the robustness, the less the initial decision reduces the effective freedom to reconfigure the system in the future.

Multi-future robustness

The definition of robustness given here is in its simplest form and begs a number of questions. Most of these can be met by appropriate answers, but one of the questions will lead on to a refinement of the definition.

The fair but answerable questions concern the lack of definition of the concepts employed. What does the 'number of options left open' mean, for example, in a situation in which the future system could in principle occupy any point on a spectrum of configurations, or where the number of alternatives is effectively infinite? Again, the 'planning horizon' could be chosen at will, and different choices could be expected to produce different robustness scores. Similarly, the notion of an 'acceptable' configuration is inherently subjective. What can an index based on such foundations tell us about flexibility?

The answer is that it can provide information on the *relative* flexibility of alternatives assessed under consistent conditions. The assumptions as to planning horizon and acceptability of options will be those which make sense to those who have the problem and the responsibility for the decision. The selection of a discrete set to represent a continuum of future options will be common to the alternative commitments under analysis. It is, therefore, quite possible to arrive at plausible flexibility rankings for the candidate decisions, and indeed to draw some broad conclusions about the orders of magnitude of differences in flexibility. What will not be possible is to derive a ratio-scale measurement of flexibility which can be traded-off explicitly against other desirable characteristics—short-run performance, for example. Such balancing of incommensurable factors remains the province of human and social judgement, as it should.

The begged question to which this simple definition of robustness provides no answer is: Under what assumptions about environmental conditions has the assessment of 'acceptability' of future options been made? A system configuration, or a policy, which can perform very adequately under some circumstances might make no sense in another future. The simple version of robustness (in practice the first to be developed) does *not* adopt an explicitly multi-future approach to planning.

A case can be made that this does not seriously undermine its usefulness. After all, a robust (under this definition) initial decision package does keep open a wide range of options which provide acceptable performance for one assumed state of the future. It is at least plausible that the more options kept open which are acceptable under the assumed future conditions, the more likely it is that one or more of them will prove to perform tolerably in the conditions which do in the end materialize. This is evidently not a rigorous argument. However, it is not unreasonable, and may be persuasive when time or resources for more extended analysis are lacking. At the least, a (single future) robust decision package can be expected to offer more directions for future development than would a conventional 'optimal' solution.

However, when there is time for fuller analysis this argument can be turned on its head. For a decision package which is in some sense 'multi-future robust' is still *more* likely to offer worthwhile options for development than would a single-future robust commitment. Additionally, we will see, introducing a multi-future perspective has other advantages.

The extension of robustness analysis to the multi-future case is conceptually simple, involving the addition of only one suffix to the previous definition. We now define the robustness of an initial decision or decision package d_i in future F_j as

$$r_{ij} = n\,(\hat{\underline{S}}_{ij})\,/\,n\,(\hat{\underline{S}}_j)$$

where $\hat{\underline{S}}_j$ is the set of all options acceptable under the conditions of future F_j, and $\hat{\underline{S}}_{ij}$ is the subset of those options which are attainable if decision d_i is taken. However, the simplicity is bought at a price. Whereas $r(d_i)$ gave us a linear array (vector) of robustness scores corresponding to the alternative decisions, the multi-future form gives us a two-dimensional matrix (r_{ij}) as shown in Figure 4. There is no longer a comparison of the alternative decision packages in terms of flexibility which is obvious at a glance. Instead there is a richer and more complex picture to analyse.

Consider the illustrative example of Figure 5. The structured information displayed here is no use for giving an answer, but may be valuable in starting a discussion. It is unlikely that decision package d_1 can be entertained; if futures F_2 and F_3 were regarded as of sufficient significance to be represented in the analysis, then the absence of any acceptable options at all under both these futures must be a crippling handicap.

However, other cases are less clear. Decision d_2 might look attractive if future F_1 was regarded as a relatively remote possibility. Further analysis and discussion might focus on this issue, including any leverage which could be exerted to prevent future F_1 from materializing. Decision d_3

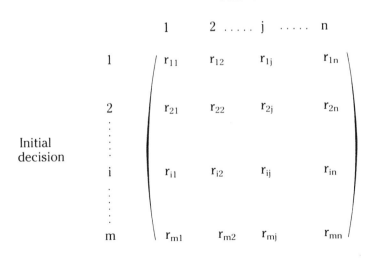

Figure 4
Multi-future robustness matrix, r_{ij}

Future

	F_1	F_2	F_3
d_1	1	0	0
d_2	0	0.9	0.8
d_3	0.6	0.6	0.6
d_4	0.8	0.8	0.3

Decision

Figure 5
An example of a robustness matrix

provides reasonable all-round coverage. How important is it felt to have many alternative options *within* each possible future? Perhaps for a future regarded as less plausible, an insurance policy of maintaining at least one viable option will be regarded as adequate. Is future F_3 such a case in point? Then decision d_4 might have the edge. And so on.

This example should bring out the potential benefit of multi-future robustness analysis. This is not that it tells those who have the problem what to do—there will in any case be many other factors to consider. It is, rather, that it can initiate a process of reflection and research, aimed at clarifying participants' understanding of the nature of the predicament which confronts them.

Ways of working with robustness

The calculation of robustness scores between 0 and 1 is not an end in itself. Robustness analysis is rather a way of working which focuses attention on the possibilities (not probabilities) inherent in a situation. There is no single algorithm-like method, giving a prescription of which analysis to perform next. The analysis will be at its most productive when it responds successively to the unfolding shape of the problem situation—both the logic of the complexities and uncertainties, and the developing perceptions which the earlier stages of the analysis have helped to activate. Some of the variety of ways of bringing out the structure of interrelationship of threats, opportunities, and decisions will be illustrated in this section.

A hypothetical example will help explore some of the potential of this approach. Consider a situation in which decisions to transform a system of interest are expected to be made in a number of stages. Early decisions

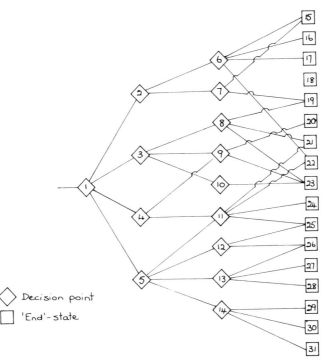

Figure 6
A three-stage planning problem

may foreclose certain future options; there may also be alternative decision routes to what is effectively the same system configuration. Figure 6 illustrates such a case, with three stages to the planning horizon. We are poised at decision point 1. The choice to be made is not which of the 'end'-states 15 to 31 should be selected, but which of the decision packages, leading to decision points 2 to 5, to commit to.

Suppose that those confronting the situation are happy to accept one view F_1 of the future of the environment of the system which concerns them. However, they feel that three categories (desirable/acceptable/unacceptable) rather than two are needed to characterize future performance. Their valuations are shown in Figure 7.

It would be possible to calculate single future robustness scores based on both the top category (two elements) or the top two categories (five elements). However, one can effectively combine the two analyses by listing for each initial decision the numbers of desirable (D) and acceptable (A) options kept open, as in Table 1. On this basis initial decision 5 has the edge.

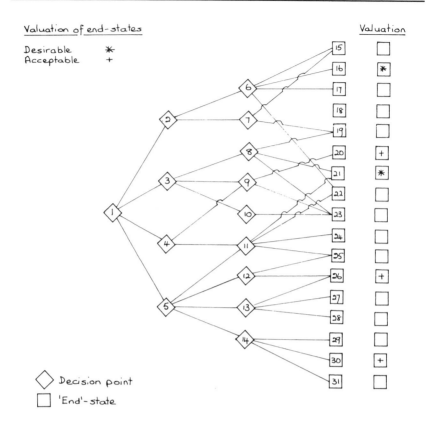

Valuation of end-states   Valuation

Desirable   *
Acceptable   +

◇ Decision point

☐ 'End'-state

Figure 7
A three-stage planning problem—with end-states valued

Alternatively, it may be felt that the 'unacceptable' group is too broad, and should be subdivided into marginal, undesirable and catastrophic, as shown in Figure 8. This concern, about how disadvantageous some of the available options might be, is undoubtedly a factor in many situations. Why? Because those engaged in forward thinking about the system are less than certain that they will be able to determine all decisions which may be taken about it in the future. Otherwise they would only need to consider the number and variety of good options: with enough of these to hand, they would never have to choose a bad one. There would, therefore, be no reason to worry about them.

Lack of future control could be a concern where an opposing faction might come to power only a little way down the road. Or the decision makers might fear that negative options carelessly left open might be

206

Table 1
Preferred options left open by alternative decisions

Initial decision	Options left open	
	D	A
2	1	0
3	1	1
4	1	1
5	1	2*

Key
D desirable
A acceptable

*One option accessible by multiple routes.

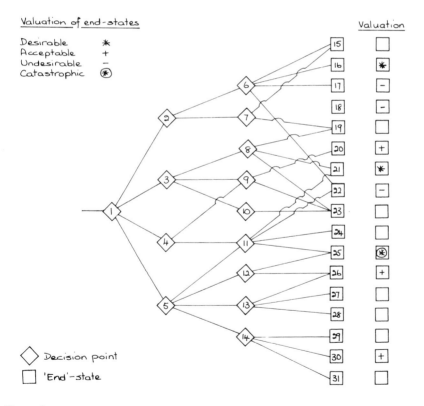

Valuation of end-states

Desirable　　　*
Acceptable　　　+
Undesirable　　　−
Catastrophic　　⊛

Valuation

◇ Decision point
☐ 'End'-state

Figure 8
A three-stage planning problem—with revised end-state valuation.

Table 2
Preferred and non-preferred options left open by alternative decisions

Initial decision	Options left open				
	D	A	U	C	
					Key
2	1	0	2	0	D desirable
3	1	1	0	0	A acceptable
4	1	1	1	1	U undesirable
5	1	2*	1	1*	C catastrophic

*One option accessible by multiple routes.

imposed on them by superior authority—for example, by governmental legislation or pressure. Attention to possible future bad outcomes could also make sense for the relatively powerless in a conflictual situation. Their leverage is limited—all the more reason for analysing current alternatives for the extent to which each curtails the scope for future distress.

Returning to our example, Figure 8 can now be summarized as in Table 2. This can now be analysed in more than one way. If only the preferred options (D and A) are taken into account, we have seen that initial decision 5 offers more future flexibility. But it also offers more opportunities than the others for eventual negative outcomes. If closing-off non-preferred options is the sole criterion then initial decision 3 is a clear winner. If, as will be most usual, some balance between threat and opportunity is appropriate, then Table 2 provides simply structured information to clarify the choices. Supplementary analyses can help to make the choice still clearer. For example, initial decision 4 can be discarded. It is dominated by decision 3, which keeps open identical preferred end-states, but has no compatible non-preferred options. Evidently in cases such as this, robustness analysis goes beyond a concern with keeping options open. Rather than option preservation we now have a broader focus on 'option management' under conditions of uncertainty.

So far, however, our example has been based on a single version of the future environment. If alternative futures can be identified (as in Figure 9, a four future case) then the analysis above can be extended further. For example, robustness scores based on the combined sets of desirable and acceptable end-states can be calculated, as shown in Figure 10(a). These indicate a clear flexibility advantage to initial decisions 4 and 5, but with decision 3 performing respectably.

The other, negative side of the coin can be inspected through the complementary concept of 'debility' (Caplin and Kornbluth, 1975). This is

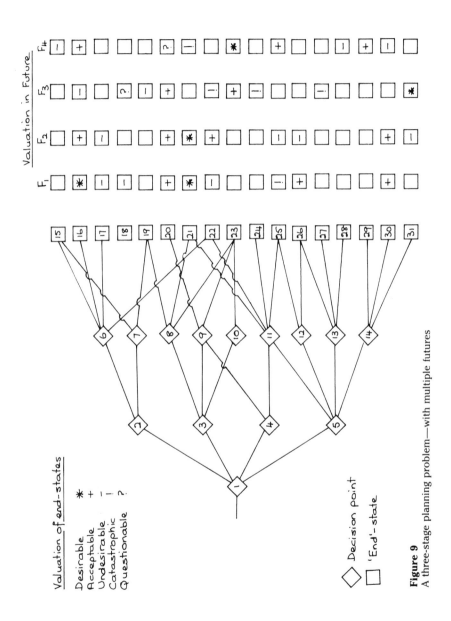

Figure 9
A three-stage planning problem—with multiple futures

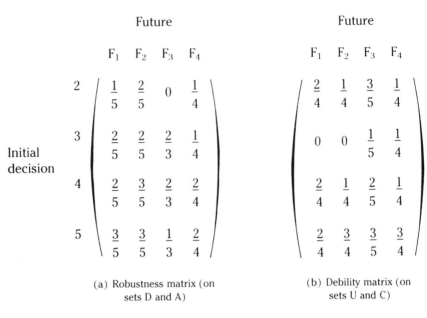

$$\text{Initial decision}\quad \begin{array}{c} 2 \\ 3 \\ 4 \\ 5 \end{array} \left(\begin{array}{cccc} \dfrac{1}{5} & \dfrac{2}{5} & 0 & \dfrac{1}{4} \\[2mm] \dfrac{2}{5} & \dfrac{2}{5} & \dfrac{2}{3} & \dfrac{1}{4} \\[2mm] \dfrac{2}{5} & \dfrac{3}{5} & \dfrac{2}{3} & \dfrac{2}{4} \\[2mm] \dfrac{3}{5} & \dfrac{3}{5} & \dfrac{1}{3} & \dfrac{2}{4} \end{array} \right)$$

(a) Robustness matrix (on sets D and A)

$$\left(\begin{array}{cccc} \dfrac{2}{4} & \dfrac{1}{4} & \dfrac{3}{5} & \dfrac{1}{4} \\[2mm] 0 & 0 & \dfrac{1}{5} & \dfrac{1}{4} \\[2mm] \dfrac{2}{4} & \dfrac{1}{4} & \dfrac{2}{5} & \dfrac{1}{4} \\[2mm] \dfrac{2}{4} & \dfrac{3}{4} & \dfrac{3}{5} & \dfrac{3}{4} \end{array} \right)$$

(b) Debility matrix (on sets U and C)

Figure 10
Option maintenance analysis

defined as the number of unsatisfactory end-states still attainable after an initial decision, expressed as a ratio of all such end-states. If we treat both 'undesirable' and 'castastrophic' end-states as unsatisfactory, the results are shown in Figure 10(b).

In contrast to robustness, it is *low* debility scores which are preferred. The superiority in this respect of decision 3 is evident. Whether this edge is sufficient to overcome the robustness advantage of decisions 4 and 5 is a matter for debate. The outcome will depend on perceptions of the plausibility of particular futures, and of whether sufficient control will be exercisable in the future to block off undesirable avenues left open by the current decision.

Sharp-eyed readers will have noticed in Figure 9 some notation for a new concept, the 'questionable' end-state whose attractiveness or otherwise in some future is uncertain or disputed. The corresponding '?' signals an area for possible further research and discussion, if that valuation seems capable of influencing current decisions. This is evidently not the case for end-state 18 in future F_3—the end-state is inaccessible from *any* of the initial decisions under consideration, so that its possible valuation is an irrelevance. The '?' for end-state 20 under future F_4 might be more significant, as this end-state is consistent with initial decision 3—a positive valuation could make the argument for decision 3 look stronger.

The 'query' symbol to flag possible further investigations has been borrowed from the Strategic Choice approach (see Chapter 6). The query can be used quite generally—for example to condition links of accessibility between successive stages of the decision process.

There will be many planning situations in which such uncertainties about links between stages become the exception rather than the rule. The time-scale may be too long for detailed causal connections and constraints to be convincing. The numbers of alternative decision paths may escalate beyond computational feasibility. And so on. Any of these conditions will rule out a method based on the elaborated sequential logic of Figures 6 to 9.

This difficulty can be resolved by retrenching back to the basic minimal requirements for robustness analysis—the identifiability of initial decision packages, of alternative future states of the system subject to intervention, and of relations of compatibility between them. These are sufficient to

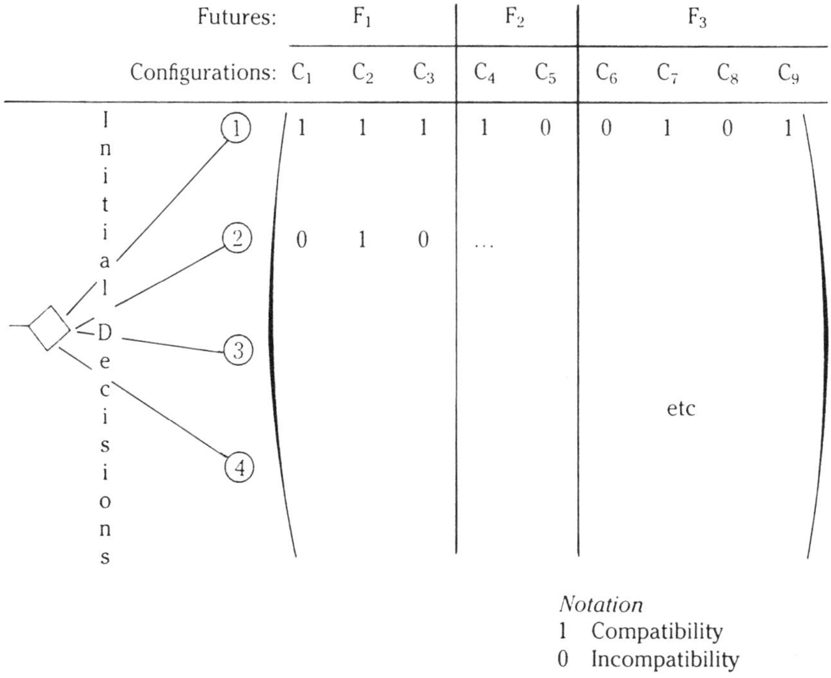

Futures:	F_1			F_2		F_3			
Configurations:	C_1	C_2	C_3	C_4	C_5	C_6	C_7	C_8	C_9
①	1	1	1	1	0	0	1	0	1
②	0	1	0	...					
③									
④					etc				

Initial Decisions

Notation
1 Compatibility
0 Incompatibility

Figure 11
Example of a compatibility matrix

maintain the bifocal approach, of assessing immediate commitments, but in terms of options left open for longer term development.

There are various ways in which this form of analysis can be structured. (For one example, see Best, Parston and Rosenhead, 1986). One approach is to generate plausible 'configurations' for the system which would function harmoniously in particular futures. For each future either one or a number of such configurations might be identified. The compatibility between each candidate initial decision and each of these configurations can then be assessed on a Yes/No basis, or a Yes/No/? basis. The results can be organized in a 'compatibility matrix', such as that illustrated in Figure 11.

'Incompatibility' in this situation cannot be taken as synonymous with 'impossibility'. The assessment must be based, rather, on the consistency of an initial decision with the developmental direction implied by a particular configuration.

The information in a compatibility matrix such as that in Figure 11 lends itself readily to the construction of a multi-future robustness matrix. However, one should not be in too much of a hurry. It may be that one configuration (or more), though generated as appropriate to a particular future, may be seen as an entirely adequate design for other futures. In this case the appropriate columns should be replicated under the corresponding futures before the robustness of initial decisions is computed.

Methodology for robustness

Much of the above discussion has proceeded, necessarily, in a virtual vacuum. In order to demonstrate clearly the various technical possibilities, the issues involved in operationalizing the approach have been neglected. However, in the realer world lists of candidate decisions or alternative futures cannot be summoned up by the magic words 'consider' or 'suppose'.

An earlier paper (Rosenhead, 1980b) has discussed some of these methodological issues at length. It is a possible reference for those who would like a more detailed presentation than can be afforded here—though it is one based heavily on the assumption that feasible decision paths can be traced through. The version of the methodology outlined in Figure 12 removes this restriction, and incorporates some other developments.

The upper part of Figure 12 is concerned with identifying initial decision packages. The lower part deals with possible future configurations of the system, and how they will behave in different futures. The left-hand side

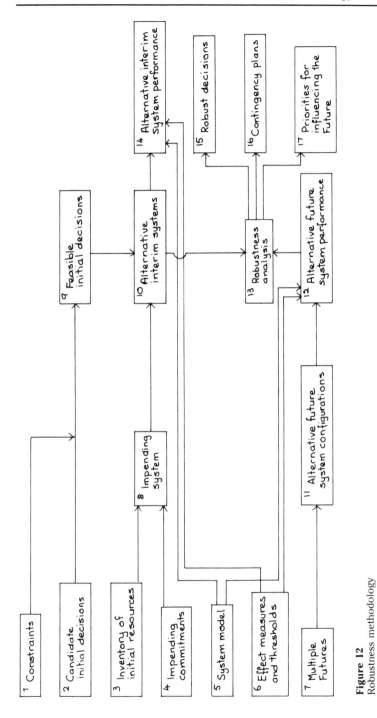

Figure 12
Robustness methodology

consists of input to the analysis, and the right-hand side presents the outputs from the analysis.

That is the quick tour. A more informative trip round the methodology might start with activities 3 and 4. Making sure that one is informed not only of the details of the existing system but also of confirmed changes which are in the pipeline is a wise precaution. Together they specify the 'impending system' (activity 8)—which will shortly be in existence independent of any of the next wave of decisions currently under discussion.

Possible initial decisions (activity 2) may be generated by those knowledgeable about the system in question or with expertise gained on similar systems; by identification of deficiencies in system performance, whether by observation or by comparative analysis; or by solicited or unsolicited proposals from interested parties. These elements will need to be composed into a manageable number of coherent alternative packages which make sense operationally and politically, and do not violate budgetary or other constraints (activity 1). Each of these alternative decision packages (activity 9) will impact on the impending system to give one possible version of the 'interim system' which will then function for some period (activity 10).

The identification of system deficiencies will already have focused attention on the need for clarity on appropriate measures of performance. In general, and especially in public sector or multiple interest group situations, such performance will be multi-dimensional. On any one dimension, the attributes of system behaviour may be rated into ordered categories, or measured on interval or ratio scales. Whatever type of measurement is adopted, it will be necessary also to identify one or more threshold levels—significant boundaries between less and more acceptable system performance (activity 6).

Robustness analysis is predicated on an ability to link decision to future consequences at some level of detail which can guide action. The system model (activity 5) organizes such understanding of cause–effect relationships. It may be a relatively sophisticated mathematical model—for example, the transportation method of linear programming used to simulate revised distribution patterns corresponding to alternative locations for an additional factory (Gupta and Rosenhead, 1968). Or it may be a comparatively simple accounting tool, balancing augmented health services against projected population forecasts (Best, Parston and Rosenhead, 1986).

One further basic input to robustness analysis is the identification of future states of the environment within which the system may have to function (activity 7). The analysis will become unwieldy and over-theoretical if it attempts to employ more than a handful of sharply contrasting alternative futures. When analytic resources are limited, a single future may serve—either a *status quo* assumption or a simple trend projection. (The justification for this short cut has been discussed earlier.)

A range of methods for identifying alternative possible futures is available, from simple brainstorming to scenario construction (Wack, 1985). The DELPHI approach can only generate expert consensus on one future state; however, if DELPHI respondents are segmented (for example, using cluster analysis—Best *et al.*, 1986), then sub-groups can be liberated to produce contrasting futures.

Robustness analysis involves the matching of early commitments against differentially advantageous future system configurations under a range of plausible future conditions. These future configurations may be constructed out of elemental decision components such as those which are candidates for immediate implementation. However, in the version of the methodology summarized in Figure 12, for each future one or more configurations are generated which could function adequately and appropriately within it (activity 11).

The performance of each of these configurations in any of the alternative futures can now be assessed via the model (activity 12). It is by testing the compatibility of these configurations with alternative interim systems (from activity 10) that robustness analysis (activity 13) can proceed.

There is no single output of robustness analysis. It is a format for exploring certain aspects of planning problems under uncertainty, rather than a method for finding an answer. Some of the types of structured information which participants may hope to have by the time they quit the process are:

- A short list of possible decision packages rated in terms of their robustness against a variety of futures (activity 15).
- A prediction of the shorter term performance improvement to be expected from implementing each of these decision packages (activity 14).
- Some guidelines as to what actions by other interests linked to the planning process would be more or less beneficial; these can serve as the basis for contingengy plans, or for incentives to encourage mutually advantageous behaviour (activity 16).
- An assessment of which of the alternative futures the system, given its current condition and evolution, is particularly vulnerable to; this can focus lobbying or opinion-forming efforts on trying to influence the occurrence of futures which, in the light of current strategy, would present particular threats or opportunities.

This brief resumé of the methodology is undoubtedly misleading. The presentation is both too elaborate, and not elaborate enough. It is insufficiently detailed because it does not specify the many necessary or possible interdependencies between activities. At an obvious level, relevant aspects of possible futures must feature in the system model. Less obviously, identified decision packages can be used to generate ideas for alternative futures, and vice versa. And so on.

The account of robustness methodology has been too elaborate, because it gives the impression of a prescribed and remorseless process, a sequence of hoops which must each be negotiated in turn and with due deference. The reality of practice is quite different. Problems can be approached in an *ad hoc* fashion, skipping over apparently daunting procedures on the basis of common sense, and producing provisional insights on the backs of only a few envelopes. Work done in one analytic area will spark off activity elsewhere in no predefined order. Analytic progress is as likely to provoke a re-examination of assumptions (with further analysis to follow) as to lead mechanically to a pre-ordained point of decision. The benefit of the process lies not merely (or principally) in the identification of robust decisions. At least as important is the achievement of the confidence necessary to take and live with those decisions. Robustness analysis and its associated technology can provide a framework for a debate in which that confidence is generated.

Discussion

Many of the general issues on the application of robustness analysis have already emerged in the preceeding sections. More will be aired in the following chapter. Only a few further aspects will be treated here.

First, an encouragement to those who have not previously employed robustness analysis. It is technically very simple. If, after you have done it, you describe your work to others, the most likely response (I have found) is 'What's so special about that?' or 'Surely that conclusion was obvious from the beginning?' or even 'I took essentially the same approach three years ago standing on my head, and never thought it was worth writing up'. Do not be put down. It will only appear obvious and commonsensical if you have fought your way to an appropriate structuring of the problematic situation.

The presentation of robustness analysis in previous sections has verged on the cumbersome. This is because of the need to handle a variety of different problem situations. There is no study in which all of these variations have been employed. Some of the variations have as yet failed to find employment in any practical application. Conversely, the language and logic are sufficiently general that any new application is quite likely to throw up a formulation which is in some way unique.

It is possible to become a robustness bore, seeing problems of uncertainty and flexibility in the most diverse circumstances. It may become necessary to remind yourself that flexibility is a means, not an end in itself. Almost always flexibility will be one of a number of considerations, among which those who must live with the consequences of decisions will have to strike their own balance. Serendipity and symbiosis not withstanding, there will in general be a cost of some kind for the maintenance of flexibility.

Even when the aspect of the problem under consideration is indeed that of flexibility, it is possible to become fixated on the available measures of flexibility rather than its reality. Each extra available option adds an equal amount to the robustness score, but that does not mean that each option has the same practical significance. Decisions need to be based on the actual options left open, not their number. For example, where options are composed of design choices in a number of interconnected decision areas (as in Strategic Choice), having a wide variety of choice in one decision area but none anywhere else might give rise to a healthy looking robustness score. This would scarcely be a good prescription for avoiding vulnerability to uncertainty. The robustness score may be regarded as a convenient *indicator* of flexibility, but its calculation does not absolve one from the need to investigate its quality and significance.

References

Best, G., Parston, G., and Rosenhead, J. (1986). 'Robustness in practice: the regional planning of health services', *J. Opl Res. Soc.*, **37**, 463–78.

Bonder, S. (1979). 'Changing the future of operations research', *Opns Res.*, **27**, 209–24.

Caplin, D. A., and Kornbluth, J. S. H. (1975). 'Multiple investment planning under uncertainty', *Omega*, **3**, 423–41.

Centre for Environmental Studies (1970). *The LOGIMP Experiment*, CES, London.

Emery, F. E., and Trist, E. L. (1965). 'The causal texture of organisational environments', *Hum. Relat.*, **18**, 21–3.

Etzioni, A. (1968). *The Active Society: a theory of societal and political processes*, Collier-Macmillan, London.

Evans, J. S. (1987). *Strategical Flexibility: a governance principle for punctuated equilibria*, Menlo Park, California, mimeo.

Friend, J. K., and Jessop, W. N. (1969). *Local Government and Strategic Choice: an Operational Research approach to the processes of public planning*, Tavistock, London.

Gupta, S. K., and Rosenhead, J. (1968). 'Robustness in sequential investment decisions', *Mgmt Sci.*, **15**, 18–29.

Holling, C. S. (1973). *Resilience and Stability of Ecological Systems*, International Institute of Applied Systems Analysis, Laxenburg, Austria.

Lee, A. M. (1976). 'Past futures', *Opl Res. Q.*, **27**, 147–53.

Rosenhead, J. (1980a). 'Planning under uncertainty 1: the inflexibility of methodologies', *J. Opl Res. Soc.*, **31**, 209–16.

Rosenhead, J. (1980b). 'Planning under uncertainty 2: a methodology for robustness analysis', *J. Opl Res. Soc.*, **31**, 331–41.

Sandberg, A. (1976). *The Limits to Democratic Planning*, LiberForlag, Stockholm.

Wack, P. (1985). 'Scenarios: uncharted waters ahead', *Harvard Business Review* Sept.–Oct., 73–89.

9
Robustness to the first degree

Jonathan Rosenhead

The literature on the practice of operational research abounds with, one might almost say consists of, accounts of decision making by large organizations. Reports of robustness analysis largely follow this pattern, dealing, for example, with breweries (Gupta and Rosenhead, 1968), chemical plants (Caplin and Kornbluth, 1975), and health systems (Best, Parston and Rosenhead, 1986). Reading between most of the lines, one can almost see the burly hard-nosed managers, waiting to be convinced before committing the sort of resources an individual worker cannot expect to earn with a lifetime of labour.

The subject of this chapter is quite different. She is, or rather was, a schoolgirl of fourteen. Her decisions would not cause concrete to rise or stock markets to fall. Her problem was—what subjects to choose for study leading to General Certificate of Education 'Ordinary Level' examinations.* But first, of course, she had to see that it was a problem.

---

*Non-British readers may find some clarification of the public examination system in England and Wales helpful. Until 1988, when new arrangements came into force, the GCE was the nationally recognized qualification for those leaving school and/or hoping to enter further or higher education. Candidates for the Ordinary ('O') Level examination were typically about 16 years old. A candidate might take separate examinations in any number of subjects, though rarely more than ten in practice. Those wishing to continue formal education would then study, normally for two further years, for a more focused set of two or three Advanced ('A') Level examinations. Many pupils at or about 16 sat for a combination of GCE 'O' Level and Certificate of Secondary Education (CSE) examinations. Assessment at grade 1 of a CSE examination was regarded as equivalent to a pass in the same subject at GCE.

Rational Analysis for a Problematic World
Edited by J. Rosenhead. © 1989 John Wiley & Sons Ltd

There are a number of reasons for using this atypical (from an OR perspective) problem situation to illustrate the application of robustness analysis. One is precisely that this *is* unfamiliar territory. If one can erode restrictive stereotypes *en passant*, so much the better. But there are other factors also. One of these is the widely understood nature and limited complexity of Sarah's planning dilemma. This avoids the necessity of describing in detail the specifics of some system which is not the principal focus of attention, but only the vehicle for a journey at a different conceptual level. Another reason is that no complicated technique, be it linear programming or cluster analysis, was performed in even a subsidiary role in this application of robustness analysis. The ground is thus relatively clear, giving unencumbered vision of the target.

The case study which follows does not extract out the 'robustness analysis' bits from their context. What is described is an interactive process of attempting to shape and reshape the recalcitrant material of real life, until we could work out what to do. Robustness analysis provided one important element of the structure we needed.

In loco parentis

Sarah is my stepdaughter. In 1976, as for some years before and after, she formed part of the nuclear family which also included her younger brother Dominic, their mother Gillian, and myself. Relations between Sarah and myself were probably no better than average for step-parents and -children, which in turn are probably no better than the average for parents and their teenage offspring. However, communication was not completely impossible.

In the spring of 1976 Sarah was in the middle of her third year at Holland Park School, a state secondary school in a central London location, catering non-selectively for more than 1800 children with a broad range of academic abilities. We learnt from her, almost by accident, that she had been asked to choose the subjects she wished to study in the subsequent two years, and that she had in fact made up her mind. The subjects she could sit at GCE or CSE at the end of year 5 would be effectively restricted to those selected now.

I cannot now remember the details of Sarah's choice. However, there was a quite striking absence of subjects which appeared likely to give openings to rewarding jobs, more advanced education, or continuing intellectual stimulation. Subjects like photography, drama, home economics were there in plenty, but did not appear to represent any coherent alternative to more academic study. Few of the subjects led to GCE examinations, and some did not lead to CSE exams either.

In discussion with Sarah it emerged that a number of factors had influenced her list—her liking for particular teachers, the inherent interest of particular subjects, what other pupils were choosing, the need to fill up the list. We suggested to her that there might be other ways of deciding, that her choices now might have vocational implications as well as intrinsic interest. (This was not the precise language that we used.) It followed that she should think about the longer term future as well as the next two years of study. However, it emerged that Sarah, like many (most?) children of her age had precious little idea what she might 'do' when grown up.

The problem was beginning to look like one of decision making under uncertainty. There was a need to make commitments now, and the uncertainty about the future suggested that there might be a case for trying to keep options open. In view of my professional interest, I proposed to Sarah that we should see if we could work together to clarify her choices. She agreed to let me try.

The analysis which follows is the product of our work together. In the original published account (Rosenhead, 1978) I claimed that she committed only an hour or so of her time to the process. I now suspect that to be an underestimate—an hour for identifying her future career possibilities, yes, but as much or more again on explaining the method and discussing the results of the analysis. My own additional commitment amounted to a few evenings extracting relevant data on prerequisites for university courses from data sources compiled for other purposes. The whole procedure was over in about a week, as it had to be to meet the school's deadline.

Structured choices

Holland Park School issued a booklet, *Choices in the Fourth Year*, from which the constraints on choice could be determined. English (leading to examinations in English Language and/or Literature) and Social Education were compulsory. Pupils in addition had to select one option from each of the six option lists in Table 1. All the subjects in one column would be taught at the same time, so that two choices from the same column would be infeasible. The risk of clashes ruling out desired combinations was reduced by the presence of more 'popular' options in two or even three option lists. Various other constraints might come into play—some subjects could accommodate only a limited number of pupils, and no subject would be taught unless at least 17 pupils opted for it.

Evidently this part of Sarah's problem was well and tightly specified. Even

Table 1
Option lists for fourth-year study

Option 1	Option 2	Option 3	Option 4	Option 5	Option 6
Science Studies	Science Studies	Needlecraft	Geography	Science Studies	Mathematics
Physics	Biology	Metalwork	Science Studies	Chemistry	Geography
Spanish (contd.)	German (contd.)	Engineering	Electronics	Classical Studies	Music
History	German (beginners)	Home Economics	Human Biology	History	European Studies
Home Economics	Mathematics	Child care	Popular Music	Home Economics	Three from
Woodwork	Needlecraft	Environmental Studies	Technical Drawing	Woodwork	1. Electronics or Typing
Art	Metalwork	Photography	Photography	Art	2. Plastics or Dressmaking
	Engineering	Sport	French (contd.)	Home Furnishing and Maintenance	3. Cinematography or Embroidery
			French (beginners)		

(From Rosenhead (1978), reproduced with permission of the Operational Research Society.)

so, the number of possible option combinations (candidate initial decisions) ran well into four figures.

The next step was to make some progress in identifying acceptable 'end-states'. Sarah might not know what she wanted to do with any certainty or clarity, but that did not mean that she had no views. For example, there were plenty of things she definitely did *not* want to be—from accountant to veterinary surgeon.

A session spent with a book called *Careers for Girls* (Miller, 1975) added further definition. She and I went through the book, flicking through the alphabetically organized pages from career to career. Some delayed us for only a matter of seconds, eliciting an instant negative from Sarah. Others caused a pause for reflection, followed by an expression of more or less guarded enthusiasm. In the end there seemed to be three levels of attractiveness, with the possible future occupations categorized as in Table 2. This format of categories emanated more from Sarah than from me. Indeed I had little idea how they might fit into the impending analysis. However, it

Table 2
Desirable occupations

Definitely (Group A)	Quite (Group B)	Marginally (Group C)
Acting	Advertising	Agriculture
Broadcasting	Air Stewardess	Beautician
Film Production	Archaeology	Housemother
Interior Decoration	Art and Industrial	Medical Laboratory
Journalism	Design	Technician
Stage Management	Barrister	Music
	Dancing	Sociology
	Mechanical Engineering	Technician Engineer
	Fashion	
	Museum and Art Gallery	
	Photography	
	Psychology	
	Social Work	
	Window Display	

(From Rosenhead (1978), reproduced with permission of the Operational Research Society.)

seemed better to reflect Sarah's perceptions as fully as possible, rather than to impose an *a priori* structure based on analytic tractability.

There will be, for any individual, many intervening life events between 'O' levels and eventual career trajectory. These events might include 'A' levels, degree or other post-school studies, false starts in employment, career switches, etc. There are an indefinite number of stages, and of alternatives at each stage. Tracing through all possible life-paths was evidently a non-starter. Instead, the approach adopted was to explore the compatibility of particular careers with specific combinations of 'O' level subjects.

For this exploration I turned again to *Careers for Girls*. For each of the careers the book also listed both minimum qualifications and any necessary training. Some of these prerequisites were expressed in terms of 'O' or 'A' level results—either the total number or specific subjects required. Others were expressed as degree requirements—either for a vocationally related degree, or for a degree in one of a number of broadly relevant subjects. Where both types of prerequisite were provided for a single occupation, it was because there were two types of entry: graduate and non-graduate. For non-graduate entry, I decided to ignore 'A' level requirements, on the assumption that transfer between subjects after 'O' level would be feasible. The resulting summary of information bearing on

Table 3
Prerequisites for desirable occupations

Occupations	No.	\'O\' level prerequisites							Degree
		Eng. Lan.	Eng. Lit.	French	Maths	Physics	Art	Other	
GROUP A									
Acting									
Broadcasting		✓	✓						Econ./Soc. Sci./History/English
Film Production	3	✓		✓					
Interior Decoration	3	✓ or Lit.			✓				
Journalism	5	✓							
Stage Management									
GROUP B									
Advertising	5	✓							or English/Psychology
Air Stewardess		✓						Geog.	
Archaeology					✓			Latin	Archaeology
Art and Industrial Design	4	✓							
Barrister									Law
Dancing									

Mech. Engineering	5	✓		✓		Mech. Eng.
Fashion	5	✓ or Lit. ✓		✓		
Mus. and Art Gallery	4	or Lit. ✓	✓	or Sci.		or Art History/ Art and Design
Photography	4	✓		✓		
Psychology	5	✓		or Sci. ✓		Psychology or Social Science
Social Work					✓	
Window Display	4	✓				
GROUP C						
Agriculture	4	✓ or Lit. ✓		✓ or Sci.		
Beautician	3	✓		or Sci. ✓ or Sci.		
Housemother						
Med. Lab. Technician	4	✓		✓ or Sci.		
Music	5			✓		
Sociology						Sociology
Technician Engineer	4			✓ or Sci.		

(From Rosenhead (1978), reproduced with permission of the Operational Research Society.)

Sarah's possible 26 future occupations is shown in Table 3. Needless to say, a number of heroic approximations, reducing the richness of the real world, were necessary to achieve this condensation.

Careers for Girls had taken us quite a long way. But it provided no mechanism for converting degree prerequisites into 'O' level requirements —though evidently 'O' levels (as well as 'A' levels) are generally necessary to gain entry to universities. To effect this mapping I turned to the *Compendium* published by the Association of Commonwealth Universities (Committee of Vice-Chancellors and Principals, 1975). This copious volume listed all first degrees available at British universities (but not polytechnics), the general requirements for entry to each university, and the specific requirements for each course of study there. Of course, the degrees so listed were those to be offered in 1976–7. Though none of us had any idea in what year, if any, Sarah would commence university studies, we were all quite clear that she was not precocious enough to gain entry in the next six months. However, degree courses are not listed, because not decided, half a decade or more in advance. So the *Compendium* for 1976–7 was the best we could do.

A number of obstacles loomed up, obscuring the map. The first was that entry requirements for a particular course at a particular university were generally expressed in terms of a minimum *number* of 'O' levels, plus a specification of particular *subjects* at 'A' level. This obstacle was side-stepped by assuming that if a particular 'A' level was called for, then the pupil (that is, Sarah) would need to take the corresponding 'O' level.

It may seem obvious, with hindsight, that this flatly contradicts the assumption on 'O' level–'A' level transfer made for non-graduate entry requirements. However, it was not obvious at the time, nor has anyone commented on it since, although this application of robustness analysis to Sarah's education has received a good deal of public exposure.

Of course, one could produce rationalizations for differences in subject switching behaviour between those intending direct entry to an occupation and their university-bound contemporaries. But I cannot swear that I had such considerations in mind, because I cannot now remember. It is more plausible, however, to believe that the contrasting assumptions were made for reasons of convenience. Non-degree entry prerequisites were most commonly specified in terms of 'O' levels, while for degree entry 'A' level requirements predominated.

Such pragmatic considerations are not unreasonable in what must of necessity be rough-and-ready analyses. Both time and resources place constraints on the detail and sophistication of what can be achieved. So too does the need to keep the argument transparent, so that the logic can be appropriated by the client. In the end the effects of the questionable assumptions may well be swamped by other factors. The balance between completeness and convenience must in general, be a matter for analytic judgement.

The other major obstacle in the way of converting university entrance conditions into 'O' level subject requirements was that universities were, and are, perversely different from each other. Consider law degrees. These were on offer from 29 universities. A sizeable minority required only four unspecified 'O' levels. However, the University of Warwick required five, and specified English Language, an arts subject, and Mathematics or a science. Other universities fell between these extremes. The same pattern of diversity recurred in all subjects.

How should this difficulty be tackled? One possibility would be to find the set of 'O' levels which would meet the requirements of all 29 universities—but the result would be so bulky a compilation of subjects as to make any child turn round and drop out. And in any case, no one needs to go to 29 universities. Another possibility would be to specify only enough subjects to make sure that at least one university would have her. After all, one is enough. But what if that one changes its admission rules, or changes the course? What if Sarah insists on moving out of London, or refuses to, or her grades aren't good enough? And so on. One is not enough.

The solution adopted was to start with the minimum requirement for a particular degree subject, and note how many universities it would gain

Table 4
'O' level requirements for degree subjects

	No. of Passes	Specified subjects	Coverage
Archaeology	4	English Language, Language	9/14
Art	4	English Language, Modern Language	7/15
Economics	4	English, Mathematics	32/40
Mechanical Engineering	4	English, Mathematics, Physics, Chemistry	27/34
English	4	English Language and Literature, French	20/31
History	4	English, French, History	22/34
Law	4	English	18/29
Psychology	4	English, Mathematics	23/36
Social Work	4	English, Mathematics	17/22
Sociology	4	English, Mathematics	24/29

(From Rosenhead (1978), reproduced with permission of the Operational Research Society.)

access to. Then the effect on university accessibility of adding relevant possible 'O' levels to the minimum requirement, first one at a time, then in pairs, was explored. This process was terminated by the law of diminishing returns.

We can take law degrees as an example. Eight of the 29 courses required only four passes, subjects unspecified. Four passes including English would give access to eighteen of the courses, far more than any other single subject. The best single subject to add to English was Mathematics, and that garnered only a further two courses, raising the total to 20 out of 29. Further extensions of the 'O' level repertoire would produce only a dribble of additional universities in twos or ones. Moving to five 'O' levels adds a few more, mostly Scottish, universities, but only when three or more subjects are specified.

Evidently a very adequate range of future choice among law degrees could be achieved with four 'O' levels of which one is English. This was adopted as the 'O' level entry requirement for law. The requirements for all degrees relevant to Sarah's careers of interest, worked out in the same way, are shown in Table 4.

Coming to conclusions

Tables 3 and 4 contain summary information about what Sarah would have to study to secure direct (non-graduate) or graduate entry to the possible occupations of her choice. But to assist in her pressing present decision problem, further processing was necessary. The next stage was to turn the logic round. Instead of listing what subjects were required for particular occupations, we examined instead which occupations should be accessible with particular combinations of 'O' levels in her satchel.

The first step was to identify the key subjects out of which any 'decision package' of 'O' levels was likely to be constructed. Evidently the subjects which had featured prominently in Tables 3 and 4 more or less nominated themselves—English, French, Mathematics, a science. Table 5 displays for each possible career the decision packages of no more than four subjects which would give access to it. (Multiple decision packages give access to the same career because, for example, if Social Work entry is possible with 'O' levels in English and Mathematics, it is also possible with English, Mathematics, and any other subject or subjects.)

The rather precise information in Table 5 was, however, only achieved through a series of further assumptions, made for simplification or for definiteness. Where there were graduate and non-graduate entry routes, we required a set of 'O' levels which would give access to both. Where there were alternative degree routes, we took as entry requirements a set of subjects giving access to at least 50 per cent of the degree subjects. The *number* of 'O' level passes required was disregarded, on the assumption that any numerical shortfall could be made good in time. These were judgements made, effectively, by myself and Sarah's mother. There is no other justification for them than that they seemed reasonable at the time— and that alternative assumptions could have been investigated in the same way.

From Table 5 it is now straightforward to read off the careers rendered accessible by each decision package of 'O' levels. The number of careers in each attractiveness class maintained by each decision package is shown in Table 6. From this table one can, in effect, compute robustness scores for any subject combination at each of three satisficing levels. Thus if only 'Group A' careers are acceptable, 'English plus a science' has a robustness of 3/6; whereas if a career from any of the three attractiveness classes will do, the robustness of the same package is 10/26 (or 12/26 if Art is also taken).

However, there were more useful things to do with the tabular information. Investigation of possible patterns in the data soon showed that the addition of 'a science' gave little extra career accessibility in any case, and none at all within Group A. So the information was further simplified, as in Table 7, to show the coverage of possible careers provided by a reduced set of decision packages excluding 'a science'. Each of these sets of 'O' levels could then be checked against the timetable constraints of Table 1. Given the incomplete specification of Sarah's programme of study (no more than three subjects out of six), and their mainline nature, there were, of course, no timetable clashes.

Table 7 consists of 'management information' bearing on Sarah's education dilemma. It did not tell her, or us, what she should study. What it did do was provide the evidence on which a balance could be struck between the number of subjects to be selected for their career potential, and the number to be chosen for their current intrinsic interest. In discussion with her mother and myself, with the analysis described here as the focus, Sarah's position on her choice of subjects shifted. In particular she came to see the value of adding to the compulsory English both French and Mathematics—which she had previously doubted. We, for our part, saw more clearly that it was unnecessary to specify all six of Sarah's options on vocational grounds. Broad coverage could be achieved with a relatively small number of strategically selected subjects.

To English, French, and Mathematics Sarah added Art, Biology, History, and Photography on the basis of personal preference. This combination, as can be seen from Table 6, permitted access to all six careers from Group A,

Table 5
Career accessibility in terms of key 'O' level combinations

Careers	Nil	French	Maths	Science	French/Maths	French/Science	Maths/Science	French/Maths/Science	Other required subjects
					Subject combinations (plus English)				
Acting	√	√	√	√	√	√	√	√	
Broadcasting ⎱ or ⎰		√	√		√	√	√	√	History
		√			√	√		√	
Film Production		√	√		√	√		√	
Interior Decoration		√	√	√	√	√	√	√	
Journalism	√	√	√	√	√	√	√	√	
Stage Management	√	√	√	√	√	√	√	√	
Advertising	√	√	√		√	√	√	√	
Air Stewardess	√	√	√		√	√	√	√	Geography
Archaeology		√	√	√	√	√	√	√	Latin
Art and Ind. Design	√	√	√	√	√	√	√	√	
Barrister	√	√	√	√	√	√	√	√	
Dancing	√	√	√	√	√	√	√	√	

Mech. Engineering
Fashion
Mus. and Art Gallery
Photography { or
Psychology
Social Work
Window Display

Agriculture
Beautician
Housemother
Med. Lab. Tech.
Music
Sociology
Techician Eng.

if Physics   if Physics   if Physics

Art

Art

(From Rosenhead (1978), reproduced with permission of the Operational Research Society.)

Table 6
Numbers of careers made accessible by alternative subject combinations

Subject combinations	Career groups		
	Group A	Group B	Group C
English	3	3	2
English, French	4 (plus History, 5)	5 (plus Art, 6) (plus Latin, 6)	2
English, Mathematics	5	7 (plus Art, 9) (plus Geog, 8)	4
English, a science	3	4 (plus Art, 6)	3
English, French, Mathematics	6	9 (plus Art, 10) (plus Geog, 10) (plus Latin, 10)	4
English, French a science	4 (plus History, 5)	7 (plus Art, 8) (plus Latin, 8)	3
English, Maths, a science	5	7 (if Physics, 8) (plus Art, 9 or 10) (plus Geog, 8 or 9)	7
English, French, Maths, a science	6	9 (if Physics, 10) (plus Art, 10 or 11) (plus Geog, 10 or 11) (plus Latin, 10 or 11)	7
Total in group	6	13	7

(From Rosenhead (1978), reproduced with permission of the Operational Research Society.)

ten from Group B, and all seven from Group C. The three inaccessible careers from Group B were effectively excluded by her failure to choose Geography, Latin, and Physics, respectively.

Afterword

At the time of writing this chapter in 1988, Sarah is 26 years old. It might be thought appropriate, therefore, to ask what happened next, and later. In

Table 7
Simplified information on career accessibility

| | Career groups | | |
Subject combinations	Group A	Group B	Group C
English	3	3	2
English, French	4+	5+	2
English, Mathematics	5	7+	4
English, French, Mathematics	6	9+	4
Total in group	6	13	7

(From Rosenhead (1978), reproduced with permission of the Operational Research Society.)

this concluding section I will attempt an answer, as well as pick out some features of the robustness analysis of her 1976 dilemma for further comment.

Life is full of uncertainties. Symbolic of this turbulence is that Sarah is no longer Sarah but Sas. More importantly, in terms of outcome, our analysis in the mid-1970s failed to take account of Mrs Thatcher or the developing crisis of world capitalism. For Sarah/Sas's generation, even a job, let alone a career, proved to be a problematic notion.

What has transpired for Sas in educational/occupational terms is this. Her attempts in French and Mathematics proved unavailing, but she secured 'O' level or 'O' level equivalent passes in English Language, English Literature, Art and History, and in Sociology which she added to her studies extra-murally in Year 5. Sas decided to stay on at school, and studied for and achieved passes in 'A' level Sociology, Politics, and History. This qualified her for admission to degree-level studies, but she declined to apply; she entered instead on an extended period of introspection, personal crisis, and unemployment.

Organizing a women-only housing cooperative brought her eventually into contact with a housing association, which is itself part of a cluster of community work organizations operating with young people in West London. For the past four years she has been working for them, first as an outreach community worker, and subsequently in a variety of roles.

So Sas has ended up, for the time-being at least, in one of the Group B (quite attractive) careers she identified at age 14. Alert readers who have already consulted Table 5 will be aware that this would appear to be an impossibility, without Mathematics 'O' level. The anomaly is, though, only apparent. Social work is a dual entry level career. Table 5 records the more stringent prerequisites for entry to be possible by both routes; Sas's non-graduate entry (see Table 3) does not require mathematics.

What has been happening to Sas since the moment of decision reconstructed in this chapter actually has precious little bearing on the validity of the method used. I summarize it here principally to dispel any doubt which silence on the subject might otherwise have provoked. This one-dimensional slice of life history does nevertheless raise a valuable issue. The question is: If the result of the analysis was to persuade Sas to study French and Mathematics, in both of which she failed to get 'O' level qualifications, wasn't the analysis a waste of time?

The answer is, I don't think so, and neither does Sas. It is not only decisions which emerge from the engagement between analyst and client. The process may be as significant as the product. In this case I believe the process of collaborating over her education choices may have contributed to a gradual improvement in our relationship. More significantly, Sas has stated on a number of occasions that the analysis of her 'O' level subjects was one of the turning points in her process of growing up. She came to see, not only that what she did now would affect her options in the future, but also that she could understand the connections well enough to make informed choices. It was a stage in feeling able to assume responsibility over her own life.

This empowering aspect of appropriate analysis is at least as important as any particular decisions which may emerge from it. Thus almost any educationalist or parent could have asserted to a child that English, French, and Mathematics are the three key 'O' level subjects. The result of our analysis was that Sas did not have to take this on trust. She understood why, so that the decisions became hers rather than ours. She could, in principle, have used the logic to explore the consequences of her subsequent educational decisions.

I am fairly sure that this did not happen at any conscious level. However, the basic logic was used again, and more than once. In 1980 Sarah's younger brother Dominic in turn confronted the choice of his 'O' level subjects, though with differences. English, Mathematics, Social Education, and a science were now all compulsory, and the simultaneously timetabled options lists had shrunk to four in number. The school had reduced in size, and some option combinations (for example History with Physics) which had previously been possible were so no longer. Other changes had also occurred in the interim—for example *Careers for Girls* had been retitled *Equal Opportunities*. But the principle difference was that Dominic was not Sarah.

Dominic was more academically oriented than Sarah. His career choices were similar in number to hers, but more tightly focused on 'professional' occupations. Furthermore, his preferences seemed to cluster them roughly into four groups (definite/likely/possible/unlikely), rather than three. Most significantly, he identified a first choice of subjects which gave us no qualms on vocational grounds. But he nevertheless had a problem. He doubted his ability to pass French and Mathematics, both of which were on his list. How crucial to his ambitions was success in these two examinations? A variant of the method developed for Sarah proved helpful. With this we were able to explore the reduction in career options resulting from failure to secure passes in either or both subjects. After passing eight 'O' levels well (but not French which he balked at) we used a further variant to examine the effects of alternative 'A' level choices.

Before this second bout with Dominic, however, I had worked with my niece Annabel on *her* choice of 'O' levels. She attended a nearby girls' public (that is, private) school with a high academic reputation. Her decision situation was different again. She was studying ten subjects, but the school would not permit her to be examined in so many. She had to find one, and preferably two, to drop. There was a lack of meeting of minds between herself and her parents on what should be sacrificed—Latin? Geography? Chemistry? Art? I was turned to by mutual agreement, as a possible way of breaking the log-jam. But in the end they resolved the issue themselves before the analysis had proceeded very far.

The main purpose of these digressions is not to introduce the reader to my extended family. It is, rather, to indicate the flexible nature of this approach to flexibility. Almost any relevant problem situation will present its own unique features. Only the very basic framework of sequentiality and option preservation (or management) is common to all applications. Particular formulations of rich variety emerge out of the combination of objective circumstances, the subjectivity of the client, and the relationship between client and analyst.

Certainly the case study of Sarah's 'O' levels has features all its own. The methodology which we evolved in use is shown in Figure 1. Evidently this bears little overt resemblance to the generic methodology sketched out in Figure 12 of the previous chapter. Interpretation can, however, reveal some regularities.

Various activities in the generic model do not feature in the analysis of Sarah's problem. The identification of an impending system (activities 3, 4, 8) was unnecessary as there were no decisions in the pipeline. Multiple futures (activity 7) were not considered—the uncertainties being managed were of Friend and Jessop's type UV (uncertainty as to values) rather than UR. Alternative interim systems (activity 10) and their performance (activity 14) did not feature, as the initial decisions as to 'O' levels were only instrumentalities towards future careers. They did not define operating systems valued for themselves. Sarah had no illusions that she could influence the context within which her decisions would become operative

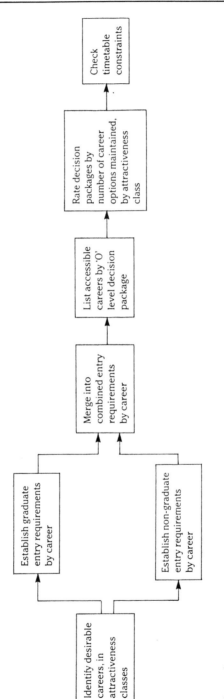

Figure 1
Methodology employed for Sarah's 'O' level choice

(activity 17), nor did we develop contingency plans (activity 16)—though we did in Dominic's case. The remaining activities can be mapped loosely on to Figure 1—but as the 'system model' is of compatibility with desired careers rather than of acceptable performance, it connects rather differently. Robustness methodology, evidently, must be regarded as an enabling framework for both analyst and client, not a prescribed straitjacket.

The integral role of the model, evident in Sarah's case as in other applications of robustness analysis, links the approach clearly to the OR tradition. OR models can in general be used in two ways—as optimizing tools for recommending decisions which are in some sense 'best', or as option scanning devices. Robustness analysis has been used on occasions in the former mode, though with 'best' reinterpreted. In Sarah's case, however, the role of the model is clearly limited to the exploration of 'what if . . .' questions about the consequences of alternative actions. Valuations of these consequences are excluded as external to the function of the model—they are the prerogative of the decision maker.

The decision-aiding approach depends crucially on its accessibility to those whose problem it is. Sarah was, aged 14, the antithesis of the normal OR client, the technically qualified or experienced manager, accustomed to the depersonalized manipulation of capital or human resources. She, therefore, posed a particularly severe test for the transparency of the robustness approach, which it appeared to pass.

Sarah was an unusual client for OR not only in her youth and limited experience, but in her gender. Just how unusual was brought home to me when I submitted the original account of this work for publication in Britain's principal operational research journal. The paper was accepted for publication; but when the proofs arrived from the printers, I found that 'she' had everywhere been replaced by 'he'. Enquiry revealed that this was not an aberration of some deranged compositor. It was a deliberate act by the editor in compliance with the house style, which called for all decision makers to be male. Publication without change of Sarah's sex was eventually agreed. But only on condition that a footnote be inserted, explaining that very similar methods would work for a boy.

This bizarre anecdote does bring out the restricted nature of OR's traditional clientele, which has been commented on elsewhere (Rosenhead, 1986). More recently there have been encouraging moves to extend the range of the subject's clients to include community groups. Transparency of methods will be at a premium. The relative accessibility of robustness analysis to Šarah suggests, therefore, that it could have a place in the repertoire of those practising community OR.

For there are a number of parallels between Sarah's life situation and those of community groups. They share a non-managerial status, and, in general, a lack of socialization into the ways of bureaucracy and processed knowledge. Community groups, too, exist to protect the interests of their members, with few resources to control except their own lives. Success for Community OR will depend on its practitioners' ability to establish committed relations with their clients; and to eschew technical solutions in favour of illuminating structures. Within this context robustness analysis may have useful services to offer. It is no easy task to keep open the options of the weak in a hostile world.

References

Best, G., Parston, G., and Rosenhead, J. (1986). 'Robustness in practice: the regional planning of health services', *J. Opl Res. Soc.*, **37**, 463–78.

Caplin, D. A., and Kornbluth, J. S. H. (1975). 'Multiple investment planning under uncertainty', *Omega*, **3**, 423–41.

Committee of Vice-Chancellors and Principals of the United Kingdom (1975). *The Compendium of University Entrance Requirements for First Degree Courses in the United Kingdom in 1976–7*, Association of Commonwealth Universities, London.

Gupta, S. K., and Rosenhead, J. (1968). 'Robustness in sequential investment decisions', *Mgmt Sci.*, **15**, 18–29.

Miller, R. (1975). *Careers for Girls*, Penguin, Harmondsworth.

Rosenhead, J. (1978). 'An education in robustness', *J. Opl Res. Soc.*, **29**, 105–11.

Rosenhead, J. (1986). 'Custom and practice', *J. Opl Res. Soc.*, **37**, 335–43.

10
The manager as politician and general: the metagame approach to analysing cooperation and conflict

Nigel Howard

Managers must coordinate and lead

Though managements's aims are concrete—to increase market share, cut costs, improve quality, and so on—they are achieved psychologically, by reaching understandings with others. It is when they 'fix' something with someone—a customer, supplier, colleague, boss or subordinate—that managers act as managers.

'Fixing' something means agreeing intentions: she now intends to do 'such and such', he will refrain from 'so and so', and each knows the other's intentions and knows that the other knows them, etc. Giving or accepting directions, reaching agreements, making commitments—all are examples of this process of fixing intentions. Doing something concrete, the technical side, comes later, as agreed intentions are carried out. But nothing actually happens in the committee room or negotiation chamber except to people's intentions and expectations.

This process of agreeing intentions between actors can be called 'politics' in a wide sense. In this sense a manager is a politician. But a manager

Rational Analysis for a Problematic World
Edited by J. Rosenhead. © 1989 John Wiley & Sons Ltd

must also show leadership. And in carrying out a strategy against competitors, rivals or others whose gain is partly the firm's loss, he or she may have to gather intelligence, plan secretly, move swiftly, and use surprise. A manager should be a general as well as a politician.

This chapter will show how a technique for analysing processes of conflict or cooperation between actors can help managers to be effective politicians and generals. Called 'metagame analysis', it was developed in the 1960s under a contract with the US Arms Control and Disarmament Agency for use on arms control problems, including the negotiations which led to the first SALT agreement. Afterwards it was used on Vietnam and the Arab–Israeli conflict, as well as other high-level policy problems, since when it has mostly been applied to business policy and·management.

Metagame analysis is 'Socratic': it asks the client questions, by answering which it (the client) educates itself. When answers are analysed, this is not so much to achieve surprising results as to summarize and state clearly what has already been sensed intuitively.

Nevertheless, it can be technically demanding, so that computer help is important, enabling a consultant to feed back results to the client straight away. A particular computer program called CONAN, which can offer assistance of this sort, will be discussed.

Actors, options, and scenarios

Suppose you have an interaction to analyse: some need either to reach understandings with others or to 'win' against them. You might be planning a marketing strategy, settling an industrial dispute, or establishing cooperation between two departments.

Begin by reviewing the issues to be decided: who will get the contract, whether there is to be a pay increase, how the work is to be shared. Make a list.

Next, ask who controls the issues—directly or indirectly. Direct control entails having authority to order something, or the ability to give it. Indirect control is exerted through threatening to react in certain ways—going on strike, say, or withholding cooperation if the issue does not go a certain way.

Each issue, then, will be controlled by one or more actors. If it is controlled by none—for example, the weather—put it down under a special 'actor' called Context.

Asking *who* controls the issues gives you a list of *actors*. Asking *how* they control them gives a list of *policy options* for each actor. In this way, though

Company A		**Girl**	
collaborate with B	1	remain faithful to boy	1
lower price	1	**Boy**	
Company B		remain faithful to girl	0
collaborate with A	1	move with job	0
adapt technology to A's	0		
Customer			
award contract elsewhere	0		
(a)		(b)	

Figure 1
Two lists of actors and options, with two scenarios

the process involves thought and discussion, you will arrive at *a list of actors and options*. Figure 1 shows two such lists.

The list of actors and options is the basic tool of metagame analysis. It describes what is called a 'situation'. Figure 1(a) is a situation of possible collaboration between two companies; Figure 1(b) is a possible pairing between a boy and a girl.

'Situations' are points of interaction between people, like those in novels or plays. Each is dated, that is it obtains during a particular time-period, a period of 'pre-play bargaining' during which no irreversible actions are taken with respect to the policy options involved. Instead, the actors are interacting to decide what to do.

We name 'actors' in bold letters in Figure 1. They are decision-making units which may be individuals or organizations—though in the latter case their preferences, attitudes, and decisions are seen as arising from game-theoretic interactions going on inside the organization.

Below each actor are shown its policy 'options', that is its possible strategic intentions for the future. Options do not exclude each other; that is, unless otherwise stated an actor may take all, some or none of its options. A particular choice of options by an actor, representing a particular 'plan', is shown by writing 1s against the options it intends taking and 0s against the rest. Note that because options are non-exclusive, a few of them can generate many possible plans.

Take stock now. At this point, merely by asking yourself the questions necessary to set up this list, you have achieved a great deal, having thought through what power is wielded by whom. The CONAN program helps to nail this down by storing the list of actors and options, and recording any extra information or explanations you wish in the form of notes attached to each actor/option. It can thus be a kind of database for strategic information.

What next? By writing 1s and 0s against each option you generate a whole column of 1s and 0s called a 'scenario'. Figures 1(a) and 1(b) show scenarios.

A scenario is, firstly, a combination of actors' plans. But it is more—for each actor it is a possible pathway into the indefinite future, representing the future the actor would anticipate if those plans were carried out. For example, the scenario in Figure 1(a) represents the future anticipated by the actors if A and B collaborate and A lowers its price while B does not adapt its technology to A's and their Customer does not award elsewhere the contract that they want. In the second situation, the scenario represents the future expected if the girl plans to remain faithful to the boy while he doesn't plan to remain faithful to her but does not plan either to move with his job.

In each case the futures the actors face are open-ended, dynamic, and multi-foliate, not simple, finite or closed. They are the future of the world, constrained only by the assumption that these particular actors will try to carry out these particular plans. Such futures the actors must consider—however briefly and inadequately—when they 'look down' different scenarios.

But bear in mind that at the time of the situation, these futures are anticipations only. In the scenario of Figure 1(b), for example, the boy hasn't yet been unfaithful—he just hasn't decided to be faithful! That is different; to have been unfaithful, as he would eventually be if the scenario were pursued, would create a different situation.

CONAN allows you to attach explanatory text to scenarios, as well as to actors and options. Deciding what explanations to input to the computer forces you to investigate and interpret different futures.

Generating, classifying, and interpreting scenarios

The list of actors and options, once achieved, is a mechanism for generating scenarios. The object is to prepare for interaction with others by looking at what may lie ahead, what they may and you should aim at, and how to exert or resist pressure.

Just generating scenarios at random helps in this because scenarios represent the objects actors strive for, the threats they fear, and the means by which they hope to achieve their ends. But it is more helpful to classify scenarios in a way that brings out their strategic roles. Finally, it is helpful to prepare for intervention by looking deeply into the interpretation of key scenarios ahead of time, rather than waiting till 'the crunch comes', as people often do.

First, how many scenarios are there?

Infeasibilities

Vast numbers of scenarios can be generated by assigning 1s and 0s to a smallish set of options—the number is actually 2 raised to the power of the number of options. But not all scenarios mechanically generated in this way could actually be carried out. In Figure 1(a), for example, A couldn't collaborate with B if B were unwilling to collaborate with A. We model this by calling such option selections 'infeasible'.

Though this seems simple, bear in mind that the infeasibility relates to actors' plans and intentions. The infeasibility of A planning to collaborate with an unwilling B is actually psychological, consisting in the fact that A can't form the intention to collaborate without belief in B's corresponding intention. Hence A's intention may be changed by B's.

This sounds odd, but is in the nature of human interactions within a given, dated situation which has not yet been resolved. In such situations anticipations are formed, collide, and re-form as actors try to reach an understanding in order to handle their interdependent futures. All the time they estimate each other's intentions through guesses, lies, revelations, promises, bluffs, and so on.

The CONAN program helps in sorting out incompatibilities between intentions. It allows the user to state that certain option choices are logically or physically impossible or perhaps just not worth considering. You can then generate and display the set of all feasible scenarios, or particular subsets of this set.

Classifying scenarios

After exploring the future by generating a number of feasible scenarios, you can shed more light by classifying them into various 'types'. These types are derived from the analysis of threats and promises described in the next section. Each type is described below and illustrated by examples.

Type 1: The *Status Quo* as it was before the situation arose

Often this is the all-noughts scenario, since it is natural to state options (which can always be stated in a positive or negative sense) in such a way that *not* taking the option means not deviating from the Status Quo. In Figures 1(a) and 1(b) the Status Quo would probably be the all-noughts scenario. Note that despite its name the Status Quo may be as dynamic, open-ended, and various as any other scenario. It simply represents the future as it was previously expected.

Type 2: The *present scenario,* incorporating present intentions

This may differ from the Status Quo, some actors having declared a change in their plans. In a strike situation, for example, the workers may have said they will be going on strike. This makes a strike part of the time-path the actors are now moving down—in other words, part of the present scenario. (*Note:* it will be different if the workers have actually gone on strike, not merely sent messages or taken other relatively costless symbolic actions. An actual strike changes the situation, requiring new assumptions about actors, options, interests, and so on.)

As actors interact within a given situation, the present scenario will change, unlike the Status Quo which necessarily remains the same. In Figures 1(a) and 1(b), for example, we may take it that the present scenario is the one shown. These intentions have been formed, though nothing irreversible has yet been done.

Type 3: The *positions* of different actors, meaning the scenarios they would like others to agree to

The word 'position' is here used as it commonly is in reporting diplomatic negotiations. Positions frequently change—are abandoned or taken up—as actors interact within the given situation. In Figure 1(a), A's 'position' (reporting only differences from the present scenario) might be that B should adapt its technology; B's, that A should not lower its price; the Customer's, that A and B should not collaborate. In Figure 1(b), Girl's position might be that Boy should remain faithful, while Boy's might be the present scenario.

Type 4: Possible *compromises* between different actors' positions

A compromise between two actors' positions, while not the position of either, is preferred by each to the other's position. A frequent benefit of metagame analysis is to reveal possible compromises between positions—or to reveal that none exists. In Figure 1(a), a compromise between A and B might consist of A not lowering price while B does adapt its technology to A's. This compromise between A and B does not, we note, involve the Customer; a compromise does not have to involve all actors.

Type 5: Possible *conflict points* actors might move to in trying to force others to accept their positions

Strikes, boycotts, stalemates, wars—or, between partners, sulks, rages, and denial of sexual favours—are examples of conflict points. When a situation develops in a healthy, normal way, actors move to conflict points only in order to induce movement to positions they prefer. Nevertheless, a genuine conflict point is sincerely meant; readers should recall how sincere they were when they last sulked with their partner! Everything, however, lies in future intentions; war has not actually broken out, though reserves may have been called up; a lease has not actually been signed on the apartment the sulking partner means to move to. These things would change the situation.

Scenarios of these different types often follow each other in a particular sequence. A harmonious Status Quo is disturbed by an actor moving to a conflict point in order to get to the 'position' it prefers. This manoeuvre may work—there may be movement to that actor's position. Alternatively, the situation may move back to the Status Quo—which will also be the 'position' of actors that prefer no change—or to a compromise.

To illustrate, consider the situation in Figure 2. Here two departments are in potential conflict. Processing is eager to use new machinery to increase its output at once. Finishing, which must process this output, wants a delay. Whether such delay is necessary is unclear: Finishing feels it is, but if forced might do without.

Faced with this problem, suppose that after due deliberation you input the actors and options shown—with notes describing what they mean. You have judged, that is, that Processing has an option to appeal to senior management against Finishing's delaying tactics. Finishing claims that accepting the increased throughput at once would mean lowering quality standards; you have judged that this is actually an option controlled by Finishing, since it would mean instructing staff to pass lower quality items.

You are, let us say, responsible to senior management for trouble-shooting production delays, so this is very much your problem. In just writing the list of actors and options you have done much to clarify the situation and prepare yourself for action. Now you want to do more. You start reviewing scenarios, and input into CONAN the columns shown in Figure 2.

Processing Dept					
increase output from new machinery now	0	1	1	1	1
appeal against Finishing	0	0	0	1	0
Finishing Dept					
accept increased throughput	0	0	1	1	1
lower quality standards	0	0	1	1	0
	(1)	(2)	(3)	(4)	(5)

Figure 2
Sequence of scenarios in a manufacturing problem

They are arranged in a sequence that you foresee might occur; some of it already has. It is, of course, a sequence of changing intentions and expectations—changed through communication and other symbolic acts. Real-world actions throughout remain consistent with (1), the *status quo* scenario that obtained until Processing declared its intention to increase output, thereby moving to (2).

The 'position' taken by Finishing is (1); Finishing accepts that there will be increased output from the new machinery but does not want it yet. But now the present scenario is (2): a conflict point that will lead to chaos if pursued, since Finishing will be refusing the output Processing intends to send.

Summing up, what has happened so far is a movement from (1) to (2). You now imagine what might happen next. You set up the next three scenarios. In (3), Finishing, realizing that the pile-up of work to be finished may prove embarrassing, has decided to accept the extra work by lowering quality standards. This is another conflict point, Finishing having moved there to increase the pressure on Processing and reduce it on itself. Finishing in fact reckons that the deterioration in quality would bring complaints which could be blamed on Processing.

You imagine next that Processing, in order to forestall this, might decide to appeal to senior management (4). In (5) you imagine that Finishing may respond to this intention (not yet carried out) by giving in and accepting the increase in work with quality maintained.

By thinking through and making notes on such possible developments in the situation you have prepared yourself still better to deal with it. You have a justified feeling that you have probably looked at all possibilities, since you cannot think of any other meaningful options and cannot juggle these to come up with other likely scenarios. Of course, this is 'probable' only. You know no more than you know, and can be surprised. But at least you will not be like the United States at Pearl Harbour—and lesser decision makers since—in not using what you know.

Scenario interpretation

Now suppose that, having done so much, you still have some time. You begin to interpret each scenario individually—as distinct from looking at a sequence of them, as we have done so far. Ask concerning each one: 'What would it really mean if these intentions were held to indefinitely?'

The point is to try to give realistic answers, noting that by fixing these actors' policy intentions you have not made the future static or deterministic—it remains a stochastic spectrum of dynamically unfolding possibilities. Actors' options themselves—just think of 'increase output' or 'lower quality standards'—are dynamic guidelines, not simple acts. And options may be overthrown despite attempts to hold to them, for example when a workforce 'drifts back' despite a union's attempt to continue a strike. These are the realistic ways to interpret scenarios.

And what use is such insight into possible futures? It helps you plan a strategy for the interaction. Looking into what would happen at a conflict point, for example, is often not done until the conflict—statemate, strike, war—has almost arrived. People feel, 'No need to think through the long-term effects of this because they won't happen, someone will give in first'.

And someone may. But since it is often the anticipated effects of not giving in that cause people to give in, such effects may be vitally important even when they never occur. It is a fallacy, in other words, to judge the importance of events by their probability of occurrence—because where we jump back to from the brink of an abyss may depend on what we see when looking into it.

Applying this, you might decide that Finishing has not thought through its refusal to accept the increased production flow from Processing. Its reaction has been, 'Processing can't do that, Finishing won't accept it,' which is why the situation is stuck for the moment at the disastrous scenario (2). If Finishing started to think what the consequences would be and how they will look to senior management should Processing stick to its guns and scenario (2) unfold, Finishing might quickly move away to (3) or even (5). By thinking this through yourself and talking kindly to those concerned you may be able to cause them to move.

Benefits also accrue from looking into non-conflict points. An actor benefits from looking deeply into the 'positions' (recommended solutions) put forward by others. It both arms itself against arguments they might use, and finds arguments to use against them. It benefits too from looking into its own 'position'. Can it be sustained long term? If not, what would its eventual breakdown lead to? These reflections may lead to a change of mind, or, if not, to better defences through foreseeing weaknesses in the actor's own position.

The general point is: scenarios will be explored in the course of the interaction as actors state positions, advance arguments, and try to make their stands credible. Such moves exert pressure through the hopes and fears aroused. By exploring scenarios beforehand you arm yourself for the fray.

Analysing threats and promises

Much benefit can be gained from what we have covered so far, that is, setting up a model of a situation and describing and classifying its elements. This enables you, using the CONAN program, to set up a useful structured database for intelligence information.

Much benefit, in other words, can be gained with relatively little effort—and the CONAN program is designed to maximize this. CONAN will also help with the more sophisticated analysis I shall now describe, that is, the analysis of threats and promises.

The object of this is to reveal the basic pressures that actors can exert on each other in the given situation. These pressures are threats and promises; other forms of pressure such as emotional persuasion and rational argument are, as we shall see, based on these. Revealing them helps you or your client to exert effective pressure on others and to resist, if you wish to, the pressures they may exert on you.

Thus you can reveal and prepare for not only threats and promises, but also the other emotional and rational pressures based on them. We will now proceed to outline how to carry out this analysis and what use it is to the manager as politician and general.

Steps in the analysis

The analysis follows the steps described and briefly explained below. The first involves the concept of 'stability'.

Step 1: Choose a particular scenario to analyse for 'stability'

'Stability' means 'acceptance by all actors as the scenario they expect'; that is, a scenario is 'stable' if each actor expects to do its part and expects others to do theirs.

A 'stable' scenario is in fact the actors' current resolution of their problem—therein lies its importance—and the threats and promises they use are designed to achieve stability at scenarios they prefer. To analyse stability is, therefore, to analyse threats and promises.

But beware. The definition of 'stability' is rather subtle. It is worth asking what it does and does not imply. First, though a stable scenario is accepted by the actors, such acceptance need not be willing; a defeated enemy, for example, may most unwillingly accept foreign rule, but if expected to continue, such rule may be stable. Next, there cannot be more than one stable scenario—a situation cannot stabilize at more than one point. (All of this follows from the definition of stability.) On the other hand, a situation may be unstable, meaning that there is at present no stable scenario; actors then either do not know what to expect of each other, or expect the wrong, or different, things.

Is a stable scenario necessarily going to be carried out? While it is stable, the actors are in the process of carrying it out, but since a scenario stretches into the indefinite future the process may not have gone far before the scenario ceases to be stable—and may then cease to be carried out. A stable scenario is necessarily the present scenario, but not vice versa; the present scenario may be unstable.

Can unstable scenarios happen? They can—this simply means that actors can be surprised by each other's actions. Conflict points are generally unstable, simply because actors stay at them in the hope and expectation that each other will move. Though unstable, they may indeed happen, to the actors' surprise: certain explanations of the First World War imply that the national leaderships involved were surprised in this way.

If actors are interrelated organizations, they need stability—that is, mutual predictability—in order to carry on their work. The opposite of stability—it may be called 'crisis'—obtains when they cannot predict each other. Crises are resolved by the actors getting together and negotiating— or by such means as defeat or elimination of some of them.

The next two steps are what you need to analyse the stability, or instability, of a particular scenario.

Step 2: Answer certain questions designed to find all 'unilateral improvements' for actors and subsets of actors from the particular scenario

These are all scenarios that are both preferred by all members of a certain subset and 'reachable' by them alone changing their plans (individual option selections). Here 'preferred' means preferred to the particular scenario, and 'reachable' means reachable from the particular scenario. The necessary questions about preferences will be put to you by CONAN, or you can work out what they are by yourself.

An example can show how this works. In Figure 3, the particular scenario is column (3). Consider the scenarios to the left of it. Scenario (1) is 'reachable' from (3) by actors A and C. Confirm this by noting that only they change plans in the transition from (3) to (1)—B's option stays at (1). Therefore since both A and C prefer (1) to (3)—check this by Figure 3(b)— (1) is a unilateral improvement achievable by A and C. Next, observe that scenario (2) is reachable from (3) by C alone—confirm that A and B have the same plans there as at (3). Hence (2) is a unilateral improvement for C, since C prefers it to (3)—check by Figure 3(b).

Unilateral improvements—also called 'improvements'—are connected with 'promises'. To make a promise is to assert the intention of making or helping to make an improvement—hoping thereby to encourage others to cooperate, either by doing their part in the improvement or by refraining

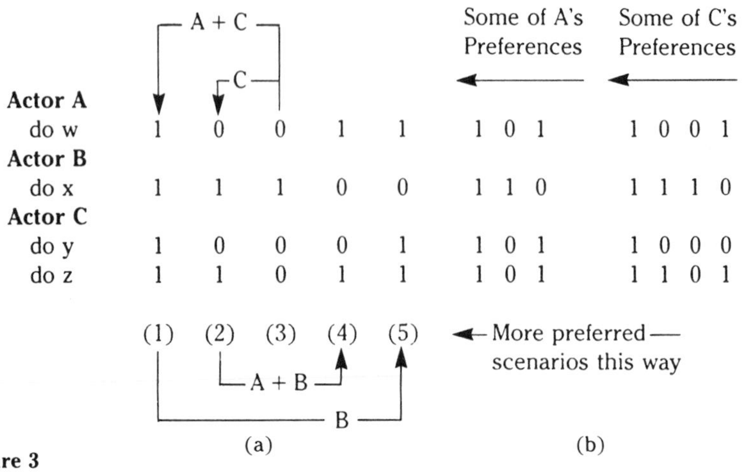

	(1)	(2)	(3)	(4)	(5)	Some of A's Preferences	Some of C's Preferences
Actor A							
do w	1	0	0	1	1	1 0 1	1 0 0 1
Actor B							
do x	1	1	1	0	0	1 1 0	1 1 1 0
Actor C							
do y	1	0	0	0	1	1 0 1	1 0 0 0
do z	1	1	0	1	1	1 0 1	1 1 0 1

— A + C —
C
A + B
B
More preferred — scenarios this way

(a)　　　　　(b)

Figure 3
Abstract game illustrating improvements and sanctions. The arrows going left in Figure 3(a) show improvements, those going right, sanctions against those improvements. Each arrow is labelled with the actors responsible for that move. The blocks of scenarios in Figure 3(b) show some of the preference rankings of A and C, with preferred scenarios written before less preferred

from adverse actions. That is why it is essential for an improvement to be 'reachable'—something the particular actor or set of actors can bring about—as well as preferred by them.

But since we are talking about changes in intentions only, this raises the question of 'credibility'. When two or more actors fix on a joint improvement—as when A and C agree to move to (1)—they have to believe each other's promise that each intends to move: their mutual promises must be credible.

The need for credibility may also arise when attempting to move away from a conflict point; the other side may need to be convinced that you mean what you say when you promise to do as they want! Of course, some improvements are inherently credible; as we shall see, these are the so-called 'willing' improvements.

In general, though a unilateral improvement from a particular scenario is not stability enhancing, its existence does not guarantee instability. First, the improvement may not be credible—actors may be unable to believe the necessary promises. Second, even a credible improvement may be deterred by the threat of certain reactions by other actors—the so-called 'sanctions' that we discuss next.

Step 3: Answer some more questions designed to find all 'sanctions' that exist to deter the unilateral improvements

Again CONAN will put the necessary questions, or you can work them out yourself. A 'sanction' against an improvement is, firstly, reachable from the improvement scenario by the actors who were not involved in the improvement—hence it is a possible reaction by them. Secondly, it is such that some actor who was involved in the improvement finds the sanction not preferred to the particular scenario—making it not worth while for that actor to have helped with the improvement.

This is less complex than it seems. Consider the improvements in columns (1) and (2) of Figure 3. A and C were the actors involved in improvement (1); and column (5) is reachable from (1) by B alone— confirm that neither A nor C changes its plan in the transition from (1) to (5). Hence since A finds (5) not preferred to the particular scenario (3)— check this in Figure 3(b)—(5) is a sanction against (1). Similarly, column (4) is not preferred by C to the particular scenario—as seen from Figure 3(b)—and since C was the 'improver' involved in the improvement (2), while only A and B are involved in the move from (2) to (4), it follows that (4) is a sanction against (2).

Sanctions are connected with 'threats', just as improvements are with promises. A threat is an attempt to convey to an intending 'improver' the intention to carry out a sanction—with the object of deterring the improvement. Again, the question of credibility arises. Does the intending improver believe that the sanction would actually be carried out?

Sanctions are stability enhancing, but do not guarantee stability any more than improvements guarantee its opposite. Put simply, stability is like a donkey walking along a path. Unilateral improvements are carrots that tempt it to stray. For each credible carrot there must be a stick to beat the donkey back. Sanctions are sticks. But the stick must be credible.

Thus credibility, while not affecting the existence of a sanction, does determine whether it can be an effective threat. The general 'law of stability' is: *for a scenario to be stable, it is necessary for each credible improvement to be deterred by a credible sanction.*

When you have found all improvements and sanctions—note that CONAN will deduce them from your answers to its questions, then display them in tableau form and state them in words—you have finished analysing this particular scenario. You know what threats must be made credible, and/or promises incredible, for it to be stable. You now cycle back to Step 1 and analyse other scenarios. When you have analysed a number of scenarios you go on to the next step.

Step 4: Draw a 'strategic map' laying out all the threats and promises actors can make to try and stabilize the situation at scenarios they prefer

But it is time to take stock before going to the next section, where strategic maps are described. We have seen how to ask questions necessary to determine improvements and sanctions. What use is this?

The answer is that the questions asked show up your own and others' strengths and weaknesses in the situation, and so help you to form an interactive strategy. If you cannot answer the questions, you will usually see their importance and want to investigate them further.

In some cases, by analysing an actor's 'position', that is, the scenario it is aiming for, you will discover that it is bound to be unstable, since there is a credible improvement from that scenario with no credible sanction to deter it. Suppose this is the case in the interdepartmental conflict of Figure 2, where your role is that of incipient trouble-shooter. Finding that the *status quo*, Finishing's 'position', is totally unstable against a move by Processing to increase output while at the same time appealing to senior management, you know what to do! With tact and discretion, you must let Finishing see this; once those concerned do so, they are bound to give in and accept Processing's 'position'.

And if your conclusion is wrong, being based on the wrong assumptions about preferences? The implementation of your interactive strategy should be at the same time a check on these assumptions! For example, tactful discussions with Finishing and Processing of what they think is likely to happen, and how they view it, will serve both purposes at once.

In another case, finding that a scenario can be stable only if certain sanctions are made credible or improvements made incredible, can show you how to undermine or strengthen it, depending on your aims. Finally, the result of analysing a conflict point is to show 'where you can get to from there', that is, what improvements are possible for all parties. This may lead you deliberately to go to one conflict point rather than another. In these ways and others, knowledge of the threats and promises necessary to make scenarios stable can help you to intervene effectively—as a good manager should.

Strategic maps and credibility analysis; emotions, irrationality, preference and option change, deceit, disbelief and rational argument in the common interest

How to draw a strategic map

Once found, the unilateral improvements and sanctions (possible threats and promises) relative to one or more particular scenarios can be summed up in a 'strategic map'. This is a diagrammatic way to communicate and discuss results.

	The scenarios	Subordinate's preference ranking	Boss's preference ranking
Subordinate improve quality of work	0 1 0	0 1 0	1 0 0
Boss fire subordinate	0 0 1	0 0 1	0 0 1

Status Quo
Improvement in Quality
Subordinate Fired

Figure 4
A simple three-scenario situation. The missing scenario, 1/1, is infeasible

To illustrate, let us take an imaginary situation. Suppose that you, the reader, are in the situation of potential conflict in Figure 4.

You are the boss (male). You are considering what to do about a female employee who has worked for you for many years, but who is refusing to raise the quality of her work to the level possible using the new technology you have installed. There are only three feasible scenarios, since the consequences of her improving the quality of her work would be that she could not be fired—partly for legal reasons, partly because you do not want to fire her.

Your preferences and hers are as shown. She is an old friend, she knew your late wife. Subordinate Fired is the least preferred scenario for both of you. As between the other two scenarios, Improvement in Quality is preferred by you to Status Quo, whereas she—who disagrees with you and considers that her work is of excellent quality—has the opposite preference.

The present scenario is the Status Quo. You have not brought up the possibility of firing her.

Getting to this simple model by asking the metagame questions has clarified the problem for you—before it was an emotional tangle of immense complexity, full of denials, evasions, and crippling doubts. But you feel the need for more self-advice.

Since you have decided on what you believe to be the correct preference ordering for yourself and your subordinate, it is a simple matter to find the improvements and sanctions. They are shown on the strategic map in Figure 5.

How do you read this map? First, *scenarios are shown by balloons*, with double lines round balloons with no improvements from them. Note that you have no improvement in moving from Status Quo to Improvement in

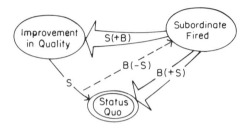

Figure 5
Strategic map of Figure 4. S stands for 'subordinate', B for 'boss'. The map shows guaranteed improvements from Subordinated Fired to the two other scenarios, and a deterrable improvement from Improvement in Quality to Status Quo

Quality—not because you wouldn't like the move, but because you don't control the necessary option.

In a more complex situation, a balloon might represent a group of similar scenarios. Generally, in complex situations with many scenarios, a certain 'art' is needed in drawing simple maps to make various different points. We omit such considerations here.

Second, arrows from one balloon to another represent *unilateral improvements*, with double-line arrows for 'guaranteed' improvements—that is, ones there are no sanctions to deter. To show the 'improvers' involved, each improvement arrow may be labelled with the names of the actors whose 'plans' change between the source scenario and the destination, followed in brackets by the names of any other 'gainers'.

In Figure 5 you can see that from Subordinate Fired, your subordinate has an undeterrable (guaranteed) improvement in moving to Improvement in Quality, your position; and you have another in moving to Status Quo, her position. This pattern, whereby each has an improvement in 'giving in' to the other, is typical of 'conflict points' such as Subordinate Fired. As both of you stand to gain from the improvements, both your names appear on the arrows, with the 'inactive gainer' in brackets. In addition, your subordinate has an improvement in moving from Improvement in Quality to the Status Quo, which is however deterrable.

Third, dotted-line arrows from improvement arrows to balloons represent sanctions by which the improvements may be deterred. Sanction arrows may be labelled with the names of the 'sanctioners'—those whose plans change between the destination of the improvement arrow and the sanction—followed in brackets with the names, prefixed by minus signs, of the 'sanctioned'. Thus here you see that your subordinate may be deterred from abandoning Improvement in Quality by the threat, if credible, that you will react by moving from there to Subordinate Fired—an available sanction achievable by a change in your plan.

Thus the map lays out the possible threats and promises that follow from the actors' preferences. It is, in all, not surprising, though it is reassuring to have it made so clear. The question is, how do you proceed to make your threats and promises credible, and your subordinate's not so? We discuss this next.

Interpreting a strategic map: credibility of threats and promises

Interpreting a strategic map means judging if and how its threats and promises can be made credible, and so deciding on the strategy and tactics you will pursue in a situation. There is a formal method of analysing credibility which can be useful here.

To show its utility, suppose first that you, the boss, make some bad decisions on the basis of a naive interpretation of the above strategic map. Then we will show how you might have done better using formal credibility analysis. Of course, a reasonably good manager would be unlikely to make such bad decisions. He or she should be able to feel how to proceed somewhat tactfully on the basis of a strategic map. However, it is plausible that errors might occur in a case like this, where a boss's personal feelings and sense of guilt over his dead wife have become mixed up in a business decision.

What then might you, the boss, conclude from the map alone, without formal analysis? Firstly, that if you want to get to Improvement in Quality you are starting in the wrong place. There is no arrow from Status Quo, where you are, to there. So you must move to Subordinate Fired—in conveyed intentions only, of course. That is, you must make your subordinate believe that she will be fired if her low-quality work continues.

Right away there is a question of credibility. Will she believe you really mean to fire her? Leaving that aside for the moment, you look at where you would be if she did believe it: at a conflict point, Subordinate Fired, with two improvements from it.

These two improvements are what metagame analysts call 'rival' improvements, meaning that each actor prefers that the other should be the one to move. So the question arises—Why should she move and not you? What determines who will be the one to move? Another question of credibility, surely, since to make her move you will have to make it credible that you will never do so.

Next, you look at a dilemma you would face should she give in and agree to move from Subordinate Fired. Suppose that she said, 'OK, I'll improve the quality of my work.' Could you believe her? What would she have agreed to?—nothing except to try to do better in future. Should she fail, it might be because she never really tried, and you would be caught in a game that could go on forever. Again you face a problem of credibility, that

255

is, the credibility of her promise to move. How do you judge this? And is there any point in extracting a promise you won't be able to believe if it is given?

Finally, if you did believe her you would be at Improvement in Quality, from where she has an improvement arrow back to Status Quo. How would you then make her believe that if she takes that arrow you will really fire her — knowing as she does what your relationship is built upon, and how having to fire her would make you suffer feelings of guilt? This, however, is really the same as the first question, that is, whether you are really able to move against your own preferences from Status Quo to Subordinate Fired — or whether such a move is not bound to be a bluff.

Thus, there are three questions of credibility on which you really should get formal advice. Instead, you decide to cut the Gordian knot. Buttoning up your feelings like a true Englishman, you walk into her office and say calmly, 'You're fired.'

Her jaw drops, she goes white. After looking at you for a moment, she bursts into floods of tears and afterwards will not look at you at all. You want to explain to her why you said that—it was only an initial move meant to establish credibility, and bargaining should follow—but she gives you no chance. After several sleepless nights you send her a bunch of flowers and arrange an opportunity to beg her forgiveness, pleading overwork.

And now you dare not mention the subject again, lest you upset her once more. The situation stabilizes more and more, till gradually you realize you have been out-gunned. Where did you go wrong?

How to establish credibility

Turning to more formal methods, you should realize that there was actually nothing wrong with your interpretation of the map. You were right about what had to be made credible and where the difficulties lay. What was wrong was your method of establishing credibility.

How then does an actor establish credibility? We shall go through the different methods available. However, we should stress that *actors may or may not be conscious of using these methods*—this varies, depending on how self-aware or 'Machiavellian' they are. We certainly do not assert that all actors are 'Machiavellian' in this sense, and when they are not, it may be more natural to talk of 'side effects' rather than 'methods'; that is, in an unselfconscious actor what we are calling 'methods' may be regarded simply as psychological and behavioural effects of the actor's attempt to be credible.

The first point about establishing credibility is that a 'willing' threat or promise, that is, one that the actor prefers to carry out for its own sake, is inherently credible. Indeed, such motivators are more naturally called 'warnings' than threats, and 'incentives' than promises—indicating their lack of a credibility problem. On a strategic map, a threat (sanction) or promise (improvement) is 'willing' for an actor if the actor has no improvement from its destination balloon.

But by this criterion (see Figure 5) your threat to fire your subordinate is unwilling, that is, you have an improvement from Subordinate Fired to Status Quo. And her promise to improve the quality of her work is unwilling, that is, she has an improvement from Improvement in Quality to Status Quo.

. How then does an actor make credible an 'unwilling' threat or promise, that is, a commitment to act contrary to its own preferences? This is where the problem lies.

There are in fact three main ways: *preference change, irrationality,* and *deceit.* Indeed, by changing its preferences an actor can make an unwilling threat or promise willing; irrationality can demonstrate a 'crazy' willingness to go against its own preferences; and finally, by using deceit, an actor can counterfeit these effects.

Moreover, these same three ways are available to an actor wishing to resist either an unwilling threat or a 'rival' improvement. To resist an unwilling threat—in the hope that it will be called off—requires an actor to go against its own preferences in accepting a sanction rather than accept the scenario offered instead. To resist a 'rival' improvement means staying at a conflict point rather than accepting the improvement being offered— in the hope, of course, that others will take the improvement being offered to them. Again, the actor in each case needs to make credible its determination to go against its own preferences—and preference change, irrationality, and deceit are the three ways to do it.

But how to change preferences? Sometimes it may be done by deliberately changing the context of the situation. Let us apply this to your case. You might increase your preference for Subordinate Fired by making efforts to find a substitute. Thus, *lateral thinking and generation of new options* may result from an actor's need to be credible.

Sometimes it will be impossible to make enough such changes, and indeed in your case you would prefer not to fire a family friend, however good a substitute you found. Can preferences be changed in any other way?

The answer is yes, but to change one's preferences without adequate external reason is essentially an irrational, emotional process. Specifically, two kinds of emotion, or a mixture of the two, are involved: '*love*', meaning positive emotion towards others; and '*hate*', or negative emotion. The mixture may be called '*love–hate*'. Such emotions are necessary for preference change and, when displayed to others, provide evidence of it.

Love is the emotion needed to make credible an otherwise incredible promise—for example, 'I'll be true to you for the rest of my life.' Hate is the emotion needed to make credible an otherwise incredible threat, such as 'I'll blow up this plane with myself on it unless you concede my political demands.' Finally, love–hate—a strong emotion that appears as a feeling of martyrdom or resentment—is the emotion needed to make credible a determination to resist others' threats and promises. It is appropriate when trying to get another actor rather than yourself to move away from a conflict point.

The point is that promises, threats, and determined resistance to them tend to fail unless made with the right emotional tone—simply because they fail to make the recipient believe that preferences have really changed that much. Thus positive and negative emotions are generated (unconsciously or otherwise) by the need to make promises, threats, and resistance to them credible.

Now preference change and its accompanying emotions are closely associated with irrationality. Many preferences, after all, derive from and are justified by an actor's philosophy, character, value-system, prejudices, and so on. To change these leaves the actor disoriented while the change is happening. Again, preference change may be only temporary, kept in place under stress of emotion and the need to convey credibility, afterwards changing back. But disorientation, emotion, and temporary preference change are all seen as signs of irrationality. Finally, irrational behaviour may serve as a substitute for preference change by giving the impression an actor is 'out of control', hence liable to do crazy things like blowing up aircraft or deciding to be true to one person! Examples of such irrational behaviour might be smashing up furniture, bursting into tears, or spending your week's wages on flowers.

Apply this to your case. Before marching into your subordinate's office you should have noted that the threat 'I'll fire you' was unwilling (check the arrows on your map). Hence the appropriate emotion to make it credible was negative, that is, anger. Moreover, since you did not want to change your preferences, or make her think you had changed them, to such an extent that you would seriously prefer to fire her, you needed to give the impression that your preferences were merely in process of changing, or had changed only temporarily. Anger and irrationality were needed to convey this complex message—that you did not want to fire her, but might feel driven to. A period of getting irrationally furious with the low quality of her work might have been appropriate. Instead, you were direct, cool, and calm, conveying the businesslike message that you preferred to fire her despite all the past. Little wonder she was upset.

Analysing next the problem of how you might believe her promise to improve her work, you see that any actual preference change on her part would have to show itself through positive emotions towards you. You should not trust her if she appears negative or resentful.

Analysing how to handle the clash of wills at Subordinate Fired, you realize that as this is a conflict point, the love–hate emotion is appropriate. A martyred, resentful attitude of 'You're creating this problem, not I. You solve it' is what is called for. Which all seems obvious once said, but was hidden from view before. You were willing to accept any offer she made, in any tone, so humbled were you. And instead of getting angry you were trying to placate her.

What about the method of deceit? Instead of going to the trouble of emotional or other preference change, might you not counterfeit them? Against this is the difficulty of deceiving one who has known you well for years, and the need to maintain a reputation for reliability with one whom you will continue to work with. More could be said about this interesting method—which incidentally is not usually called 'deceit' by those practising it—but in your case you may be right to dismiss it.

But from the possibility of deceit something follows. *Disbelief* is in general both a consequence of deceit—in that where deceit is called for, disbelief is called for on the other side—and itself a way of resisting unwilling threats and rival improvements. Disbelief may indeed eliminate the basic distinction between 'willing' and 'unwilling' threats and promises, since there is always reason for 'willingness' to be disbelieved.

Not only this, but any attempt to increase credibility may have the opposite effect—because it may generate disbelief! In particular, threats, by suggesting the possibility and need for resistance, may always have the effect of evoking resistance and resentment. There is in fact always likely to be a *reaction against explicit threats and promises*, both as a consequence of disbelief and because such a reaction is itself a method of resistance against unwilling threats and rival improvements. Applying this to your case, you see that your biggest mistake may simply have lain in making your threat so explicit.

Explicit threats may work— they have the advantage of clarity. But they need a Hitler, a Thatcher or a Murdoch to make them work—an actor who is prepared to back them up to the hilt. And still they leave resentment.

But what can you do, if indeed all attempts to increase credibility may have the opposite effect? Is not this an ultimate dilemma? It is resolved by the final method of establishing credibility, that of *rational arguments in the common interest.*

These resolve the dilemma by elevating the dispute to a higher level. Observe first that the existence of an unwilling threat or promise implies that the actors have a common interest—in the threat not being, or the promise being, carried out! Hence an actor may always make its threat or promise crystal clear while presenting it not as such, but as an argument in the interest of both parties. Such an argument, if sincere and persuasive, both makes it harder for the arguer to give in—it would be contradicting its own rationality—and easier for the recipient—it is conceding to reason, not pressure.

Explicitness of threats and promises is avoided, while clarity about consequences to individuals is retained, by these arguments in the common interest which treat the actors as one player. For just as it is true that 'every player is a game'—meaning that an actor's preferences and decisions arise from an internal game within that actor—so it is also true, where there are common interests, that 'every game is a player'. It is just as valid to discuss strategy on the higher level as on the lower, and this is what a good leader does—while letting each actor in the lower level game digest the implicit threats or promises that are being made to itself.

Of course, rational arguments at the level of the common interest can and should be presented with the appropriate emotions and so forth at the level of actors' individual interests. There is no contradiction here, just a difference of levels.

You apply this to your situation. You schedule a meeting with your subordinate to talk about company policy. Working yourself into a passion, you appeal for her help in getting everyone to adapt to new technology and higher standards, so that the firm can compete and everyone's job be secure. You are well prepared with a totally rational answer to everything she says, delivered in emotional tones and referring only to the firm's interests, not to yours or hers. You sound angry when you say that those who cannot adapt will have to be fired. (She does not think you have even thought of firing her; but she thinks of it.)

You will judge the adequateness of her response both by her tone of warm cooperation and the rationality of the reasons she gives.

Conclusion

The manager as politician and general must deal both with strategy and with relations between human beings. These factors cannot be separated, and it is the aim of metagame analysis to show how both may be handled within one structured approach.

Further reading in metagame analysis

Paradoxes of Rationality: Theory of metagames and political behaviour by N. Howard, MIT Press, 1971 summed up initial research in metagame analysis, for the US Arms Control and Disarmament Agency. 'The present and future of metagame analysis' (*European Journal of Operational Research*, **32**, 1987) covers some of the latest research into credibility, emotions, and so on.

Some books by K. J. Radford, particularly *Managerial Decision Making* and *Complex Decision Problems* (Reston Publishing, Reston Va., 1975 and 1977), discuss a simplified form of the analysis that also elaborates and extends it in practice. N. M. Fraser and K. W. Hipel, in *Conflict Analysis* (North-Holland, Amsterdam, 1984), present metagame analysis more rigorously, with further developments.

Those interested in the CONAN computer program and the continuing development of metagame analysis and the theory of emotions, etc., can subscribe to the *CONAN Newsletter*, published by Nigel Howard, 10 Bloomfield Rd, Birmingham B13 9BY, England.

11

The CONAN play: a case study illustrating the process of metagame analysis

Nigel Howard

Introduction

This case study illustrates metagame analysis and the use of the CONAN program. It is written in the form of a play for two reasons, one major and one minor.

The minor reason is that metagame analyses are usually confidential, for the same reason that analyses of the hand of a bridge player in a game still going on would be confidential. Metagame analyses tend to remain current for long periods, which means that case studies have to be either out of date or so altered as to be unrecognizable. To adopt a fictional form seems a good compromise. The reader should understand that the events described resemble actual ones, yet none of my clients will recognize this as their problem.

A more important reason for writing a play is that the usual literary forms of reporting case experience do not convey the reality and significance of what I have called 'Socratic' consultancy, that is, the process of asking a client questions, by answering which the client, or client group, educates itself. The separate stages of model building, model manipulation, and derivation of conclusions are amalgamated into a single investigatory

Rational Analysis for a Problematic World
Edited by J. Rosenhead. © 1989 John Wiley & Sons Ltd

process in which clients, not consultant, own the model. After all, every-thing in it was put there by them, to reflect their thinking!

The problem is that as such processes are written up conventionally, it can easily seem that the consultant has done nothing; that is, he has not got beyond describing the problem. My play should show how the con-sultant's role can be as vital as that of Socrates in educating the youth of Athens.

A play can also bring out, indeed dramatize, the importance of the discussions between members of the client group that are evoked by the metagame questions. As the external game is analysed and a policy emerges, internal conflicts between members of the group are 'played out' and resolved. Of course, these internal games are not analysed overtly: you cannot analyse a game you are playing, because of the possibility of deceit! They are resolved, rather, by focusing on the common external problem, exchanging copious information, and allowing no internal-game strategies except rational arguments in the common interest.

There are two elements in the play which, it should be said, are not at all essential to the metagame process. One is Nathan's use of the 'manage-ment cross'. This is merely his way of grasping the context of the situation. The other is the fact that they are engaged in a 'training' exercise. This is merely the way this analysis came about, though it is true that metagame analysis is a good tool for management training.

Notice that Nathan uses the techniques of metagame analysis flexibly, skipping steps when there is a time constraint, and trying to get the most out of the session for the benefit of the client. This is in the nature of interactive consultancy, done 'on the hoof'.

The play has been performed several times in different versions, and I will follow convention in noting that the original cast, when it was prem-iered at the Operational Research Society National Event on Metagame Analysis at Aston University, Birmingham, in July 1986, were Raul Espejo, Mike Luck, Derek Powell, and myself. To my three co-actors, many thanks! On stage the action was interrupted from time to time by Derek waving his hand, causing the others to freeze in position while he explained the process and the use of the CONAN program. Here these interruptions are replaced by short sections headed 'Explanation'.

The play

The scene is a conference room, with a flip chart and a personal computer. Ray *and* Mark *come in, carrying coffee in plastic cups.* Ray *is red-faced and abrasive,* Mark *lofty and calm.*

RAY [looking round]: He's not here yet. Now, Mark, just what is all this about? A training exercise? Is that what you said?

MARK: Well, sort of.

RAY: Sort of? Look, Mark, I have problems I need to talk over with you. Introducing the new machines has set off more trouble with the maintenance people. We need to get together—urgently.

MARK: Good! This is a chance to do it!

RAY: I don't mean get together for a training exercise! We need to decide tactics and strategy.

MARK [calmly]: Yes, Ray. Let me explain. As personnel director of this firm I have to work with you on employee relations problems. I also have to run training programmes.

RAY: Yeah, so? And I'm a plant manager with an employee relations problem! These chaps have started a go slow, and I'm not interested in training right now. Can't we put off meeting with this—what is it?—*metagame* expert until we've sorted out what to do?

MARK [firmly]: The point is, I'm combining my two functions in one. The session this morning is meant to give training in how to deal with people—and remember it's company policy that you've got to have your quota of training, same as all of us. But this CONAN training works by taking as an example an actual situation you're in. So we'll take your current crisis as an example and kill two birds with one stone! What's wrong with that?

RAY [giving way rather reluctantly to Mark's superior status]: Okay, but I don't want to waste too much time on the training side of it. Let's stick to discussing the hole we're in over this go slow.

MARK: Don't worry. You'll find we discuss it all right.

RAY: H'm, well. CONAN, did you say? Is that what this thing is called? I thought it was called metagame something or other.

MARK: It seems CONAN is the name they've given to their computer-aided way of doing metagame analysis.

RAY: Computers, eh? [He walks over and stares rather fretfully at the computer. Picks up a floppy disk. Reads.] The CONAN system.

Nathan *enters behind him, and he turns round quickly.* Mark *greets* Nathan *and brings him forward.*

MARK: Ray, this is Nathan.

NATHAN: Good morning. [He looks keenly at Ray. Nathan is a lean, serious-looking person.]

RAY [waving the disk]: CONAN. An acronym, I suppose. What does it stand for?

NATHAN [going past Ray to the flip chart and testing out pens]: Cooperation or conflict analysis. When you're dealing with people, those are the alternatives. You can cooperate or get into conflict.

RAY [doubtfully, looking at Nathan's back]: Well, I suppose that's one way of looking at it. [Turning to Mark] How are we going to handle this? Remember, we need to spend time on my problem.

MARK: I shan't forget. [To Nathan]: Ray has just been bringing me up to date on the situation with his maintenance staff. The situation's blown up as I suspected it might. Can we take that as our case study?

NATHAN [inserting disks in the computer]: Certainly we can.

RAY: It's more than a case study! We've got to decide what do to about it. The idiots have started a go slow!

NATHAN [turning and facing them across the table, flip chart on one side of him, computer on the other]: Well, why don't we get cracking?

Ray *and* Mark *look uncertainly at each other, then sit down at the table.*

NATHAN: Let me explain what we're going to do. The object of this, as a training event, is to strengthen your ability to handle people and situations. To do this, we're going to take a current situation and analyse your handling of it. That will (a) help you with handling that situation, and (b) help in general with other situations.

Mark *looks at* Ray, *who nods briefly.*

NATHAN: The situation we're going to analyse is the problem with the main-tenance workers in Ray's group—am I right?

RAY [hurriedly breaking in]: Right. Do you want me to tell you about it? This is a group of six workers. Andy Saxe is their unofficial leader. They not only maintain the new machinery, they set it up as well. They think they should be on a separate wage scale. I agree with them—the job is now much more skilled. If we don't pay more we may not be able to keep or replace them.

MARK: Yes, Ray, but we've just negotiated new company-wide scales with the union. We can't upgrade your six men now, it's out of the question—would reopen the whole thing.

RAY: If they keep on with their go slow it could delay the X24 contract! It could end up costing us five million pounds!

MARK: But the grade they're asking for doesn't exist! In effect, the new agree-ment would be shown up as meaningless, and we'd be back into fire-fighting dozens of problems with small groups all over the company.

Ray *glares fiercely at* Mark, *who gives him a hard, cool look in return.*

NATHAN [after looking from one to the other]: Right, that's fine. Can we just take all that under advisement for the moment? Let me explain the first step we're going to take in analysing this situation. [He writes on the flip chart.]

NATHAN: The first step is: *place the situation in its organizational context.* So. I'm placing you two in the middle of a cross we call the 'management cross'. This is where you're being crucified! Above you are the people who control you; below, the people you control; to the left the ones who supply you; to the right, the ones you supply.

All right, who controls you?

RAY: The board.

NATHAN [agreeing]: You have to have your decisions approved by the board, naturally. However, you are the ones in touch with the situation, so your advice, if you can argue for it, will probably prevail. [They nod.] In any case, your job is to decide what advice to give to the board! Below you are the workers—including Andy and his five men. To the left, your various suppliers and, of course, the union—they supply labour at a negotiated rate. To the right—who? Who are your customers?

MARK: Several big ones, Defence—and a couple of nationalized, soon-to-be-privatized industries. And some big firms.

NATHAN: In any case, the point is there is this particular contract—for the X24. The danger is that it might be delayed, with penalties accruing.

RAY [disgustedly]: That's right!

NATHAN: Okay, having got an idea of the organizational context—although we'll come back to it as necessary—I want to say something.

Look at the management cross. You can see that your job as a team of two people—in fact anyone's job—has two sides to it. One is the 'technical' side, consisting of what you do by yourself, in the middle of the cross as it were: the other is the 'political', or 'people' side, which consists of reaching the right *understandings* with people on the arms of your cross. That's just as important!

MARK: What you call politics is practically the whole of a senior manager's job.

NATHAN: Exactly! As you go lower down the management hierarchy the 'technical' side seems more important. But actually 'politics'—having effective understandings with others—is an essential part of everyone's job, even right down to the bottom of the organization.

RAY [unexpectedly]: I agree. That's the point of the single-status organization. Everyone needs to take a managerial attitude to his or her job.

MARK [mildly]: It's company policy, actually.

RAY [with sudden exasperation, realizing that they are being side-tracked]: So—where's it getting us with *my problem*?

NATHAN [smoothly]: Let's see. Your current problem involves relationships up, down, left, and right on the management cross. Looking up, you've got to sell your strategy to the board, to get their backing—whether you hold out against Andy and his five or whether you give in. Looking to the right, the union plays a part—it presumably doesn't like what Andy's doing.

MARK: It's hopping mad!

NATHAN: And to the left, your customer plays a part—he'll insist on his pound of flesh if you fall down on the contract.

RAY [sardonically]: He will, he will.

NATHAN: But of course the main problem is downwards—with Andy and his five and perhaps with the other workers. Do they support Andy?

RAY: There's some sympathy with them.

MARK [with interest]: Is there? I suppose there are other groups that might want to go the same way.

RAY [not certain about this]: Well, maybe . . .

MARK [emphatically]: This could be disastrous.

Ray *looks at him and shakes his head briefly.*

NATHAN [after observing this exchange]: Well, we're here to see if we can avoid disaster! We've located our situation on the management cross. Now we've got to analyse it.

RAY: So—what do we do next?

Explanation

Nathan now asks Ray and Mark a series of questions about *what* are the issues in this situation, *who* has power to decide them, and *how* they would exercise that power. This evokes much discussion and valuable exchange of information between Ray and Mark. Finally, they are satisfied with the list of actors, options, and scenarios shown in Figure 1—although Nathan explains that the list need not be final, they will be able to come back to change it later if they wish. Nathan has used CONAN to set up this list on the computer screen and add notes attached to each actor and option. These sum up the information and insights, often newly arrived at, that Ray and Mark have given out. Now Nathan has written the actors and options on the flip chart.

	Go Slow	Dismissal	Strike	Go Slow, Six Covered
The Company				
1 concede	0	0	0	0
2 dismiss the six	0	1	1	0
The Six				
3 go slow	1	1	1	1
The Union				
4 call for a strike	0	0	–	0
The Workers				
5 strike	0	0	1	0
6 cover for the six	0	0	0	1

Figure 1
List of actors and options representing the company's situation, with four scenarios considered by the client group

The actors and options are fairly self-explanatory. Notice that it has been decided that two kinds of strike are possible—an official strike if the union calls for a strike and the workers obey, an unofficial one if the workers strike without the union issuing a call. The way in which the option 'Cover for the six' was arrived at is interesting. It had not previously occurred to Ray or Mark as a possibility. It arose from Nathan putting the question, in a search for new options—is there any way that the contract could be completed on time assuming that the go slow continues? It then struck Ray that it would be possible for the other workers to keep the machinery going in the short term without the six maintenance men.

The scenarios shown in Figure 1 have also been input into the computer, after further discussion. They have been picked out as being probably of interest, worth discussing, and interpreting. They are in fact different kinds of 'conflict point', none representing a satisfactory resolution of the problem. Nathan has just finished writing them on the flip chart.

Ray jumps up, comes forward and stabs his finger against the Go Slow scenario.

RAY [with disgust]: Exactly. That's where we are now—a go slow. That scenario is one where we're likely to be late with the contract—and lose millions.

MARK [still calm]: But the board has decided that we can't continue to give in— we've got to get tough with these unofficial splinter groups. These six people are losing nothing by going slow except a bit of overtime. I think they should be dismissed. [As he says this Nathan points to the Dismissal scenario.]

269

NATHAN: Which might lead to the other workers going on strike. [He moves his finger to the Strike scenario.]

MARK: Yes, they might go on unofficial strike, or the union might call for a strike, and they might vote in favour. It's a risk we've got to take. It makes little difference, actually, whether there's a strike or just a go slow, the contract will be delayed just the same. Of course, we'll do our best to fend off a strike, but [To Nathan] as in the case we looked at last week, it's a matter of standing firm against blackmail.

RAY: What case was that?

MARK: Oh, we were using the method to look at our marketing strategy. It helped the board to decide it had to face down our American friends.

NATHAN [a bit concerned at this]: Yes, but the method doesn't *always* tell you to be aggressive! It depends on your situation. Let's wait and see what we get this time.

MARK: Oh, quite, yes.

NATHAN: And now—may I ask about this other scenario, where the workers might cover for the six maintenance men.

RAY: That could save the contract for us.

MARK: It could?

RAY: Oh, sure. If the other workers really pitched in, we could swing it. [Nathan points to the Go Slow, Six Covered scenario on the flip chart.] But would they?

MARK: Would they pitch in? Heaven knows! But I think the point is we have to show them leadership, that we mean what we say. That means no giving in, regardless. I'm speaking for the board.

NATHAN: This is going to be interesting. But first, let me get this clear. As I understand it, the uncertainty as to whether the go slow would mean delaying the contract is largely taken up by the reaction of the other workers. If they cover for the six, the contract will probably be on time. If they don't, it won't. [The other two nod.] So that's an important option. Now, the next step . . .

Explanation

Nathan, seeing that time is short, skips discussion of any further scenarios and moves on to the stage of analysing actors threats and promises. This involves, first, choosing a particular scenario to analyse. He advises them to choose the current crisis at Go Slow, an important 'conflict point' which is also the present scenario.

	Go Slow	Concede
The Company		
1 concede	0	1
2 dismiss the six	0	0
The Six		
3 go slow	1	0
The Union		
4 call for a strike	0	0
The Workers		
5 strike	0	0
6 cover for the six	0	0

Figure 2
Two scenarios to be compared in regard to the preferences of the company

When this scenario is input, the CONAN program responds with a number of questions about actors preferences; that is, it wants to know the preferences of various actors for various other scenarios, compared to the scenario Go Slow. Nathan, after looking at the computer screen, decides that the most meaningful question to put first to the client group is about the company's preferences for the second scenario shown in Figure 2. This is not one of the scenarios previously considered, but probably should have been had there been more time. It is, as far as Nathan can see, the 'position'of the six. He writes it on the flip chart and gives it the title Concede. He explains that the computer wishes to know which scenario is preferred by the company—Go Slow or Concede.

NATHAN: So which of these is preferred—assuming, as it seems we must, that the Go Slow would almost certainly mean delay with the contract?

There is a dramatic pause, during which Ray shoots sidelong glances at Mark.

MARK [loudly and firmly]: The board has decided it will put up with the go slow rather than concede.

RAY [quietly]: Did you persuade it to that view?

MARK: Well, yes.

NATHAN [after looking from one to the other]: But, may I make a point here? We aren't asking what the board has decided to do—we're asking about its preferences between scenarios. These aren't necessarily the same. The board may decide to put up with the go slow for strategic reasons, even though it doesn't like it! That will come out in the analysis. But there's a distinction between putting up with something you don't like and actually liking it! That's the distinction you're being asked to make here—in confidence, of course. To answer it, the usual way is to weigh up pros and cons. Pro the concession is, of course, to complete the contract on time. Con it is to maintain the wage structure you've just negotiated. How do these factors weigh against each other?

Ray *looks at* Mark, *who is silent.*

NATHAN: You see what I mean?

MARK [grimly]: I see what you mean.

NATHAN: Well—let me make another point about the identity of actors. We've defined an actor here—the company. But we have an axiom, 'Every player is a game,' meaning the preferences and strategies of an actor are determined internally by a game going on between different parties within that actor. Now doesn't it seem that an internal game is just what we have in this case? It seems that you and Ray disagree, with Ray attaching more importance to the contract. But it's the board, finally, that will decide! So it's a question of estimating how the preference—not necessarily the action—would finally be judged by the board.

MARK [heavily]: The board attaches a lot of weight to the contract. [Hurriedly] But it does agree that we must stand firm.

NATHAN: I think, then, that it's a question of standing firm for strategic reasons, and the actual preference, in terms of pros and cons, would be for concession. Let me repeat, this doesn't mean that you have to concede!

MARK [slowly and reluctantly]: Okay, I agree with that. I guess the board's preference for Go Slow has to be based on the belief, or hope, that the six will give in. If we discount that, then certainly we prefer Concede.

NATHAN [after a pause]: Okay—and I think that probably the same preference is shared by all the actors ... Certainly it is by the six.

RAY: And by the other workers! The main thing for them is to have the dispute over—they have bonuses to earn if the contract's completed on time.

NATHAN: And the union? [Taking their silence for consent]: Even though you said it was hopping mad at the six's action?

MARK: Even though—? Oh, yes. After all, if the six succeed the union will have *carte blanche* to go at us for more concessions. It's the go slow it doesn't like.

	Go Slow	Normal Working
The Company		
1 concede	0	0
2 dismiss the six	0	0
The Six		
3 go slow	1	0
The Union		
4 call for a strike	0	0
The Workers		
5 strike	0	0
6 cover for the six	0	0

Figure 3
Scenarios to be compared in regard to the preferences of the six

NATHAN: So it's a preference for everyone, I think.

He inputs this preference judgement into the computer, waits a while, presses another key and writes his next question on the flip chart. Again the computer has asked about a new scenario—the second one in Figure 3—which he recognizes as the position of the company and gives the title Normal Working. His question is: which of the scenarios in Figure 3 is preferred by the six? As Nathan writes these two columns on the flip chart, Mark gets up and starts walking around with his hands behind his back.

NATHAN [with his eye on Mark]: So the question now before us is—do the six prefer the go slow for itself, or for strategic reasons?

RAY: They must be concerned about the contract being on time. Of course they must, they have bonuses at stake like everyone else! And anyhow they're losing overtime while they go slow.

NATHAN: So when we consider preferences for scenarios, the six are in a corresponding position to the company. They too would prefer to concede, in the sense of ceasing to go slow, rather than hold out at the current scenario. They're going slow for strategic reasons, to try to force you to concede, not for preference reasons.

RAY: Of course. That's right, isn't it, Mark?

MARK [stopping to look at the flip chart, then giving an objective answer]: It is. The union and the workers would prefer normal working too, of course. [He resumes pacing up and down.]

	Go Slow	Dismissal
The Company		
1 concede	0	0
2 dismiss the six	0	1
The Six		
3 go slow	1	1
The Union		
4 call for a strike	0	0
The Workers		
5 strike	0	0
6 cover for the six	0	0

Figure 4
Scenarios to be compared in regard to the company's preferences

NATHAN: Great! [Goes to the computer and inputs this assumption. Looks at the screen for a moment.] H'm, that's a good question. [Writes on the flip chart the scenarios in Figure 4.]

NATHAN [pointing to the second scenario]: This is the scenario in which the company shows tough and dismisses the six. Presumably, from what you've been saying, the board would prefer this scenario, under present circumstances, to the go slow—provided at least that there was no strike?

RAY: How's that? We've said that, as far as preferences go, the board would prefer to concede.

NATHAN: Yes, fine, but that's not the question now. The question is—given no concession and given continuation of the go slow, would they *then* prefer to dismiss the six?

RAY [thoughtfully]: They would, I suppose—so long as it didn't provoke a strike.

NATHAN [back at the computer]: Okay, so that is preferred, provided there's no strike. [He operates the computer.] Now, what's left? [He presses a key.] H'm, that's something. [Goes back to the flip chart and writes up the two columns in Figure 5.]

NATHAN [pointing to second scenario]: This is the scenario in which the other workers cover for the six. Here's my question. The company would naturally prefer the workers to cover for the six—but what about the workers? Would they prefer to do it—so that the contract wouldn't be delayed?

Mark *stops in his stride and stares at the flip chart.* Ray *raps sharply on the table with his pen. A short, intense pause.*

	Go Slow	Go Slow, Six Covered
The Company		
1 concede	0	0
2 dismiss the six	0	0
The Six		
3 go slow	1	1
The Union		
4 call for a strike	0	0
The Workers		
5 strike	0	0
6 cover for the six	0	1

Figure 5
Scenarios to be compared with respect to the other workers' preferences

RAY [carefully]: Perhaps. I think at the moment they're waiting for management's reaction.

NATHAN: Again, please remember we're not asking about actions, but about preferences between scenarios. They may be deterred from acting at the moment—but what about these scenarios? If they cover, the contract is on time, they get bonuses...

RAY: They do indeed.

NATHAN: ...If they don't, what do they get? Are they sympathetic to the six's claim?

MARK [to Ray]: You said they were.

RAY: I think there's some sympathy, but not that much. They're waiting to see how it goes. I think if they were sure management would stand firm...

MARK: Which we will.

RAY: ...and if the maintenance men aren't dismissed ... I'm afraid the men'd be bound to take their side if the six were dismissed!

Mark *looks sharply at* Ray.

NATHAN: Okay, so can we put it in as preferred provided there's a zero against dismissal?

RAY [looking at Mark]: I think so.

MARK [tensely]: Yes. Makes sense.

Explanation

Nathan inputs this assumption, and the computer asks more questions. Many of these are interesting, and give rise to further interaction and exchange of information between Ray and Mark. All are relevant, or the program—which constantly recalculates the minimum further information it needs to perform each step of the analysis—would not ask them. Many of the answers, however, are fairly obvious: these Nathan quickly answers on his own, just mentioning them to his clients as a check on his thinking.

Asking these questions, many of which are seen to be important when asked, but which Ray and Mark would not have put so clearly to themselves or each other, is a major benefit of the analysis. The program's analytic output, on the other hand, is rather too technical for Nathan to want to show to Ray and Mark. It is easier to communicate with them through 'strategic maps' drawn from the analysis.

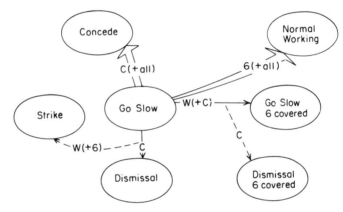

Figure 6
Strategic map showing analysis of Go Slow scenario

The play resumes as Nathan finishes drawing the map in Figure 6. In this map, as explained in the previous chapter, improvements (preferred scenarios obtainable by unilateral action) are shown by firm arrows labelled with the names of the 'improvers' followed by the bracketed names of all others that benefit from the improvement. Sanctions (reactions that would deter improvements) are shown by dotted arrows. Improvements with no sanctions to deter them are shown by double-line arrows.

RAY [after standing up, leaning across the table to get a better look, then sitting down slowly]: Okay, what does it all mean?

NATHAN [expansively]: This sums up the whole analysis of the Go Slow scenario.

From Go Slow, there are four improvements, of which the best two—for everybody, this is something they all agree on—are the two at the top, to Concede and Normal Working. The trouble is, these are what we call *rival improvements*—meaning that the actors have a reason to stay where they are because each wants the other to be the one to move. The company's objective is Normal Working—but the six have to be the ones to move to get there. And the six's objective is Concede—but the company has to move if it is to get there! So each may stay where it is, on the hot seat, hoping the other will be the one to move! Sitting on this hot seat, they're likely to feel a mixture of emotions. Anger, when they think of how they must hold out against the temptation to give in. Goodwill and cooperativeness, when they think of how much they want the other to give in. But the less they communicate, the more that negative feelings will predominate, because then the priority is to be the one that holds out longer!

RAY [explosively]: There's damn all communication going on at present!

NATHAN: Then anger is likely to be growing on both sides.

RAY: How right you are!

NATHAN [after pausing to absorb the compliment]: As for the other improvements, they, unlike the first two, are not 'guaranteed'; they can be deterred by threats. Let's take the workers improvement first—where they move to cover the six, and so save the contract and their bonuses. On the assumptions you've made, they can be deterred from this by the 'threat' (whether or not it's intended by management as a threat) that the company may move to dismiss the six! I think perhaps this identifies the feeling one of you expressed—I think it was you, Ray—that the workers were waiting to see how management was going to react. They're being deterred, at present, from moving to cover the six by the 'threat'—so called—of management action.

Ray *looks at* Mark, *who is now sitting down and looking rather morose. There is a pause.*

MARK: Go on. I'm listening.

NATHAN: The other improvement—by the company in moving to dismiss the six—is also deterrable, by the threat of a strike, official or unofficial. Official action would require the union and the workers to act, unofficial action only the workers; in either case, the workers' will to act is essential. Of course, this threat has to be credible, and I think, Mark, that it's largely because you're not sure of the credibility of that threat that you've hesitated so far to carry out the policy you got the board to agree with—get tough and dismiss the lot of them!

MARK [unwillingly]: I think—you're right.

NATHAN: So that explains why we're stuck, for the moment, where we are—on the hot seat of Go Slow! The improvements at the top aren't being taken because they're rival improvements. And the improvements down below are being deterred. Of course, the scenario isn't stable!—a scenario with rival improvements from it is usually unstable, because of course it's *not* being accepted by the parties—on the contrary, each is doing what it is doing *because it expects the other to change.* So it's unstable—which doesn't mean it can't happen. It's like a jeep trundling towards a cliff edge with two passengers in it, each refusing to be the one to steer! You may well go over the cliff edge—delay the contract—even though that is unstable and nobody wants it.

RAY [fascinated]: But what's your advice to someone sitting in such a jeep?

NATHAN: Well, the first question is, can you get to a better jeep? Sometimes you can—and in this case I think it's possible—here. [He stabs with his finger at the Go Slow, Six Covered scenario.] But it may not be possible, so I'll answer the question generally as follows. When you're stuck in the jeep, be emotional but friendly and advance as many *rational arguments in the common interest* as you possibly can as to why they—the other side—should be the ones to steer. And listen to, and answer fully and carefully, every rational argument they put forward! The more rational arguments in the common interest you can nail down on your side, the more difficult you make it for yourself to give in—and the easier you make it for them! That's why rational arguments—got from OR studies, or from wherever else you like—are vitally important. But they must be used in the right way, backed up by the right sanctions.

RAY [soberly]: I see.

There is a pause. Then Mark *stands up and goes to the flip chart. From this point on he tends to take charge of the meeting, making decisions and reasserting his authority as a director.*

MARK: Okay. So if we are in a confrontation, that's how we should handle it. That's right, I think. That should be our approach, Ray, not to continue with this lack of communication, but sit down and talk it over with them. Point out as reasonably as we can that it's out of the question for us to make an exception for them, however strong their case, but they'll just have to wait till their position is reviewed within the newly agreed pay scales. Make it stick.

RAY: The trouble is, they've got a strong case.

MARK: Ours is stronger. We can answer them and make it stick.

RAY [agreeing, while feeling there is something more to be said]: Okay, it can't do any harm. Maybe they'll give in. Whereas if we carry on as we are doing . . . [He gives an eloquent shrug.]

MARK [dismissing him]: I agree. [Turning to Nathan] And now—let's get on to the other possibility you mentioned. Can we get to a better jeep?

NATHAN: A better jeep? Yes, I think we should analyse this particular scenario . . . [He points to Go Slow, Six Covered.]

Explanation

It is back to the computer now to analyse another scenario! This time, however, there are fewer judgements to be made, as the program stores and uses all judgements made previously. Nathan completes the analysis and illustrates it by adding a few more arrows to the strategic map already on the flip chart. The result is the map in Figure 7.

Mark *is standing next to the flip chart as* Nathan *finishes drawing on it.*

MARK: So where is the better jeep? Explain it to me.

NATHAN [points to 'Go Slow, Six Covered']: Here it is, a much better jeep. From here there is *no* improvement to the solution they want. That's because on the assumptions you've given me, you prefer this scenario to the concession —your reason being that after all, with the others covering for the six men, it'll probably mean the contract finishing on time. So *you* prefer this to the concession, and *you* have to be active if there is to be a concession,

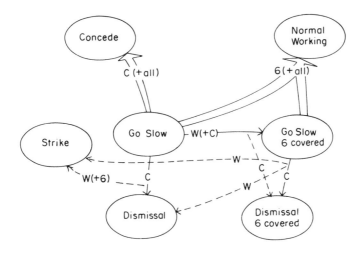

Figure 7
The 'better jeep': strategic map of the two scenarios, 'Go Slow' and 'Go Slow, 6 Covered'

consequently there is no improvement from here to the concession! Consequently, they have to be the ones to give in—you can't and won't. There are just two problems. [He pauses, thinking.]

MARK [patiently]: Yes. What are they?

NATHAN [beginning to sound rather academic]: Well, one is not too difficult, you can probably get over it all right. I mean the fact that the workers might not want to go to this scenario—might not want to start covering for the six men—simply because they're deterred by the threat that you might dismiss the six. And that threat is very credible, because it's doing something you want to do anyway—it's a 'willing' threat, not an 'unwilling' one. It's the board's decision, I think you said, isn't it?

MARK: It is.

NATHAN: Well, it won't do.

MARK [amused]: I think I see what you mean. But just spell it out for us.

NATHAN: Quite simply—do you want the other workers to cover for the six? You must—it makes your position much stronger.

MARK: We do.

NATHAN: Then on the assumptions you've made, you must convince the workers you're *not* going to dismiss the six men.

A pause. Mark *turns to* Ray.

MARK: He's right, it makes sense.

RAY [enthusiastically]: I think it does.

NATHAN: That way you're bound to win—I assume the workers will take your word for it and be persuaded to cover for the six—except for the other problem . . .

MARK: What's that?

NATHAN: Well, we've said that when you're in a dangerous jeep, you should use rational arguments in the common interest, accompanied by appropriate emotions, to make it credible that you won't give way. These are good ways to win—but you can also use deceit! Deceive them into thinking that you do actually prefer the conflict point—Go Slow—to giving in, and then they must give in!

MARK: I don't think we could try to make them believe that. The whole workforce knows how much the contract matters to us—we've told them so.

NATHAN: No, and of course you want to get to your better jeep instead. The point is, however, that where there's a reason for deceit, there's a reason for *disbelief*! Suppose now that you are here, at the scenario Go Slow, Six Covered. Even if you didn't prefer this scenario to Concession, you would *have reason to pretend you do*. Therefore, you're likely to encounter disbelief! Let's see—the six will know that their work is being covered—but they may not believe that that's enough to guarantee the contract being finished on time! Right? Unless you can persuade them it is, and so persuade them that you really do prefer Go Slow, Six Covered to conceding, they're likely to continue going slow.

MARK [reasonably]: But that won't matter too much, in those circumstances. If the others cover for the six men, we are in fact likely to fulfil the contract on time—that's the main consideration.

NATHAN [collapsing with his argument]: Well yes, that's true.

MARK [pointing to the flip chart]: No, the important thing is to move from here to there—you've convinced me of that now, and of the way to do it. Are you happy about that, Ray?

RAY [grinning broadly]: I'm *very* happy.

MARK: So am I. I think this day's session may have saved us from sacrificing five million pounds in order to try to show we're tough.

RAY: Whereas what really appears as tough is to win!

MARK: Exactly. And now—I think we must be about finished for today . . . [He turns to see if Nathan agrees with this.]

RAY [breaking in as he sees an opportunity to get away]: Are we? Well that's great—I'm going to head right back to the plant and start implementing this analysis. I'll assure the men that management is not going to fire anyone— then maybe get some lateral thinking going about how to get the contract done on time.

MARK [heartily]: Okay.

RAY [shaking hands with Nathan]: I can't thank you enough. It's been exhausting—feel like my brain's been through a wringer—but well worth while.

NATHAN [showing signs of wanting to carry on]: Okay, well I'll go ahead and finish the model on my own—there are one or two loose ends to tie up, but I don't think they'll make much difference. But, of course, I'd like another session to present the finished model and discuss it with you. And to draw out the training implications—so that you can generalize from this experience and learn from it.

MARK [reassuringly]: That's fine—as we arranged it.

RAY [still shaking hands with Nathan]: Goodbye, and thanks very much. [Exits with a cheery gesture to Mark.]

MARK [watching Nathan, who is looking a little uncertainly at the door through which Ray has gone]: Well? How do you feel? Are you satisfied with how it went?

NATHAN: I don't know. [Pointing to the audience] Let's ask them!

At which point the actors stop acting and begin discussing the play with the audience...

12
Modelling interactive decisions: the hypergame focus

Peter Bennett, Steve Cropper, and Chris Huxham

Introduction

Like others described here, our approach aims to help with decisions variously termed 'wicked', 'complex' or 'messy'. In these situations, objectives cannot easily be quantified, subjective judgement is important, and there may be no precedents to guide action. Our specific concern is with situations under the partial control of several parties, each with a stake in the outcome, and some power to affect what happens. Often, each side's decisions will depend on the choices (or predicted choices) of others: we say that their decisions are 'interactive'. Usually, the parties' aims or interests differ, giving at least some potential for conflict. But conflict is seldom absolute: there will also be some common interests, and gains to be made by cooperating. So though our concern is with 'conflict' in a general sense, it is not just with obvious, hostile conflicts. It is with threats and promises, bluff and counterbluff—or conversely, attempts to coordinate actions—and with negotiation and bargaining, under conditions ranging from goodwill to outright enmity. Such situations are marked by questions such as:

'What will their reaction be if we go ahead with this?'

'If they don't help now, the whole project is in jeopardy, so why aren't they going along with us? Is someone else holding them to ransom?'

'How can we steal a march on the competition for this contract?'

'Making concessions now might undermine our colleagues' position—can we agree a joint approach?'

'How can we limit (or encourage) the spread of disruptive action?'

'If we fight, who will support us? At what price?'

Implicitly or explicitly, such questions often form part of the cut and thrust of decision making in many different settings—in business, national, local or international politics, voluntary organizations or, for that matter, academia. However, some decision makers are more obviously concerned with interactive problems than others. Within organizations, these are likely to be either at the top of the hierarchy, or with a high degree of local autonomy, particularly where responsibilities include competitive strategy or the resolution of internal disagreements. Between organizations, likely users are those seeking to coordinate joint projects, negotiate partnerships or resolve disputes. A final class of users are those acting outside any large, formal organization—individuals or small groups trying to manage their own decisions more effectively, and for whom a 'conflict' perspective may be particularly relevant (Rosenhead, 1986).

The methods to be described below offer ways of analysing interactive decisions, using (amongst others) the ideas of *hypergame analysis*. The rest of this introductory section outlines the general 'view of the world' underlying this approach, and the sorts of help that can be offered to decision makers.

The hypergame approach rests on four presumptions. Firstly, it embodies a 'pluralist' view of the world, in which many actors—individuals, groups, and organizations—can make choices to advance their own aims and interests. Their aims may be altruistic (or vindictive) rather than self-centred; they may also be imprecise, changeable, and subject to internal conflict. Though we are mainly concerned with deliberate decisions, we are certainly not confined to narrow models based on 'rational self-interest'.

The second presumption is that decisions taken by each actor very often affect the well-being of others. Even if choices are *made* independently, without consultation or reference to anyone else, their consequences usually make actors *interdependent*; A's actions affect B, who can in turn affect A. The actors may manage their interdependence to their own advantage, or unwittingly create outcomes intended by no one.

Thirdly, actors often hold different views of situations in which they are involved. For example, relevant parties can be perceived in various ways, a point which can affect one's whole definition of the problem. Thus, a local council is often seen simply as 'the council' by members of the public. But those within it, or with particular reasons for dealing with it (for example leaders of pressure groups, or businessmen negotiating contracts) tend to see far more differentiated (and differing) structures of officers and councillors, departments, committees, and so forth. This emphasis on differing problem constructions—shared with the SODA/Cognitive Mapping approach (see Chapters 2 and 3)—differentiates hypergames from other game-based approaches.

These three points underpin hypergame theory. In developing the approach in practice, we have also been at pains to stress a fourth: that each actor is commonly involved in complex systems of related decisions. A national union leader, say, believes that the union should support one local branch in a dispute, avoid getting embroiled in another, and prepare for a probable fight over a national pay claim. This last will need inter-union support, and relations with other unions are strained. There are factions within the national committee. She is due to retire, and is determined that her deputy should not succeed her. Delaying retirement would help achieve that, but she would like to spend more time with her husband. And so on. . . . It could be misleading to analyse any one of these interactions in isolation, but of little help just to insist that 'everything is connected to everything else'.

Having outlined the presumptions behind the hypergame approach, it is also important to stress a wider point. We see hypergame modelling as one element in an overall approach to helping with complex problems which may involve conflict, uncertainty, differences in perception, and other difficulties. Many other theories and models are highly relevant to interactive decisions. Some come from within the field of conflict studies—for example, models of how conflicts develop and change over time. Others come from approaches developed quite separately from conflict analysis as such, some of which are described elsewhere in this volume. Strategic Choice and Robustness Analysis (Chapters 6–9) concentrate on managing uncertainty and maintaining flexibility. Cognitive Mapping and other methods within SODA (Chapters 2–3) provide ways of accessing and using the different problem definitions typically held within groups. We regard these perspectives as complementary, not exclusive. Our overall approach is, therefore, to use elements of these different strands of analysis in combination (Bennett, 1985; Bennett and Cropper, 1986). We return to the theme of combining methods later in this chapter, and in the case study that follows.

How, then, can hypergames help? What 'help' means will depend greatly on *whom* one is trying to help—especially in a conflict. Analysis done for one side will obviously differ from work to support mediation (Bennett, 1988). Both differ again from research at a distance, carried out without direct involvement with any of the parties—who may nevertheless use it for their own purposes. In offering direct assistance, the main concern of this chapter, the types of help that are appropriate also depend on the client's own position. (For the less powerful, analysis itself can provide one form of empowerment: understanding the 'game' becomes the prelude to changing it.) Nevertheless, it will be useful to set out four general types of help, relevant to a wide range of settings (Bennett and Cropper, 1986).

Firstly, a consultant can help clients to articulate and think through their problems. Like other contributors to this volume, we generally aim to work *with* clients (especially in small, relatively informal groups), rather than primarily carrying out analysis *for* them. Provided that potential clients are prepared to work in this way (not all are) one can thus take the role of 'process manager', seeking to facilitate debate and decision. The consequences of shared assumptions can be brought to the surface, as can disagreements about what 'the problem' is. A seemingly mundane but important function can be to record ideas in a convenient form.

At the next level, though the analyst will not usually have any expertise on the specific problem in hand, he or she can be a valuable generator of new ideas—ideas that may challenge current thinking. Being an outsider can in itself provide opportunities to put forward a fresh view. In addition, the analyst may have encountered other situations from which analogies can be drawn, while general theories about the nature of conflict and about decision processes provide a further basis for suggestions.

A third form of help is that of setting problems in a structured format. To quote Phillips (1982), the analysts 'contribute the form of the model and the problem owners provide content'. This is a role going beyond pure facilitation, while stopping short of providing expertise on the problem itself. The analyst comes armed with ways of conceptualizing problems—a range of 'relevant' questions, and models to encapsulate the answers given. These help to draw attention to particular aspects of problems, as well as to express clients' views.

Finally, more formal analysis of key aspects of the situation can be undertaken, often revealing points that would not otherwise have been picked up. Most importantly, models can be built up to incorporate different hypotheses about the situation—for example about other parties' aims or possible strategies. Analysis then helps in testing alternative assumptions, and in searching for responses effective in a variety of possible cases.

The relative importance of these roles can vary widely, even in the course of a single piece of work. The distinctions between them also blur;

for example, using a 'structured format' may lead one to ask questions that already imply a 'fresh view'. In particular, trying to apply the models described here 'forces' questions about the interactions of different parties' decisions—whether or not these were already at the forefront of clients' thinking. Though the first two forms of help may be informed by the hypergame perspective, it contributes more directly to the latter two. Both here and in Chapter 13, we thus emphasize these last two forms of help—problem structuring and formal analysis.

The next two sections will describe the various forms of model used within the hypergame approach, while that following discusses how these can be used as part of a practical methodology for helping with decisions.

Modelling interactions: simple games and hypergames

Hypergame analysis has its own range of models for representing interactive decisions. In this section, we gradually introduce this repertoire, starting from the simplest. We thus start from the basic model of interactive decisions provided by game theory, then show how simple hypergames can allow for differences in perceptions amongst the actors involved. In the course of this, we also set out various ways of representing games or hypergames ('matrices', 'trees', and 'tableaux'), each with particular advantages and disadvantages. Though we shall use simple illustrations of various types of model, the process and purposes of modelling are largely left to one side here, to be taken up in the next section.

The 'game' model

To describe something as a 'game', in this context, is not to imply that it is trivial, or that there must be winners and losers. In this respect, the name is unfortunate. Rather, a game is simply a model of interactive decisions, consisting of 'players', 'strategies', 'outcomes', and 'preferences'.

The *players* are simply the interested parties; those who have a stake in what happens, and some power to affect events. They may be individuals, groupings such as committees or cabinets, or entities such as companies, councils, unions or nations.

Each player has various *strategies*, representing possible courses of action. Often, moves can be made at various stages in the game: technically, each strategy contains a complete recipe of moves. (Do 'a' initially, then do 'b' if he does 'x', but do 'c' if he does 'y' or 'z', then ...)

A choice of strategy for each player defines an *outcome* of the game. To complete the model, we specify how good or bad each outcome is for each player. Originally, it was supposed that this could be measured, in terms of utility values. Simpler models are now often used, based on *preference orderings* for each player which rank outcomes from 'best' down to 'worst'.

In such a game, the players' aims may conflict to a greater or lesser extent. At one extreme, in 'zero-sum' games, one player's gain must always be another's loss. At the other extreme, players' aims exactly coincide. Between these are mixed-motive games, in which players may be torn between conflict and cooperation.

Analysis normally assumes that each player knows everyone's available strategies and preferences, but not what the other(s) will choose to do. In two-player zero-sum games, an optimal strategy for each player can be shown mathematically to exist (Von Neumann and Morgenstern, 1944). But outside the world of parlour games, zero-sum cases are fortunately rare. (If an 'elegant' victory with fewer overall casualties is preferred, even military conflicts are no longer zero-sum.) Mixed-motive games are much closer to the real world of partial conflict, threats and promises, bargaining and negotiation. Here, the neat mathematical results disappear. The role of the model can best be seen in terms not of getting right answers, but of helping to clarify the structure of the situation, complete with any dilemmas and difficulties.

As we shall see, games can be represented in several forms. We first illustrate the most common 'matrix form', using a standard game known as *Prisoners' Dilemma*. This gets its name from a story about two criminals held on suspicion of having jointly committed a serious crime. The District Attorney has insufficient evidence to gain convictions on this charge, though he can convict each of a lesser offence. So the prisoners are isolated in separate cells, and offered a choice. Each can confess to the serious crime ('squealing', and so implicating his partner) or remain silent (cooperating with the other). The deal put to each is as follows: if one confesses while the other does not, the first goes free, while the other has the book thrown at him (say, fifteen years). If both confess, each gets a severe sentence, but with some reduction for confessing (say, ten years in gaol). If both remain silent, each will be convicted of the minor crime (two years behind bars).

The logic of the prisoners' problem can be laid out as in Figure 1. A's strategies are shown down one side of a matrix, B's along the other. (A three-player game would have a 3-D matrix, and so on.) Figure 1(a) shows the four outcomes that can result from their choices: the entries in each box show the penalties each of them would suffer. This clarifies the structure of the problem. But to go further with analysis, we need some information or assumptions about which outcomes each player would

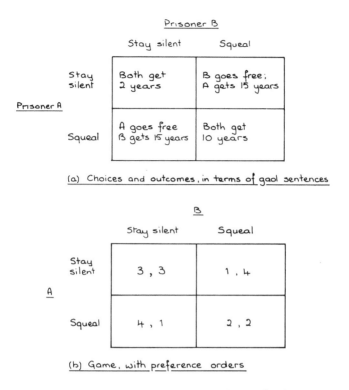

Prisoner B

Stay silent   Squeal

Prisoner A

	Stay silent	Squeal
Stay silent	Both get 2 years	B goes free; A gets 15 years
Squeal	A goes free B gets 15 years	Both get 10 years

(a) Choices and outcomes, in terms of gaol sentences

B

Stay silent   Squeal

A

	Stay silent	Squeal
Stay silent	3 , 3	1 , 4
Squeal	4 , 1	2 , 2

(b) Game, with preference orders

Numbers show each player's preference for the outcomes, ordered from 4 ('best') down to 1 ('worst'). A's preferences are shown on the left in each case.

Figure 1
'Prisoners' dilemma' game

prefer. This, of course, depends on their aims. If we suppose that each mainly wants to minimize his gaol sentence, their preferences will be ordered as follows, from 'best' down to 'worst':

> I squeal, he stays silent (so I go free).
> Both of us keep silent (I get 2 years).
> Both of us squeal (I get 10 years).
> I stay silent, he squeals (I end up the 'fall guy', getting 15 years).

This gives the game of Figure 1(b), in which the preferences are shown by means of numbers—4 for 'best' down to 1 for 'worst'. We could equally well have used some other, non-numerical symbols—such as those used in the 'robustness' diagrams of Chapter 8.

The dilemma facing the prisoners is as follows. Knowing what the game is, A may well reason: 'I don't know what B will do, but there are two possible cases. If he stays silent, confessing gives me my best outcome ('4' instead of '3'). If he confesses, then by doing the same, I at least avoid my worst outcome. Either way, I do better by confessing.'

A has a so-called 'dominant strategy': one that pays off whatever B chooses. B's position is analogous, and A knows this. So it seems 'rational' for each to squeal—and to expect the other to do so. However, they then do worse (2, 2) than they would if each cooperated with the other and stayed silent (3, 3). In real terms, each gets ten years behind bars instead of two! Despite this, (2, 2) is the only *equilibrium* in the game: an outcome which neither player could improve on by changing his or her choice unilaterally.

This, and similar 'paradoxes of rationality'—to use Howard's apt phrase —have generated a voluminous literature (see Hardin, 1968; Howard, 1971; Axelrod, 1984). Various criteria have been proposed for defining when outcomes are 'stable'. Roughly, a stable outcome is one likely to persist because no player would gain by initiating a move away from it. The idea of 'equilibrium' noted above provides one definition of stability, but considers only unilateral changes of strategy. Wider criteria have been developed, to take account of other players' possible responses to any initial change. Some of these criteria arguably remove the dilemma in the game above, by making mutual cooperation stable too.

Analysing games for stability can help in predicting final outcomes. Just as importantly, it provides insight into why outcomes may be stable or unstable, and into the threats, promises, and arguments players might use. Simple models such as Prisoners' Dilemma can also be extended in many ways (by allowing some communication, for example). An impressive range of situations have been modelled in these terms—from biological evolution to arms races and trade wars, from the establishment of trust in business to unofficial truces in the trenches. One fascination of such models is the unearthing of common features in problems which at first sight seemed quite unrelated.

The basic hypergame model

Despite its intellectual power, Game Theory has been criticized as over-idealized, irrelevant, and even malign. Without attempting to review the arguments here, critics seem to be on firm ground in at least one respect. Game models normally assume that the same game is seen by all participants. A cursory study of the real world—and many far-from-cursory studies (for example, de Rivera, 1968; Jervis, 1970)—suggests that this is seldom true. Decision makers may indeed conceptualize problems in terms similar to those of game theory, but they typically see *different* games. Furthermore, this can be important in determining what actually happens. So it is better to model such situations not as a single game, but as a collection of subjective games. This is the fundamental idea of hypergame analysis.

The hypergame model shares with the simple game model the basic concepts of players, strategies, and outcomes. But it is now necessary to specify the strategies and preferences each player believes everyone (including self) to have. In effect, this means that there are separate games for each player. As will be seen from the following two examples, these can differ as to perceived preferences, available strategies (and hence outcomes), or both.

Our first example comes from a classic cautionary tale in international relations (Rapoport, 1960). A and B are rulers of two nations, each desiring peace but suspicious of the other. A search for 'security' prompts an arms race, in which each side sees itself as reacting to the threat of the other's weapons. In its extreme form, the story ends with a 'mad dash to the launching platforms'. This situation has often been modelled by the Prisoners' Dilemma game (usually with 'disarm' as the 'cooperative' strategy, though the model can be adapted to cover more specific proposals). But the Prisoners' Dilemma model applies only to players who would like, above all else, to gain an arms lead. Suppose, however, that A and B genuinely want mutual disarmament, but don't trust each other. Still keeping things artificially simple, we can model such a situation as follows. Let us suppose that each player has the same straight choice—arm or disarm—and that each sees these as the strategies available to both. These perceived strategies, and their outcomes, are shown in Figure 2(a). Let us further suppose that A, being 'genuinely peace loving', has the following preference order:

Mutual disarmament.

Arms lead for A (A arms, B disarms).

Arms race.

Arms lead for B (A disarms, B arms).

Alas, this is not how B sees matters; he believes that A would most prefer an arms lead. In A's preferences *as seen by B*, the first two outcomes are, therefore, reversed. If A perceives B in the same way, the hypergame of Figure 2(b) results.

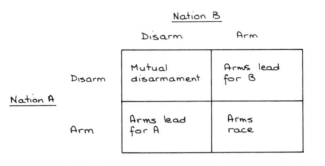

(a) Choices and outcomes (as seen by both sides)

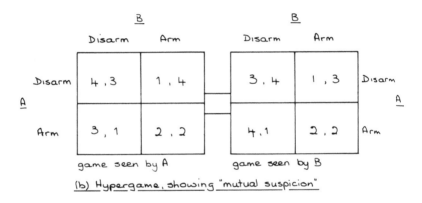

(b) Hypergame, showing "mutual suspicion"

Figure 2
Simple hypergame model of an arms race

In this model, both 'arms race' and 'mutual disarmament' are stable. Neither side has a dominant strategy, but A *perceives* 'arm' to be a dominant strategy for B. Believing that whatever he does, it will pay B to arm, A 'has' to arm too, to avoid his worst outcome. So does B, on the basis of his beliefs about A. The result is an arms race nobody wanted, while each side's actions only serve to confirm the other's suspicions. It is not the intention to argue for this as *the* model of any current arms race, though it has some plausibility as a partial explanation (Bennett and Dando, 1982; Plous, 1985). Rather, it provides a simple model of mutual distrust, in which competition can persist even if each side would really like nothing better than to stop. The driving force is not desire for superiority, but fear of being left behind.

Let us now look at a second example of a hypergame, this time showing how one can model cases in which players misconstrue what others are able to do. One result of this can be 'strategic surprise', in which one player uses a strategy unseen or discounted by others. There are many examples in military history (see, for example, Bennett and Dando, 1979), but contemporary and 'peaceful' examples also exist. A recent example in the field of land-use planning concerned a major site on London's South Bank known as Coin Street (Cropper, 1986).

Coin Street had been a source of controversy for many years. Lying within Greater London, it straddled the boundary between two boroughs, so that three local authorities held statutory planning powers. Many different development proposals had been made; all had foundered through changes in the economic climate and in political control of the councils. In 1980, the Secretary of State for the Environment intervened. At this point, several commercial property developers were seeking to build offices, while a local community group (with support from two of the councils) had put forward a scheme for public housing. Following a Public Inquiry into thirteen different planning applications, the Secretary of State rejected them all. In his judgement, the office proposals represented gross over-development, while the scheme for housing would generate insufficient employment. He laid out guidelines for further proposals. Two contenders, Greycoats Commercial Estates and the Association of Waterloo Groups (AWG)—the foremost commercial developers and the local community group—set about revising their plans, each aiming to become sole developer of the site.

We take up the story at this point, by considering the possible actions of three main participants: Greycoats, AWG, and the Secretary of State.

Greycoats and AWG each had to decide how far to modify their proposals: the Secretary of State would then reconsider. This much seems to have been seen by all. As Greycoats and AWG perceived matters, each could make a range of modifications. For illustrative purposes, we shall consider just two broad alternatives: to make only minor changes to their earlier proposals, or to make major changes to meet the new guidelines as closely as possible. It is also clear that both saw three possible moves for the Secretary of State: to accept Greycoat's proposal, accept AWG's, or reject both. The possible outcomes can be visualized as in Figure 3.

We consider the analysis of this game later. For present purposes, the main point of interest is that the Secretary of State chose to do something quite unforeseen by the other two players. That *both* schemes could be approved had been regarded as beyond the realms of possibility (see, for example, GLC, 1979). But this is exactly what the Secretary of State did—to

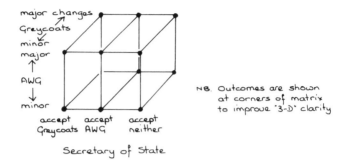

Figure 3
'Coin Street' example: matrix of choices as seen by developers (AWG and Greycoats)

almost universal annoyance and confusion:

> This even-handedness has annoyed the planning authorities, confused the developers, and exasperated the community groups who fail to see how their predominantly residential scheme could possibly be married with [Greycoats'] grand design. (Planning, 1983)

Perhaps the choice need not have come as such a shock. (If both schemes were broadly acceptable, approving both might improve the chance of one or other being implemented.) But the decision was totally

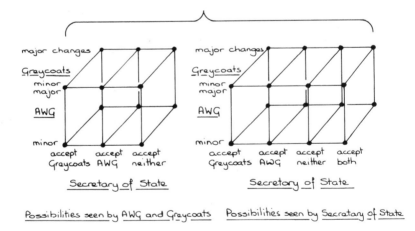

Figure 4
Outline hypergame model for 'Coin Street' case: matrix form

294

unexpected. In matrix form, the hypergame has the structure shown in Figure 4.

In this case, however, matrices do not provide the most helpful representation of the model. We shall continue with this illustration to explain why, and to consider two other representations.

Alternative representations: trees and tableaux

Although matrices provide an economical way of representing simple interactions, trees help to show sequences of decisions more directly. Each branch in the tree represents a possible action under the control of a specific player, shown in the order in which choices are to be made. 'Chance' events can also be included, as possible actions of a player called 'nature'. (For the purposes of the model, one decision comes 'after' another if the player making it knows what move has been made at the 'earlier' branch.) The end points of the tree are outcomes: as before, we suppose that players have preferences for these. The complete tree then represents a game: in a hypergame, there are subjective game trees for each player, just as with matrices.

Consider, for example, the matrices of Figure 4, used to model the Coin Street case. As they stand, these take no account of the sequence of choices. While the two developers had to make their moves simultaneously, the Secretary of State would then make his decision after seeing both their proposals. One way of modelling this is to expand the matrix, with conditional strategies for the Secretary of State. (One such strategy would be to 'choose AWG if both make major changes; choose AWG if only AWG makes major changes; otherwise reject both'.) Or the simple matrix could be used as a rough basis for verbal argumentation. A tree, however, provides a more convenient way of showing the decisions. Figure 5 shows the sequence of moves as seen by each side. The dotted line around Greycoats' two decision points means that this decision is made in ignorance of AWG's choice. (Since their choices are simultaneous, it makes no difference which is drawn at the top of the tree.)

To avoid devoting too much space to this illustration, we complete and analyse just the developers' part of the hypergame, on the left of Figure 5. Each developer had an obvious incentive to meet the new guidelines, but neither wanted to move too far from its original proposal. For AWG, introducing other uses would mean giving up valuable housing space, while toning down the scale of the offices would mean less profit for

Greycoats. The outcomes can be arranged into five main types, in decreasing order of preference:

1. Own proposal accepted, with minor changes.
2. Own proposal accepted with major changes.
3. Both rejected, after minor changes to own proposal (which at least leaves the issue open).
4. Both rejected, after major changes to own proposal.
5. Other proposal accepted, own rejected.

The outcome reached would, of course, depend on the Secretary of State. So far as the developers knew, he had no prejudice towards either proposal. If either were substantially changed while the other were not, he would presumably prefer the former. If both were modified, he might prefer either: if neither were, he would probably reject both again. Figure 6(a) shows the left-hand side of Figure 5 expanded to include preferences consistent with these assumptions (a fuller analysis would explore the consequences of various possible preferences). Each outcome has three preference rankings, one for each player. As before, more highly preferred outcomes are shown with higher numbers.

Trees can be analysed by working backwards from their end points. That is, we consider the last choice available in each branch, and find the best move for that player to take if that point were to be reached. Assuming that this best choice would be made (if that point were reached), and that all the players can predict this, we then look at the next-to-last decision, and so on back up the tree. In this case, the first step is to consider the Secretary of State's final choice in each possible case. For example, let us look at the branch of the tree where AWG opts for major change and Greycoats for minor. The Secretary of State's best move—as indicated by the preference entry '4'—would then be to choose AWG. Predicting that he will do so allows us to 'roll back' this part of the tree, replacing its three branches with this one outcome. Figure 6(b) shows the result of performing this roll back for each of the branches. This now effectively leaves us with a two-player game, shown in both tree and matrix form. Since the remaining decisions are simultaneous, we cannot usefully roll back the tree any further.

Note that if both schemes undergo major change, the Secretary of State is seen to have no clear preference. This incompleteness in the ordering means that one can only say that one of two final outcomes would occur; beyond this, his choice can be considered as a chance event. This makes the developers' decision apparently rather difficult. To decide whether they would prefer the uncertain outcome '4, 1 or 1, 4' to that of '3, 3', they would have to weigh up the chance of being chosen by the Secretary of State

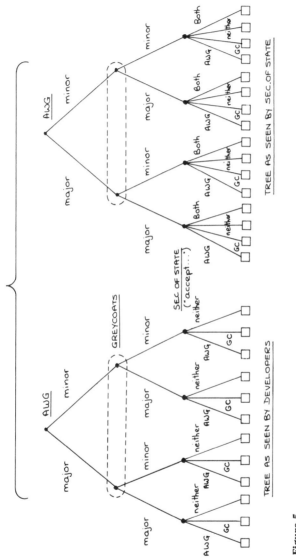

Figure 5
Outline hypergame model for 'Coin Street' case: tree form

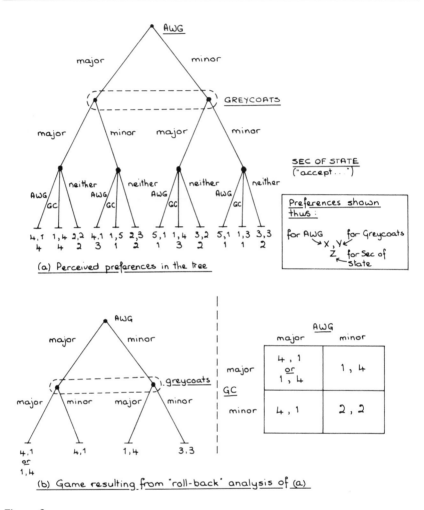

Figure 6
Coin Street: Analysis of the developers' game tree

against the undesirability of making major changes. However, the crucial point is that only major change will result in any chance of success. Regardless of how the uncertain preference order might work out, making major change represents a dominant strategy for each developer. Not surprisingly, this is what they both did.

The effects of their having overlooked the Secretary of State's eventual move can be modelled by completing and analysing the full hypergame. While space precludes more detailed discussion, it is significant that for

Greycoats in particular, the outcome 'both schemes approved' was far from satisfactory. As the situation unfolded, it became clear that this was essentially as bad as outright rejection. (The decision allowed local councils sympathetic to AWG to re-enter the game in a more powerful role, and in essence it was AWG's scheme that eventually prevailed.) Had the possibility of 'two approvals' been realized and examined, Greycoats might well have preferred to make only token amendments or even to withdraw altogether, thereby saving time, effort and hence money.

So far, we have introduced two alternative ways of representing both games and hypergames—matrices and trees. While trees are helpful in showing sequences of choices, they rapidly become cumbersome as the number of moves increases. Similarly, it is difficult to draw matrices with more than two or three players. Before moving on, in the next section, to extend the hypergame model itself, it will be useful to introduce a third format designed to overcome this size limitation. Developed as part of the 'Analysis of Options' or metagame method (Howard, 1971), this is based on the notion of a *tableau of options*. Briefly, this works as follows. Players (participants) are listed, each with various options—possible courses of action, formulated as simple 'yes–no' alternatives. Outcomes (or 'scenarios') are columns constructed by specifying 'yes' or 'no' for each and every option, usually by writing 1 for 'yes' and 0 for 'no'. Typically, some outcomes are taken to be infeasible (e.g. logically or physically impossible). These are separated out prior to further analysis.

This approach is discussed much more fully in Chapters 10 and 11. To give a brief illustration here, Figure 7 shows a simple tableau for the Coin Street case. The participants and options are self-explanatory. Two scenarios are shown for illustration: in the first, AWG makes major changes, Greycoats minor, and the Secretary of State nevertheless rejects both. The second is similar, except that AWG has made only minor changes. Some infeasible outcomes are shown to the right. Two of them express the assumption that whatever else happens, no party can make changes defined as both major and minor. Taking the hypergame perspective, the players' perceptions are modelled by introducing separate tableaux. Just as with matrices and trees these may differ from each other. Here, the difference between the developers' perception and that of the Secretary of State can be neatly modelled as a difference in infeasibilities, as noted on the figure.

Whether the tableaux for the various participants are similar or different, analysis serves to establish the stability of outcomes by finding any 'improvements' from the outcome for any participant, and then considering what 'sanctions' other parties might have to prevent this. This approach can be a helpful way of managing 'combinatorial' complexity resulting from

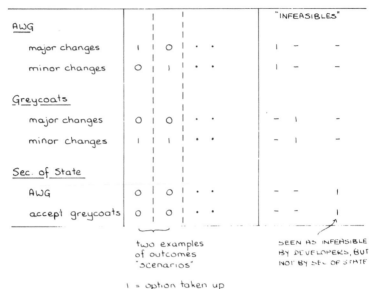

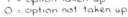

Figure 7
Partly-completed option tableau for the 'Coin Street' example

trying to take account of many possible actions, each of which might or might not be undertaken. In the Coin Street case, for example, the tableau method would be particularly useful were we to examine in more detail the various possible changes that AWG and Greycoats could make. It is a format lending itself to the use of computer software, both to help build up models of particular situations and to analyse them. The CONAN program referred to in Chapters 10 and 11 provides a good example of such software, while we briefly outline the use of another program in Chapter 13.

To summarize, we have so far introduced three ways of representing games or hypergames: matrices, trees, and tableaux. While matrices provide the most compact visual representation of simple interactions, trees highlight the sequencing of decisions through time. Tableaux allow us to deal with relatively many players and possible courses of action.

Extending the hypergame model

The basic hypergame framework has been extended in a number of ways, two of which are important here. One of these is to allow for more radical differences in players' perceptions (Bennett, 1980, 1986). The second is to consider systems of linked interactions, rather than just isolated hypergames. Both of these extend the range of models used within the hypergame approach.

Radical differences in perception

In the versions of a hypergame outlined so far, there must be some possible actions (strategies, moves or options) common to all the players' games. Otherwise—so far as the model is concerned—they would not interact at all. This implies that the games must be defined in roughly similar terms. Often, this is plausible enough, especially where actors have similar backgrounds and training. But sometimes, they may have radically different views of the world, and disagree as to what the whole conflict is about. For example, it has been suggested that US leaders took the Vietnam War to be 'about' containing communism, whereas the North Vietnamese saw the issues primarily as national unification and self-determination.

We thus need to allow for the games seen by various parties to be defined in quite different terms, while still being 'linked' in the sense that moves made in one game can affect the others. Two specific sorts of difference are of particular interest. Firstly, players may disagree as to *who the relevant parties are* (Bryant, 1983). Secondly, there may be disagreement about *the authorship of actions*: who was responsible for an event. (This can happen even if everyone sees the same overall set of players.) Just prior to the Falklands/Malvinas War for example, General Galtieri reportedly felt that the USSR might be prepared to sink a British carrier, with the Argentine taking credit (Haig, 1986). In the more 'peaceful' context of corporate takeover battles, it has become almost commonplace for shares to be bought up by 'mystery' buyers actually supporting one side. Equally, however, confusion over attributions and/or cast lists can happen unintentionally (see, for example, Bowen, 1981).

Intentionally or otherwise, such differences can affect the whole way in which the situation is defined. For example, among statements about the 1980 'riot' in the St Paul's area of Bristol, 'the community' is defined variously as: (a) both 'blacks' and 'whites' living in the area; (b) the 'black' and 'West Indian' community; and (c) the people living in St Paul's, together with the police—'community police', who 'act in the community and are respected members of community bodies'. Not surprisingly, different accounts of the riot following from these definitions then offer contrasting versions of events, and contrasting perceptions of the ways in which they were managed or mismanaged by specific actors. The differences can be dramatic. For example

> The first [definition] puts the blame on the rioters and sees solutions at the level of police strategy. The second blames discriminatory state practices (in policing and finance) and proposes positive intervention, in terms of policy and provision for St Paul's. (Potter and Reicher, 1987).

To set up a hypergame model, we need not decide which world-view, if any, is 'correct'. The approach is rather to seek out accounts about how the world is seen, and then model what happens when the holders of these different views interact with each other. Finally, we should stress that in emphasizing how actors' perceptions can differ, our claim is not that radical differences must exist. It is rather that they may do so, that this may affect what happens, and that our models should allow for such possibilities. In general, we argue for a presumption of difference between world-views. This is based not only on studies of particular conflicts, but also on a general view of individuals as active interpreters of the world, constructing their own theories (see especially Kelly, 1963 and Eden in Chapter 2 of this volume). Our aim is to carry this presumption as far as possible while still using game-based models. If and when perceptions turn out to be similar, it is easy enough to simplify the model.

Modelling systems of interactions

The ability to model radical differences in perception brings the hypergame notion nearer to the real world, while still retaining its basic structural simplicity. So far though, we have still been concerned with modelling single interactions, considered in isolation. In real life, as we have already remarked, actors are often involved in many related decisions, each having a bearing on choices in the others. (Recall the union leader in the Introduction to this chapter.) For the analyst, this leads to a dilemma. Attempting to build a single game or hypergame which takes account of all the various interrelated choices would lead to models of fantastic complexity. Yet we do not wish to ignore relevant cross-linkages altogether. To help strike a balance, models have been devised to represent systems of interactions in simple, diagrammatic ways, helping us to picture the wider context of specific interactions. Two such modelling methods have been developed specifically to aid hypergame analysis.

The first of these methods is termed *Preliminary Problem Structuring* (PPS), and focuses on the patterns of interactions amongst actors. As

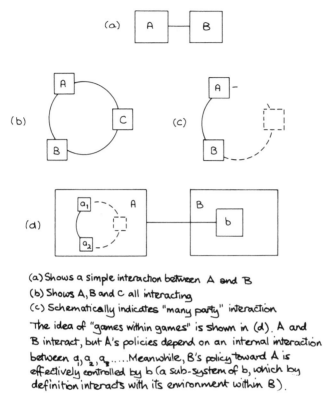

(a) Shows a simple interaction between A and B
(b) Shows A, B and C all interacting
(c) Schematically indicates "many party" interaction
The idea of "games within games" is shown in (d). A and B interact, but A's policies depend on an internal interaction between q_1, q_2, q_3 ..... Meanwhile, B's policy toward A is effectively controlled by b (a sub-system of b, which by definition interacts with its environment within B).

Figure 8
Preliminary problem-structuring notation (PPS)

outlined in Figure 8, players are joined by lines representing interactions over particular issues—in other words, showing where the main games or hypergames are. Because players can be defined in either more or less aggregated terms, there are typically 'games within games'. PPS allows one to display these as a background to further analysis, rather than considering just one level.

The use of PPS can be illustrated by a study of problems faced by a Borough Council in an area of London badly hit by the loss of traditional industries (Bennett and Cropper, 1987). In response to this, the Council had devised a programme of industrial development, including some Council factory-building. More recently, changes in the Council's political control (and in the property investment climate) had led to a shift in emphasis. The new administration was unsympathetic to planning, favouring reliance on market forces. This was reflected in its attitude to the Planning Department in general, and to the industrial development programme in particular. Planning Officers had nevertheless fought hard to protect the programme, while necessarily adapting it to emphasize the role of the private sector. Council action still included the purchase of unused land and its arrangement into usable 'packages' prior to sale. This much was agreed to be essential. But there were further, more contentious, decisions to be made. In particular, the Council could also 'improve' sites prior to sale—for example, by providing road access, or dealing with hidden gas mains. The need for this was a subject of disagreement between departments. Roughly, while the planners argued that developers would only buy improved sites, the Valuer's Department insisted that sites would sell anyway. The issue was compounded by a long-standing territorial rivalry between these (and other) departments competing for influence, in which control of local industrial development represented an important prize.

Through discussing the situation with the planners primarily responsible for the industrial programme, it became clear that they attached significance to a host of different, but linked, interactions. At one level, they saw the Council as a body interacting with various external agencies such as landowners and property developers—some heavily influenced by further 'games' with their sources of finance. However, they also perceived a complex system of interactions taking place within the Council, and serving to determine its policy. Figure 9 shows parts of a PPS diagram devised to help picture these 'internal' interactions. Figure 9 (a) represents interactions (within the Council as a whole) between Planning and other departments, and between each department and the elected councillors. Figure 9(b) shows in more detail how the Planning Department interacts with the councillors, primarily via a key contact member on the Planning Committee. (He himself was involved in other political games—with his party, his constituents, and so on—which also affected his behaviour toward his Department. Though omitted here for simplicity, these could be represented in a similar way.)

The second method is based on the notion of a *decision arena*. Where PPS focuses attention on patterns of linkage between actors, the arena model primarily addresses the nature of the interactions. As with PPS, the 'building blocks' are interactions over specified issues. Relevant information is then structured as in Figure 10. On one side of each arena are shown starting conditions, to do with the parties' available options, their preferences, beliefs, particular strengths and weaknesses, and so on—what each side 'takes into the arena'. On the other are outcomes—possible results of

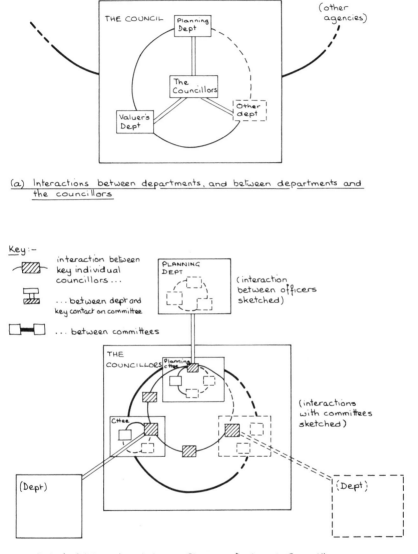

(a) Interactions between departments, and between departments and the councillors

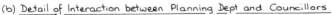

(b) Detail of Interaction between Planning Dept and Councillors

Figure 9
Parts of a PPS diagram

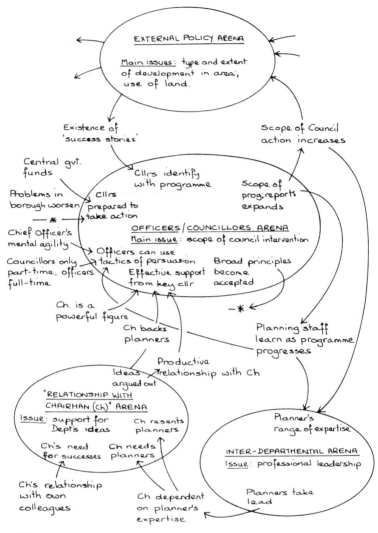

Figure 10
Extracts from a 'decision arena' model

the parties having gone through an interaction. Factors affecting the starting conditions appear as input, the wider consequences of particular outcomes as output. Because an outcome of one arena can affect the starting conditions of others, this provides for links between arenas (and for reflexive links back into the same arena). Figure 10 shows a simplified example taken from the same case as before, this time representing one planner's view of the political system. This model concentrates on one arena, that in which planning officers and councillors argue over the appropriate scope of council intervention. Input and starting conditions are shown on the left of the arena, some possible outcomes and output on the right. Some other linked arenas are shown in outline. (Note that these roughly correspond to interactions appearing in the PPS diagram.) For example, one output from the central arena is that the scope of council action increases: this in turn serves as an input into the 'interdepartmental' arena (tending, in fact, to strengthen the Planners' position relative to other departments), and into the 'external policy' arena (making the Council a more active participant in the land-use and development 'game'). Conversely, this last arena also affects the first; the existence of 'success stories' tends to make councillors identify with the industrial programme, altering their attitude towards it.

This completes our review of models used within the hypergame approach. Our final section will now consider how these ideas, and others, can be used together to help with complex decisions.

Using models to help with decisions

We now put some flesh on the general principles advanced in the first section of this chapter, showing how the models described above can be used. First, we describe a process designed to help tackle complexity. We then set out specific ways of using models with clients, relating these to two 'forms of help' discussed earlier: problem structuring and formal analysis. We also place the use of these models within a wider repertoire of methods.

An approach to tackling complexity

Recognizing that different sorts of model (game-based and others) cope better with different kinds of complexity, we aim to use them together in a flexible way. Furthermore, the intention is that modelling should contribute to a learning process for both clients and analysts. These aims lead to an approach quite unlike the fixed recipe that might be suggested by the formal apparatus of game theory ('Define all the players, strategies, preferences ... analyse the game to find the answer'). Such an approach would be unhelpful (in any of the senses of 'help' discussed earlier). It would, in any case, be quite impracticable. Even in 'simple' interactive decisions, there tend to be so many possible combinations of moves that comprehensive analysis is out of the question (Rapoport, 1960). Instead, it seems more helpful to aim for 'requisite' models, good enough to serve as guides to action. With this in mind, we have designed a methodology that is 'mixed-scanning, iterative, and piecemeal'.

At its simplest, a *mixed-scanning* approach means moving judiciously between a broad overview and more detailed, but narrow, analysis (Etzioni, 1967). We can do this by varying both the level of aggregation of actors and options and the scope of models. For example, very many players often appear in clients' initial accounts. It is then usually desirable to simplify before moving further, to avoid becoming swamped by complexity. This can be done by narrowing the model—focusing in, say, on a key inter-action between two or three actors. Or the broad view can be maintained at the expense of detail. Players may be aggregated together, and internal interactions ignored for the time being. Overall, mixed scanning aims to maintain a creative tension between breadth and detail.

In a learning process, models must be open to revision, with opportunities for this built into the methodology. As in Strategic Choice, modelling is thus an *iterative* (or 'cyclical') process. Cycles occur within the construction of particular models. In building up a tableau, for example, consideration of feasible and infeasible outcomes may lead one to redefine the options to produce a neater model. They also occur between models. For example, consideration of options available in a hypergame may lead to a revision of the PPS structure within which the hypergame had been embedded. Our general preference is to start with broadly defined models, deferring consideration of detail until a rough structure has been agreed, but these early models are often altered almost beyond recognition later on.

We have already stressed the need for multiple alternative models, to express different hypotheses about a situation. *'Piecemeal'* modelling goes further, by suggesting that different representations can usefully be used alongside each other, rather than searching for a single, 'best' model. Each model can be used to bring out a different facet of the situation—such as the timing of decisions, or the linkages between them. Within hypergame modelling, trees, matrices, and tableaux may be used together (as illustrated on a small scale in our 'Coin Street' study). They may also be used alongside quite different types of model, such as those described elsewhere in this volume, allowing analysis of each to inform the others.

Our aim is thus to tackle complexity using a mix of models, each in itself comparatively simple. Throughout, there is a constantly shifting balance between the need to capture the complexity of issues, and the need to keep models tractable and comprehensible. As clients and analysts work together, the key choice at each point is that of what to include explicitly in each model, and what to treat as 'background'. We shall now examine this process in more detail.

On the process of working with clients

To say that clients and analysts 'work together' on problems covers a multitude of possibilities. Where, for example, does information to start the process come from? Does the analyst work entirely 'on the hoof' with the client group, or with individuals, or in the 'back room'? We would not want to prescribe set choices; each analyst will find particular ways of working most helpful with different sorts of client. Nevertheless, we can set out a general view of the processes of problem exploration, problem structuring and analysis, and the relationships between them—though discussing each in turn may make the methodology seem deceptively linear.

The most important initial source of information is likely to be the clients' own 'tacit knowledge' (Polanyi, 1958; Eden, Jones, and Sims, 1979): hence the importance of exploring this and structuring it in a convenient form. At the problem-exploration stage, game or hypergame models *can* be used with client groups from the start (as in the 'CONAN Play' of Chapter 11). In order to access the variety of views held within groups, however, we wish to avoid forcing their problems into a pre-ordained mould. We usually prefer to start by exploring individuals' views in some depth, without yet introducing a pre-selected problem structure explicitly. Cognitive Mapping provides an appropriate medium for this, whether or not the subsequent steps of the SODA methodology are to be followed. So mapping can be a natural precursor to hypergame modelling. There are exceptions, particularly if the client is a single individual (removing any need to explore intra-group differences), or if initial accounts are already clearly couched in terms of actors, options, and preferences. The case study of Chapter 13 provides just such an example.

Exceptions aside, we start problem structuring in hypergame terms as an experimental, 'backroom' activity carried out by the analyst(s) in parallel with the process of exploring clients' views. The aim is to find models representing relevant parties, interactions, and issues in broad terms. These help to organize data, to select relevant information from more general background, and so provide reference points for any more detailed analysis. Both the PPS and Decision Arena methods are designed specifically for this role. But trees, matrices, and tableaux can also be used for problem structuring, especially by using partly defined models. For example, drawing up a rough tableau or matrix (without yet considering preferences) can help to sort out what feasible outcomes may exist. Similarly, trees can be used simply to help visualize how decisions unfold. We should also stress again that game-based models form part of a wider range. For example, if the forms of uncertainty dealt with in Strategic Choice seem of more importance than conflict as such, we should certainly use ideas taken

309

from that approach (Matthews and Bennett, 1986; Bennett and Cropper, 1989).

Some provisional problem-structuring models are next introduced to the client group, and from now on work is primarily carried out with the group as a whole, the models providing a 'common currency' for discussions. But it is still helpful to carry out occasional backroom work; time away from the clients is useful, to experiment with and review the models used. Guided by the framework, we start to ask more specific questions—both of the clients and, in backroom work, of the data. Which actors are centrally involved in which issues? What 'internal games' might affect the behaviour of a given organization? What factors are likely to influence a given actor's aims?

From this problem-structuring phase, we often move on to more formal analysis. This involves focusing on one or more specific interactions, each with actors and options defined at one particular level. For the time being, the 'rest of the world' is treated as constant background. As noted before, such simplification can involve working with a more narrowly defined problem, losing detail, or both. The criteria used in choosing foci are often similar to those found in Strategic Choice: the importance of outcomes to the client, the urgency of decisions, and their impact on other decisions. Our own perspective leads us to stress an additional criterion. This is that the client should be directly involved in the interaction(s) chosen, either by being a major player or, failing that, by being able to take some contingency action to deal with the side effects of others' battles.

Several of the above points can be briefly illustrated by some analysis of a problem of 'bad neighbourliness'. The 'client' in this case was a single individual, who saw himself as suffering from unacceptable noise and disturbance. He gave an initial description which included a multitude of actors more or less directly involved. After discussion using PPS as a vehicle, a central interaction between the client and one other individual was chosen for more detailed examination. Having selected this focus, we formulated the available actions in very broad terms to build an initial formal model. A simple matrix was drawn up to reflect the nub of the conflict: this then served as a basis for examining more detailed and 'realistic' options in a tableau. Later again, an attempt was made to place these in the context of the wider set of interactions: it was now easier to see how and when more distant participants would be significant.

In moving to formal models, we need some direct indication of parties' preferences. There are various ways of feeding preferences into the model: by repeatedly comparing pairs of outcomes, by prioritizing options, and so on. It is seldom necessary to define complete preference orders. Detailed preferences are often irrelevant to the results of analysis, and substantial blocks of outcomes may be left with equal rankings. Some general indication of preferences will have come already from problem exploration and structuring. Where necessary, this can be augmented by direct questioning, and by other methods. In particular, if the reasons for clients' expressed preferences (or perceptions of others' preferences) are non-obvious, it can be helpful to step back to explore factors that might underlie these. A convenient way of doing so is again provided by cognitive mapping. Maps of argumentation expressed about specific outcomes serve to set out the perceived consequences of parties' actions, to help see why outcomes might be good or bad from particular points of view. Used in this way, maps serve to make explicit the argumentation behind hypergame models: Chapter 13 provides an example.

All these processes of structuring and analysis tend to pinpoint questions that *cannot* be answered with any confidence. In building up a PPS diagram, for example, we may find issues of probable relevance to current decisions, but be unsure who are the main parties involved. While trying to set up formal models, we may uncover major uncertainties about other actors' preferences, or (say) their perceptions of our client's strategies. A key role of analysis is thus to suggest what the most crucial areas of ignorance (or disagreement within the group) may be. By constructing and comparing alternative models, we can start to see which uncertainties are most likely to affect the course of events. These can be given priority for further investigation. At any given point, analysis proceeds on a 'what if . . .' basis. Indeed, the analyst may well end up in a 'devil's advocate' role, challenging assumptions previously held with confidence. The modelling process itself provides a framework for asking about the effects of change. What if a participant were to leave the 'game'? What if participants of a certain type were to become involved? What if others' preferences or perceptions were to change in a certain way? Can we devise moves that would bring about (or prevent) any of these changes?

In all of this, a crucial issue is that of how to arrive at games which might be perceived by other parties. The difficulty, of course, is that when working for a particular participant or group, direct access to other participants may be shut off. Two approaches can be adopted. One is to try to construct perceived games for each participant from scratch, making no prior assumption about similarities between them. Provisional ideas can come from whatever intelligence is available, from interpreting behaviour to date, from initiatives designed to test others' views, or from setting up special internal procedures to simulate others' points of view (see, e.g. Radford, 1984; Huxham and Eden, 1987). A less radical approach is to start with models expressing one view (normally, the client's), and then to investigate others by considering plausible differences from it. This provides a fairly quick form of piecemeal 'assumption busting' or contingency analysis, but will be inadequate if other parties have drastically different definitions of the situation. Some mix of these approaches is normal in practice, the balance depending on the time and resources available, and on some reasoned argument about the likelihood of radical differences in perception.

Having drawn up specific hypergames, the technical notions of dominance, stability, and so on are brought to bear in formal analysis proper, using matrices, trees, or tableaux. (We often continue to use different types of model 'piecemeal', to take advantage of the strengths of each.) Using models to analyse the effects of possible threats, promises, bluffs, and so on can often lead to 'non-obvious' conclusions. For example, analysis might suggest that an outcome dismissed intuitively as implausible is nevertheless likely to happen under certain circumstances; that a result thought to be obtainable unilaterally is dependent on others' actions; that an apparently powerful threat can be evaded; or that 'irrational' moves by others have a predictable logic of their own. Such conclusions are not necessarily superior to those arrived at intuitively (by clients or analysts), but they do provide additional food for thought in re-examining assumptions, conclusions, or both.

Summary

We have described an approach to modelling interactive decisions, based upon the idea of a hypergame. Within this is a repertoire of model types—matrices, trees, and tableaux—that can be adapted to deal with more or less radical differences in perception. It is also useful to expand this repertoire in two ways. The first is through 'problem structuring' models directly related to the hypergame perspective, such as those of Decision Arenas and PPS. We then have a wider range of methods, each emphasizing different aspects of interactive decisions. The second extension is to treat the hypergame approach itself as part of a wider set of methods, to be used in combination with quite different approaches to complex decisions, such as Cognitive Mapping or Strategic Choice.

References

Axelrod, R. (1984). *The Evolution of Cooperation*, Basic Books.
Bennett, P. G. (1980). 'Hypergames: developing a model of conflict', *Futures*, **12**, 489–507.

Bennett, P. G. (1985). 'On linking approaches to decision-aiding; issues and prospects', *J. Opl Res. Soc.*, **36**, 659–69.

Bennett, P. G. (1986). 'Beyond game theory—where?', in *Analysing Conflict and Its Resolution: some mathematical contributions*. (Ed. P. G. Bennett), OUP, Oxford.

Bennett, P.G. (1988). 'Hypergames as an aid to mediation', in *New Approaches to Mediation* (Eds. C. Mitchell and K. Webb), Greenwood Press, 1988.

Bennett, P. G., and Cropper, S. A. (1986). 'Helping people choose: Conflict and other perspectives', in *Further Developments in O.R.* (Eds. V. Belton and R. O'Keefe), Pergamon, Oxford.

Bennett, P. G., and Cropper, S. A. (1987). 'Maps, games and things in-between', *EJOR*, **32**, 33–46.

Bennett, P. G., and Cropper, S. A. (1989). 'Uncertainty and conflict: Combining conflict analysis and strategic choice', *J. Behavioural Decision-Making*, in press.

Bennett, P. G., and Dando, M. R. (1979). 'Complex strategic analysis: A hypergame study of the fall of France', *J. Opl Res. Soc.*, **30**, 23–32.

Bennett, P. G., and Dando, M. R. (1982). 'The arms race as a hypergame', *Futures*, **14**, 293–306.

Bowen, K. C. (1981). 'A conflict approach to the modelling of problems of and in organisations', in *Operational Research '81* (Ed. J. P. Brans), North-Holland, Amsterdam.

Bryant, J. (1983). 'Hypermaps: A representation of perceptions in conflicts', *Omega*, **11**, 575–86.

Cropper, S. A. (1986). 'Modelling Land Use Planning and Development as Social Exchange', Unpublished Phd. Thesis, University of Wales.

Eden, C., Jones, S., and Sims, D. (1979). *Thinking in Organisations*, Macmillan.

Etzioni, A. (1967). 'Mixed-scanning: A "third" approach to decision-making', *Pub. Admin Rev.*, December.

Greater London Council (1979). 'Land at Stamford Street, Upper Ground, Coin Street, etc.', PC 371; Report to Planning and Communications Policy Committee, GLC, London, 1.2.79.

Haig, A. (1986). *Caveat: Realism, Reagan and Foreign Policy*, Wiedenfeld and Nicholson.

Hardin, G. (1968). 'The Tragedy of the Commons', *Science*, **162**, 1243–8.

Howard, N. (1971). *Paradoxes of Rationality*, MIT Press.

Huxham, C. S., and Eden, C. (1987). 'Gaming, competitor analysis and strategic management', International Symposium on Future Directions in Decision Management, Toronto, August 1987.

Jervis, R. (1970). *The Logic of Images in International Relations*, Princeton Univ. Press, Princeton, NJ.

Kelly, G. A. (1963). '*A Theory of Personality: the psychology of personal constructs,*' W. W. Norton & Co.

Matthews, L. R., and Bennett, P. G. (1986). 'The art of course planning: Soft OR in action', *J. Opl Res. Soc.*, **37**, 579–90.

Phillips, L. (1982). 'Requisite decision modelling: A case study', *J. Opl Res. Soc.*, **33**, 303–12.

Planning (1983). 'King faces design issue as Ayatollah moves on', *Planning*, **501**, 11.

Plous, S. (1985). 'Perceptual illusions and military realities' *J. Conflict Resolution*, **29**, 363–389.

Polanyi, M. (1958). *Personal Knowledge*, University of Chicago Press, Chicago.

Potter, J., and Reicher, S. (1987). 'Discourses of community and conflict: the organisation of social categories in accounts of a "riot"', *Br. J. Soc. Psych.*, **26**, 25–40.

Radford, K. J. (1984). 'Simulating involvement in complex situations', *Omega*, **12**, 125–30.

Rapoport, A. (1960). *Fights, Games and Debates*, Univ. Michigan Press, Ann Arbor.

de Rivera, J. (1968). *The Psychological Dimension of Foreign Policy*, Merrill, Columbus, Ohio.

Rosenhead, J. (1986). 'Custom and practice', *J. Opl Res. Soc.*, **37**, 335–44.

Von Neumann, J., and Morgenstern, O. (1944). *Theory of Games and Economic Behavior*, Princeton Univ. Press, Princeton, NJ.

13
Using the hypergame perspective: a case study

Peter Bennett, Chris Huxham, and Steve Cropper

Introduction

This case study will show how some of the ideas introduced in the preceding chapter can be applied to a real problem. Our intention is to demonstrate how different aspects of the situation are brought to the fore by various models, within a 'piecemeal, iterative, mixed-scanning' approach. Our example is a problem that was faced by one of the writers (PGB)—who was thus the 'client' for the study—as chairman of a sporting organization. The analysis was carried out jointly with one of the other authors (CSH). The description given here will not focus on the process of client–consultant interaction. Those issues discussed in Chapter 12 specifically concerned with helping groups are largely irrelevant here, given a single (and atypical!) client. We have included a fair amount of technical detail on each model, for those who may wish to use this chapter as a guide to analysis. In this respect, it should be noted that such details are much more easily digested by the clients and analysts involved in building the models up, than by readers of a retrospective account. Those seeking a general illustration of the approach should find it possible to skim over this detail.

Let us start with the problem that faced the client. This can be summarized by the following statement (in which proper names have been changed to protect confidentiality):

The 'Albatross' is a class of sailing dinghy, widely used for racing, and the problem concerned the venue for the class World Championship. The affairs of the class are organized nationally by the English Albatross Association, through an elected committee. There are similar associations in other countries where the Albatross is sailed, notably Wales, Sweden and America, though the English Association is by far the largest. These associations in turn belong to an international Federation. World Championships, lasting a week, are normally held each summer. The venue roughly rotates between the four main countries, with the national Association making arrangements with some suitable sailing club to run the event.

The problem concerned the next championship due to be held in Wales. Until late in the preceding summer, all had seemed to be progressing as normal. The Welsh Association had apparently made preliminary arrangements with a club at Llados to run the event, and matters had been left in their hands. But as time passed, the English committee had become increasingly anxious to receive confirmation of venue and notice of dates. Would-be competitors needed to book their holidays, and other fixtures had to be finalized. Furthermore, the Swedes were simultaneously organizing their own National Championship, also open to UK competitors. A clash of dates here would be disastrous. But no firm answers were forthcoming from Wales. Meanwhile, English class members had been showing some reluctance to go to Wales anyway, for various reasons including distance. But our committee was committed to promoting the event as hard as possible. A good turnout was seen as vital to the class.

Out of the blue, in October, came a startling call from the Welsh Association chairman. He reported great difficulties with Llados, putting the whole event in doubt. No agreement had been reached with the club on crucial financial and organizational issues. The club itself seemed to be divided into factions for and against running the event, with neither firmly in control.

This left us with *very* little time, for several reasons. Apart from championships, the class holds 'open meetings' at different venues most weekends: chains of decisions rested on the championship issue. (For example, a special Southern Area Championship had been arranged on the assumption of the major championship being in Wales. If, say, the latter were to be moved to England, it would be better to omit the area event. The possible dates of two other open meetings in turn depended on that decision.) Such issues always involve negotiation—sometimes delicate—with the clubs concerned. The risk of a clash of championships with the Swedes was increasing all the time, since they were also under pressure to fix their dates. Such a clash had happened once before, resulting in a last-minute cancellation amid much bitterness. Finally, another danger loomed. If Llados were not to run the event, it might be too late to find any other venue. In short, someone had to do something, and quickly—but what?

Our problem thus concerned a small-scale voluntary organization (with a few hundred members) rather than affairs of state or of some major corporation. It was nevertheless real enough, causing much worry and concern to people deeply committed to the success of the class. Our description reflects the subjective views held at the time by one such actor, as chairman of the English committee. As the study unfolds, we hope that readers will be able to recognize features also met in quite different contexts. 'Conflict', in the everyday sense, was not much in evidence. The main actors were all 'on the same side' in working for the success of the Albatross class. Nevertheless, the situation was one in which different actors could influence events, and were likely to have differing preferences and, perhaps, beliefs. In terms of the 'problem settings' outlined in Chapter 12, we thus saw an interactive decision problem, to which hypergame models should be applicable. In passing, we should also note the potential for more overt conflict, as time ran out. Already, differences within the English committee had started to surface, with some taking a much less sympathetic view towards the Welsh.

This chapter reports various stages of study and analysis in the order in which they were carried out, showing how the principles set out in the preceding chapter were applied in this particular case. These are presented in terms of four broad steps. The first of these involved problem structuring from a hypergame perspective, leading to a choice of problem focus, and a preliminary examination of some broad options and outcomes. The second step was to use cognitive maps to express and explore argumentation underlying the client's own view of the problem, and assumptions about the situation that might be held by other parties. The third step was to carry out some analysis of 'games' as seen by the client, using both tableau and tree formats. Finally, this was extended to some hypergame modelling and analysis.

Each of these steps is set out below, together with our reasons for taking it. Especially, it is significant that in this case, our approach to hypergame modelling concentrated mainly on building up the 'game' as seen by the client. We only then concentrated on how others' perceptions might plausibly differ from this, rather than trying to build others' games from scratch. (In other words, we tended towards the 'less radical' of the two approaches set out in Chapter 12.) A final introductory point should also be stressed. Though we have laid out the four steps in order here, in reality we moved through these in an iterative way. Figure 1 shows the main links moving 'forward' through the steps. In addition, earlier views of the problem (including the description given above) changed as we cycled through the process. It is not surprising if later observations on the problem occasionally contradict earlier ones. Rather than rewriting material to give some *post hoc* impression of 'consistency', we will note the main changes in view as the story unfolds.

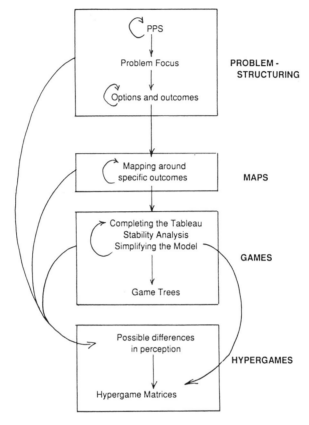

Figure 1
Overview of modelling process

Problem structuring

The description of the problem given above represents the client's view prior to any explicit analysis. Clearly, in this case, the client's starting 'script' showed a game-like structure. That is, he already saw the problem in terms of relevant actors, issues, and at least rough options and outcomes. We cannot be sure to what extent this reflected the nature of the problem, rather than the client's conceptual style. In any event, it allowed us to proceed straight away to use game-based problem structures.

Of the types of model described in Chapter 12, the Preliminary Problem Structuring notation was particularly appropriate to this case, as several 'levels' of interaction appeared significant. Client and analyst therefore

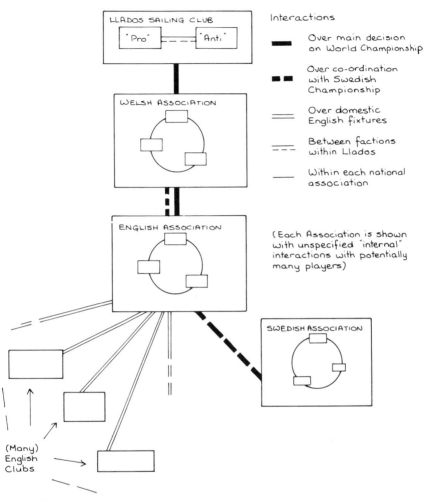

Figure 2
PPS diagram: the problem as initially perceived

worked together to produce PPS diagrams showing key actors perceived, and interactions between them. The main structure to emerge at this stage (after much discussion) was as in Figure 2. This shows the following interactions:

1. Between the English Association, the Welsh Association, and the Llados Sailing Club, over the issue of when and where the championship should be held.

2. Between the English, Welsh, and Swedish Associations, attempting to avoid a clash of championships.
3. Between the English Association and English clubs, over the 'domestic' fixture list.
4. Within Llados Sailing Club between (to us, rather mysterious) factions 'pro' and 'anti' staging the championship.
5. Within each of the Association committees.

This was not intended as a definitive picture of the problem as perceived —let alone of the 'whole' problem in some global sense. As will be seen, this view changed significantly in the course of further analysis. But already, the process of constructing the diagram had served to draw attention to some important points not mentioned in the client's initial description. In drawing the diagram so as to show direct lines of communication between the actors we noted, for example, that the English Association was not in direct communication with Llados, but only via the Welsh Association. Similarly, the Welsh and Swedish Associations were communicating only via the English—the only one of the three *not* due to be running a championship!

Rather than trying to look at all these interactions in detail, our next step—in line with the 'mixed-scanning' methodology—was to choose a problem focus on which to concentrate, recognizing that this could be extended or changed later on. The issue of championship location and timing was clearly of paramount concern, on the grounds both of its direct importance and urgency for the client, and its impact on related choices. So we chose to look more closely at the interaction between the English and the Welsh Associations and Llados Sailing Club (each as 'unitary actors') over this issue. For the time being, we agreed to consider other interactions only in so far as they affected this central problem.

The choice of a focus allowed us to flesh out this central issue by considering some specific options and outcomes. That is, we wished to examine what actions each actor might take, what might result from various combinations of these actions, and how. Of the models described in Chapter 12, the tableau provides a convenient way of building up a model of problems involving several players, each with several options that may be interdependent. As this seemed just such a case, we set about building a tableau to describe the 'game' currently seen by the client. Later, this would also provide one basis for constructing games that might be seen by other participants.

Tableaux can be used in two ways, each pursued in turn here. One is to generate and examine outcomes of particular interest, to see how these might arise or be ruled out. This partial and selective exploration we class as a continuation of problem structuring. The other, which will be considered shortly, is to generate all outcomes arising from given assumptions about options and their compatibility. This can be used to check whether any important outcomes have been missed out, and as the first step in formal analysis. As usual, the process of tableau construction was itself cyclical. The format provided a framework for discussing options and outcomes, both being continually redefined to express the points made by the client in as neat and coherent a way as possible. By the end of this discussion, the client's view of the main actions open to each side was expressed by the following options:

Llados Sailing Club	1. Propose definite championship arrangement.
Welsh Association	2. Agree to Llados's proposal (if one is made).
	3. Withdraw from Llados.
	4. Seek alternative Welsh venue.
	5. Take offence at English.
English Association	6. Support event in Wales.
	7. Stage an English National Championship.
	8. Stage World Championship in England.

The options used at this stage were defined quite broadly—one could, for example, go into much finer detail on the timing of actions. This fits in with our general practice of deferring considerations of detail until a rough framework has been established. Some options will be explained further below: first, however, we should recap the overall logic of the model. Each option represents an action that can be taken up or not. (Thus, Llados can make a definite proposal or not, and so on.) If independent, 8 options would give rise to $2^8 = 256$ possible outcomes, but in practice, we felt that many combinations could be more or less firmly ruled out as infeasible. Through discussing these, we built up a provisional picture of possibilities and impossibilities.

One result of this appears in Figure 3. The outcomes and infeasibilities displayed were chosen to express points of particular significance to the client. Outcomes are shown as columns of 1s and 0s, indicating options taken up or not. Thus, the first column represents the *status quo*, in which Llados had not made a definite proposal, the Welsh Association had taken no firm decision, and so on. Some comments are attached to each outcome. These annotations were important in capturing argumentation as it unfolded, providing much richer information than a bare tableau would have done. The six outcomes differed radically from each other, and the client felt intuitively (and as will be seen, wrongly) that they covered all the

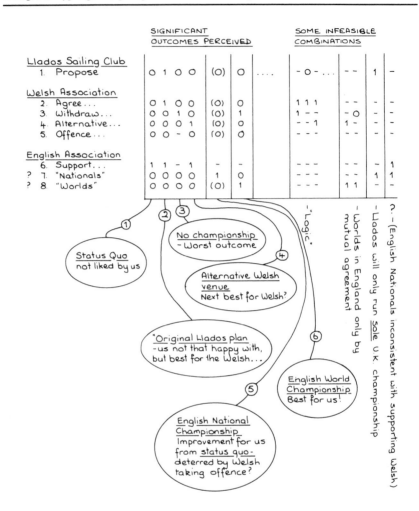

Figure 3
Some options and outcomes in the championship issue

main possible results, from which other outcomes would differ only in detail.

To the right of Figure 3 are some combinations judged to be infeasible, with explanations for their infeasibility. The first three seemed to be ruled out by the way the options were defined—by the internal 'logic' of the model. For instance, the first column states that the Welsh cannot 'Agree' and 'Withdraw'; this is so whatever other options are taken up (a point represented by the dashes in the rest of the column). Other infeasibility

322

assumptions represented more subtle interdependencies of decisions. Two are worth some explanation, which will also help to clarify certain options. One possibility might be to hold the World Championship in England (option 8). Constitutionally, however, such a change could be made only by mutual consent—i.e. if the Welsh were to forego their turn. A pair of columns thus tells us that 8 is feasible only if the Welsh withdraw from Llados *and* do not seek another venue.

The other point concerns the possibility of holding an English National Championship (option 7), a type of event also lasting a week. In principle, the English could decide to do so unilaterally. However, Llados had previously agreed to consider hosting the World event only as the sole major UK championship (fearing that otherwise, very few English would attend). Hence 1 is seen as incompatible with 7. Mounting a National Championship would pull the rug from under the feet of the Welsh Association, ending any chance of agreement with Llados. For the English, this would have considerable immediate advantages, but what of longer term relations with the Welsh? Such an action would break an informal understanding that there would be no 'rival' week in England, and would almost certainly cause considerable offence. Finally, the question marks against both 7 and 8 reminded us that time for finding a new venue was rapidly running out: these options would individually become infeasible.

Using maps to express argumentation

Having identified some significant outcomes, the next task in game or hypergame analysis is usually to consider how the client sees the preferences of the various parties. In this case, some assumptions about preferences had already been strongly implied in his description. But it was often unclear to the analyst why the client regarded outcomes as 'good' or 'bad' (even for the English committee). To get a more coherent picture, it was appropriate to step back temporarily from the game/hypergame framework, and to explore factors affecting preferences. As noted in the previous chapter, mapping can provide a useful way to express the argumentation behind hypergame models. Here, mapping was used, first to help examine key parties' preferences as seen by the client, and then to explore why different views might be held by other actors.

We did this by taking various outcomes represented in the existing tableau and building cognitive maps to help elaborate and express how the client saw the consequences of these outcomes, and why they might be welcome or unwelcome. Figure 4 shows one of the maps that resulted. It is based around the *status quo* outcome, showing some (generally unsatis-

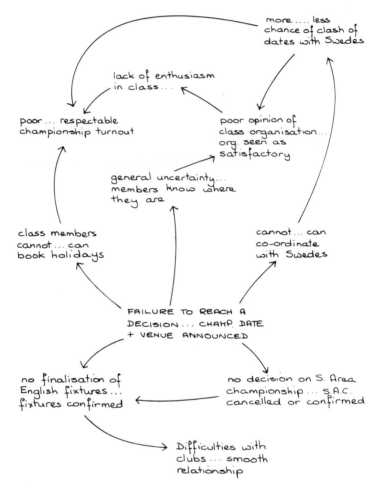

Figure 4
Map based on an outcome (1): 'Why the status quo is undesirable'. In this diagram, arrows should be read loosely as 'leads to' and dots as 'rather than'. Many of the concepts are in two parts, intended to highlight contrasting states of affairs as seen by the client. For example, the concept in capitals may be read as 'failure to reach a decision *rather than* championship date and venue announced'. Wherever arrows join two concepts in this map, the first part of one leads to the first part of the second; the second parts of the concept are linked similarly. The argumentation at the centre of the map thus expresses the view that 'failure to reach a decision' will lead to 'general uncertainty'; by contrast, a 'championship date and venue announced' would let members 'know where they are'. For a fuller description of mapping notation, see Chapter 2.

factory) consequences from the point of view of the English committee. Other maps were developed to express the client's reasoning about other outcomes, and his views about other actors' preferences for these.

Exploring other actors' possible preferences led us naturally into trying to envisage the situation seen by them. Figure 5, for example, shows an attempt to look at the outcomes involving a championship in Wales, from the point of view of the Welsh Association. This represents an attempt to

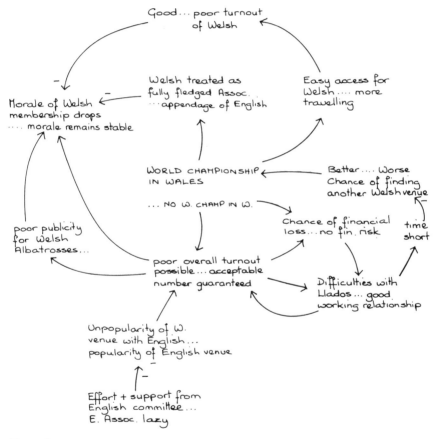

Figure 5
Map based on outcomes (2) and (4): Argumentation attributed to Welsh on having World Championship in Wales. A minus sign attached to an arrow indicates that the *first* part of one concept leads to the *second* part of the other. At the top left, for example, the argument is expressed that (other things being equal), the Welsh being treated as a 'fully-fledged Association' would help their members' morale to remain stable, whereas treating their Association as an 'appendage' would cause morale to drop. In all other respects, the map should be read exactly as for Figure 4.

think, not just about another actor's preferences, but about its whole viewpoint. We have used the term 'role thinking' to express this idea—analogous to the more familiar 'role playing', but without physically acting out other parties' behaviour. Within this, the hypergame perspective leads us to pay particular attention to their possible views about one's own side. Here, for example, the exercise drew attention to the idea that the Welsh might rather resent the (much larger) English Association, and perceive a tendency to treat the Welsh as a mere appendage. This could in turn affect Welsh preferences on the issue of the championship, which might be seen as symbolic of Welsh independence.

Analyses of the client's game

Armed with provisional assumptions about perceived actors, options, outcomes, and preferences, we moved on to the stage of formal modelling. As explained earlier (see the third box of Figure 1), we first continued with the 'game' seen by the client, temporarily ignoring the complexity arising from other actors', probably differing, perceptions. Even so, the 'piecemeal' methodology involved using several models alongside each other, in particular the use of both tableau and tree formats.

Completing and analysing tableau models

Continuing first with the tableau format of Figure 3, the first step in formal analysis was to find all feasible outcomes for the game. This was a job for the computer: we used Fraser and Hipel's (1979) program. (Howard's CONAN program, which is arguably superior, was not yet available to us.) Various assumptions about infeasibilities were explored. Given those that seemed most plausible to the client, the program listed 25 possible outcomes. Although these mainly consisted of the expected 'minor variations' on the six already considered, there was one striking exception. This concerned the possibility of having both a World Championship in Wales and an English National Championship. Though this had been considered briefly in passing, the client had discounted it—partly because of Llados's known insistence against 'two championships', and partly because having two events just seemed too 'silly' to be a likely outcome. Rather to his surprise, however, this appeared as a feasible outcome in the model. On reflection, this seemed to point to something overlooked before. Given the possibility of other Welsh venues, a 'two championships' outcome might happen as a result of each association becoming committed to its own plans in an uncoordinated way. On further reflection, the client felt that this outcome, though undesirable, would at least be preferable to that of no championship. It might even be quite a good result if the English could continue to support the Welsh event, though as will be seen later, such support would present problems. In other words, the analysis pointed to a set of issues not hitherto explored. Later on, we extended this train of thought to consider what might happen if the English and the Welsh ended up trying to stage their own World Championships. This, however, we leave until the section on hypergame analysis.

The next stage in analysing the game seen by the client was to consider the preferences of the various parties. Having explored these informally using the maps already described, the task was now to use these arguments to rank the 25 outcomes in order of preference for each player. Here, as often, it was convenient to use a mix of methods to do so. In considering preferences to be attributed to the Welsh Association, for example, the 25 outcomes were first roughly ordered in blocks according to whether the result would be (in decreasing preference):

1. a World Championship (only), in Wales;
2. an English National Championship too, but with English support for the 'Worlds';
3. a World Championship (only), in England;
4. an English National Championship only;
5. as (2), but without English support;
6. no championship.

We then examined individual outcomes to decide on orderings within the groups, and to consider changes in ranking on other grounds. Several possible orderings, differing in detail, were considered for each player, and the games analysed for stability (again using Fraser and Hipel's program).

In the course of this analysis, we also found that the structure of the model could usefully be simplified. So far, we had considered three players: the English and Welsh Associations, and Llados. While believing that Llados was still deciding whether to make an offer, we had very little information about their preferences (in other words, about what affected Llados's 'internal' games). Llados's decision seemed to depend on other parties' actions only in one respect: that they would definitely pull out if any other UK championship were announced. For the purposes of analysis, this could be expressed by treating Llados as a source of difficulty for the Welsh Association rather than a separate player. This simplification would be a particular asset when other forms of complexity—notably the existence of differing perceptions—came into consideration. As shown in Figure 6, this change involved some reformulation of the Welsh Associa-

FEASIBLE OUTCOMES
(Listed in order of preference for English)

INFEASIBILITIES
Assuming agreement with Llados *is* possible

WELSH ASSOCIATION

1/2. Stage event at Llados?	0	1	0	0	0	0	0	0	0	0	0	0		1	1	0	1	1	–	–	–	–	0
3. Seek alternative venue	0	0	0	0	1	0	1	1	1	1	0	0		1	–	0	–	–	–	1	–	1	–
4. Take offence	0	0	0	1	1	0	0	1	1	1	0	1		–	–	–	–	–	–	–	–	–	0

ENGLISH ASSOCIATION

5. Support Welsh event	0	1	0	0	1	1	1	1	0	0	0	0		–	0	1	–	–	–	–	–	1	0
6. Stage National Champ.	0	0	0	0	1	0	1	1	1	1	0	0		–	1	–	1	1	–	1	–	0	–
7. Stage World Champ.	1	0	1	1	0	0	0	0	0	0	0	1		–	0	–	1	1	1	1	–	–	–

PREFERENCES

English	12	11	10	9	8	7	6	5	4	3	2	1	
Welsh	8	4	12	7	5	11	10	9	6	3	1	1	

12 = most preferred
1 = least preferred
for each party

STABILITY

	·	U	·	U	·	U	·	U	U	U	U	U

(U = Welsh would gain by moving)

ANALYSIS

	·	U	·	U	·	U	·	U	U	U	U	U

(U = English would gain by moving)

	S	x	S	x	x	x	x	x	x	x	x	x

(S = Stable outcome: neither side would gain by initiating a move away)

Figure 6
Stability analysis for simplified model

tion's options, combining their first two options into that of 'stage event at Llados'. Infeasibilities—based on the same assumptions as before—are again shown on the right. In this simplified model, twelve feasible outcomes then remain, shown on the left. In addition, the Welsh 'Llados option' is noted as being of doubtful viability anyway, given the uncertainty about Llados's willingness to host a championship under any circumstances. In other words, we assumed that in some circumstances, Llados would not offer to run a championship, but never that they definitely would.

Analysis of tableaux tells us which outcomes are stable, in the sense that no player would benefit by moving, taking into account the others' possible responses. If the assumptions underlying the model are reasonable, such results give a preliminary indication of what might be expected to happen in reality. Here, it is easiest to explain the analysis using the simplified model of Figure 6. The letters along the bottom of the tableau show whether either player would gain by initiating a move away from each outcome. If so, the outcome is labelled 'U' (for 'unstable'); if neither would gain, the outcome is stable ('S'). Here, there are two stable outcomes: that of a single championship at Llados (if feasible); and that of a World Championship in England. Though in this version of the model, these are the most highly preferred outcomes for the Welsh and English Associations respectively, the same result holds for several variants on the preferences shown.

Using game trees

While stability is significant in choosing outcomes that one might sensibly aim for, this does not mean that there is necessarily any easy way of getting there. An aspect of the problem not yet considered was the order in which decisions would be made—a crucial part of the client's dilemma. Models failing to capture this, while useful in clarifying options and outcomes, could be only of limited help in deciding what to do. Given that the number of moves considered here was reasonably small, we introduced game trees to examine the sequence of possible decisions. The task of developing trees was simplified by having options and infeasibilities already defined. Especially, the infeasibility of option combinations could be represented by cutting off appropriate branches, an approach which allows the tree to be simplified as it is constructed.

An important point about this case was that the order of the decisions could itself be varied. As we have seen, part of the dilemma for the English Committee was whether to take some action at once, or wait for the Welsh. Two types of tree were, therefore, developed. The first type considered the decisions in the order they *should* have been taken, with Llados first

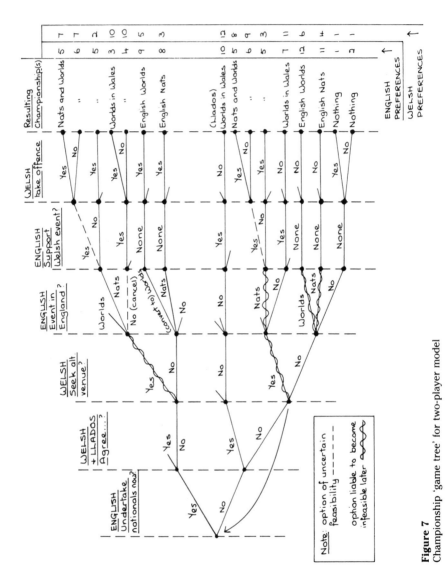

Figure 7

Championship 'game tree' for two-player model

deciding whether or not to make a proposal, the Welsh Association then deciding whether to accept, and the English stepping in if necessary. More interesting, however, was a second type, shown in Figure 7. This is a development of the previous two-player model, drawn specifically to clarify the English dilemma of whether to make the pre-emptive move of arranging a National Championship. Other decisions, both English and Welsh, follow on in turn. The outcomes at the end of the tree can take account of the order in which decisions are made (especially, outcomes in which the English undertake a National Championship immediately are not the same as those in which they do so after waiting for the Welsh decision).

This second model thus contains a somewhat richer set of sixteen outcomes, as compared with the twelve in the two-player tableau of Figure 6. To help keep track of what each outcome means in terms of championship locations, these are summarized on the right of the tree. Preferences for the English and Welsh Associations are shown, based on essentially the same argumentation as before (several variants were again produced). Finally, the tree was elaborated to convey two further points. The first was that if both the English and Welsh Associations initially did nothing concrete, the system would cycle back to the start, with each party facing the same decisions over again. The second point, however, was that this could not go on for ever. Eventually, in the absence of firm action, branches of the tree would disappear as alternative venues became impossible to find. But it was far from clear when this would happen.

Various trees of both types were analysed as outlined in Chapter 12, working backward from the last set of decisions. Without going through the results in detail, these showed how the uncertain time dependence of options lay at the heart of the English problem. An initial English move to undertake a National Championship would lead almost certainly to an eventual result of a World Championship in England, but with the Welsh taking offence. The latter might just possibly be avoided through later moves, but these were of doubtful feasibility (and desirability). The best attainable outcomes lay in the bottom half of the tree—which involved waiting for the Welsh. But this carried the danger of commitment by default to 'Llados or nothing'. As a result of factors beyond the English Association's control, this could easily end up as 'nothing'. Relative security lay in the top half of the tree: at least something could be guaranteed by moving fast.

Hypergame modelling

We had already noted, at various points, the strong possibility of actors other than the English committee seeing the championship problem in rather different terms. Would this matter, or not? Some attempt to explore the possible consequences of such differences was essential. So far, such considerations had not entered into our formal models: overcoming this limitation required a move from games to hypergames, as indicated in the last box of Figure 1. In Chapter 12, we noted two approaches towards setting up formal hypergames. One is the 'radical' approach of defining games for each party from scratch, making no prior assumption about similarities between them. The alternative is to start with the client's game and then consider how others' perceptions might differ, as a relatively quick form of 'assumption busting'. The choice between these in general depends both on the time and resources available, and on reasoned argument about the likelihood of radical differences in problem definition.

Within the problem focus presently chosen, the main actors here were (primarily) the English and Welsh Associations and (possibly) Llados Sailing Club. On balance, it seemed likely that these held roughly similar definitions of the situation, though there might well be specific points of difference. All had been concerned with running sailing events for some time, and had common experiences of the problems entailed. The Welsh committee seemed to be in an analogous position to the English, subject to many of the same worries, pressures, and hopes. Many of the key individuals knew each other personally, and most came from roughly similar backgrounds. While not guaranteeing similarity in view, these arguments, combined with the need for fairly quick, simple analysis, led us to adopt the less radical approach.

Even when starting from a given viewpoint, however, the hypergame approach itself encourages one to consider many specific differences of view that might occur. Prior to formal hypergame modelling, each part of the study so far was deliberately challenged by trying to look at how other player's perspectives might differ—remembering that the English committee's perspective should not be regarded as any more 'correct' than anyone else's. Having run through the possibilities that resulted, we would decide which differences merited modelling as formal hypergames.

Sources of difference: challenging the models

We began this part of the process by returning to our initial problem structuring. We had already noted that the PPS diagram of Figure 2 was drawn from the perspective of the English committee (more specifically, its chairman). Attempting now to envisage the Welsh committee's point of view, it seemed that an interaction with the Welsh clubs over their fixture list would be significant for the Welsh committee. They might also have a more detailed model of Llados's internal game, though this seemed doubtful on the evidence available. A more detailed version of Figure 2 would also have shown a finely differentiated structure within the English committee, with the Welsh remaining a virtual 'black box'. Presumably, this would be reversed for Welsh committee members. Such points would probably represent differing degrees of attention given to parts of an overall situation, rather than fundamental disagreement. As such, we would not have expected them greatly to influence the results of analysis. The structure of the situation as seen by Llados was more difficult to hypothesize, given the lack of any direct dealings with the club. But a worrying possibility that had at least to be entertained was that the club might see the class as a monolithic structure, not appreciating the relative autonomy of its national associations.

Moving on to the tableaux and trees, each part of these—feasible options, preferences, and so on—was now subjected in turn to scrutiny, examining how the games seen by other actors might be different. Focusing still on the English–Welsh interaction, we concentrated on possible differences in perception between the two Associations. This extended the process, already begun, of building multiple alternative models. For example, where the feasibility of an outcome had already been considered dubious, one could ask 'What if the English committee assumed it feasible, the Welsh infeasible?', so generating the outline of a hypergame. However, this 'what if' approach was now taken much further, subjecting even assumptions so far considered secure to critical scrutiny and debate. The main possibilities brought up by this process fell into three categories.

Firstly, English and Welsh perceptions of each other's preferences could vary, both regarding championship venues *per se*, and regarding the amount of goodwill around. What if, for example, the Welsh were less keen to find an alternative Welsh venue than the English supposed? Conversely, what might happen if the English belief that the Welsh also regarded 'no championship' as the worst outcome were mistaken? What if the Welsh believed that the English really wanted to go to Wales?

Secondly, perceptions of the feasibility of options and outcomes might vary. Most notably, the Welsh committee might believe that the English could not arrange a championship venue in time, so that it was up to the Welsh Association to find one. (In the game seen by the Welsh, the English would have only one choice—whether or not to 'support the Welsh'.) Conversely, the Welsh might perceive that the English had plenty of time and could afford to wait for them a good while longer. (They would thus not see the 'time dependence' of options in the English tree of Figure 7.) Similarly, was our impression correct about the seriousness of their difficulties with Llados?

Finally, there seemed to be clear dangers of misunderstanding as parties started to make decisions public. Consider, especially, the English option of 'supporting' a championship in Wales. The English committee might genuinely see itself as having offered support to the best of its (limited) power, while the Welsh interpreted the result as half-hearted and unsupportive. Similarly, what is a 'definite proposal' on championship arrangements? A proposal seen as 'definite' by the Welsh Association (or by Llados) might seem too vague to be acceptable to the English.

Hypergame analysis

Any of the above possibilities could be explored through formal hypergame analysis. As always, however, our effort was selective, concentrating on those cases that seemed to be most relevant to the decision in hand. Here, one hypergame will illustrate both the general form of analysis and a point of particular concern.

Introducing different perceptions obviously increases the complexity of formal models, whether matrices, trees or tableaux. To compensate for this it is often helpful to choose a problem focus narrower again, or to ignore detail. Such was the case here. As we have seen, the most pressing problem for the English committee—in the absence of firm news from Wales—was whether to carry on waiting, or to arrange a championship in England. Focusing on this aspect of the dilemma, and again temporarily leaving aside tactical detail on the timing of moves, the immediate alternatives open to each side appeared to be as shown in the matrix in Figure 8. For the

		Welsh	
		Insist on trying to hold Worlds	Forego Worlds if English hold a championship
English	Hold on	Status Quo: Welsh Worlds or nothing	Status Quo (but English free to act)
	Announce Nationals	Worlds and Nationals	English Nationals only
	"Announce" Worlds in England	Constitutional crisis!	Worlds in England

Figure 8
Immediate game, showing outcomes in terms of planned events

purposes of this model, we assumed that these alternatives were seen by both associations. As will be seen, the hypergame to be considered has at its heart some possible misperceptions of preferences.

Figure 8 shows three strategies for the English Association: to 'hold on' for the Welsh, or to announce its intention to run either a National or World Championship. By concentrating on announcement of intentions, we aimed to model the consequences of the moves immediately available. As will be recalled, announcing a championship in England would (we believed) cause Llados to break off their negotiations with the Welsh Association. For the English, this might be successful in inducing the Welsh to move aside—but were the risks worth taking? This was the question on which we wished to concentrate. The idea of announcing a National Championship came straightforwardly from our previous discussion: that of 'announcing' a World Championship was new, and requires some explanation. As noted before, the English could only *hold* a World Championship if the Welsh consented to forego their turn. But we considered that it would be feasible unilaterally to 'announce' a World Championship, in the hope of forcing the Welsh to abandon their plans completely. At least, the possible consequences of such a move seemed worth considering.

Two strategies, meanwhile, were considered for the Welsh, insistence on trying to hold a World Championship (at Llados or, if necessary, elsewhere), or foregoing the Welsh 'turn' if a championship in England were to be announced. The presumed outcomes of these various choices are shown in the matrix. These roughly correspond to those in previous models, with one exception—that of a 'constitutional crisis'. If the Welsh stuck to their guns in the face of English attempts to arrange a World Championship, this would lead to a constitutional crisis of epic proportions—at least, relative to this small world.

In considering preferences for these outcomes, we started by assuming that the 'constitutional crisis' would be worst for both sides. Perceived preferences for other outcomes were initially based on those of Figure 7, making the further assumptions: (a) that the Welsh would take offence at an English announcement; and (b) it would be impossible for the English to support the Welsh in the 'two championships' outcome. The resulting game seemed to be an accurate reflection of the current English perceptions. This is shown on the left of Figure 9. (As compared with Figure 7, the numbering of the preferences reflects the fact that there are only six outcomes in this model.)

Consider the alternatives open to the English in this game. If they were to continue holding on, the Welsh would have no incentive to move: the best hope for the English would be an eventual finalization of plans at Llados (admittedly a dramatic improvement on the *status quo*, but beyond English

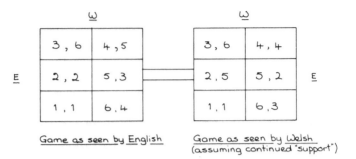

Figure 9
A possible English–Welsh hypergame

control to implement). 'Announcing' a World event would produce a situation akin to a game of 'Chicken', in which at least one side would have to lose face to avoid joint disaster. There was no way of telling whether an English announcement could carry sufficient credibility to induce the Welsh to back down first—the intuitive answer was 'no'. Furthermore, such a plan would be very vulnerable to the English having misperceived Welsh preferences. With pride at stake—and with some justice—the Welsh might actually prefer to ride out a crisis rather than back down. What, we asked, would happen then? Hypergames models of this situation were produced, all of which predicted disaster for the English. (Since this conclusion is hardly surprising, these are not reproduced here.) With constitutional legality pitted against force of numbers, one end result could even be two rival 'World' Championships.

We thus rapidly moved back to consider the option of announcing a National Championship. At first sight, this course of action looked much more promising. Though it would again lead to a situation akin to 'Chicken', the result of neither side backing down would be distinctly less disastrous than before. Furthermore, a National Championship was something that the English Association could genuinely and publicly commit itself to. Were such a commitment to be believed, then (in the game as seen by the English) the Welsh Association could only improve its own position by giving way, moving from (2,2) to (5,3). From there, it would be to both parties' advantage for the English to move to (6,4). In other words, a World Championship would be held in England, by something like mutual consent. But this line of argument was again vulnerable to the possibility of having misperceived Welsh preferences, and we used hypergames to explore this. As a specific example, we asked 'what if' the Welsh believed that if the English had a National Championship they would still support a Welsh event. (Such a belief would not have been far from the truth: as the tree in

Figure 7 shows, the English could only gain by trying to offer support if the Welsh event went ahead.) Given this belief, the Welsh game would be as on the right of Figure 9. In the resulting hypergame, the English attempt at inducement would again fail, this time because the Welsh would have no incentive to respond. By announcing a National Championship, the English would give the Welsh, in their game, a choice between (2,5) and (5,2); the former, preferable for the Welsh, was to be gained by sticking to their plans. The result would be a 'two championships' outcome slightly worse for the English than the *status quo*.

From considerations such as these, a potential way forward for the English committee began to emerge. Our analyses had pointed out various dangers of making a pre-emptive move. Some way had to be found of minimizing these, while also avoiding the danger of ending up with no championship through inaction. If the Welsh were to be persuaded to step down, it would be necessary for them to believe (rightly or wrongly) that the English could not support both theirs and another championship. At the same time, it was important to move in such a way as to avoid offending the Welsh as far as possible. This might be achieved by emphasizing the (perfectly genuine) English fear of ending up with no event, and stressing continued support for the Welsh if arrangements could be made quickly. These points eventually coalesced around the idea of giving the Welsh a specific deadline, beyond which the English committee would consider itself free to announce a National event. This plan, and its results, are summarized briefly in the next section.

The decision

So what did the English Albatross Committee actually do? In making the decision, the concept of a *commitment package* was used. Devised as part of the Strategic Choice methodology (see Chapter 6), as a way of dealing with uncertainty, the commitment package provides a convenient way of formulating sets of decisions to be implemented through time. Decisions can be immediate, delayed, and/or contingent on events: the package will include both actions and explorations of various types. The development of packages specifically to deal with conflict as well as uncertainty is a current area of research (Bennett and Cropper, 1986, 1989). Here, the general commitment package concept proved useful in devising a way forward for the English committee, bearing in mind the complexities discussed above.

The 'package' actually adopted is summarized in Figure 10. This categorizes decisions into immediate, contingent, and delayed, shown on the vertical

	ACTIONS	MESSAGES	EXPLORATIONS
Immediate ("do now")	Commitment now to having champ date + venue approved at next cttee mtg (4 weeks) Procedural decision: authorise small group to negotiate with English clubs Avoid any firm commitment to a championship in England for next 3 weeks Preference amongst possible English venues, if available, agreed	To Welsh Assoc: English support for event in Wales guaranteed only for another 3 weeks Stress difficulty of English supporting two championships in one year	Informal exploration of possible championship date with several known English clubs Attitude of other National Associations
Contingent ("do if")	1/ If firm date + venue from Welsh received within 3 wks: (a) Support Welsh proposal (b) Confirm arrangements for southern area event 2/ If not: (a) Firm up date with most promising English club straight away (b) leave World/National status of above event for latter negotiation (c) Cancel Southern Area event	To Welsh Assoc: (case 1) Confirm arrangement and English committee support (case 2) Announce plan for event in England, stress regret at necessity for this, continued general support To other National Assocs: keep informed of general situation.	Explore (with Welsh) how to make event more attractive to English Will Welsh be prepared to recognise event in England as 'World Championship'?
Delayed ("do later")	Above decision (either way) to be finalised at next cttee meeting Announcement to be agreed for broadcast to members	To other National Assocs: Immediately after next meeting: confirm championship date + venue To (English) members as above; If necessary 'sell' idea of going to Wales as fully as possible	

Figure 10
English committee's decision expressed in (modified) commitment package form

axis. The other axis has headings for actions, messages, and explorations. The explicit inclusion of 'messages' is additional to the usual Strategic Choice formulation. Both in this and in specific content, the package strongly reflects the interactive nature of the situation. As much as a response to uncertainty, it can be seen as a game plan—especially the ultimatum given to the Welsh, with subsequent decisions contingent on their response. It also represented an attempt to balance crisis management with the preservation of reasonable relations with the Welsh, with—in all honesty—an emphasis on the former. Perhaps most importantly, it provided a clear framework for the

English committee, within which decisions were discussed, improved, and rapidly agreed. The result was then acted on by the committee, with full agreement and some enthusiasm. The decisions 'worked', at least at a tactical level. The Welsh accepted the deadline, then subsequently acknowledged their inability to meet it. Explorations had by then established a feasible championship venue in England. This was immediately taken up, whereupon the Welsh agreed to the event having 'World' status. Within three weeks, the crisis had been resolved satisfactorily from the English point of view. In due course, the championship was held, and proved reasonably successful. Meanwhile, the Welsh seemed to accept that English decisions had been driven by necessity rather than by malice.

Concluding comments

Leaving the immediate decisions to one side, one can ask what was learnt about the problem in the course of the study. Despite the considerable amount of problem 'pre-formulation' on the client's part, aspects of it were clarified, and a few genuine surprises emerged. We have tried to indicate what was gained from particular models in the course of the narrative, and to give some impression of how the client's view of the problem evolved. We have already emphasized that the various models informed one another as part of an iterative learning process, and Figure 1 showed how we moved 'forward' through types of model. But it is also worth noting some of the main ways in which earlier views were modified by later analysis.

The initial PPS exercise (as in Figure 2) had already elicited some peculiarities of the problem known to the client, but not mentioned in the initial description (for example, the lack of any direct communication between the Welsh and the Swedes). Subsequent parts of the study, however, suggested several ways in which this picture could usefully be extended and modified. The mapping exercise, for example, drew attention to a further level of interaction. Several of the maps had constructs such as 'poor (or good) opinion of committee held by class members', and it was realized that the relationship between each committee and its 'constituency' represented an important concern, hitherto largely unexplored. (Figure 2 acknowledges 'internal interactions' within each Association, but gives them no specific substance.)

Most significantly, analysis later drew attention to a continuing 'oddness' about the perceived problem structure. Why was the championship issue a problem for the English Association? Logically, it seemed to be the responsibility of the Federation. Having been mentioned briefly, this had not even emerged as a player. The immediate answer was that in practice, all normal business was conducted at a national level: over the years, the English Association had (as the largest) tended *de facto* to take on the Federation's role too. On a day-to-day basis, this had mattered little. In the current crisis, it meant that no agreed mechanism was in place for resolving international issues. Furthermore, this confusion of roles might well compound any possible resentment of the English on the part of other associations. This aspect was something which had been largely over-looked. While little could be done about it in handling the immediate problem, the position of the Federation clearly warranted serious consideration in the longer term. Otherwise it would only be a matter of time before similar problems recurred.

To summarize, this case provided a good illustration of some aspects of our methodology. Attention was given in turn to broad-brush representations, and to more detailed analyses. Rather than attempting to produce a 'definitive' picture at each stage, insights gained at any point were used to revise what had gone before. In short, the process was 'piecemeal, mixed scanning, and iterative'. Consequently, we have also been able to illustrate most of the individual types of analysis mentioned in Chapter 12. It should be reiterated, however, that this was a fairly simple problem, highly 'pre-structured' by the 'client'. This feature heavily influenced both the choice of starting point (going straight into PPS), and the overall balance between different parts of the methodology—especially the late and relatively limited formal consideration of differing perceptions.

References

Bennett, P. G., and Cropper, S. A. (1986). 'Conflict and uncertainty', O.R. Society Annual Conference, University of Kent, Sept. 1986.

Bennett, P. G., and Cropper, S. A. (1989). 'Uncertainty and conflict: Combining conflict analysis and strategic choice', *J. Behavioural Decision-Making* (in press).

Fraser, N. M., and Hipel, K. W. (1979). 'Solving complex conflicts', *IEEE Transactions SMC-9*, **12**, 805–15.

14
Diverse unity: the principles and prospects for problem structuring methods

Jonathan Rosenhead

This book has presented six different methodologies for structuring problems and decisions. Each has been described both in general (in terms of aspiration, terminology, method, and process), and in application.

The new paradigm is still in the making, and it is too early for any definitive stock-taking. However, it may help the reader if in this final chapter at least some of the threads are drawn together. We will highlight in particular the features which the methodologies have in common, and then return to more general issues about the significance of these developments for the future of rational analysis.

Contrasts and congruences

There are some evident contrasts between the methodologies described in earlier chapters—they take different situations as their fields of application, and handle them in differing ways. These contrasts often appear large to the authors, as they read and react to each other's work. They will, however, seem less significant to the reader than certain overriding similarities between the methods described—similarities which are in fact

Rational Analysis for a Problematic World
Edited by J. Rosenhead. © 1989 John Wiley & Sons Ltd

even greater than might appear, as the authors have been encouraged to concentrate on the more distinctive aspects of their respective approaches in order to avoid too much overlap. In this section I will try to draw out these common features behind the diversity of methods.

Points of focus

Certain of the methodologies have a concentration on particular types of decision or problem situations, while others make fewer assumptions about the internal structure of situations for which they can be of use. In the latter category it is reasonable to place Strategic Options Development and Analysis (SODA), Soft Systems Methodology (SSM), and Strategic Choice. Yet in another sense each of the methods does provide a general problem structuring facility. Each deploys a repertoire of methods, any one of which may (or may not) be applied at some point in the course of a study. Many of them are quite eclectic in their willingness to take other approaches under their wings.

Though most of the methodologies have origins in operational research, they have tended to move away in varying degrees from the simple decision orientation of traditional OR. Thus, in the case of the two game-theoretic approaches—Metagame and Hypergame Analysis—decisions are of central concern. But they do not feature as alternatives to be assessed against each other. The focus is rather on helping to improve decision making by analysing the quite complex interactive *process* through which decisions emerge.

SODA shares this emphasis on process but, despite its OR pedigree, employs a technique which is not predominantly decision focused. This technique, cognitive mapping, centres as much on identifying organizational goals as it does on decision options. This contrasts with the approach of Strategic Choice and Robustness Analysis, whose emphasis is (more conventionally in an OR sense) on the choice between candidate decisions. Preferences, values, rankings, and the like do, of course, feature —but as means of comparing or excluding various decision options rather than as subjects of equivalent status.

SSM makes a further contrast. Emerging from the somewhat different background of the systems approach, and indeed system design, the concern is more with how systems could work better, than with what decisions to take. The very word 'decision' is strikingly absent from the account Peter Checkland provides of it—we get no nearer than 'systemically desirable and culturally feasible changes'.

Such differences in origin and formulation do not detract from the overall homogeneity of the approaches. SSM and SODA will serve as an example. Despite their distinct theoretical bases, in systems thinking and in social psychology, they are widely perceived as closely aligned in style and purpose—indeed their principal authors have played down any incompatibility (Checkland, 1985; Eden, 1985).

Products, process, and complexity

Another, related, way of understanding the diversity within the unity of these methodologies is to consider their orientation towards either visible or invisible products. (For a fuller account of these concepts, see the Chapters 6 and 7 on Strategic Choice.) For most of the approaches—SSM, SODA, metagames, and hypergames—the outputs are skewed to a greater or lesser extent towards the invisible end of the spectrum. Though recommended actions and policy changes—the visible products—can be expected to emerge, they do so largely as an indirect result of the core methodology. The more direct effect is on the outlooks, perceptions, and appreciative judgements of the participants. These are the invisible products of the application of the methodology. With Strategic Choice and Robustness, recommendations as to action are generated more directly in the process of applying the methodology. The relative prominence of visible products in these cases is, in fact, a fairly logical consequence of their explicit focus on the act of commitment to decision.

I have already suggested, in Chapter 1, that an emphasis on decision process (and hence on invisible products) gives *technique*, in the sense of manipulation of abstract representations, less work to do. It is the *process* which, in its own way, performs crucial tasks which would otherwise fall to technique. However, this idea can be broadened out to discriminate *within* the set of problem structuring methodologies.

It can be argued, perhaps, that there is a significant cleavage in the types of problem situation addressed by the problem structuring methodologies. In one case the problematic situation is problematic principally because of lack of clarity or communication about objectives, purposes, 'what business we are in', etc. In such situations, methods where products are largely invisible—interaction facilitated, understanding shared—are both necessary and sufficient. SODA and SSM seem to fall largely within this category.

In other cases, however, the problem situation may embrace very considerable degrees of complexity, which are not easy for decision makers to assimilate. For difficulties arising principally from complexity, it can be argued that a more elaborate technique is needed. Such techniques need bear little resemblance to the algorithms of the orthodox paradigm. With no remit to search for the unique optimum, they can avoid baroque impenetrability. Technique is required, simply, to structure and reduce complexity to a point where the decision process can appropriate it. The participants in that process may then feel able to act on the resulting understanding. Alternatively, the provisional understanding may provoke a refocusing of the problem, which may in turn benefit from further analytic effort.

At the strategic level, complexity arises less from sheer number of options than from interactions between different decision makers and from compounded uncertainties. However, these two sources of complexity produce different challenges to technique, which are reflected in particular problem structuring methodologies. The technical aspects of Hypergame and Metagame Analysis take as their subject matter the multiple possibilities of conflict and cooperation between at least semi-autonomous decision makers, as well as their accompanying dimensions of emotion and irrational behaviour. For Strategic Choice and Robustness Analysis, technique is used to engage with the complex interactions between possible combinations of interventions in the system under study, and the uncertainties which surround them. In each of these cases, the higher level of formal technique and of visible outputs represents, not a question of taste or of random variation, but a response to a different category of problematic situation.

If juggling with complexities presents difficulties for the individual, it is still less feasible in a group situation. Yet working with groups is a common characteristic of the methodologies described in this book. Some of the methods can certainly be used with or by an individual working alone—witness the case studies of Robustness and Hypergame Analysis. Further, the CONAN computer program for Metagame Analysis, and the user-friendly software now emerging for Strategic Choice, can enable individuals to use the approaches in isolation. However, this is seen as a supplement to, rather than a substitute for, group working.

Robustness Analysis is the approach least orientated to working with groups—though its transparency of method makes it easily accessible to non-specialists. By contrast, many of the developed methods (and a sizeable chunk of the technology) of SSM, SODA, and Strategic Choice would be rendered irrelevant in working with an individual decision maker. The workshop format is the norm. It is worth noting that of these three, Strategic Choice is distinctive in aiming to 'structure complexity' rather than 'clarify objectives'. The provision of a general-purpose methodology, whose structuring of complexity can be adopted by lay groups and used in progressing their own understanding, represents a very considerable achievement.

There is ample scope for diversity of method. Indeed there is strength in it. One solitary problem structuring method, however beneficial, would come to act as a blighting new orthodoxy on what is still an under-developed area. And viewed in the context of the orthodox paradigm, the similarities amongst these alternative methodologies are more striking than their divergencies.

The six dimensions

Consider the extent to which the approaches conform to the six character-istics of an alternative paradigm of decision aiding, identified in Table 2 of Chapter 1. A number of these dimensions have already been touched on in the preceding discussion. Explicit clarification of *conflict* is limited to the two game-theory based contributions, but the use of simpler more trans-parent models is evident in all the methodologies. Similarly, handling of *uncertainty* and the preservation of options is most explicit in Strategic Choice and Robustness Analysis. But none of the other approaches assumes a certain future which is to be planned for. Again, the three methods based inherently on group working clearly take participants as *active subjects*. But the other approaches offer substantial scope for active participation—through transparency of representation, focus on the immediate commit-ment, and so on.

Compare this with the opportunities for participation available with any method based on the use of quantitive algorithms. These are largely restricted to legitimation of the project, validation of assumptions, supply of data, and acceptance (or otherwise) of results. This is a crude caricature of the relationship of client to model wherever the practitioner within the orthodox paradigm is reasonably sophisticated. But the analyst has to fight against the deficiencies of the paradigm—involving, for example, elaborate manoeuvres to establish client trust in a fundamentally incomprehensible technique.

Other characteristics of the alternative paradigm identified in Chapter 1 feature strongly in the problem structuring methodologies. The pursuit of *optimality* is absent from all of them, and with it the need for trade-offs or single objectives. Strategic Choice and Robustness in particular utilize 'satisficing' to identify a range of acceptable schemes, while Metagame and Hypergame Analyses employ game-theoretic logic to produce not—or not directly—an assessment of alternative strategies, but an understanding of human behaviour in the decision-making process.

Data requirements are also much reduced in all of the methodologies. In part this is a result of operating at the strategic level. It is useful here to think in terms of the 'mixed scanning' model of planning (Etzioni, 1968). Mixed scanning endeavours to overcome some of the practical and politi-cal objections, sketched out in Chapter 1, to both rational comprehensive

345

planning and its competitor, disjointed incrementalism. Planning (or 'scanning') is seen as occurring at two levels: the strategic and the incremental. The former sets the broad directions; the latter implements the resulting policy in a responsive way. Detail, then, which is of the essence at the incremental level, should be excluded when strategic issues are under consideration. The data hungry methods of the orthodox paradigm of rational analysis must be eschewed at the strategic level. In this way both information overload and detailed inflexible prescriptions can be avoided.

Problem structuring, of its nature, occurs predominantly as an element of high level, strategic scanning. Shaping the context of understanding is not re-initiated every time events deviate to some extent from what might have been expected. Adaptation of programmed activities can occur at the incremental level, within the policy context already established. So problem structuring methodologies will be applied primarily at a level where extensive detail and data, of the sort generated in routine operations, will be unavailable, irrelevant, or both.

Mixed scanning is explicitly espoused only by Hypergame Analysis (see the account in Chapter 12). However, the importance of moving up and down between levels of generality and specificity is emphasized in several of the other approaches described in this book. In Robustness Analysis, a relative lack of detail is made possible by the concentration on the immediate commitment, which enables potential later decisions to be handled in a more approximate way.

The reduced data intensity of these methods does not result only from their strategic domain of application. It arises also from their project of assisting rather than replacing judgement. The methods must be able to receive inputs and provide outputs in a variety of forms—hard and soft, relatively objective or explicitly subjective, cardinal or ordinal. Much of the information required and manipulated by these approaches is not 'data' in the numerical/statistical sense in which this word is commonly used.

There is one characteristic remaining out of the six identified for the alternative paradigm—its ability to facilitate *bottom-up planning*. This point is addressed directly only by SODA, through its amalgamation of individual cognitive maps into a single strategic map. Other approaches, however, help bottom-up planning more indirectly, through their user-friendly transparency, but not through any particular formulations.

Perhaps, though, the distinctive decision orientation which many of these methodologies share is itself such a formulation. The orthodox paradigm, and its problem solving methods, starts with abstract objectives from which concrete decision options are then deduced. By contrast, most of the methodologies in this book, as we have already seen, start with concrete decision options available to one or more participants in the problematic situation. These decisions are then analysed for feasibility, compatibility, etc., in ways which make use of preference information but without assuming any overarching objectives. This provides the conceptual freedom, not yet fully exploited, to develop the methodologies for use in bottom-up planning.

A conclusion supporting this view is reached by Jackson (1988). Starting also with the six dimensions of the alternative paradigm, but employing a different argument, he finds that the problem structuring methodologies (which he calls 'enhanced OR') have much to offer the alternative clientele of community operational research. These are community groups organized to advance or protect the common interests of their members. Typically they have limited resources and no hierarchical management structure, and operate through consensus and democratic procedures. The strength of such groups depends on cementing internal unity, and their weakness limits the chance of success without negotiation and coalition formation. Evidently top-down planning can have limited applicability here, and the scope for analysis in bottom-up mode could be considerable.

These are encouraging reflections, but constitute in large part speculations about what might be. Nevertheless, three of the six methodologies forming the core of this book are illustrated by case studies for unconventional clients—three straws in the wind?

Issues for rational analysis

The previous section has explored similarities and differences, both within the alternative paradigm of problem structuring methods, and between that paradigm and the orthodoxy which it is challenging. This discussion has already touched on a number of themes identified in Chapter 1. Others are worthy of further consideration, now that the substance of the methodologies is, so to speak, available in evidence. The field is new, underdeveloped, and changing fast. It would be at variance with its prevailing critical spirit if the book were to end on a complacent note. It would also do the field a disservice. There are important issues as yet unresolved. They can and will be worked out in practice, forming indeed points of departure for new developments, provided that critical attention is focused on them. In what follows I will try to raise such issues, even where I can offer no more than pointers to where a resolution might lie.

The role of the consultant

One group of issues concerns the role of the consultant, internal or external, who deploys problem structuring methods. For the consultant who offers problem *solving* methods, there is no ambiguity. She is an expert in particular types of complexity. Her mode of operation is to extract relevant information from participants with minimum interference to the system under study; the intended impact on the system is via recommendations reached through manipulation of that information.

Those who advocate the use of problem *structuring* methods do so out of an awareness of the inadequacy of this 'expert in complexity' model. The supposedly 'non-expert' participants in any decision process have their own forms of knowledge about the system and the issues to be faced, which are not capturable in any analyst's coarse mathematical net. One possible conclusion is that the consultant's role should be that of 'expert in process'. This method of working, 'process consultancy', aims to surface the knowledge available to a group by skilfully promoting interaction. The consultant acts as a catalyst, employing both sensitivity to cues and acquired process management skills. This is the route adopted, for example, by practitioners of Organizational Development (OD) (Huxham, Cropper, and Bennett, 1989).

There may be a temptation amongst some, especially those who have worked at some time within the orthodox paradigm, to react against its simplistic excesses. Concentration on process (as in OD) may come to be seen as a virtue; on substance (as in orthodox OR) as almost a vice—at least for problems concerning non-routine aspects of human activity systems. However, a dialectical understanding of their relationship is crucial. Both OD and OR have their particular domains—and there is a yawning gap between where neither principle alone is sufficient. This is the domain of planning or design under conditions of complexity, uncertainty, and conflict. Handling only what Checkland calls (following Blackett) 'the logic of situations' leads to the sterility discussed at length in Chapter 1. Handling only the process aspects leaves the tangled chaos of interacting factors, and participants' perceptions of them, to the mercies of *ad hoc* simplification. The perplexing labyrinth demands structuring, not just facilitation.

The opportunity and challenge confronting rational analysis is to pick up not just one of these opposing poles, but both. The role of the consultant cannot be that of process consultant only, or of expert in complexity only. Only when these two aspects are united can purposeful interventions in the mess, the wicked problem, be executed with some confidence, and prepared in a way which increases participants' abilities to handle future problems (see Eden, 1987).

Techniques, tools, and methodologies

The creative tension between process and content must be a shaping force in the development of problem structuring methodologies. Some formal tools are required for the structuring of substance, but these must not impede facilitation of process. Indeed the tension will be resolved most fruitfully when the tool or technique itself constitutes what Eden calls a 'facilitative device'. This may take the form of a computer with its software and output; or the consultant may call up different items from a technical repertoire sufficiently simple to obviate the need for computer manipulation.

Operational research, through its over-reliance on techniques, has helped to get them a bad name. Some of those analysts who, realizing this, help to celebrate or create the new generation of problem structuring methods, verge on techno-phobia. (This is *not* true of the contributors to the present volume. Each of the methodologies described here incorporates a technique element, and acknowledges its essential contribution.) Because technique orientation drove out problem orientation over the past three decades, they now see all techniques as inherently suspect, if not worse. Each problem, it is asserted, should be tackled without preconceptions, or pre-investment in technical apparatus which may bias the approach.

There are some provoking aspects to this attempted proscription. Thus, to some for whom techniques are beyond the pale, 'tools' are apparently quite acceptable. Tools, in this context, are self-contained computer packages or systems which can be delivered to the users. (The design of such tools should be carried out in close rapport with at least one user, but that is a separate issue.) The acceptability in principle of tools appears to lie in their passage to the direct control of the users, to employ as and how they see fit.

The defensibility of this position of 'methodologies—good, tools—why not?, techniques—never' seems to me very dubious. The packaged assumptions and structure of a computerized tool constitute a preconceptualization of subject matter no less questionable than in the techniques of OR. Indeed, the tool is perhaps more insidious, on account of its shining user-friendly façade. Inside the tool there is always a technique, with its power but also its accompanying limitations.

Equally, a great divide of acceptability between methodologies and techniques seems hard to sustain. A technique, in this context, is an ordered series of calculations. A methodology is an ordered sequence of processes (some of which may or may not incorporate techniques). Each is constructed and elaborated because it is thought to apply potentially to a significant class of problem situations. Though there are evident differences between techniques and methodologies, there are enough parallels to discredit any simple claim to moral superiority. It would be a case of the straitjacket calling the manacle tight.

Creative cooking

What feature of any preconceptualization of a class of problematic situations makes it more enabling than restrictive? Surely it is the flexibility with which practitioners can adapt it while handling the particularities of a given case. The most productive view of any available methodology is to view it as a repertoire, not a recipe. This is a theme running through many contributions to this book, but it is one which is often ignored in practice. Relative novices grasp at the relative certainties of an ordered sequence of stages. The great chef, familiar with culinary materials, does not cook to a recipe, but his cook-book enables many others to do so.

One solution to this dilemma could lie in trainee analysts learning through apprenticeship (Huxham, Cropper and Bennett, 1989). But this imposes a dampening effect on the spread of any new methodology, unless a number of separate foci of infection can be spawned. In fact there seem to be appreciable difficulties in securing transfer of methodologies away from their originators. The phenomenon is quite general—witness the case of Ackoff's 'idealized planning'.

Various explanations of this transfer problem are possible, from the sales resistance of analysts brought up in a different culture, to the inherent problem of transmitting craft (as opposed to technical) knowledge other than by shared experience (see Cropper, 1987). But whatever the causes, one effect has been to generate a certain scepticism. If the only practitioner much in evidence is the person who invented, developed, and now lives by the methodology, how do we know that it isn't just a case of a guru with a gimmick?

Of course, we don't. And, indeed, gurus and their associated gimmicks are far from unknown in management pastures. The rich pickings attract them. For those as yet unexposed to a particular methodology, the claims made for it may be close to unverifiable. This is particularly so for approaches whose products are primarily invisible, necessarily attestable to only by direct participants. To an outsider, this may seem akin to mystical experience.

Scepticism is reasonable, but paranoia is not. Reasonable doubters might find the following guidelines helpful. Be prepared to give a methodology the benefit of the doubt, and perhaps a trial, provided:

- it is not just the guru who proclaims its success;
- the evidence of client satisfaction amongst individuals not otherwise noted for their gullibility suggests that the benefits may not be restricted to the mystical sphere;
- the logic, in a general sense, by which the approach is claimed to produce

benefits is accessible to and survives attack with the weapons of educated common sense.

Undoubtedly the originator of a methodology will employ the approach in an individual manner. He or she may well achieve superior results with it through greater virtuosity, authority or even charisma than other consultants. Personal variation of this kind is not a skeleton in the methodological cupboard. An optimizing technique *should* be the same whoever uses it, a problem structuring methodology should not. For a problem structuring methodology, the consultant is commonly a participant in an evolving interpersonal process. His or her individual characteristics, therefore, can affect both the value of the methodology, and the eventual outcome (see Cropper, 1984). In practice, even for the supposedly objective optimizing techniques, craft skills are extremely important, from model construction to the interpretation of results.

Helping to shape perceptions of a problematic situation is not, then, a neutral and objective activity. The consultant, especially when operating in facilitative mode, makes, whether deliberately or otherwise, considerable personal inputs. This view was certainly expressed following a recent conference demonstration of several problem structuring approaches (Huxham, Cropper and Bennett, 1989). One 'guinea pig' client said that on several occasions it appeared that the consultant 'was deciding which concepts were important'. Another was concerned about the possibility of too much 'haste to get away from the original vagueness'. A comment on one of the methodologies was that it 'is a good way of getting clients to accept (possibly as their own) the consultant's ideas about the world'. Eden and Simpson (not involved in these sessions) are explicit in Chapter 3 about their deliberate choice on personal grounds of who to adopt as client from within the organization, and indeed of what projects to take on. The analyst/facilitator/consultant is a factor in the situation, and can have multifarious influences. Since this is so, it is probably better that these choices are made consciously than inadvertently.

Subjectivity and objectivity

It follows from this argument that problem structuring methodologies have a double measure of subjectivity. The subjectivities of the participants are commonly a key ingredient of their subject matter; and there is also considerable scope for subjective variation in the way the methods are applied. Indeed, an early joint presentation of several of these methodologies was at an event titled 'Practical approaches to subjectivity in OR'.

351

Subjectivity is a delicate subject in the OR context. With its natural science heritage and orientation, many OR practitioners would prefer to— and prefer to believe that they do—deal only in objective facts. The reaction (Machol, 1980) of a distinguished academic, ex-President of the Operational Research Society of America, to a case study reported by one of the contributors to this book, exemplifies the attitude: 'didn't say anything about anything ... time for someone to stand up and shout that the emperor isn't wearing any clothes ... no content in any of this ...', and so on.

This syndrome of doubting the validity of any factor which is not rooted in objective fact and capturable in numbers, is at one extreme, to which problem solving methodologies provide an overdue antidote. Perhaps Checkland's account, here and elsewhere, of the theoretical underpinnings of SSM provides the strongest medicine. He stresses interpretations, images, world views; his models of purposeful activity are compared not with 'reality', but with perceptions of that reality. Social reality, he writes, is not given; it is 'continuously constructed and reconstructed by communication between individuals' (Checkland, 1981). He criticizes 'old-style OR and management science' for concentrating heavily on the 'logic of situations'; SSM by contrast is struggling to cope with the 'myths and meanings' by which people make sense of their perceptions of the world (Checkland, 1985).

This polar opposition between objectivity and subjectivity parallels that between content and process which we explored a little earlier. A method rooted in one pole, alone, gravely handicaps itself for significant classes of the most demanding problem situations. Can the two opposites, then, be united? Farkas (1984), in a difficult and challenging article, proposes such a renewal of systems analysis (that is, of operational research) based on a materialist dialectic, which would encompass the way in which values and objective factors determine each other. Though the approaches in this book strike a variety of different balances between the objective and the subjective, none attempts this organic bonding.

Farkas draws our attention, also, to what he terms 'objective irrationalities' which stem from 'the basic contradictions of the socio-economic structure of societies split by conflicting interests'. In other words, conflict (one of the diagnostic signs that problem structuring methods might be appropriate) exists of a type which is not capable of being willed away by a change of perception. This more entrenched conflict arises out of institutionalized clashes of material interests.

The more major of these oppositions—based on class, gender, and race—shape the development of all our societies. Rational analysis is not above these battles. Its very existence has been called up by the antagonistic way in which productive forces have been organized. The different forms of analysis—Dando and Bennett's (1981) orthodox, reformist, and revolutionary paradigms, for example—constitute differing responses to these fluctuating struggles (Rosenhead and Thunhurst, 1982; Rosenhead, 1989).

This argument is rather abstract, but it has very concrete manifestations. Orthodox OR, in particular, has developed in a form best suited to provide a control function in hierarchical organizations. It has been quite inappropriate to the problem situations of democratically run organizations with little in the way of resources to control. Needless to say, it has been employed scarcely at all in such contexts.

Methods for alternative clients

I have discussed this bias in the clientele of operational research at length elsewhere (Rosenhead, 1986). The alternative practice of working with community groups was pioneered by Ackoff (1970) in the Mantua ghetto of Philadelphia. It has been taken up most significantly by the community operational research movement in Britain (Jackson, 1987a, 1988; Thunhurst, 1987). There are aspects of self-interest in this development—for example, the appeal of an analytically unexplored territory of pristine new problem situations. But the principal motivation has been outward looking: the desire to contribute not just to a more 'efficient', but also to a less exploitative and a fairer world. Appropriate analysis can help to empower the underprivileged.

Earlier in this chapter I suggested that problem structuring methodologies might be particularly suitable for planning with and for community groups. However, are all the methods equally appropriate? Suppose that a community group which is one of the weaker parties to a multi-faceted power struggle—an example of what Jackson (1988) calls a 'coercive' problem environment—is open to the thought that analysis may have some help to offer. Suppose again that the only method which is not completely mystifying involves, say, the various parties engaging jointly in workshop-format discussions. The method aims to find a resolution through mutual adjustment of perceptions. In these circumstances the potential client might be well advised to show the potential consultants the door.

Why? Because under conditions of inequality, weaker parties can easily be disadvantaged in a participative planning exercise (Jackson, 1982; Rosenhead, 1984). Ideological assumptions, embedded in the methodology, may bias the type of outcome which is possible. Supposedly neutral consultants may have past obligations or future expectations from those participants with greater power and resources. Inequalities of power are likely to be reflected also in inequalities of 'communicative competence', due to a variety of socio-cultural factors. Participation under these conditions may undermine the development of that self-reliance which could improve chances of success in future bouts.

Joining in such an enterprise may, nevertheless, taken in the total context, be better than any other option open to the disadvantaged potential client or it may not. The choice will depend on the client's reading of that context. How, when, and where to engage in negotiations, or in particular analytic manoeuvres, is a political act. What form of analysis could help *this* decision along?

To address this question, let us return again to Dando and Bennett's (1981) three-way split into orthodox, reformist, and revolutionary paradigms. One way of distinguishing between them is through their concepts of control. The orthodox, 'hard' systems paradigm can be seen to correspond to control through a 'command' relationship; the reformist paradigm lends itself to control through manipulation; and the revolutionary paradigm to self-control, that is, emancipation (Rosenhead, 1985).

These broad-brush generalizations undoubtedly oversimplify. For example, the reformist paradigm, with its commitment to participation, has some potential for emancipation as well as for manipulation. Nevertheless, one may perhaps identify problem structuring methods more closely with the (manipulative) reformist than with the (emancipatory) revolutionary paradigm. That is, they are most apt to generate a managed and structured participation, unthreatening in its essentials to the *status quo*. Our putative client, aiming at upsetting the power balance, may indeed fail to find a developed approach designed to serve his or her purpose. The revolutionary paradigm is as yet defined more by its characteristic clienteles and its empowering client–analyst relationship than by any distinctive methodology. This is a weakness, and an area for further creative work. But it is not a fatal weakness: almost any method can at a pinch be turned to account, despite its design defects. Radical re-use of existing technology offers many possibilities.

Looking outward

The issues discussed in the previous section are in a sense internal and subordinate questions. Given that the case for problem structuring methods is established, these questions become important—is this the right way to do it? How can we understand better what happens when we apply one of the approaches? And so on.

But that case, though gaining ground, is far from universally accepted, even among practitioners. The failures of traditional operational research, of 'hard' systems methods, to gain access to the more significant problems of complexity, uncertainty, and conflict have been protracted and recurrent. Nevertheless, there are still those who believe that the answer lies in more of the same.

Two prominent examples will emphasize the point. The opening address (Cyert, 1981) to the 1981 Conference of the International Federation of Operational Research Societies acknowledged the fact that 'operational research has not yet proved itself at top management level'. The distinguished speaker held that the greatest successes of OR had been with well-structured problems, the solution of which 'have enabled operations research to reduce the areas of management that are left completely to judgement'. He proposed that an extension of this approach into the areas of management strategy and organizational design, where models were still thin on the ground, could make the breakthrough. While he did not believe that judgement could ever be eliminated, 'reduction should continue to be our objective'.

The second exhibit, from the end of the same decade, does not even acknowledge that there is a problem. A Vice-President of IFORS, in an open letter circulated through the Federation, celebrated the 'impressive weaponry' forged by the battalions of OR academics and the phalanx of practitioners (Ridgway, 1988). The quality and rigour of the former was outstanding 'and bears comparison with the traditional hard sciences'. An upbeat view of the future for OR was in order because of the realization of the 'science fiction dream' of automated factories, space travel and global communications, and the computers which made them possible. In a deliberate echo of a resonant Churchillian phrase, he concluded 'today, we have the men and the tools for whatever task we set ourselves. We have a world looking to us for our dedication—the solution to many pressing problems. The torch of World War II has been ably passed on.'

'Let's get on with it and do it well!'

It is probably kinder to regard this rhetorical flourish as designed to encourage the troops. Certainly, pressing problems exist in plenty, but for OR the problem is that so few of them are offered to, or even seem tractable by, its traditional methods. A break with its judgement-reducing, hard science orientation will be needed first.

At present the potential for rational analysis of social problems which defy pre-formulation is thwarted by practitioners who do not recognize the possibilities of tackling such situations; by practitioners who believe that they can be tamed by traditional methods; by teachers who help to

355

produce the next generation of convergent thinkers; and by clients who, perhaps not surprisingly, are unaware that operational research and the systems movement have anything else to offer. Evidently there are exceptions amongst practitioners, teachers and clients, and their number is growing. The purpose of this book is to help this process on its way.

There are now a number of distinctive alternative strands in the rational analysis of social and organizational problems. Not all have been described in this volume. Is there a *modus vivendi* between these various tendencies from which the activity as a whole would benefit? Jackson (1987b) strongly advocates a pluralist strategy as offering the best future prospect. The separate strands should not merge, make take-over bids, or retreat into isolation. They should rather engage in constructive debate on theoretical and practical issues for mutual development and the progressive identification of respective domains of application.

The existence of multiple strands should not be seen as a threat from which to retreat hastily into a monolithic fortress or an unprincipled marriage of convenience. It is an asset and a sign of health. Diversity offers a variety of developmental possibilities, and a broader based contribution to the many problems—of prediction and control, of mutual understanding, of emancipation—which could benefit from analytic assistance.

A constructive route forward is of importance not just for those who are academics and practitioners in the various strands of rational analysis. The elaborately complex and interconnected societies which are lurching erratically towards the twenty-first century need the services which such a professional community can potentially provide. So far they have been made available principally, though still inadequately, for the control problems of the unitary managements of hierarchically structured work organizations. Beyond them lies a vast, almost analytically unexplored swampy terrain—the strategic choices confronted by those managements, the dilemmas of community-based organizations, the social problems which afflict advanced societies, the global issues of harmony, equity, and survival.

Questions of economic development, energy policy, unequal opportunities, hunger, law and order, health care provision, industrial relations, ecology and the like dominate the news. All involve debate, organization, and commitment under conditions of ramifying complexity, uncertainty, and conflict. The outcomes of these complex processes condition the lives we lead, and our prospects for the future. Yet the formation of policy, the design of organizational instruments is guided at best by partial and biased analytic tools, lacking the systemic and systematic dimension. The scope for improvement in the analytic component of deliberative processes at every level in society is almost unlimited.

The unexploited potential of rational analysis is both an opportunity and a responsibility for its exponents. To take up the challenge, a renewal of methods is a prerequisite. This book indicates some fruitful ways forward.

References

Ackoff, R. L. (1970). 'A black ghetto's research on a university', *Opns Res.*, **18**, 761–71.

Checkland, P. (1981). *Systems Thinking, Systems Practice*, Wiley, Chichester.

Checkland, P. (1985). 'Some reflections on the Henley Conference 1985', *J. Opl Res. Soc.*, **36**, 854–5.

Cropper, S. (1984). 'Ways of working: fine tuning our ideas about OR methodology', Univ. Sussex, Brighton, mimeo.

Cropper, S. (1987). 'The complexity of decision management: some elements of a theory of decision management practice'. Presented at International Symposium on Future Directions in Decision Management, Toronto, September 1987.

Cyert, R. M. (1981). 'The future of operations research', in *Operational Research '81* (Ed. J. P. Brans), pp. 1–10, North Holland, Amsterdam.

Dando, M. R., and Bennett, P. G. (1981). 'A Kuhnian crisis in management science?', *J. Opl Res. Soc.*, **32**, 91–103.

Eden, C. (1985). 'Perishing thoughts about systems thinking in action', *J. Opl Res. Soc.*, **36**, 860–1.

Eden, C. (1987). 'P x C — the future consultant?' Presented at International Symposium on Future Directions in Decision Management, Toronto, September 1987.

Etzioni, A. (1968). *The Active Society: a theory of societal and political processes*, Free Press, New York.

Farkas, J. (1984). 'Change in the paradigms of systems analysis', in *Rethinking the Process of Operational Research and Systems Analysis* (Eds. R. Tomlinson and I. Kiss), pp. 125–34, Pergamon, Oxford.

Huxham, C., Cropper, S., and Bennett, P. (1989). 'Decision aiding demonstrated!', *OR Insight*, **2** (2), 15–21.

Jackson, M. C. (1982). 'The nature of "soft" systems thinking: the work of Churchman, Ackoff, and Checkland', *J. Appl. Sys. Anal.*, **9**, 17–29.

Jackson, M. C. (1987a). 'Community operational research: purposes, theory and practice', *Dragon*, **2**, 47–73.

Jackson, M. C. (1987b). 'Present positions and future prospects in management science', *Omega*, **15**, 455–66.

Jackson, M. C. (1988). 'Some methodologies for community operational research', *J. Opl Res. Soc.*, **39**, 715–24.

Machol, R. E. (1980). 'Comment on "Publish or Perish"', *J. Opl Res. Soc.*, **31**, 1109–10.

Ridgway, F. J. (1988). 'The resurgence of operations research', Letter from the President No. 30, IFORS, Lyngby, Denmark.

Rosenhead, J. (1984). 'Debating systems methodology: conflicting ideas about conflict and ideas', *J. Appl. Sys. Anal.*, **11**, 79–84.

Rosenhead, J. (1985). 'A system of systems conferences', *J. Opl Res. Soc.*, **36**, 849–54.

Rosenhead, J. (1986). 'Custom and practice', *J. Opl Res. Soc.*, **37**, 335–43.

Rosenhead, J. (1989). 'Operational research at the crossroads: Cecil Gordon and the development of post-war OR', *J. Opl Res. Soc.*, **40**, 2–28.

Rosenhead, J., and Thunhurst, C. (1982). 'A materialist analysis of operational research', *J. Opl Res. Soc.*, **33**, 111–22.

Thunhurst, C. (1987). 'Doing operational research with the community', *Dragon*, **2**, 143–53.

Index

Note: 'OR' means 'operational research' in this index